Governmental Intervention in Foreign Trade in Archaic and Classical Greece

Mnemosyne

Supplements

History and Archaeology of Classical Antiquity

VOLUME 312

Governmental Intervention in Foreign Trade in Archaic and Classical Greece

By

Errietta M.A. Bissa

BRILL

LEIDEN • BOSTON
2009

This book is printed on acid-free paper.

Library of Congress Cataloging-in-Publication Data

Bissa, Errietta M. A.
Governmental intervention in foreign trade in archaic and classical Greece / by Errietta M.A. Bissa.
p. cm. – (History and archaeology of classical antiquity 312)
Includes bibliographical references and index.
ISBN 978-90-04-17504-4 (hardback : alk. paper)
1. Greece–Commerce–History. 2. Greece–Economic policy. I. Title. II. Series.

HF375.B57 2009
382'.30938–dc22

2009015839

ISSN 0169-8958
ISBN 978 90 04 17504 4

PRINTED IN THE NETHERLANDS

εἰς μνήμην Ἀμαλίας Γ. Μπίσσα (1951–2001)

CONTENTS

LIST OF TABLES

ACKNOWLEDGEMENTS

This work is the result of an exploration into the Greek economy disguised as a PhD thesis at University College London between 2003 and 2007. It and I are in debt to the people and institutions that made this exploration both possible and enjoyable. First and foremost, I owe an immeasurable debt to my supervisor, Professor Hans van Wees, for his willingness to listen, comment on and criticize ideas and arguments and, most of all, for his unstinting support and gentle encouragement throughout.

I owe a debt of gratitude to Professor Simon Hornblower for his support, criticisms and patience during the four years of my doctorate. My profound thanks to Professor Dominic Rathbone and Professor Edward Harris for their comments, criticisms and suggestions. I would also like to thank Professor Mike Edwards for his comments on a draft of the grain chapters and Professor Michael Crawford for his gentle criticisms on an initial draft of the conclusion. Further, I would like to express my gratitude to the publisher's reviewer for their helpful comments and suggestions. My profound thanks to Professor Fritz Graf for his guidance and teaching in my epigraphic forays.

I would like to offer my humble thanks to the librarians and support personnel of the Institute of Classical Studies in London for providing a true home during my research. My thanks also to the personnel of the library of the British School at Athens, the library of the Techniko Epimeleterio in Athens and the library of the Greek Institute of Geology and Mineral Exploration. I would also like to thank Dr. Maria Oikonomakou of the 2nd Ephorate of Prehistoric and Classical Antiquities for her response to my inquiries regarding the Thorikos bowl and Mr. Nikos Koupetoris for his answers regarding traditional boat-building. I owe a special debt to a number of Greek farmers who indulged me in remembering the conditions, crops and farming ways of modern Greece in the early 20th century, foremost among them my grandmother, Mrs. Areti Lalapanou.

My profound thanks are owed to fellow-students and colleagues for their willingness to listen and comment on a number of papers in conferences and seminars during my research. I owe a great debt to Miss Charlotte Greenacre not only for her willingness to discuss any and all subjects regarding Greek trade but also for her comments and suggestions in the copy-editing of this book.

Further, I would like to thank the History Department of University College London for its support during my research. I owe a debt of gratitude to my colleagues of the Classics Department in the University of Wales Lampeter for their unstinting support during the revision and publication of this work.

I owe a very special thanks to the Classics graduates of the class of 2007/2008 in the University of Wales Lampeter, and particularly to Mr. Finlay Jones, for illuminating me on the difficulties faced by students with little or no Greek and suggesting simple and viable solutions to making this book more accessible to all students.

Last, but most certainly not least, I owe the greatest debt to my family for their support, help and love throughout.

As always, and rightly, all mistakes and miscomprehensions are my own.

EB
Lampeter, January 2009

ABBREVIATIONS

Agora 17	Bradeen, D.W. (1974) *The Athenian Agora: Results of Excavations Conducted by the American School of Classical Studies at Athens. Vol. 17, Inscriptions: the Funerary Monuments*, Princeton
Agora 19	Walbank, M.B., Lalonde, G.V. & Langdon, M.K. (1991) *The Athenian Agora: Results of Excavations Conducted by the American School of Classical Studies at Athens. Vol. 19, Inscriptions: Horoi, Poletai Records, Leases of Public Lands*, Princeton
BMC	*Catalogue of the Greek Coins in the British Museum* (1879–1929), London
FGrH	Jacoby, F. (1923–1958) *Die Fragment der griechischen Historiker*, Berlin
IACP	Hansen, M.H. & Nielsen, T.H. (2004) *An Inventory of Archaic and Classical Poleis*, Oxford
IEph	Wankel, H., Merkelbach, R. et al. (1979–1981) *Die Inschriften von Ephesos, I–VII*, Bonn
IG I^3	Lewis, D. et al. (1981–1998) (eds.) *Inscriptiones Graecae: Inscriptiones Atticae Euclidis anno anteriores*, 3rd edition, Berlin
IG II^2	Kirchner, J. (1913–1940) (ed.) *Inscriptiones Graecae: Inscriptiones Atticae Euclidis anno posteriores*, 2nd edition, Berlin
IG V(1)	Kolbe, G. (1913) (ed.) *Inscriptiones Graecae: Inscriptiones Laconiae et Messeniae. Fasc. 1*, Berlin
IG XII(2)	Paton, G.R. (1899) (ed.) *Inscriptiones Graecae: Inscriptiones insularum maris Aegaei praeter Delum. Inscriptiones Lesbi Nesi Tenedi*, Berlin
IG XII(5)	de Gaertringen, F.H. (1903–1909) (ed.) *Inscriptiones Graecae: Inscriptiones insularum maris Aegaei praeter Delum. Inscriptiones Cycladum*, Berlin
IG XII(7)	Delamarre, J. (1908) (ed.) *Inscriptiones Graecae: Inscriptiones insularum maris Aegaei praeter Delum. Inscriptiones Amorgi et insularum vicinarum*, Berlin
IG XII Suppl.	de Gaertringen, F.H. (1939) (ed.) *Inscriptiones Graecae: Inscriptiones insularum maris Aegaei praeter Delum. Supplementum*, Berlin
IGCH	Thompson, M., Morkholm, O. & Kraay, C.M. (1973) *An Inventory of Greek Coin Hoards*, Oxford

IOSPE	Latyshev, V. (1885–1901) *Inscriptiones antiquae orae septentrionalis Pontis Euxini Graecae et Latinae*, Leningrad
LGPN	*Lexicon of Greek Personal Names* Project
LGPN Vol. 1	Fraser, P.M. & Matthews, E. (1987) *Lexicon of Greek Personal Names I: Aegean Islands, Cyprus, Curenaica*, Oxford
LGPN Vol. 2	Osborne, M.J. & Byrne, S.G. (1994) (eds.) *Lexicon of Greek Personal Names II: Attica*, Oxford
LGPN Vol. 3a	Fraser, P.M. & Matthews, E. (1997) (eds.) *Lexicon of Greek Personal Names III.A: Peloponnese, Western Greece, Sicily and Magna Graecia*, Oxford
LGPN Vol. 3b	Fraser, P.M. & Matthews, E. (2000) (eds.) *Lexicon of Greek Personal Names III.B: Central Greece: From the Megarid to Thessaly*, Oxford
LGPN Vol. 4	Fraser, P.M. & Matthews, E. (2005) (eds.) *Lexicon of Greek Personal Names IV: Macedonia, Thrace, Northern Regions of the Black Sea*, Oxford
LSJ	Liddell, H.J. & Scott, R. (1996) *A Greek-English Lexicon*, 9th edition, Oxford.
McCabe *Samos*	McCabe, D.F., Brownson, J.V. & Ehrman, B.D. (1986) *Samos Inscriptions: Texts and List*, Princeton
McCabe *Teos*	McCabe, D.F. & Plunkett, M.A. (1985) *Teos Inscriptions: Texts and List*, Princeton
ML	Meiggs, R. & Lewis, D. (1988, revised edition) *A Selection of Greek Historical Inscriptions to the End of the Fifth Century* BC, Oxford
Nomima I	Van Effenterre, H. (1994) *Nomima: recueil d'inscriptions politiques et juridiques de l'archaïsme grec.* 1, Rome
Pauly-Wissowa	Pauly, A. et al. (1894–1980) (eds.) *Paulys Realencyclopädie der classischen Altertumswissenschaft: neue Bearbeitung*, Stuttgart
RO	Rhodes, P.J. & Osborne, R. (2003) *Greek Historical Inscriptions 404–323* BC, Oxford
SEG	*Supplementum Epigraphicum Graecum* (1923–) Amsterdam
Tod II	Tod, M.N. (1948) *A Selection of Greek Historical Inscriptions Vol. 2: From 403–322* BC, Oxford

AUTHOR'S NOTE

An effort was made to distinguish between restored and unrestored text in the translation of inscriptions, thus restored text is found in square brackets ([]). Since the differences between English and Greek mean that such efforts are merely estimations, I have intended this distinction between original and restored text to be a guide aimed to assist students with little or no Greek.

Regarding the names of people and places in the Greek world, I have preferred to transliterate as per the Greek rather than provide latinised versions, except for those names and places where the latinised version has become so ingrained that providing a direct transliteration would seem odd to the reader. The choice may seem arbitrary at times and for that I apologise to those who may find it disconcerting. Regarding the titles of ancient sources, I have followed the titles used by the Loeb Classical Library with the aim of making the works easier to find for students.

INTRODUCTION

οὐ γὰρ ἔστι πόλις οὐδεμία ἥτις οὐ δεῖται εἰσάγεσθαί τι ἢ ἐξάγεσθαι.
For there is not a single polis that need not import or export
[Xenophon] *Constitution of the Athenians* (= Old Oligarch) 2.3.1

These words of an Athenian pamphleteer are one of the most illuminating statements on the economic position of the polis. Import and export were part of life in the world of archaic and classical Greece, where political fragmentation created a unique distribution of available resources. In a world where one could barely travel a day without crossing a border, exchange of commodities was an unavoidable necessity and self-sufficiency an utopian ideal. In the modern world, exchange equals trade to a large extent but that was not necessarily the case in archaic and classical Greece. The two main questions posed in this work are, firstly, how important a part of exchange was trade in the archaic and classical periods and, secondly, what was the role of the state, if any, in foreign trade.

The Ancient Economy

In order to understand the ancient economy, we need to know the part played in it by trade and traders; in order to understand the role of trade and traders, we need to hold some view of the ancient economy. K. Hopkins[1]

Keith Hopkins articulated perfectly the ideological problem of studying Greek trade, since one has to subscribe to one of the two positions of the debate on the 'ancient economy,' which is the unequal continuation of the famous *oikos* debate that marked nineteenth century scholarship. Until the late nineteenth century, ancient history had remained aloof from the growing interest in economic motives in studying and explaining past and contemporary societies. The ancient world was given a place in the

[1] Hopkins (1983: ix).

economic evolution of societies by Marx and his followers but ancient historians and philologists did not become embroiled in the wider economic debate until Karl Bücher's effort to identify the Greek economy with a closed household economy.[2] Bücher's attempt met with immediate resistance by the leading scholars of the time, most importantly Eduard Meyer. As Austin rightly noted, the reactions to Bücher's propositions led to a greater evil.[3] The polarization between Meyer and Bücher and their followers on the function of the *oikos* in society and economy gave birth to extreme positions, such as Meyer's infamous comparison between 16th century CE Europe and fifth-century Athens.[4] In the first half of the 20th century CE, in the light of political and social upheavals in Europe, the 'modernist' approach seemed to have won the day and was expressed masterfully in Rostovtzeff's vision of the ancient world as amenable to the application of modern economic theories.[5] Both sides of the debate limited their vision to the question of modernism or primitivism without allowing the Greek world a measure of independence from other eras and societies. The situation changed, if with considerable delay, with Hasebroek's seminal *Trade and Politics*, which followed the teachings of Weber, based on the formalist/substantivist division in economic anthropology, in favour of a more substantivist approach to the evolution of the economies.[6] Weber moved the limelight from economic proceedings to the role of the economy in society and particularly on to the social perspectives that dictated economic relations in the ancient world. Hasebroek in his work reacted to the negativism and theorising of the modernists of his time, who tended to ignore the specific evidence of the sources in favour of their own theories. Hasebroek focused on the role of non-citizens in trade and manufacture in the polis and concluded that the polis neither had nor pursued any economic policy and that this failure was due to the lack of nationalised trade or manufacture.[7] The work of Weber and Hasebroek provided the study of the Greek economy with one of its most fundamental bases: that the economy was a part of the polis and any study of the economy without a study of the polis was

[2] Bücher (1893).

[3] Austin & Vidal-Naquet (1977: 4).

[4] Meyer (1924: 118–119).

[5] Rostovtzeff (1941); Rostovtzeff in spite of writing after Hasebroek is probably the best example of the modernist approach.

[6] Hasebroek (1928). I use here Polanyi's theoretical distinction to mark the break with the strict primitivism and modernism of the previous era.

[7] Hasebroek (1933).

doomed from the start. Irrespective of whether one agrees with the conclusions reached by either Weber or Hasebroek on specific issues of the economy of the polis, their fundamental change of perspective from a freestanding economy to an economy inextricably tied to the polis as an idea and an institution holds true under any scrutiny.

The theories advanced by Weber and Hasebroek were further systematised by Karl Polanyi. Polanyi created a system distinguishing modern and primitive economies according to their relation to their societies. Thus, the modern economy was deemed a 'disembedded' economy, while primitive economies were 'embedded' in society; in other words, the economy was judged according to the closeness of its relation with society and social norms.[8] For Polanyi the Greek economy was clearly embedded, thus consigned to being primitive and, consequently, had no understanding of economics. Austin, closely following Polanyi's model, tried to explain the fact that the Greeks both knew and understood economic motives by proposing that they did not realise them as economic in their own right but merely as an extension of politics.[9]

Polanyi's disembedded/embedded division is theoretically correct but its application to the practice of economics is more difficult. Our knowledge of the ancient, or indeed any pre-modern, economy is dependent on practice, not theory, yet our understanding of the modern economy as disembedded is more dependent on economics as a science rather than on economic practice. Baeck's view, as a modern economist rather than an ancient historian, that the *oikonomia* was "not an independent analytical sphere of thought" sums up perfectly the shift in modern thought that enables such distinctions today.[10] How far economic factors were realised independently of politics by the Greeks can be debated endlessly since the polis was by definition a political entity.[11] The fundamental division that exists today between state and people would be incomprehensible to the Greeks because of the very nature of the polis; economic factors affected all in the polis and as such were an immediate political concern. The same mode of thought is readily recognisable in modern poli-

[8] Humphreys (1964); Polanyi (1957).

[9] Austin & Vidal-Naquet [(1972, original French edition) (1977: 10)]. Note that Austin was writing before Finley's *Ancient Economy*. Both were clearly influenced by Polanyi and his ideas of the embedded economy, although Austin kept a more cautious attitude than Finley.

[10] Baeck (1997: 147).

[11] On the opposite interpretation of the close relation between politics and the economy in the polis, see Finley (1985: 156).

tics where the economy is a major cause of political and social concern, not unlike the Greek understanding of the economy as a political issue. An ordinary taxpayer in the modern world would have great difficulty in recognising the modern economy as disembedded from society, and economic policy is a major concern for voters worldwide. Disregarding the particular concerns of ancient historians and particularly historians of the economy, the roots of the debate can be interpreted as an evolution in post-Aristotelian analytical thought rather than as an evolution in the nature of the economy itself.

In spite of the work of Hasebroek and the theoretical framework advanced by Polanyi, the literature of the period was marked by a definite modernist perspective, best illustrated in the works of French, Starr and, later, Hopper.[12] The reaction to extreme modernism continued and found its most powerful adherent in Moses Finley. Finley proposed a purely substantivist model of the ancient economy advocating a change from wealth to status, social and/or political, as the prime mover of the economy.[13] The origins of Finley's thesis lie equally in the theoretical position of Karl Polanyi outlined above and in Finley's own work on landed loans in classical Attika, where he attempted to show that such loans were mainly non-productive.[14] Finley's vision of the Greek economy was masterfully presented in his seminal work, *The Ancient Economy*, where he attempted both to disprove the extreme modernist thesis of the Greek economy as a formalist economy and put forward his own model of a status-based non-capitalist economy.[15] Finley's model depends on three main axes, all three relating to specific lacks in the ancient economy and ancient thought.[16] The first is the lack of a large unified economic space evidenced by a system of interdependent markets. Finley argued, using as a case study the grain trade in classical Greece, that changes, or perceived

[12] French (1964); Starr (1977); Hopper (1979). Of particular interest is Hopper's *Trade and Industry*, which completely ignores any theoretical framework for either trade or industry in the Greek world, preferring a clearly descriptive, and summary, approach.

[13] Finley (1970).

[14] Finley (1952).

[15] Finley's earlier works, such as the *World of Odysseus* (1954), also operate under the same general principles but it is not until the *Ancient Economy* that the full model is presented.

[16] Note that I will, as much as possible, confine myself to Finley's examples and evidence on the Greek world, rather than the Roman world, since I think that one of the main weaknesses of Finley's model is the idea of an 'ancient economy' per se. On this issue see further below page 15.

changes, in demand did not influence supply.[17] The second axis, to which Finley devoted most of his *Ancient Economy*, was the lack of a productive mentality on the part of the Greeks and the Romans. Finley centred his argument on the attitudes of the elite and their unwillingness to override moral issues in favour of productivity, although, as he noted, acquisitiveness was part of elite mentality in Greco-Roman antiquity.[18] His main points illustrating the lack of a productive mentality on the part of individuals were the lack of an organised large-scale industry, the unwillingness of the Greeks and the Romans to pursue technological advances as a means of increasing productivity and the lack of credit-based institutions.[19] The third axis, which is the most pertinent in the present work, is the lack of state interest and intervention in the economy as evidenced by the lack of direct taxation and the lack of meaningful intervention in trade and manufacture.[20]

Finley rightly noted that the authority of the state in classical Greece was total and there was no aspect of public or private life where the government did not have the potential or the authority to intervene.[21] The lack of polis interest in the economy is seen through the lack of specifically commercial clauses in *symbola* agreements and the absence of formal treaties relating to commercial benefactions, such as the one between Athens and the Spartokids.[22] Finley pays specific attention, following to an extent Hasebroek's example, to the fact that a large part of trade, particularly Athenian trade, was in the hands of metics and foreigners.[23] A particularly potent point made by Finley is the apparent inability of the polis to create different tax regimes for foreigners and residents, imports and exports or necessary and luxury commodities, or to institute a direct taxation regime that would alleviate its financial problems in times of crisis and create permanent public savings.[24] The polis also did not realise or utilise the possible effects of monopoly on production, recognising merely the fiscal benefits of monopoly, particularly of coinage.[25] Finley

17 Finley (1985: 177–179).
18 Finley (1985: 60–61).
19 Finley (1985: 121–122, 147–149).
20 Finley (1985: 175–176).
21 Finley (1985: 154).
22 Finley (1985: 162).
23 Finley (1985: 163–164), using as evidence Xenophon's *Ways and Means* and the lack of any radical proposals in the pamphlet, such as the abolition of the *metoikion*.
24 Finley (1985: 164, 174–175). On this issue, there may be clues that there were different tax-regimes outside Athens (see page 161).
25 Finley (1985: 166–168).

recognised the permanent intervention of the Athenians in their grain supply but considered it a unique set of measures adopted by a unique polis.[26] Finley isolated important parts of state intervention in the modern age and highlighted their absence from Greek antiquity, thus arguing in favour of a deliberate disregard for economic considerations by the polis, as well as a simultaneous inability of the government to assist the progress of the economy towards the modern model.

Finley's model quickly achieved the status of orthodoxy and gave new impetus to the debate on the Greek economy.[27] The extent of the model's canonical status is probably best seen in Goldsmith's survey of pre-modern economies, where under a clearly formalist presentation, Finley's model is upheld as the only existing explanation of the Athenian economy.[28] Yet the reaction to Finley and the status-based economy has been equally strong, particularly in the last fifteen years, with a variety of studies tackling particular aspects of the model. The best example of the nature of the continuing debate is the almost simultaneous rival expositions on credit and lending in Athens by Millett and Cohen.[29] Such works have become the norm in the post-Finley era with specific studies concentrating on particular aspects of the Greek economy, mainly the Athenian, aiming to explore issues, which were highlighted in Finley's work, either against the status-based orthodox model or in favour of it.

The debate still rages under three distinct headings. On the one hand, followers of Finley have attempted both to explore specific issues and to test Weberian and Finleyan models on specific aspects and case studies in the Greek economy, such as Millett's work on credit, Garnsey's exposition on food crises and Moller's work on the status of Naukratis.[30] In a similar vein and in response to initial criticisms of Finley's model as ignoring the Hellenistic period, some scholars, side-stepping Finley's own argument that the Hellenistic kingdoms did not impact on his model since they belonged to the oriental economies, have proposed various models in an effort to prove the importance of status over profit in the Hellenistic

[26] Finley (1985: 169–170).

[27] For Finley's thesis as orthodoxy see Hopkins (1983: xi); Patterson (1998: 157). It has been argued that Finley's work was the culmination, and indeed end, of the debate [McClellan (1997: 172)].

[28] Goldsmith (1987: 16–33).

[29] Millett (1991); Cohen (1992).

[30] Millett (1991); Garnsey (1988); Moller (2000).

kingdoms, mainly Ptolemaic Egypt, and refute Rostovtzeff's modernist approach.[31]

At the other end of the spectrum, there has been an effort to reconcile the great insight initially of Hasebroek and then Finley on the paramount importance of status as an economic force in the Greek world, and the evidence of economic processes and the power of the market, as exhibited in the literary sources and the archaeological record. In what can best be called a neo-modernist approach, a variety of works has concentrated on interpreting the existing evidence in an anti-Weberian protest against ideal-types and exploring new avenues in both quantitative and case-study research. Thus, Cohen explored the importance of banks and banking in fourth-century Athens, Osborne proved the interdependence of markets through pottery evidence for the archaic period, Foxhall argued in favour of widespread market related imports in the archaic period and Shipton proved that elite investment in Athens was more oriented towards manufacture than land.[32] Within this approach also fall works which have tried to distance themselves from the debate on the nature of the economy, concentrating instead on specific source material, such as Stroud's *editio princeps* of the grain-tax law of 374/373.[33]

Of particular interest for this work are Bresson's criticisms of Finley's thesis concerning the role of the state in the economy and particularly in price-fixing and market creation.[34] Bresson has tried to show that Finley's model is too strict and primitive-oriented for the testimony provided by the sources and in some respects he has succeeded, particularly in relation to markets and the use of revenues by the poleis.[35] His most impor-

---

[31] Finley (1985: 183): "There was therefore no 'Hellenistic economy;' from the outset there were two, an ancient sector and an Oriental sector". For the various models, see Samuel (1983), where economic stability rather than economic growth is the main goal of Ptolemaic policy, Bingen (1978) that stable revenue not economic growth was the goal, Turner (1984) with an incredibly interventionist state with an almost nationalised industry sector and, finally, McClellan (1997) where it is argued that the Ptolemies were not totally successful in arresting production growth. Interestingly, while all these proposals profess to follow Finley's vision, they inexplicably manage both to argue in favour of rational and specific state intervention and to presume the existence of interdependent markets. Finley's own argument remains the best defence of his thesis relating to the Hellenistic period.

[32] Cohen (1992); Osborne (1996b); Foxhall (1998); Shipton (2000, especially pp. 94–95).

[33] Stroud (1998).

[34] Market creation (Naukratis): Bresson (2000: 13–84); Price-fixing: Bresson (2000: 183–210).

[35] Bresson (2000: 247–257).

tant contribution to the debate is Bresson's discussion of the Aristotelian view of the relative importance of exports and imports in the polis. Bresson effectively demolishes the primitivist thesis that the polis was uninterested in exports and shows conclusively that Aristotle, as well as other sources, clearly show that the polis had a vested interest in exports, as well as imports.[36]

However, Bresson's view of the economy is in many ways restrictive, since he does not adequately differentiate between the different types of polity in the Greek world and the types of intervention available to and used by them. Bresson's work is valuable to the study of the various types of economic proceedings in the Greek world and in the matter of co-operation between polities, especially in his work on Naukratis. However, his exploration of the theme is in many ways fragmented and his outlook is heavily influenced by the legacy of Hasebroek and Finley in looking closely at the personnel of trade and their position in society, rather than on policies and their changes.[37]

Another key matter in the post-Finley era has been a discussion of the validity and applicability of economic and anthropological models on the ancient economy. In an effort to move beyond the narrow confines of the debate and bring the study of the economy back into the mainstream of ancient history, works such as those by Whittaker and Davies have called for the re-evaluation of existing and proposed models and have explored the uniqueness of the Greek, and Roman, economy as a theoretical field.[38] This theoretical and methodological discussion reveals the inherent duality in the post-Finley era on both sides of the debate between the theoretical basis of study and the practical antecedents. In other words, while both sides of the debate are theoretically dependent upon the status-based economy model, either to support or to disprove, the practical aspect is readily traced back to the earlier work of Moses Finley on the *horoi*, which highlights the need for further study on all aspects of the Greek economy.[39] Finley never realised his grand plan of a series of detailed studies on aspects of the economy before producing an overarching model but in the thirty-five years since the *Ancient Economy*, work has concentrated on achieving that ambition. The study of the Greek economy today, in spite of its debts to the works before 1973,

---

36 Bresson (2000: 109–130).
37 Bresson (2000: 65–70, 95–99).
38 Whittaker (1995) focusing on the Roman world and Davies (2005).
39 Finley (1952: vii): "this book is intended as the first of several volumes".

is shaped by and around Finley, a situation best articulated by Geoffrey Lloyd in a recent exposition: "the *Ancient Economy* contributed hugely in opening up debate, Finley himself never imagined that it closed it."[40]

Theory and Methodology

Exploring any aspect of the Greek economy today necessarily refers back to Finley and his views on the subject. In the simplest of terms, to paraphrase Hopkins, in order to understand the ancient economy, we need to know the part played in it by trade and traders; in order to understand the role of trade and traders, we need to hold some view on the *Ancient Economy*. Finley's model has several problems, both theoretical and methodological; both categories are equally important in acquiring a view on the validity of the model.

The first of Finley's main arguments was the lack of a system of interdependent markets in the Greek world, which automatically relegates the Greek economy into the category of primitive. Even if we ignore the fact that interdependence of markets has been shown through pottery evidence for the archaic period, and thus logically continued to exist in the classical, Finley's own examples do not stand up to scrutiny.[41] Finley rightly noted that statistical evidence that would enable a specific answer to the question is unlikely to be discovered and that the only viable alternative mode of inquiry is to analyse the factors of trade. The prime cited example of the supposed lack of influence of the consumer on the producer is the grain supply of Athens, based on the situations described in Lysias 22 and Demosthenes 56.

Demosthenes 56, which provides the bulk of Finley's argument, is a pseudo-Demosthenic *paragraphe* speech from the 320s BCE, where Athenian investors are trying to recover their loan from a trading venture in Egyptian grain. An initial problem with Finley's argument is that the speech does not refer to regular market conditions but conditions of widespread famine throughout the eastern Mediterranean. This is not a case of demand failing to influence supply but rather supply influencing demand, since not only local production in Greece and the Aegean was affected by the drought but also that in the main exporting regions, Egypt and the Black Sea. Certainly, the situation as portrayed in Demos-

[40] Lloyd (2002: xviii).
[41] On archaic interdependence of markets, see Osborne (1996b).

thenes 56 is not one of an independent scheme or effort to defraud the consumer by the supplier but a scheme rising from a specific set of crisis circumstances. As is argued later, the main reason that Kleomenes manages to succeed in his scheme for more than one sailing season is the widespread drought which made supply so small that whatever the price asked by the producer, the price paid by the consumer would be higher, thus enabling traders to pay higher prices for the product and still make a profit.[42] Secondly, the first part of Kleomenes' scheme directly involved the correlation of prices between exporter and importer, since the scheme recognised the increased demand and subsequent increase in prices paid by the importers, and correspondingly increased the price of grain for export in Egypt.

Turning to Lysias 22, this genuine speech of Lysias is of the accuser in the trial of a number of Athenian *sitopolai* (grain-dealers) accused of creating a cartel and illegally buying grain in bulk, thus creating crisis-circumstances in a normal period.[43] Finley argued that the devices employed by the *sitopolai* to keep prices high in Athens, including creating a cartel, had no influence that can be proven on production in the Black Sea and Egypt. First, the *sitopolai* in Athens are not "producers and shippers" as Finley says, on the contrary it is the shippers that support the action against the *sitopolai*; the *sitopolai* are part of the apparatus of the consumer not the producer.[44] Secondly, the infuriated response of the *emporoi* implies an expectation of correlation of prices between the producer and the consumer, since we are left to infer that the scheme of the *sitopolai* kept prices in the *emporion* lower than they should have been under free market conditions. Furthermore, there is no reason to assume that schemes like that of the *sitopolai* in Athens, with their very short duration, should in any way influence the production of Egypt or the Black Sea. Finley cites as a comparison a similar scheme in early modern Amsterdam, which would influence production in Poland, but the situations are not comparable.[45] Amsterdam was the clearinghouse for the rest of Europe; if the scheme of the *sitopolai* had taken place in its ancient equivalent, Rhodos or Byzantion, then Finley's argument would work, but it took place in Athens, which was not a clearinghouse for

[42] See further page 165.

[43] Note that throughout, I take Lysias 22 to be an actual speech delivered in court, not a rhetorical exercise.

[44] Finley (1985: 178).

[45] Finley (1985: 177).

grain but a major consumer. Accordingly, demand as perceived by the producer did not change. For production to increase or decrease, there must be a perceived change in demand. As long as there are multiple markets, which was the case in the Greek world, then small changes in demand would change production only in the long-term. To provide a hypothetical example, production in the Bosporan Kingdom would be affected if Athens was totally removed from the network, thus removing its demand. If the scheme of the *sitopolai* was allowed to continue unchecked, not because it would affect actual demand but as it would make the *emporoi* avoid Athens, this would affect the perceived demand on the network.

The main axis of Finley's argument concentrates on elite mentality, which he argues was acquisitive but not productive. The main problem with this argument is that it concentrates on the elite and the moralising views of the philosophers, rather than on the society as a whole and the actual practice of both elites and non-elites in the Greek world. The lack of organised large-scale industry and the perceived unwillingness of the elite to invest rationally, even in land, for moral reasons, are both issues that have to be qualified. As Finley himself admits, moral reasons notwithstanding, land remained a very lucrative investment in the ancient world, thus that a portion of the elite preferred to invest in land makes perfect economic sense.[46] The lack of rationality in investment is shown only through Roman paradigms, which fall outside the scope of this work. Shipton in her study of public land leases has shown conclusively that such investment appealed widely in Athens and not merely to the liturgical class.[47]

Further, from fourth-century Athens we have evidence of citizens preferring to invest in ventures other than land without that affecting their elite status. An obvious example is Pasion, who after attaining citizenship did not change his investment regime from manufacture and banking to land, although according to Finley's model that is what any self-respecting member of the elite would have done. Yet given the special status of Pasion's life, Demosthenes' father is a better example, since he was a member of the liturgical class and a respected member of the community, yet his investments were exclusively in the fields of manufacture and finance. Finley's argument that Demosthenes does not refer to depreciation ignores the genre in which the information is

[46] Finley (1985: 121–122).
[47] Shipton (2000: 48–49).

found.[48] A steady unchanging return was necessary for Demosthenes' case, since depreciation or loss of profits in any form would vindicate the case of the defendants.

Finley bases a considerable part of his argument on the moral value of agriculture against trade or manufacture.[49] The validity of assuming that a philosophical moral position either influences investment or represents the actual practice of persons is questionable. The sources are referring to an innate contempt on the part of the traditional aristocracy for people who have acquired wealth from trade, manufacture and finance; the difference with the modern attitude towards the nouveau riche is difficult to distinguish. Social attitudes, then as now, are not as easy to categorise. Kephalos may have been a manufacturer but he was clearly accepted in upper-class salons, interestingly so was Socrates, a true *banausos*. It cannot be fully ascertained whether Pasion and Phormion found the same decree of acceptance in the Athenian upper classes, yet their initial status as slaves and non-Greeks may have been much more potent in their relations with the Athenian upper classes than their profession.

One rightly wonders how the upper-class students of Socrates, who had never worked a day in their lives, managed to so completely condemn *banausia* and never feel any concern or remorse that they automatically condemned their philosophical inspiration. Agriculture was certainly the most natural and valid form of wealth acquisition and surely it created the right lifestyle of leisure; yet, one would feel slightly more comfortable if the sentiment was voiced by a subsistence farmer, not an absentee landlord. Finley quotes Plato, Aristotle, Cato and Cicero, not the unknown litigant of Demosthenes, who can boast that he has left the high seas for the last seven years to take up a life of money-lending on the happy shores of the Piraeus. He, too, may have thought that agriculture is the most natural of occupations, yet that did not affect his investment regime as far as we can tell.

Finley is right in pointing out that the Greek world did not exhibit, to the best of our knowledge, an organised large-scale industry in the modern sense or a guild structure of the medieval type. The main argument is the lack of any polis known specifically for its manufacture rather than for its agricultural produce, thus making the city a centre of consumption in

[48] Finley (1985: 116). Note that amortisation is not mentioned in Demosthenes, since there were no loans to repay.

[49] A good example is Finley (1985: 122) quoting Aristotle *Oeconomica* 1343a25–b2.

the Weberian model rather than one of production.[50] While Finley is correct that Athens never became Flanders, guild halls have not been found in excavations, nor is any polis particularly noted for its manufacture, all these statements need qualification, most importantly, the meaning of manufacture and what constitutes a manufactured product. Finley's own words, clearly based on the [Aristotelian] *Oeconomica*, make his position clear:

> Essentially the ability of ancient cities to pay for their food, metals, slaves and other necessities rested on four variables: the amount of local agricultural production, that is, of the produce of the city's own rural area; the presence or absence of special resources, silver, above all, but also other metals or particularly desirable wines or olive-bearing plants; the invisible exports of trade and tourism; and fourth, the income from land ownership and empire, rents, taxes, tribute, gifts from clients and subjects. The contribution of manufacture was negligible; it is only a false model that drives historians in search of them where they are unattested, and did not exist.[51]

The first and second of Finley's categories are of particular interest in this case, since they highlight the primary issue when researching manufacture, not its existence but its definition. Today ascertaining manufactured products as against natural products is easy; a car is a manufactured product, so is a computer, a book or a pen. The lexical meaning of manufacture is "the making of articles, especially in a factory etc."[52] There is an obvious problem when attempting to categorise articles in such a way; tobacco is a natural product, yet cigarettes are not, similarly for oil and wine. Neither oil nor wine is a natural product, yet apparently they are not manufactured either, at least according to Finley. Processing of foodstuffs, like that of tobacco, is considered part of a country's industries in modern economics. So, when an Athenian bought a jar of wine, he was not buying a product of the earth but a manufactured article, and similarly with a jar of oil or perfume, a bar of soap, a chair, or indeed garum or salted fish from the Propontis. A fresh fish in the market at Athens is a natural product, preserved tunny from Kyzikos is not. Similarly, grain from the Bosporan Kingdom is a natural product but *semidalis* (fine flour) from Phoenicia is not.

Finley, quoting Xenophon *Ways and Means* 4.4–6, further postulates that demand for manufactured products was essentially inelastic, thus,

---

50 Finley (1985: 134–139).

51 Finley (1985: 139).

52 *Concise Oxford Dictionary*, 9th edition, s.v. manufacture I.

the demand was predominantly local, and consequently, the ancient city was a consumer city and manufacture was negligible.[53] The passage from Xenophon, however, is not as clear-cut as that, except of course if one quotes selectively. Xenophon does not refer to coppersmiths or ironsmiths only, since he goes on to state that the same is true of grain and wine, and when production becomes too great, many leave agriculture to engage in trade, retail and finance:

> And when there are many coppersmiths, the value of copperwork falls, and the coppersmiths close down, the same with the ironsmiths; and when there is much grain and wine, the value of the produce falls, and agriculture brings little profit, then many leave agriculture and turn towards trade, retail and lending; but as much as more silver ore is found, so much more silver is made, so many more people get involved in mining.[54]

Xenophon is addressing an Athenian audience and it is interesting that he does not mention oil or honey, the other products, apart from silver, for which Athens was known. The ancient city consumed but there is little evidence to suggest that it did not produce also, and while some cities certainly did not produce manufactured products, as some countries today do not, others did.

Concerning the lack of major technological advances, which Finley argues are a good indicator of the essential non-productive thought and practice of the Greeks, it is worth pointing out that while the Greeks did not pay as much attention to technology as the modern western world does, there were certainly technological advances during the period. The modern western world has witnessed more technological advances in the last 200 years than in the whole of human history, whether that is a sign of an advanced economy or merely the culmination of the advancement of analytical and scientific thought is an issue that needs be further investigated.

The other major argument that is thought to prove the unproductive economic practice of the Greeks is the lack of credit-based institutions.

---

[53] Finley (1985: 135).

[54] Xenophon *Ways and Means* 4.6–7: καὶ γὰρ οὐδ' ὥσπερ ὅταν πολλοὶ χαλκοτύποι γένωνται, ἀξίων γενομένων τῶν χαλκευτικῶν ἔργων, καταλύονται οἱ χαλκοτύποι, καὶ οἱ σιδηρεῖς γε ὡσαύτως· καὶ ὅταν γε πολὺς σῖτος καὶ οἶνος γένηται, ἀξίων ὄντων τῶν καρπῶν, ἀλυσιτελεῖς αἱ γεωργίαι γίγνονται, ὥστε πολλοὶ ἀφέμενοι τοῦ τὴν γῆν ἐργάζεσθαι ἐπ' ἐμπορίας καὶ καπηλείας καὶ τοκισμοὺς τρέπονται· ἀργυρῖτις δὲ ὅσῳ ἂν πλείων φαίνηται καὶ ἀργύριον πλέον γίγνηται, τοσούτῳ πλείονες ἐπὶ τὸ ἔργον τοῦτο ἔρχονται.

Cohen very convincingly showed that the Athenians in the fourth century had credit-based institutions in the form of banks, which supported trade and manufacture.[55] On the other hand, both Finley's work on the *horoi* and Millett's work on lending patterns in Athens have made it clear that a large part of loans were for personal reasons.[56] Finley's insistence on excluding maritime loans from his discussion effectively restricts the available evidence to only one part of the credit spectrum in the Greek world. It would be impossible to study modern credit institutions if the spectrum of data was restricted to personal loans and credit-card transactions. The balance of the studies on credit and lending in Athens has shown that the Athenians borrowed both for personal non-productive reasons and for business purposes. The situation seems not much different from modern credit transactions, where people borrow both for personal reasons and for investment purposes.

The third axis of Finley's model concerns specifically the intervention of the state in the economy. This part of the Greek economy has been sadly neglected, since detailed studies on aspects of the behaviour and role of the state in the economy are rare. This work attempts to explore one particular aspect of the role of the state: its behaviour in relation to the foreign trade of necessary commodities.

Beyond the specific theoretical problems of Finley's model, there are several points of disagreement on methodology. Firstly, there is Finley's insistence on the idea of the 'ancient economy,' which has been a systemic fiction in Greek and Roman history since the 19th century CE. After 1973, historians have followed Finley's substantive model, which distinguished the 'Greco-Roman Economy' chronologically, culturally and geographically. Recent studies in the history of classical scholarship have highlighted that Finley was a product of his times and their politico-ideological climate.[57] The turn of the century witnessed the advent of a different approach to ancient history in general, one of integration and the demolition of artificial boundary constructions, geographical, cultural or chronological.[58] Arguments for connectivity and the blurring of artificial distinctions have brought about the call for a redefinition of the ancient economy as an integrating framework for a better understanding

---

55 Cohen (1992).
56 Finley (1952: 81–83); Millett (1991).
57 Nafissi (2005).
58 Horden & Purcell (2000) is the turning point.

of the ancient world including all its individual components, from the Near East to Britain and from the Bronze Age to the end of the Roman Empire.[59]

The ancient economy as visualised by Finley ignores not only the connections between the broader Mediterranean region and its immediate neighbours, but also the deep economic ties, and their necessity, between the various cultures. Simultaneously, it creates an artificial economic entity, which in spite of Finley's admission of its artificial quality, has dominated the study and exposition of economic functions in the ancient world.[60] The idea of the 'ancient economy' not only ignores the larger picture but also disregards the smaller component pictures. The classical Greek economy and economic processes were different from the Roman ones in the same way that politics and political processes were different.[61] While similarities between the two systems were in existence and can be mapped and identified, the overall framework of economic development was different. Further, even within the Greek world in the classical period there were considerable differences in the economic systems and processes of the various poleis, as there were differences in the economy of any one polis at different times within the period. Moreover, while it is possible to identify patterns of economic behaviour within a specific period and area, it does not mean that there were no exceptions within that economic system. A consequence of Finley's vision of a unified model for the Greco-Roman worlds is its static character. Finley believed that an economic model should reflect the 'dominant' behaviours in the economy.[62] By advocating a model of one dominant mode of behaviour

---

[59] Manning & Morris (2005).

[60] Finley (1985: 29).

[61] To provide only one example of the fusion that Finley consistently employed: "Or, should we place the stress on the universal Greek restriction of land ownership to citizens, or in the two second-century attempts to compel newly created Roman senators from the provinces to acquire estates in Italy?" (1985: 156). The two situations are inherently different. For the Greek world, even if the restriction were universal, which has not been proven to my knowledge, the background of the practice differs sharply from that of the Romans. There are valid strategic reasons for the restriction of ownership to citizens and equally valid political ones. In the modern world, where land ownership is not restricted (although there are exceptions, such as the modern Greek restriction on foreigners owning property in the border provinces), there have been incidents of immigrants forced to abandon their holdings, such as when the US forced immigrants of Japanese descent to abandon their holdings in WWII. Land-ownership is an issue greater than mere investment; a point that Finley ignores when criticizing Xenophon's proposal on allowing metics to own houses (1985: 163).

[62] Finley (1985: 29).

for the economy of the Mediterranean world throughout the Greco-Roman period, Finley disregarded the inherent fluctuations of any economy.

Another problem with Finley's idea of the 'ancient economy' is the problem of exceptions. Finley consistently insisted on ignoring any practice or evidence which did not follow his model of a status-based economy.[63] Exceptions will exist in any system, since alternative patterns are the safety valves for any system to avoid stagnation and adapt to changes. On the one hand, the study of these exceptions is as necessary as that of the rules, for thus we can better understand the system. On the other hand, to be able to distinguish between rules and exceptions, there must be data that throw both into relief. Demosthenes' father invested in manufacture and finance and so did Pasion, Andokides became a trader during his exile and after his return invested in tax-farming, Nikias invested considerably in the mining industry and his descendants in the fourth century continued the trend. The balance of the evidence is not as unambiguous as the philosophers, or the status-based model, would have us believe. Whether the attitude of these people was exceptional in classical Athens is something that needs further study; it is unwise to assume the exceptionality of these cases because of moralising statements in the philosophers.

A further problem of Finley's model is the insistence on considering certain types of evidence and methods of inquiry better than others. The exact use of sources and evidence as well as the types of method employed for analysis and interpretation of data are necessary methodological decisions. Finley, as others before and after him, embraced some types of evidence, for example philosophical writings, while excluding others, for example pottery.[64] Finley's reaction to the abuse of pottery evidence was justified, yet the exclusion of pottery robs the student of the economy of a

[63] For example (1985: 164): "Xenophon's argument about the limitless demand for silver is a rare and rudimentary exception." Yet interestingly both surviving political pamphlets are concerned with the polis' choice of revenue, albeit from different perspectives. Also, (1985: 170): "Just price was a medieval concept, not an ancient one, and this interference by the state, altogether exceptional in its permanence, is a sufficient measure of the urgency of the food problem." Interestingly, just price was not an ancient concept and is exceptional where found, although the Athenians not only legislated on profit margins and fixed public grain prices to what was considered just by the assembly, but the Teans also legislated against artificial increase of prices. If every piece of legislation which we know is an exception, then the rule can only be inferred ex silentio.

[64] Finley (1985: 33) for the main cautionary example. In the years since Finley it has become accepted that pottery evidence cannot be uniformly excluded, see Morley

vast set of surviving data. Similarly, it has become almost an urban legend in Greek history that statistics are non-existent, unreliable and unusable for the study of economic and social phenomena.[65] The main reason for avoiding the use of statistics is that the surviving data is incomplete, and thus no analysis will be full. That is true, but since the possibility of a full set of data appearing is remote, not using the available data is nonsensical. A partial picture is better than none, and the existing data and their statistical analysis will provide the partial picture, which otherwise would be unknown to us.[66]

Governmental Intervention

Beyond the theoretical and methodological problems of Finley's model, a major issue is clearly economic: governmental intervention. Finley argued that there was only limited and occasional governmental intervention in trade.[67] Previous scholars, who like Finley followed Polanyi's theory, relegated governmental policy to a minor import policy concentrating on grain.[68] The aim of this work is to explore the role of the state in foreign trade in the archaic and classical periods.

An issue that needs be clarified at this initial stage is the use of the words state and government in this work. The definition of the polis as a state has been an issue of debate among scholars with differing opinions based on the historical evolution of the European state and the concept of state in the modern period.[69] Recently, Berent argued in favour of viewing the polis as a stateless society based on the relative lack of institutionalisation in the polis and the lack of a fundamental divide between state and citizens, which is a major concept of government and politics in many modern states.[70] This argument has been adequately refuted by Hansen in a number of studies, which highlight the similarities

(2007: 6). However, there have been alternative suggestions as to how amphorae are not trade indexes, in this case for Rome: Whittaker (1989).

65 Quantitative studies are a necessity in ancient economic history, as Finley recognised in an earlier study: Finley (1965: 35).

66 Osborne (1991: 139).

67 Finley (1985: 155).

68 Austin & Vidal-Naquet (1977: 113). For a re-iteration of that thesis, see Morley (2007: 4, 57).

69 For a review of the main recent arguments, see Faraguna (2000).

70 Berent (1996: 39, 58–59).

between the polis and the early modern and modern state in relation to both government and its power over the people and the concept of state as comprising territory, government and the body politic.[71]

This work follows Hansen's view of the polis as a state, albeit with important differences from the early modern and modern states.[72] More importantly, as testified by the title, this work is concerned mainly with the role of government in foreign trade, in other words with the role played by institutions, laws and inter-polity relations and agreements in foreign trade. Since the focus is not exclusively on the polis but also on other types of polity, both Greek and oriental, in the Greek world and its fringes, the term government is preferred to encompass the different types of constitution and authority exhibited in the different polities from Athenian democracy to tyrannical and monarchical regimes. However, mainly for the polis but also to some extent for other polities, particularly the Greek ones rather the oriental, the state is understood to be the combination of institutions and the body of citizens, since decision making, especially in democracies and relatively open oligarchies, is dependent upon the will of the people as a whole rather than upon that of a superimposed and independent government.

There is a fundamental distinction which has failed to come up in discussions of trade and the economy in the Greek world, that between intervention and involvement. Intervention is when the government seeks to influence the economic behaviour of citizens, while involvement is when it engages itself in economic activity and transactions. Thus, legislating on the import of grain is an act of intervention, similar to providing *ateleia* (exemption from taxes/dues) to an exporter. On the other hand, the ownership of mines by the polis makes the government involved in the mining industry, and when the Spartans buy gold from Kroisos, the involvement of the government in the transaction is full and clear.[73] The issue of government intervention in the economy, particularly in trade, has been debated, for governmental non-intervention is considered a major sign of a primitive or unevolved economy according to Polanyi's theory.[74] Yet discussions seem to ignore governmental involvement. Governmental involvement and governmental intervention can be simultaneous operations and are not mutually exclusive.

---

[71] Hansen (2002: 26–30), Hansen (1998).
[72] Hansen (2002: 41–42).
[73] See further page 45.
[74] Finley (1985: 154–155); Austin & Vidal-Naquet (1977: 112).

Nevertheless, the equilibrium between involvement and intervention is the key to the state's role in the economy.

Methodologically there are some initial bases to be established. Firstly, and possibly most importantly, an initial assumption in this work is that the practice of the economy reflects economic thinking. Thus, the practices of governments are studied in detail rather than the moralising and utopian concepts of the philosophers. This initial assumption firmly places this work within the neo-modernist approach and opens it to attack on the matter of the existence of a theoretical superstructure for the actions of governments. Finley distinguished between economic policy and political actions with unintended economic consequences, thereby relegating many measures and decisions with an economic dimension to irrelevance.[75] This work seeks to answer whether in practice there was intervention and involvement by the Greek governments and in what ways this was done. Motivations, policies and theoretical superstructures for such intervention and involvement are inferred from the actual measures.

Secondly, the chronological focus of the investigation is intentionally narrow, covering only the archaic and classical periods. Economies change and adapt to different circumstances, social and political. The advent of Alexander, and more importantly the Successors, changed the face of the Greek world, thus creating different economic networks. While there are instances of intervention in the Hellenistic world, such as the *sitonia* or the Delos timber and charcoal regulations, which would be of use in this work, the economic networks and political circumstances in which they belong are radically different from those of the archaic and classical periods.

Even, however, within the archaic and classical periods, changes occurred and when possible they are pointed out and discussed; thus, for example, the economy of Athens changed drastically at the end of the fifth century with the loss of empire. It must be pointed out that at no point are the conclusions reached in the work considered to apply by default to other periods. Geographically, as much of the Greek world as possible is covered within the constraints of the evidence, including non-polis polities. The Greeks were not uniformly organised in polis structures, and thus the study of non-polis polities both within and at the borders of the Greek world provides necessary points of comparison. It must be

[75] Finley (1985: 155).

noted that comparisons with later periods or other geographical regions are avoided, since the political, social and economic circumstances of the Greek world in the archaic and classical periods are not found, to my knowledge, in any other historical period or geographical region.

Thirdly, in the use of the evidence and examples, I have departed significantly from the use advocated by Finley, since, as mentioned above, the exceptionality of any given example should be judged not individually but within the body of data. Additionally, even exceptional or unique cases can be used to throw light on the rules of the general economic environment. Concerning the silence of the sources, the initial assumption is that the evidence is lost not lacking: I have tried to avoid arguments from silence, preferring to concentrate on the existing evidence. Thus, I have deduced measures or policies where possible; where there is no evidence, no conclusions are drawn. Thus, for example, it is argued that Corinth was chronically deficient in local grain, but given the absence of evidence on any policy or measures concerning grain supply, no conclusions are drawn on the possible measures that the Corinthians could have taken. This source-based approach is open to the accusation that the study concentrates on exceptional polities or circumstances. This is a fundamental methodological issue on the validity of arguments from silence, where I wish to make my position clear: arguments from silence are not valid.

The aim of the work is achieved by the discussion of four commodities: gold, silver, timber and grain. The four commodities were not chosen randomly but for their potential as essential commodities to the polis. Gold and silver (or their mutual alloy electrum) were the metals of coinage, a state initiative by definition. Specific types of timber were used in the construction of warships, and naval warfare was a major element of military reality in our period. Grain, finally, was one of the main staples of the ancient diet and its supply was a political concern. In the trade of such necessary and important commodities, the polis or polity was most likely to play a role, either as importer or as exporter.

The role of the government in trade is clearly divided between two major spheres of commerce: imports and exports. The state could be involved or intervene in both. For the state as exporter, there are various issues to explore. Firstly, the producers with capability of export for each commodity must be identified, both geographically and politically. In other words, not only must the regions of export be identified but also the political status of the communities involved. As was mentioned above, the Greek world was an amalgam geographically and politically. The poleis interacted not only with each other but also with non-Greek tribes of interior and coastal areas, non-Greek poleis, Greek and non-Greek kingdoms. Both the geographical positioning of the resources and the political status of the communities dominating them played a role in the trade of these commodities and in their availability as exports.

Secondly, the form of export must be identified. For each commodity, the form of export is different. For example, gold and silver could have been exported as bullion, artefacts or coins. The form of the exportable commodity answers major questions as to the role of the state in the export of the commodity. Taking as an example silver, the export of bullion meant considerably more intervention and knowledge of export by the state than the export of coins, which was largely outside the power of the polis, since they were available on the open market.

Thirdly, the extent of public control on exportable surpluses of these commodities must be discovered, and how the poleis or polities exercised such control. A major issue is whether the state controlled surpluses through ownership of resources and whether such ownership was translated into direct exploitation. Further, the influence of the state on the production of the resources must be explored. The government could exert considerable influence on production through legislation or incentives, and, more importantly, could even encourage the production of particular commodities. Lastly, the role of the government in the disposition of the surpluses must be considered. The type of disposition adopted by a polis or polity can provide important information on the amount of direct intervention employed by the government.

On the other side of the fence, poleis and polities were also importers. The first step in exploring the role of the government in imports is to identify which states had regular or permanent shortages of a commodity. The identification of importers and the exploration of the relative volume of imports depend on the commodity discussed. In the case of grain, for example, regular shortages were dictated by the ratio between population size and cultivated territory. For silver, on the other hand, population and territory have no consequence on imports. In that case, the relative volume of minted coins provides the best method for identifying importers and the volume of their imports.

More importantly, the extent of the intervention of the government, if any, on the import of any given commodity must be discovered. The government had at its disposal a variety of means to encourage or ensure import of a commodity. The polis or polity could intervene forcefully in import by coercing or obliging exporters through seizure of marketed surpluses, conquest of the resource territories or simply by treaty with the exporter. Another form of intervention, though not as forceful, was to offer honours or incentives to attract exporters. The government could also intervene internally to ensure successful import of commodities by encouraging private local traders to import specific commodities or by encouraging production of exportable commodities, which would naturally attract traders. Lastly, the government could take the import of a commodity into its own hands by directly importing specific commodities.

Each of the four commodities provides information about particular stages of the journey of the commodity from production to consumer and more importantly relates to specific types of governmental involvement in trade. Silver and gold are counterpoints, since survival has dictated that one is known from exporter's point of view, the other from the importer's. Silver informs us of the system of production within those systems, while providing vital clues as to the importance of exportability of commodities to the polis within a framework of maximum involvement but minimum intervention. Gold informs us of imports from a practical viewpoint since it exemplifies the varied means of acquisition and highlights the effects of random opportunity. Timber and grain are complementary because both are known principally from the importer's point of view but some evidence on the exporters and their actions has survived. Timber informs us of the practicalities of commercial transaction completion and focuses on maximum intervention through monopolies. Grain on the other hand, informs us of commodities as part of political and social causation and on the relative intervention-involvement equilibrium of the state in its role as regulator.

For anyone familiar with Finley's work, the choice of commodities may seem counter-productive and the scope of this work expressly limited in its ambition. Necessary commodities for the well-being of the polis were admitted by Finley to have been of interest to the polis and having been targets of greater degrees of intervention.

The choice of commodities was deliberate and had specific aims. It is not the intention of this work to single-handedly vanquish Finley's model based on state intervention. That would be a mistake of epic proportions. Finley's work provides the necessary axis for working on the Greek economy, and even in disagreement it is a basis for further study. This work is attempting to fill a hole in modern scholarship regarding specifically those commodities that both sides of the debate agree were important to the polis. At the same time, this is an attempt to display a methodology of researching the economy through commodities, whose main tenet is in-depth research into the specific commodity rather than a discussion of unconnected pieces of information concerning intervention in the trade of the commodity.

The study of the Greek economy and particularly trade has been limited, hampered, in my opinion, by the insistence of scholars on answering particular questions without delving into the greater picture. A simple example is the trade in silver and the role of the government within it. There is no surviving literary or epigraphical evidence of overt governmental intervention; no legislation, no import or export regulations etc. Thus, scholarship was led to believe in minimal, if any, involvement by the polis and a haphazard means of acquisition for the minting of coins. By casting a wider net through researching the individual exporters and importers and the means, quantities and mechanisms of trade, then a different picture emerges. The quantification of hoard data to reflect upon quantity of minting is not something that could obviously be related to governmental intervention or indeed the mechanisms of the trade in silver rather than other commodities, which is why such an avenue of research had not been attempted before. Yet through a type of research seemingly unrelated to the object at hand, it becomes clear that in spite of the lack of literary or epigraphical evidence, the polis was heavily involved in the trade in silver and it is impossible to substantiate the argument in favour of a haphazard means of acquisition.

The consequence of this example, and a similar case could be made for timber and grain, is that methodologically we need to look at the trade of a commodity from producer to consumer as a whole in order to answer the specific questions we have. Theoretically, in regard to the debate, this is a major issue, since scholarship has been obsessed with legislation and specific intervention techniques based on texts. The example of silver shows that the polis was involved and intervened, and yet no text or inscription of such intervention survives. Thus with this presentation of alternative evidence, gold and silver enter the debate, where before they had been on the fringes or completely ignored. Yet they should not have been, since they, and particularly silver, are clearly a governmental matter because coinage is a state initiative.

There is, of course, a negative consequence of this method. The amount of data one has to present is a lot larger than it would have been with any of the traditional methodologies. Additionally, much of it appears unremarkable or not quite relevant. As always, however, there is a silver lining. On the one hand, it helps with the overall picture regarding intervention in relation to the lack of data and the tinier pieces of evidence that are otherwise ignored. On the other hand, it provides information on places and circumstances that have not been presented before, precisely because the methodology of other works has been more concentrated on specific pieces of evidence. Governmental intervention was part of the economy and economic networks as a whole and thus must be studied within this greater spectrum rather than as a separate and isolated part.

By concentrating on four commodities that both sides of the debate agree were important, have been researched before and yet for which it is still possible to present new information, new techniques and new interpretations, and to create a model for intervention that is larger, more detailed and more inclusive of different forms of intervention and different types of state, is very important to the debate. It shows that there is ample scope for research into intervention and into trade as a whole and, more importantly in my view, that we need to expand our scope further and become more methodologically inclusive of types of evidence and types of research into the evidence in order to acquire a better understanding of the Greek economy.

In the simplest of terms, if we have been missing out on commodities that we all, wherever we fall in the primitivist-modernist spectrum, agree are important and which have been in the forefront of the discussion, then how much have we missed regarding other, less important and less researched, commodities? As was mentioned above, it is not the intention of this work to make Finley obsolete, even if such a thing were possible, nor is that its ambition. Finley, the scholar even if not the model, has been the major influence on this work. Finley's never achieved 1952 plan of specific in-depth studies as necessary building blocks for the creation of an overall model remains equally relevant and necessary today, as it was then. This discussion of the four commodities is not an anti-Finley demonstration or a platform for proposing a modernist model of the ancient economy. It is simply a presentation of a methodological model of research and the filling of a gap in modern scholarship regarding governmental intervention.

PART 1

GOLD AND SILVER

GOLD AND SILVER: PROLEGOMENA

Exchange is a common feature of human societies. In some societies, exchange transforms from direct to indirect, requiring the use of money. Money is the means of unlimited exchange based on the calculation and recognition of value without direct correlation of need. In the archaic period, in the Greek world and some non-Greek states in Asia Minor, a specific type of money spread, coinage. The distinguishing feature of coinage as against other types of money was its exclusive issue by the state.[1] The degree of monetization found in the Greek world has been debated by scholars, but for the purposes of this work the pervasiveness of monetization is immaterial, since the investigation focuses on the role of the state.[2] However, it must be stated that it is assumed throughout that there existed at least a minimal degree of monetization in the archaic period and a basic degree in the classical.

Coinage in the Greek world was a state issue and as such the procurement of precious metals for it was a state concern, either by their own means for the few states that controlled relevant resources, or from external sources.[3] The following chapters explore the role of the state in the trade of precious metals, gold and silver, especially in relation to precious metal coinage.

Silver was the coinage metal par excellence in the Greek world, particularly after the middle of the sixth century. Gold, on the other hand, was particularly important in the archaic period as the main constituent metal of electrum and continued to be used in some parts of the Greek

---

[1] Schaps (2004: 179).

[2] The most important work on the issue is Kraay (1964), especially pages 84–88, where is it argued that the low level of fractions minted by Greek poleis shows a very low level of monetization. However, recent research has shown that the level of fractions was considerably higher than those Kraay knew from the archaic period onwards, showing that the level of monetization was higher throughout the archaic and classical periods: Kim (2002).

[3] There are a few disputed cases from the time of early coinage, e.g. The Phanes coin, which has been thought to be that of a private individual, possibly a merchant. However, it is equally possible that one of the poleis followed the Lydian system of inscribing the name of the minting official: Kraay (1976: 24–25).

world in the classical period. The study of both commodities, as that of most commodities, suffers from a lack of adequate evidence and to some extent a lack of interest within modern scholarship. The literary evidence consists of various brief references in the sources and of part of Xenophon's *Ways and Means*, relating to the marketability and uses of silver. The epigraphic evidence relates mainly to the Athenian exploitation of the Laurion mines in the fourth century. There is, however, a large body of material evidence in the form of coins and mining installations. In both areas, more archaeological research is necessary, specifically on the provenance of coinage metals and on mining installations beyond Laurion and the Huelva. Since precious metal deposits are not widely found in the Mediterranean and its periphery, this study begins with the identification and discussion of states that had access to resources of precious metals, with specific attention paid to the regime of exploitation of silver in Athens and the role it played in its economy. Then the states that minted in silver or gold but did not have their own resources of metal, which consequently may have imported, are examined through the information provided by their coinages mainly on what they imported, how they did it and to what extent trade played a role in acquisition.

CHAPTER ONE

THE EXPORTERS OF GOLD AND SILVER

The rarity of gold and silver in the Mediterranean and peripheral regions, along with the low cost of labour, made the exploitation of even the smallest deposit economically viable, while the limited technology available made exploitation less productive and, consequently, the product more valuable.[1] Since not all deposits known to modern geology in the Mediterranean and peripheral regions were exploited in the archaic and classical periods, the selection of deposits examined is based on three alternative criteria: first, mention in the sources, second, evidence of ancient workings and, third, probability, which applies only to specific gold alluvial deposits that were easier to exploit.[2] The deposits are examined from west to east.

The Iberian Peninsula has both gold and silver deposits, of which those in the Huelva region were particularly important in the ancient world. In the beginning of the eighth century, the Phoenicians established colonies and trading posts in the region, while, traditionally, the mines were known to the Greeks from the late seventh century.[3] Iberian metals are at the centre of the debate on the interaction between Greeks and Phoenicians in the western Mediterranean, which relates mostly to early colonisation but also expands to later eras and encompasses diverse

[1] Gold is less rare today due to the discovery of massive gold deposits in the Americas, South Africa and Australia in the early modern period and the advances in mining technology in the last century. Out of an estimated 116,000 tons of gold produced in the world since prehistoric times, only 10,000 were produced before the Middle Ages: Bache (1987: 3).

[2] The gold deposits exploited by the Greeks were either alluvial, which were the most productive quantitatively, or veins, which were underground and, thus, harder to exploit. Vein deposits harder to exploit: Bache (1987: 27); Yannopoulos (1991: 3–4); Williams & Ogden (1994: 14); Forbes (1971: 159, 161). Even as recently as 1989 CE, 58% of world production came from alluvial deposits: Eliopoulos & Konstantinides (1989: 69). Note that the quality of alluvial deposits is generally less than that of vein deposits: Yannopoulos (1991: 25).

[3] Gold: Strabo 3.2.8, 3.4.2; Posidonius F89.168; Agard & Emberger (1989: 21–24); Lyritzis & Lyritzi (1985: 79); Vázquez Guzmán (1989: 114–115, 153, 156–158). Silver: Herodotos 1.163.2–3, 4.152.3; Dominguez (1999: 301); Morgenroth (1999: 395).

themes, from Phokaian settlement abroad to Herodotos' credibility, with the aim of establishing which of the two cultures was the dominant power in the western Mediterranean.

Aubet argued convincingly for the eighth century that Phoenician expansion was peacefully connected to Euboian activity in the western Mediterranean.[4] In the late archaic and classical periods, the intermittent conflicts between the Greeks, mainly of Sicily, and Carthage certainly created periods of strained relations. However, the many finds of Greek pottery in Iberia throughout the classical period show considerable contact between Greeks, Phoenicians and natives, particularly relating to the metal trade, since many of the finds were discovered in the Huelva.[5] Cabrera agued that the finds do not prove Greek trade with Iberia but can be explained by Phoenician trade with the area.[6] However, Greek pottery is generally accepted to be evidence of direct trading contacts with Greeks, except in cases of isolated finds.[7] The Phoenician presence in Iberia does not exclude a Greek presence either there or in other areas of the Mediterranean.

For the classical period, Cabrera argued that the development of Laurion negated any need for Iberian silver in the eastern Mediterranean.[8] This argument is very difficult to substantiate at present without an extensive study of the metallic provenance of silver artefacts. More importantly, Laurion had a major competitor in the eastern Mediterranean, the Thracomacedonian region, which should have been more directly affected by the development of Laurion, yet apparently suffered no adverse effects. Additionally, the western Greeks would still need metals, of which the most likely supplier remained Iberia. The imports of Greek pottery in Iberia testify to Greek trading contacts with the region, while the large number of finds in the Huelva points directly towards metals being the main reason for such contact. Further, the Greek settlements on the east Iberian coast, such as Ampurias, show the considerable interest of the Greeks, especially the Massaliotes, in the region.[9]

---

[4] Aubet (1993: 315) against Burkert (1992: 21).

[5] Dominguez (1999: 301); Treister (1996: 188–189); Shefton (1994: 72); Boardman (1999: 213).

[6] Cabrera (1998: 193), Cabrera specifically considers Greek pottery to have been Phoenician gifts to the native elite but the context of many finds in industrial settings precludes this.

[7] A suitable example is of course Al-Mina: Boardman (1994: 140); Graham (1997: 250).

[8] Cabrera (1998: 197–198).

[9] Hodge (1998: 161–167).

Gaul has several gold deposits in the Salsigne area, and although there is no evidence of exploitation before the Roman period, there is extensive evidence for quantities of gold being in circulation among the natives; the nearest Greek polis was Massalia, which had commercial contacts with the Gallic tribes.[10]

In Italy, the Salassi tribe, who were Gallic, exploited deposits at the foot of the Alps near the River Adige in the second century.[11] This deposit could have been exploited earlier and gold could have entered the Greek world through Etruria, since the Etruscans had settlements in the Po Valley and a thriving precious metal industry.[12] In Sardinia, there were silver mines that were exploited in the fifth century, possibly by the Phoenicians.[13]

Illyria had silver mines in Damastion, which could be identified with modern Argyrokastro.[14] These mines have been connected in modern scholarship with Epidamnos and the conflict between Corcyra and Corinth; and possibly Damastion, through Epidamnos, was one of the suppliers of silver to Corinth in the fifth century.[15]

The Thracomacedonian region was particularly rich in precious metal deposits. The Macedonian Kingdom had at least one and possibly three gold deposits, in the Gallikos River, the Axios River and Mount Dysoron. The Gallikos deposit is mentioned in the sources and numerous ancient workings were observed there in the early twentieth century CE.[16] The exploitation of the other two deposits in the archaic and classical periods cannot be ascertained without further archaeological investigation.[17]

---

[10] Poseidonios FGrH87 F169; Diodoros 5.27.1. Forbes (1964: 168); Treister (1996: 148); Agard & Emberger (1989: 21–24); Bache (1987: 48–53, 99); Bouladon (1989: 42, 44–45, 71). Archaeological evidence from Gaul suggests that gold was widely used by the native population: Hodge (1998: 115).

[11] Strabo 4.6.7. Forbes (1964: 168); Zuffardi (1989: 222–224, 238, 241, 243).

[12] Athenaios 1.28b. Treister (1996: 252) proposed that the Greek poleis of Italy and Sicily in the fourth century imported silver from Calabria, but the evidence of mining operations there in the classical period is still insufficient.

[13] Treister (1996: 186); Healy (1978: 53).

[14] Strabo 7.7.8; Shepherd (1993: 106–107). Argyrokastro, meaning "silver castle" in modern Greek, is modern Gjirokaster in Albania. Note that Finley (1965: 17–18) does not think that there were mines in Illyria.

[15] Coin analysis of Corinthian coins has shown that before the Peloponnesian War Corinth imported ⅓ of its silver from Athens; the other suppliers remain unidentified: Kraay & Emeleus (1962: 35); Hornblower (1991b: 17); Boardman (1980: 285); Shepherd (1993: 106).

[16] Scylax *Periplous* 66.7; Strabo 7.F21. Treister (1996: 184); Liatsikas (1939: 559); Georgalas (1921: 10–11).

[17] The Axios deposit needed no permanent facilities: Mastoris et al. (1979: 276).

In the Chalcidice, two areas had gold and silver deposits: Mount Stratonike and the Lagkadas basin. On Mount Stratonike, the two main mining areas were Olympias and Skouries, where extensive remains of ancient exploitation have been found.[18] The nearest polis to both sites was Stageira but the best candidate for domination was Akanthos, the largest polis in the eastern Chalcidice and a prolific minter.[19] In the Lagkadas basin, remains of ancient exploitation have also been found; the deposit belonged either to Apollonia or to Lete.[20] Healy and Treister have argued that these deposits were not exploited before 383 and that they belonged to either Olynthos or Macedon (under Philip II) based on the speech of the Akanthians in Sparta as reported by Xenophon, which does not mention any gold mines:[21]

> What is the hindrance (to their expansion), since there is timber for shipbuilding in the land, and there are monetary revenues from many harbours and *emporia*, and there are many people and an abundance of grain?[22]

The Akanthian speech, however, refers specifically to the resources of Olynthos and the allies it is trying to attract, Potidaia and the poleis of the peninsula of Pallene:

Dysoron: Barbaressos (1933: 1219–1220); Demou (1989: 214–215); *Επεξηγηματικόν τεύχος του μεταλλογενετικού χάρτου της Ελλάδος* (1973: 212); Mpitzios (1989b: 43–44); Mposkos (1982/1983: 97–98). Ancient slag heaps in Dysoron, need for further analysis: Papastamataki (1975: 34).

[18] Slagheaps: Papastamataki (1975: 32), (1979: 869). Skouries exploited for gold: Oikonomou-Eliopoulou et al. (2000: 150); Mpitzios (1989b: 42). High copper content in the slag is the result of incomplete smelting, a usual practice by the Greeks when exploiting a precious metal deposit with a high base metal content as for example silver and lead in Laurion: Papastamataki (1979: 879–880). Ancient mine shafts and galleries in Olympias: Papastamataki (1975: 30–31), (1979: 868, 881).

[19] Akanthos was clearly more powerful than Stageira and exploitation of these gold (and silver) deposits would explain both the amount of coinage minted by Akanthos and the tribute (5 and 3 talents) it paid to Athens in the 5th century: Hansen & Nielsen (2004: 559, 613).

[20] Two ancient galleries and one shaft (from archaic to Hellenistic periods): Vavelidis (1990: 173).

[21] Treister (1996: 186); Healy (1978: 46–47); Shepherd (1993: 104). Note that each account mentions different deposits, belonging to different poleis and for different periods.

[22] Xenophon *Hellenika* 5.2.16–17: τί γὰρ δὴ καὶ ἐμποδών, ὅπου ξύλα μὲν ναυπηγήσιμα ἐν αὐτῇ τῇ χώρᾳ ἐστί, χρημάτων δὲ πρόσοδοι ἐκ πολλῶν μὲν λιμένων, ἐκ πολλῶν δ’ ἐμπορίων, πολυανθρωπία γε μὴν διὰ τὴν πολυσιτίαν ὑπάρχει;

> Since they also have Potidaia, which is at the isthmus of Pallene and the poleis inside it (i.e. the peninsula) are their vassals.[23]

Yet the deposits were within the spheres of influence of Akanthos and Apollonia, the poleis whose representatives make the speech. Since there is no reason to suppose that the Akanthians and the Apolloniates would mention their own resources in the speech, the mines may have been exploited before 383.

Lake Prasias on the Strymon boasted one alluvial gold deposit in Nigrita, where numerous ancient workings have been found, and one silver deposit, mentioned by Herodotos as particularly rich.[24] The area was traditionally dominated by Thracian tribes, probably the Edoni, but there was a brief period of Macedonian domination in the early fifth century, while after its foundation the area probably belonged to Amphipolis.[25] The Pangaion precious metal deposits are among the best known in the ancient world. Silver was mined in modern Nikisiani and Palaiochori. Ancient remains of gold exploitation have been found in modern Nikisiani, Mesorope and Philippoi, while the sources also mention three mining areas, Philippoi, Daton and Scapte Hyle; Philippoi can be identified with modern Philippoi. Since Scapte Hyle was exploited by the Thasians, it could be identified with Mesorope near Neapolis, the primary Thasian colony in the area.[26] The sources give contradictory accounts of the location of Daton but if its connection with the Edoni is credible, then it could be identified with Nikisiani near Amphipolis.[27] In the early archaic period control of the district belonged to the Thracians, but after its foundation Thasos forcibly took control of part of the area; Nikisiani, Palaiochori and Philippoi probably belonged to the Thracians and Scapte Hyle to Thasos.[28] Athens in the 460s tried to dominate the

---

[23] Xenophon *Hellenika* 5.2.15: ἐπεὶ δὲ καὶ Ποτείδαιαν ἔχουσιν ἐπὶ τῷ ἰσθμῷ τῆς Παλλήνης οὖσαν, νομίζετε καὶ τὰς ἐντὸς ταύτης πόλεις ὑπηκόους ἔσεσθαι αὐτῶν.

[24] Gold, ancient remains: Mastoris et al. (1979: 287–288); Georgalas (1921: 19); Kelepertzis (1980: 19). Lake Prasias: Herodotos 5.17.2; Shepherd (1993: 96).

[25] Macedonian domination: Hammond (1979: 102).

[26] Herodotos 6.46.2–3.

[27] Of the various conflicting sources, I follow Herodotos, as the nearest chronologically. Connection with the Edoni: Herodotos 9.75.1. Connection with Neapolis: Strabo 7.F33, F36, F32. A Thasian colony: Zenobius 3.11. Identification with Philippoi: Harpokration s. v. Δάτος; Appian 4.13.105. Contradicting Diodoros (16.8.6), who mentions specifically that Krenides was renamed Philippoi and does not mention Daton. Leake (1835: 223–224); Pauly-Wissowa s.v. Daton.

[28] Archaic conflict between Thasos and Thracian tribes at the time of settlement: Archilochos F102, 105, 291. Thracian holdings: Herodotos 7.112; Lavelle (1992: 17).

whole area but succeeded only in wresting Scapte Hyle from Thasian control. After the foundation of Amphipolis and especially during the Peloponnesian War, specific spheres of control cannot be ascertained. The dissolution of the Athenian Empire could have enabled Thasos to regain its possessions; however, the anti-Thasian stance of Neapolis in the last decade of the Peloponnesian War suggests that the ownership of Scapte Hyle could have been in dispute.[29] The Thracian tribes probably never lost control of their mines; if they did, they had certainly regained it by 382, while the Thasians had control of Krenides and the surrounding area for some time before the middle of the fourth century.[30] In the second half of the fourth century, control of the whole area passed to Macedon through conquest.

The exploitation regime practiced by Thasos and the Thracians is unknown, although the Thracians certainly disposed of some of their surplus through coinage.[31] The tradition of Peisistratos' exploitation of mines in the Pangaion area suggests that the Thracians were not averse to leasing out concessions.[32] Since the Thracians in the fifth century were particularly hostile to encroachment of their mining areas as seen in the Ennea Hodoi episode, it is probable that Peisistratos fitted into an existing system of concessions and was certainly not perceived as hostile. In all probability, the concession carried a monetary recompense to the tribe in control of the area, rather than some future reward of a more nebulous nature, as suggested by Cole.[33]

For the later part of the fifth century, Thucydides' testimony suggests that Athenians with familial ties to the region had control of the mines of Scapte Hyle:

> At that point Brasidas was concerned about the help coming from Thasos with the ships and feared Thucydides, who had the concession of the gold mines in that area of Thrace and, thus, influence over the best of the mainlanders ...[34]

---

[29] IG I^3 101.

[30] Thracians: Xenophon *Hellenika* 5.2.17. Krenides: based on numismatic evidence, see Hammond (1979: 358).

[31] Austin & Vidal-Naquet (1977: 57); Boardman (1980: 132); Hornblower (1991: 63).

[32] Herodotos 1.64; [Aristotle] *Constitution of the Athenians* 15.2.

[33] Cole (1975).

[34] Thucydides 4.105.1: Ἐν τούτῳ δὲ ὁ Βρασίδας δεδιὼς καὶ τὴν ἀπὸ τῆς Θάσου τῶν νεῶν βοήθειαν καὶ πυνθανόμενος τὸν Θουκυδίδην κτῆσίν τε ἔχειν τῶν χρυσείων μετάλλων ἐργασίας ἐν τῇ περὶ ταῦτα Θρᾴκῃ καὶ ἀπ' αὐτοῦ δύνασθαι ἐν τοῖς πρώτοις τῶν ἠπειρωτῶν ...

The exact system of exploitation cannot be reconstructed but Thucydides' words do offer a glimpse of the type of exploitation. Thucydides clearly suggests that Athens owned the mines and that he had control of the works. Such a system is similar to the lease system practiced in fourth-century Athens for the Laurion mines, although it seems that, unlike the fourth-century leases, in the holdings in Thrace areas of exploitation were leased, rather than individual mines. A lease system would not only be consistent with latter Athenian practice but also account for the gold from these mines found in the Athenian treasury.[35]

After the Macedonian conquest, ownership of the mines passed to the Macedonian king. The exact system of exploitation is unknown but Diodoros' testimony of Philip's investment to increase production suggests a more direct involvement by the Macedonian government in exploitation:

> After these he went to the polis Krenides, which he enlarged with a number of settlers and renamed it Philippoi after himself. At the gold mines near the city, which were small and unimportant, he enlarged the infrastructure to the extent that they brought him revenue of over 1000 talents. From these he quickly collected much wealth, and due to the amount of wealth, he led the Macedonian kingship to great power. He minted a gold coinage, which was called after him Philippeion, and with this he created a large force of mercenaries and bribed many Greeks to become traitors to their fatherlands.[36]

Specifically, Philip is said to have increased profit from the mines through increased investment in infrastructure and to have received 1000 talents from this investment, which he used to mint a gold coinage. Even if the figure itself is spurious, the connection between the proceeds and the *philippeion* suggests that the king exploited the mines directly rather than through leasing; probably the same was true of the earlier exploitation of the Lake Prasias mine by Alexander I.[37] If Philip employed

[35] IG I[3] 376.105, 118.

[36] Diodoros 16.8.6–7: μετὰ δὲ ταῦτα παρελθὼν ἐπὶ πόλιν Κρηνίδας ταύτην μὲν ἐπαυξήσας οἰκητόρων πλήθει μετωνόμασε Φιλίππους, ἀφ' ἑαυτοῦ προσαγορεύσας, τὰ δὲ κατὰ τὴν πόλιν χρύσεια μέταλλα παντελῶς ὄντα λιτὰ καὶ ἄδοξα ταῖς κατασκευαῖς ἐπὶ τοσοῦτον ηὔξησεν ὥστε δύνασθαι φέρειν αὐτῷ πρόσοδον πλεῖον ἢ ταλάντων χιλίων. ἐκ δὲ τούτων ταχὺ σωρεύσας πλοῦτον αἰεὶ μᾶλλον διὰ τὴν εὐπορίαν τῶν χρημάτων εἰς ὑπεροχὴν μεγάλην ἤγαγε τὴν Μακεδονικὴν βασιλείαν· νόμισμα γὰρ χρυσοῦν κόψας τὸ προσαγορευθὲν ἀπ' ἐκείνου Φιλίππειον μισθοφόρων τε δύναμιν ἀξιόλογον συνεστήσατο καὶ τῶν Ἑλλήνων πολλοὺς διὰ τούτου προετρέψατο προδότας γενέσθαι τῶν πατρίδων. Treister (1996: 184).

[37] Hammond (1979: 360), (1989: 178–180); Borza & Thomas (1995: 42–43). For the

leasing as the main method of exploitation, then the investment in infrastructure is difficult to understand, since it would be expected for the lessees to make such investment, especially in the opening of *kainotomiai* (new cuttings/mines). Further, Diodoros' comment on the speed with which Philip amassed this wealth ("he quickly collected much wealth") also implies direct exploitation. Certainly, the disposition of the surplus as coinage made the effects of the conquest of the region and of the increased exploitation widely felt.

The island of Thasos also had gold and silver deposits, which were a major source of revenue.[38] Both Herodotos and Thucydides attest the state ownership of these mines but whether the Thasian state exploited the resources directly or used a leasing system is not certain:

> In the next year it happened that the Thasians seceded from them due to a quarrel about the *emporia* opposite in Thrace and the mine they possessed.[39]
>
> That revenue came from the mainland and the mines.[40]

In eastern Thrace, the gold deposit in the river Ardas probably belonged to the Thracian tribes of the area, either the Koilaletai or the Bennoi; the nearest poleis were Maroneia and Ainos.[41]

Siphnos was the main precious metal producer in the Aegean in the archaic period.[42] The mines contributed greatly to the wealth of the island:

---

opposite view, on the use of leasing for exploitation, see Hatzopoulos (1996: 434–435) based on Livy 45.29.11. Livy refers to the status quo at the time of Perseus at the end of the Hellenistic period, which may imply that there had been a change in the exploitation regime of the mines in the intervening period.

[38] Herodotos 6.47.1–2. Gold mines in the acropolis and in modern Kinyra: Tsompos et al. (1989: 84); Vavelidis & Amsutz (1983: 385, 387, 389); Higgins & Higgins (1996: 120); Wagner et al. (1989); Papastamataki (1985: 49–50). Treister (1996: 25) identified modern Potamia near Kinyra with ancient Ainyra. Silver mines on the western side of the island: Treister (1996: 187).

[39] Thucydides 1.100.2: χρόνῳ δὲ ὕστερον ξυνέβη Θασίους αὐτῶν ἀποστῆναι, διενεχθέντας περὶ τῶν ἐν τῇ ἀντιπέρας Θρᾴκῃ ἐμπορίων καὶ τοῦ μετάλλου ἃ ἐνέμοντο.

[40] Herodotos 6.46: Ἡ δὲ πρόσοδός σφι ἐγίνετο ἔκ τε τῆς ἠπείρου καὶ ἀπὸ τῶν μετάλλων.

[41] Pliny *Natural History* 23. 66. Healy (1978: 46); Shepherd (1993: 103); Eliopoulos & Konstantinides (1989: 78–79); Orfanos (1985: 22); Michael (1989: 98); Mpitzios (1989a: 315), (1989b: 42–43).

[42] Gold mines: Pausanias 10.11.2. Pausanias also mentions that exploitation stopped due to flooding (traditional date 516) but modern investigations showed that only the mine at Ayios Sostis could have been in danger of flooding, so probably the ore had run

> At that time, the Siphnians were in ascendance. In fact, they were the richest of the islanders, because there were on the island gold and silver mines. The mines were so productive that from the tenth of their *ginomena*, the Siphnians built a treasury at Delphi as rich as any other. They used to divide the *ginomena* amongst themselves.[43]

Although Herodotos does not mention the amount of profit, the overall impression is of great wealth. The state ownership of the mines is evident in the text but the specific exploitation regime employed depends upon the interpretation of *ginomena*, which can mean either the revenue accrued by the state through leasing the mines or the entire profit of the industry if the state exploited the resources directly.[44] However, since direct exploitation and the subsequent monopoly are attested only in monarchical states, it is safe to assume that the Siphnians employed a system of diffused exploitation. The disposition of surpluses preferred by the Siphnian state was direct distribution to the people, thus allowing substantial quantities of silver to enter the market, creating additional wealth for those not directly involved in the mining industry. Part of the surplus was disposed of in religious and civic functions, such as public buildings and a treasury at Delphi.[45] Finally, part of the surplus was exported, most notably to Aigina, where 18 % of its archaic coinage was made of Siphnian silver.[46] The form of export as bullion or coins is a matter of conjecture but bullion is the better option of the two. Export in the form of coins is less probable not only because the amount of Siphnian coins minted is very low in comparison to those of Aigina but also because there has been no adequate explanation of the extra costs accrued by the suggested process of minting, melting and reminting.[47]

Athens was the greatest silver producer in the eastern Mediterranean in the classical period. The Laurion mines were exploited intermittently

---

out by the end of the archaic period: Higgins & Higgins (1996: 177); Treister (1996: 188); Healy (1978: 46).

[43] Herodotos 3.57: Χρημάτων γὰρ ἐδέοντο, τὰ δὲ τῶν Σιφνίων πρήγματα ἤκμαζε τοῦτον τὸν χρόνον, καὶ νησιωτέων μάλιστα ἐπλούτεον, ἅτε ἐόντων αὐτοῖσι ἐν τῇ νήσῳ χρυσέων καὶ ἀργυρέων μετάλλων, οὕτω ὥστε ἀπὸ τῆς δεκάτης τῶν γινομένων αὐτόθεν χρημάτων θησαυρὸς ἐν Δελφοῖσι ἀνάκειται ὅμοια τοῖσι πλουσιωτάτοισι· αὐτοὶ δὲ τὰ γινόμενα τῷ ἐνιαυτῷ ἑκάστῳ χρήματα διενέμοντο.

[44] The only related use of *ginomena* I found was products of the earth as agricultural produce, ex. IG XII Suppl. 345 and Plutarch *Solon* 24, while in Aristotle *Oeconomica* 1346a6–9, the word is used generically.

[45] Herodotos 3.57.

[46] Treister (1996: 188); Kraay (1959: 3) (1976: 45); Price (1981: 51); Papadopoulos (2002: 42).

[47] On this see further page 84.

from the Bronze Age onwards.[48] The classical exploitation started in the late archaic period contemporaneously with the minting of the early Athenian owls.[49] The continuous exploitation of the mines in the classical period has been questioned by Hopper who argued that the lack and fragmentation of the available evidence on Laurion reflects not the state of the sources but the nature of the exploitation itself.[50] Archaeological research has shown that Laurion was an industrial area for the whole of the classical period, but the type of remains surviving and the natural indestructibility of the mines cannot prove continuity of exploitation.[51]

For the fifth century, Hopper argued that Laurion was abandoned sometime after the Persian Wars due to Athenian interest in the Thraco-macedonian sources, based on the lack of references to Laurion between Aischylos' *Persians* in 472 and the last quarter of the century, when the loss of Amphipolis to Brasidas spelled the end of Athenian domination of the area. The lack of references to Laurion in Perikles' speeches at the beginning of the Peloponnesian War is considered of special import.[52] The problems with Hopper's argument are many. Firstly, full Athenian domination of the Strymon and Pangaion areas cannot be postulated before the foundation of Amphipolis in 437. Secondly, the Pentekontaetia is a badly documented period known only from Thucydides' brief account and later references; more importantly, Laurion was outside the scope of Thucydides' account, whose focus was the empire.[53] The lack of references in Perikles' speeches in the beginning of the Peloponnesian War or in Thucydides' account of the resources of Athens for the war is expected since Thucydides focuses on the empire. The only possible reference to internal revenues is the quite vague 'apart from their other revenues' in the following passage:

> He gave advice urging the same things as before: to prepare for war, bring in the movable property from the fields and not to rush into battle but to enter the city and guard it, further to get the fleet ready for on that depended their power. Also he urged to keep in hand the allies, thinking that their power was dependent on them and on the money from them, especially in war where success depended upon counsel and money. He

[48] Kakavoyiannis (2005: 93–96); Dayton (1978: 235).
[49] Kraay & Emeleus (1962: 16).
[50] Hopper (1961: 143, 145).
[51] Hopper (1968: 293–302); Jones (1982).
[52] Hopper (1961: 143–147).
[53] Thucydides 1.97.2: "and provide evidence of how the empire of the Athenians came to be."

> said that there were annually 600 talents of revenue coming in from the allies apart from their other revenues.[54]

However, the passage does not create the impression that Thucydides is here referring to internal revenue. Perikles' strategy as described by Thucydides is based upon, and targets, the empire. In the text, the weight falls upon the navy and keeping the allies in hand, revenue being specifically mentioned as the key issue regarding the empire. This emphasis on the empire and its revenues is the immediate backdrop of any interpretation of the phrase: "He said that there were annually 600 talents of revenue coming in from the allies apart from their other revenues." Consequently, it follows smoothly in Perikles' argument that the 'other revenues' are also imperial revenues. These lesser imperial revenues are not mentioned in Thucydides but may be partly reconstructed from other sources, such as the pseudo-Xenophontic *Athenaion Politeia*, where the financial rewards of imposing judicial disabilities on the allies are mentioned:

> Of these that is how the Athenian *demos* profits from the fact that the trials of the allies take place in Athens. Firstly, the revenue to the polis from the *hekatoste* at the Piraeus increases, secondly the boarding houses do very good business, then there is revenue from the hiring of teams or slaves, lastly the heralds also do well from the allies' arrival here.[55]

It appears that Thucydides at no point mentions internal Athenian resources, focusing instead on the proceeds of the empire, which, on the one hand, seems a major omission but, on the other, represents admirably the Periclean strategy and its rationale.

For the role of the Laurion mines in the Athenian economy it is better to turn to the passages were the mines are mentioned, such as in the second Peloponnesian invasion of Attika:

---

[54] Thucydides 2.13.2–3: παρῄνει δὲ καὶ περὶ τῶν παρόντων ἅπερ καὶ πρότερον, παρασκευάζεσθαί τε ἐς τὸν πόλεμον καὶ τὰ ἐκ τῶν ἀγρῶν ἐσκομίζεσθαι, ἔς τε μάχην μὴ ἐπεξιέναι, ἀλλὰ τὴν πόλιν ἐσελθόντας φυλάσσειν, καὶ τὸ ναυτικόν, ᾗπερ ἰσχύουσιν, ἐξαρτύεσθαι, τά τε τῶν ξυμμάχων διὰ χειρὸς ἔχειν, λέγων τὴν ἰσχὺν αὐτοῖς ἀπὸ τούτων εἶναι τῶν χρημάτων τῆς προσόδου, τὰ δὲ πολλὰ τοῦ πολέμου γνώμῃ καὶ χρημάτων περιουσίᾳ κρατεῖσθαι. θαρσεῖν τε ἐκέλευε προσιόντων μὲν ἑξακοσίων ταλάντων ὡς ἐπὶ τὸ πολὺ φόρου κατ' ἐνιαυτὸν ἀπὸ τῶν ξυμμάχων τῇ πόλει ἄνευ τῆς ἄλλης προσόδου.

[55] [Xenophon] *Constitution of the Athenians* (= Old Oligarch) 1.17–18: πρὸς δὲ τούτοις ὁ δῆμος τῶν Ἀθηναίων τάδε κερδαίνει τῶν δικῶν Ἀθήνησιν οὐσῶν τοῖς συμμάχοις. πρῶτον μὲν γὰρ ἡ ἑκατοστὴ τῇ πόλει πλείων ἡ ἐν Πειραιεῖ· ἔπειτα εἴ τῳ συνοικία ἐστίν, ἄμεινον πράττει· ἔπειτα εἴ τῳ ζεῦγός ἐστιν ἢ ἀνδράποδον μισθοφοροῦν· ἔπειτα οἱ κήρυκες ἄμεινον πράττουσι διὰ τὰς ἐπιδημίας τὰς τῶν συμμάχων.

> The Peloponnesians, after they had laid waste to the plain, went to the area called Paralos up until Laurion, where the silver mines of the Athenians are. Firstly, they laid waste to the land, which looks towards the Peloponnese, and then the one towards Euboia and Andros. Perikles, who was general then also, as to whether the Athenians should not go out against the enemy, had the same opinion as in the previous invasion.[56]

Here Perikles' insistence that the Athenians should not sally from the walls in defence of the region and the Peloponnesian choice to target the southern Paralos first illuminate the importance of the mines in the eyes of the Athenians. The resurgence of Laurion in the sources in the last quarter of the century coincides with the reappearance of written sources at the time, not the loss of Amphipolis.[57]

For the fourth century, Hopper suggested that the mines remained disused from the end of the Peloponnesian War until the early 360s, explaining the resumption of silver minting in the 390s as the result of Persian support; without specific archaeological evidence, the argument cannot be substantiated.[58] Moreover, the lack of any such reference in Aristophanes, our main source for the recall of plated coins, is at the very least curious if the new Athenian owls were made of Persian silver.[59] For the remainder of the fourth century, the *poletai* records and various references in the sources show that the mines were working.[60] Overall, the evidence does not suggest discontinued exploitation of the Laurion mines in the classical period, except during the Dekeleian War and the early 390s. The exploitation regime and disposal of the surplus of the Laurion mines are discussed in the next chapter.

Greece and the Aegean had several minor precious metal deposits; information on their exploitation has not survived. A gold veinlet deposit in Kalliana near Karystos in Euboia has yielded remains of ancient exploitation but these have not been dated, while Aristotle referred to a deposit in Samos, which has been doubted in modern scholarship but is

---

[56] Thucydides 2.55: Οἱ δὲ Πελοποννήσιοι ἐπειδὴ ἔτεμον τὸ πεδίον, παρῆλθον ἐς τὴν Πάραλον γῆν καλουμένην μέχρι Λαυρείου, οὗ τὰ ἀργύρεια μέταλλά ἐστιν Ἀθηναίοις. καὶ πρῶτον μὲν ἔτεμον ταύτην ᾗ πρὸς Πελοπόννησον ὁρᾷ, ἔπειτα δὲ τὴν πρὸς Εὔβοιάν τε καὶ Ἄνδρον τετραμμένην. Περικλῆς δὲ στρατηγὸς ὢν καὶ τότε περὶ μὲν τοῦ μὴ ἐπεξιέναι τοὺς Ἀθηναίους τὴν αὐτὴν γνώμην εἶχεν ὥσπερ καὶ ἐν τῇ προτέρᾳ ἐσβολῇ.

[57] Note that Thucydides mentions the mines as a major resource of the Athenian state in the speech of Alkibiades at Sparta (6.91.7).

[58] Hopper (1953: 248–249).

[59] Aristophanes *Frogs* 718–737, *Assemblywomen* 815–822.

[60] Agora 19.P5–51; Xenophon *Ways and Means* 4; [Aristotle] *Constitution of the Athenians* 47.2; Demosthenes 37.

geologically probable.[61] Silver deposits were possibly exploited in Melos, Kimolos and Methymna in Lesbos.[62]

The Black Sea had several precious metal deposits, mainly of gold. The main gold deposits were in the Colchis, Lake Van and Dacia. Colchis has been traditionally associated with gold resources, especially those of the tribe of the Soanes, but recently this association has come under attack, mainly by Gocha Tsetskhladze.[63] Tsetskhladze suggested that the colonisation of the area was not connected to its gold resources but to increased pressure by the Lydians and Persians on the Asia Minor metropoleis, arguing that the Asia Minor metropoleis had local gold resources in the Paktolos and Thasos, and thus did not need further resources.[64] The motive of any colonising venture is debatable, if indeed any single motive can be attached; however, Tsetskhladze's proposal has merit since increased pressure by the eastern kingdoms could explain the large number of colonies sent by the Asia Minor poleis, especially Miletos. On the other hand, the Asia Minor poleis did not have local gold resources in the Paktolos and Thasos because neither deposit belonged to them. The example of Thasos shows that it should not be assumed that mines in one polis (Siphnos) stopped others in the same region (Paros) from trying to settle in areas with similar resources. Thus, the gold resources of the area could have motivated colonisation to some extent. Further, Greek settlement in the Colchis was commercially oriented, as a recent comparison between the settlement pattern of the Colchis and the Crimean Bosporus has shown.[65]

[61] Kalliana: *Επεξηγηματικόν τεύχος του μεταλλογενετικού χάρτου της Ελλάδος* (1973: 214); Georgalas (1921: 7); Mpitzios (1989b: 41, 44); Theofilopoulos & Vakondios (1982: 27, 29–30, 35, 37, 39–40); Trikkalinos (1961: 395–396). Samos: Aristotle *Fragmenta Varia* 8.444.572; Treister (1996: 186); Healy (1978: 46). On the geology of Samos: Mpitzios (1989a: 319), (1989b: 51).

[62] Melos: Aristotle *On Marvellous Things Heard* 44; Treister (1996: 186). Kimolos: Shepherd (1993: 112). Methymna: Treister (1996: 186); Healy (1978: 53).

[63] Strabo 11.2.19, Appian *Mithridatic Wars* 103, Pliny *Natural History* 6.14, 6.30, 33.52. The Soanes exploited the alluvial deposits of the area using sluices lined with animal skins, which could be the grain of truth behind the myth of the Golden Fleece.

[64] Tsetskhladze (1994), (1995: 307, 323–325), (1998: 64–65). Tsetskhladze (1994: 114) is right to criticize modern scholars for using the Argonaut myth as evidence of Greek knowledge of the Colchian resources in the Bronze Age; however from the eighth century onwards, there is evidence that the Greeks knew of the gold resources, traded in the area and had themselves made the connection between Colchis and the Argonaut myth (Eumelos F2).

[65] Koshelenko & Kuznetsov (1996). It seems that the colonies in the Colchis were *enoikismoi* rather than *apoikiai*: Gabelia (2003: 1217).

The deposits of Lake Van and the Karebech Mountains were in the territory of local tribes, the Chalybes and probably the Taochoi, which had relations with the Greeks from the pre-colonial period; the nearest Greek poleis were Trapezous and Amisos.[66] The deposits in Dacia are among the richest in Europe and numerous old workings have been found, mainly in Maramureş and Roşia Montana; the earliest date of exploitation has not yet been confirmed.[67] The deposits were in the territory of local tribes and evidence from hoards suggests relations with Histria and Macedon in the classical period.[68] Finally, the Greek poleis of the Crimean Bosporus, Pantikapaion and Theodosia, were probably the entrance point of gold from the deposits of the Ural and Altai Mountains, where numerous old workings have been found.[69] The precious metal industry of the area and the suggestive griffin legend on the coinage of Pantikapaion support the theory that gold was imported through the Crimea into the Greek world.[70]

Asia Minor had two gold-producing regions: the Troas and the Tmolos-Paktolos. In the Troas, the only ascertained deposit was in Astyra near Abydos, which was probably exploited from the fifth century.[71] A gold deposit is often mentioned in connection with Lampsakos but there is neither archaeological nor geological evidence of its existence; possibly this was only a small rare mineral deposit, since the sources refer

[66] Chalybes: Aristotle *On Marvellous Things Heard* 26. Syspiritis: Strabo 11.14.9. Forbes (1964: 162); Healy (1978: 47).

[67] Dumitru (1993: 52–53). For Roşia Montana, unconcluded archaeological investigations of the mines found objects from the third century but the archaeologists cautioned that the dating is not yet secure: Cauuet (2002: 65).

[68] Lockyear (2004: 65).

[69] Ural Mountains: Smirnov (1989: 279). Kochkar and Berezovo: Smirnov (1989: 359–360). Altai Mountains: traditionally Aristeas was the first Greek to have contact with the area particularly with the Issedonians (modern Saka), who had relations with the Greek World since the seventh century (Pausanias 1.24.6).

[70] On the relation between the legend of the griffins as mythical guardians of gold and the Altai Mountains, see Mayor (1994: 53–56); Williams & Ogden (1994: 13). Treister (1996: 178) argued that the precious metal industry in the Bosporus used material from the deposits of Asia Minor and the Aegean but the Bosporus was at the end of a major trade-route with the east and there were closer areas from which to acquire gold (including the southern Black Sea) than to assume a tortuous route of imports through the Asia Minor metropoleis.

[71] Xenophon *Hellenika* 4.8.37; Strabo 13.1.23. Cook (1973: 290, 366); Forbes (1971: 166); Treister (1996: 188); Shepherd (1993: 223); *Arsenic, Mercury, Antimony And Gold Deposits Of Turkey* (1970: 21). Modern Kalekayasi and Sarikaya: modern exploitation has destroyed any signs of ancient mining. The first mention of the mines is in Xenophon, but the Abydene fifth century gold coinage suggests that the mines were exploited earlier.

to precious stones from the site not gold.[72] The Tmolos-Paktolos region includes three deposits exploited in antiquity: Karşikaya, Salihli and Tire.[73] The deposit of Karşikaya, which is not mentioned in either sources or scholarship but has been confirmed archaeologically, was probably in the territory of Smyrna. Karşikaya may be particularly important in the study of the provenance of Asia Minor coinage, since it is the only deposit in the region within the territory of a Greek polis rather than in the hands of the Lydians.[74] Salihli is the famous Paktolos River deposit often mentioned in the sources, while old workings suggest the exploitation of Tire on the slopes of Tmolos near the Cayster River; both deposits belonged to the kingdom of Lydia.[75]

The Lydian state intervened in the production and export of gold as early as the reign of Kroisos:

> Kroisos made these proposals through his messengers and the Lakedaimonians having heard of the oracle to Kroisos welcomed the Lydians and made an alliance with them; they had also in the past received benefits from Kroisos. When the Lakedaimonians had sent to Sardis to buy gold, which they wanted to use for a statue of Apollo, the one that now stands in Lakonia in Thornax, Kroisos as they were buying it gave it to them as a gift.[76]

This is the earliest case of an official commercial transaction between states in the Greek world, and as such its importance is paramount.[77] The first and most important question is the authenticity of the story,

---

[72] Theophrastos *On Stones* 32; Pliny *Natural History* 37.74. Treister (1996: 186); Healy (1978: 46).

[73] Treister (1996: 172) mentions a particularly rich gold deposit on Mount Tmolos near Ephesos, for which he does not give an exact location; there are no deposits near Ephesos (the nearest are on the southern slopes of the Tmolos Mountain, which have yielded no old workings and even if exploited in antiquity would belong to Lydia).

[74] *Arsenic, Mercury, Antimony And Gold Deposits Of Turkey* (1970: 22).

[75] Athenaios 5.36; *Scholia in Lycophronem* 272.4a, 27210b; Herodotos 1.69.4, 1.93.1, 5.101.2; Pliny *Natural History* 33.66; Strabo 13.1.23, 13.4.5. Forbes (1971: 166); Healy (1978: 46); Shepherd (1993: 225); Treister (1996: 172).

[76] Herodotos 1.69: Κροῖσος μὲν δὴ ταῦτα δι' ἀγγέλων ἐπεκηρυκεύετο, Λακεδαιμόνιοι δὲ ἀκηκοότες καὶ αὐτοὶ τὸ θεοπρόπιον τὸ Κροίσῳ γενόμενον ἥσθησάν τε τῇ ἀπίξι τῶν Λυδῶν καὶ ἐποιήσαντο ὅρκια ξεινίης πέρι καὶ συμμαχίης. Καὶ γάρ τινες αὐτοὺς εὐεργεσίαι εἶχον ἐκ Κροίσου πρότερον ἔτι γεγονυῖαι· πέμψαντες γὰρ οἱ Λακεδαιμόνιοι ἐς Σάρδις χρυσὸν ὠνέοντο, ἐς ἄγαλμα βουλόμενοι χρήσασθαι τοῦτο τὸ νῦν τῆς Λακωνικῆς ἐν Θόρνακι ἵδρυται Ἀπόλλωνος, Κροῖσος δέ σφι ὠνεομένοισι ἔδωκε δωτίνην.

[77] State-to-state transactions were common in earlier periods in the Near East as seen in the transactions between Kings Solomon and Hiram, which were a permanent arrangement: *Kings* 1.5.7–12; Elat (1979, especially p. 545).

since Herodotos is more than a century removed from the event. The authenticity of the story is shown by the reference to the statue of Apollo and its placement in Herodotos' own day. The involvement of the Spartan state in the transaction is testified by the use of 'the Lakedaimonians' and by the supposed influence of the event on Spartan foreign policy. The commercial nature of the transaction is testified by the use of the words 'buy' (ὠνέοντο) and 'buying' (ὠνεομένοισι). Although Kroisos presents the gold as a gift, the purpose of the Spartans in going to Lydia was to buy the gold, not engage in gift-exchange. The passage further testifies that the supplier of the Spartans was the Lydian state itself, not some private trader in Sardis. The use of 'as they were buying it' (σφι ὠνεομένοισι) as the stage for Kroisos' gesture implies that the gold belonged to Kroisos, and thus was at his disposal to give as a gift. The state probably owned the deposits, as was common in the ancient world. Additionally however, the state-to-state transaction with Sparta and the evidence of ownership of large reserves of bullion by the Lydian kings suggests that the deposits were directly exploited, not leased out as was common in polis government.[78]

Briant has argued that the exploitation of the Lydian resources was in the hands of private individuals, who merely turned over part of their profits to the king, using as evidence the story of Pythios.[79] However, Pythios in Plutarch is specifically referred to as the governor of the city under the Persians, which clearly implies that the mines were in the control of the government, especially since he is shown as able to coerce citizens into working the mines. Direct exploitation of resources is attested in the Persian Empire in the cases of the iron mines of Niriz, the stone quarries of Wadi Hammurat and the naphtha fields of Susiana.[80] Such direct exploitation of natural resources appears to have been a feature of oriental kingships from an earlier period, as seen in the direct exploitation of the timber resources of Urartu and Subria by Sargon II.[81]

Further, the large reserves of bullion of the Lydian kings suggest strongly that the form of gold in the Lydo-Spartan transaction was bullion not coinage. More importantly, the transaction suggests that disposition and export of surpluses of gold and electrum were directly controlled

[78] Herodotos 1.51, 6.125.

[79] Briant (2002: 401) based on Plutarch *Moralia* 262d–263c.

[80] Susiana: Herodotos 6.119; Wadi Hammurat: Posener (1936: 179–180), Goyon (1957: 1–9, 128–130); Niriz: Persepolis Tablet 52, Cameron (1948: 166).

[81] Parpola (1987: no. 98); Lafranchi & Parpola (1990: xxv, nos. 33–34).

by the king. The setting of the transaction, possibly in the king's court so that Kroisos could observe and interfere in the transaction, suggests that judicious politically motivated gifts were a valid method of disposing of surpluses.

Cyprus was famous for its mineral wealth including a gold deposit in Kokkinoyia near Skouriotissa, which was probably in the territory of Soloi.[82] Egypt was a major gold producer in the Mediterranean and was in contact with Greeks from the early archaic period. Gold and grain were the major commodities Egypt could offer to the Greeks, along with lesser items such as papyrus, scarabs and other luxuries, and although scholarship has concentrated on the grain trade, gold must have been an item sought by the Greeks, especially in the archaic period when there was relatively little need for imported grain.[83]

---

82 Aristotle *Fragmenta Varia* 6.37.266, referring specifically to mines on Mount Trogodos. Bache (1987: 37); Hadjistavrinou & Constantinou (1982: 266); Forbes (1971: 166).

83 Hekataios FGrH1 F25.475; Diodoros 3.12.1, 1.49.2, 1.33.3; Agatharchides FGrH86 F19. Penhallurick (1986: 7); Shepherd (1993: 265); Forbes (1964: 162, 164). On the possibility of gold imports from Egypt see page 73. The gold deposits of India, Arabia and the Red Sea were known to the Greeks but it is doubtful that gold from these sources reached the Greek World in the archaic and classical periods. India: Herodotos 3.102; Strabo 15.1.30, 15.1.44; Megasthenes F39a, F1; Arian *Indica* 15.6; Diodoros 2.36.2; *Scholia in Theocrinem* 17.106/107; Bache (1987: 42–43, 145); Forbes (1964: 165). Arabia and Red Sea: Poseidonios FGrH87 F38; Diodoros 3.12.1, 2.50.1; *Paraphrases in Dionysium Periegetam* 933–953; Agatharchides FGrH86 F23.10; Cornelius Alexander F18; Bache (1987: 48–53); Forbes (1964: 164–165).

CHAPTER TWO

THE ATHENIAN SILVER INDUSTRY

Mineral wealth was a very important source of revenue for an ancient state, as the pseudo-Aristotelian *Oeconomica* informs us:

> Thirdly that of the polis. For this type of administration the major revenue is that of the special products of the country, then from the *emporia* and dues and lastly from the internal revenues.[1]

The author defines earlier the special products as "the one of the special products of the country, be they gold, or silver, or copper, or whatever else it produces."[2] Unfortunately, for the majority of silver and gold producers in the Greek world, very little information has survived relating to the role of the precious metal industry in their economies and the role of the state in production and export. The sole exception is Athens, from where both literary and epigraphical evidence on the mining industry and the role of silver in the economy is available. However, the evidence suggests that the Athenian government played a minor role in the actual export of silver, which immediately raises the question of the reason for such minimal intervention. The aim of this chapter is to discuss the role of the government in silver mining, the revenue it accrued from it and the role of silver in the economy of the polis, as well as to explain the absence of the government from export itself.

The state was involved in the production of silver at the most basic level, since the mines were public property. In Athens, known mines were leased to individuals and permission for exploration had to be granted, also under the lease arrangements. Yet the involvement of the state did not end there but extended also to regulating the exploitation itself, mainly through legislation. The mining laws themselves have not survived, but a summary of the legislation has:

---

[1] Aristotle *Oeconomica* 1346a6–9: Τρίτον δὲ τὴν πολιτικήν. Ταύτης δὲ κρατίστη μὲν πρόσοδος ἡ ἀπὸ τῶν ἰδίων ἐν τῇ χώρᾳ γινομένη. Εἶτα ἡ ἀπὸ τῶν ἐμπορίων καὶ διαγωγῶν. Εἶτα ἡ ἀπὸ τῶν ἐγκυκλίων.

[2] Aristotle *Oeconomica* 1345b33–35: ἡ ἀπὸ τῶν ἰδίων γινομένη, οὗ μὲν χρυσίον, οὗ δὲ ἀργύριον, οὗ δὲ χαλκός, οὗ δὲ ὁπόσα δύναται γίνεσθαι.

> Consider also the mining law. And from this law also, I will endeavour to show you that this trial is not admissible, and that I am more worthy of praise, not malicious accusations. Read. *Law.* This law mentions specifically which are the cases that are called *metallikai.* If someone ejects another from his workings, then the law makes him a defendant. But not only did I not eject him, but I made it possible for him to keep what another was trying to take away and I became his vendor when he asked me. Yes, he says, but if one commits other injustices concerning mines, then the cases can be admitted. You are right, Pantainetos! But which are those? If one smokes out another, if one makes an armed attack or if one bores beyond the boundaries. These are the other offences. But none of these did I commit against you. Unless of course, you think that when someone is trying to recover what he lent to you, he is making an armed attack. If such you think, then you can bring mining suits against all those who risk their own money.[3]

The law forbade the ejection of a lessee from a mine, the smoking out of a rival mine, an armed attack against another mine and an illegal expansion of a mine into another mine's territory. There may have been other provisions in the mining law, but the importance of the legislation rests not on its specific provisions but on its general spirit. The legislation has the specific target of protecting the mines and miners. From the state's point of view, as ultimate owner of the mines, the protection is that of an important investment. The state's income from the mines came in the first instance from the leases; an ejection of lessees either by a smoking trick or by force would reduce the income from them. Such incidents would not only deprive the state of the lease of the mine in question but also would deter future prospectors from trying their luck in the industry. An illegal expansion of a mine is a direct threat to the revenue of the state since the lessee would have greater income but would not reimburse the state for it, especially if the expansion is against an unworked mine. The mining legislation of Athens supervises the industry, aiming at protecting the resources of the state, but more importantly present and future revenues.

---

[3] Demosthenes 37.35–36: Λαβὲ δὴ καὶ τὸν μεταλλικὸν νόμον· καὶ γὰρ ἐκ τούτου δείξειν οἴομαι, οὔτ' οὖσαν εἰσαγώγιμον τὴν δίκην, χάριτός τ' ὢν μᾶλλον ἄξιος ἢ τοῦ συκοφαντεῖσθαι. λέγε. ΝΟΜΟΣ. Οὗτος σαφῶς ὁ νόμος διείρηκεν ὧν εἶναι δίκας προσήκει μεταλλικάς. οὐκοῦν ὁ μὲν νόμος, ἐάν τις ἐξίλλῃ τινὰ τῆς ἐργασίας, ὑπόδικον ποιεῖ· ἐγὼ δ' οὐχ ὅπως αὐτὸς ἐξίλλω, ἀλλ' ὧν τοῦτον ἄλλος ἀπεστέρει, τούτων ἐγκρατῆ κατέστησα καὶ παρέδωκα, καὶ πρατὴρ τούτου δεηθέντος ἐγενόμην. ναί, φησίν· ἀλλὰ κἂν ἄλλο τι ἀδικῇ τις περὶ τὰ μέταλλα, καὶ τούτων εἰσὶν δίκαι. ὀρθῶς γ', ὦ Πανταίνετε· ἀλλὰ ταῦτα τί ἐστιν; ἂν τύφῃ τις, ἂν ὅπλ' ἐπιφέρῃ, ἂν ἐπικατατέμνῃ τῶν μέτρων ἐντός. ταῦτ' ἐστὶν τἄλλα, ὧν οὐδὲν δήπου πέπρακται πρὸς ὑμᾶς ἐμοί, πλὴν εἰ τοὺς κομιζομένους ἃ προεῖντό σοι, μεθ' ὅπλων ἥκειν νομίζεις. εἰ δὲ ταῦθ' ἡγεῖ, πρὸς ἅπαντας τοὺς προϊεμένους τὰ ἑαυτῶν εἰσί σοι δίκαι μεταλλικαί.

The interest of the state in the mining industry was intimately connected to the revenue and wealth it generated. The first reference of revenue from the mines of Laurion implies great income for the state:

> Another of Themistocles' opinions before this resulted in great good, it was when the Athenians had lots of money in the common fund from the mines of Laurion and they planned to distribute it to all to the amount of 10 *drachmai* each. At that time Themistocles had counselled the Athenians to stop the distribution and to make with this money 200 ships for the war, the one against Aigina.[4]

Although Herodotos does not mention the exact amount in this passage, it is implied, from his earlier reference to the citizen population of Athens as 30,000, that it was 50 talents.[5] However, it must be noted that the revenue of the mines could have been larger and that the fifty talents were the ultimate surplus after the government had appropriated part of the funds for other purposes. More importantly, if the connection of this incident with the beginning of exploitation of Contact III is valid, then this was only the start of considerable revenue for the state, since Contact III contained the most and best ore.[6] The importance of revenue from the mines is also shown by Alkibiades' speech in Sparta, where Laurion is mentioned first among the revenues of the Athenians:

> The revenue from the silver mines of Laurion and from land and the courts, which they now have, will be immediately taken from them, especially the revenue from the allies will dry up, since the allies, seeing that you are now committed to total war, will not be diligent.[7]

The main source on the state revenue from the mines is the fourth-century mining leases in the *poletai* accounts (367–300). Only thirty of the 68 original lists have survived, all but one in fragments. Unfortunately, none of the leases records the final amount of revenue for the year,

---

[4] Herodotos 7.144: Ἑτέρη τε Θεμιστοκλέϊ γνώμη ἔμπροσθε ταύτης ἐς καιρὸν ἠρίστευσε, ὅτε Ἀθηναίοισι γενομένων χρημάτων μεγάλων ἐν τῷ κοινῷ τὰ ἐκ τῶν μετάλλων σφι προσῆλθε τῶν ἀπὸ Λαυρείου, ἔμελλον λάξεσθαι ὀρχηδὸν ἕκαστος δέκα δραχμάς· τότε Θεμιστοκλέης ἀνέγνωσε Ἀθηναίους τῆς διαιρέσιος ταύτης παυσαμένους νέας τούτων τῶν χρημάτων ποιήσασθαι διηκοσίας ἐς τὸν πόλεμον, τὸν πρὸς Αἰγινήτας λέγων.

[5] Herodotos 5.97.

[6] [Aristotle] *Constitution of the Athenians* 22.7; Hopper (1961: 141–142); Cunningham (1967: 156).

[7] Thucydides 6.91.7: καὶ τὰς τοῦ Λαυρείου τῶν ἀργυρείων μετάλλων προσόδους καὶ ὅσα ἀπὸ γῆς καὶ δικαστηρίων νῦν ὠφελοῦνται εὐθὺς ἀποστερήσονται, μάλιστα δὲ τῆς ἀπὸ τῶν ξυμμάχων προσόδου ἧσσον διαφορουμένης, οἳ τὰ παρ' ὑμῶν νομίσαντες ἤδη κατὰ κράτος πολεμεῖσθαι ὀλιγωρήσουσιν.

which has given rise to a debate on the importance of the revenue to the state. The two main issues debated are the meaning of mine classifications recorded in the leases and the frequency of payment.[8]

The leases record four types of classifications, the *kainotomiai* (new cuttings), the *ergasima*, the *anasaxima* and the *palaia anasaxima*, in direct conflict with the account in the *Constitution of the Athenians*, which mentions only two classifications, the *ergasima* and the *sugkechoremena*: "... and the leased mines, the *ergasima* leased for 3 years and the *sugkechoremena* leased for ... years."[9] The meaning of the classifications has a direct impact on the potential revenue from the mines, since the classification reveals the potential of the mine according to the state, and the length of the lease. The debate centres on the interpretation of the word *ergasimon*, which can mean either 'working' or 'workable.' If 'working' is the right interpretation, as Crosby and Hopper argued, then not only were there very few fully active mines but also their price was fixed, and thus the revenue from them was quite low.[10] The alternative interpretation of 'workable', advocated by Aperghis, reverses the situation completely since *ergasimon* denotes only potential, in line with the paucity of such mines in the leases and their low payments.[11] Aperghis' argument is very convincing and fits the available evidence, especially given that a century of previous exploitation meant new mines must have been both rare and risky, something reflected in the low number of *kainotomiai*.

The surviving prices in the leases are in their majority either 20 or 150 *drachmai* with some scattered prices considerably higher. Whether these prices represent one-off, yearly or prytany payments is debated. Both Crosby and Aperghis have argued in favour of yearly payments, supposing that the total revenue from the leases could not have been sizeable based on the following passage from Xenophon's *Ways and Means*:[12]

---

[8] A further issue debated is the length of the lease for the various classifications. Since the leases provide no help in this matter and the text of the *Constitution of the Athenians* is corrupt, the issue must remain in doubt among 3, 7 and 10 years' lease for the non-*ergasima* mines. On the solutions proposed see Rackham (1952: 130–131, n. 2, b); Crosby (1950: 199–200); Hopper (1953: 237).

[9] [Aristotle] *Constitution of the Athenians* 47.2: καὶ τὰ πραθέντα μέταλλα, τά τ' ἐργάσιμα τὰ εἰς τρία ἔτη πεπραμένα, καὶ τὰ συγκεχωρημένα τὰ εἰς [·] ἔ[τη] πεπραμένα. Crosby (1950: 196). Note that the meaning of the words *anasaxima* and *sugkechoremena* is not known: Hopper (1953: 203).

[10] Crosby (1950: 201–202); Hopper (1953: 203, 234–236).

[11] Aperghis (1997/1998: 5, 7).

[12] Crosby (1950: 203–204); Aperghis (1997/1998: 16–17).

> I believe on the silver mines that if they are organised as they should, then there will be great proceeds from them excepting any other revenues.[13]

This argument from silence is particularly weak since, as Hopper rightly noted, Xenophon in the *Ways and Means* is concerned with creating new revenues from the mines and, thus, would not be concerned with existing revenues that were well known to his audience.[14] More importantly, the balance of evidence clearly suggests that revenue from the mines was considerable and that the leases were a major part of the overall revenue, since they were the most easily controlled. On the one hand, the lease prices recorded in the literary texts are considerably higher than those recorded in the leases, namely 9,000, 2,000 and 18,000 *drachmai*, of which the latter was only part of the overall price.[15] Interestingly, assuming a 10 year lease, the prices mentioned in the speeches are not widely disparate from those in the leases, if these represent prytany payments, since 20 *drachmai* would be translated as 2,000 over the ten years and 150 as 15,000. Additionally, it is mentioned specifically that payments were made in parts (*katabolai*), thus, precluding the possibility that the prices recorded in the leases were one-off payments: "... who carried the part-payment to the city for the mine ..."[16]

On the other hand, estimates of the total revenue from specific leases do not appear to have been extraordinary amounts. In the only complete inscription that has survived (367/366), the total sum of the leases in the inscription is 3,690 *drachmai*.[17] Crosby calculated the total for stele XVI (342/341) at three talents.[18] For 367/366, the total revenue of the state in case of prytany payments for that year would be 6 talents 900 *drachmai*, while for 342/341 it would be 30 talents. Since the *poletai* accounts record the new leases sold each year, the revenue for the government would be the total of all the currently running leases, not merely those sold in the particular archon year. Thus, if we assume a ten year lease period for the majority of the mines, in any given year the government would

[13] Xenophon *Ways and Means* 4.1: Τά γε μὴν ἀργύρεια εἰ κατασκευασθείη ὡς δεῖ, πάμπολλα ἂν νομίζω χρήματα ἐξ αὐτῶν καὶ ἄνευ τῶν ἄλλων προσόδων προσιέναι.

[14] Hopper (1953: 238–239).

[15] Demosthenes 37.22, 40.52, 42.3.

[16] Demosthenes 37.22: ὃ ἔφερεν καταβολὴν τῇ πόλει τοῦ μετάλλου.

[17] Agora 19.P5.

[18] Crosby (1950: 203). The total is of course conjectural since not only is the size of the stone estimated but also there could be prices beyond 20 and 150 *drachmai* apart from the one surviving price of 6,100 *drachmai*.

receive income from 10 accounts; consequently, if the totals were similar to those recorded, then in 367/366 the total income would reach 61 talents 3,000 *drachmai* and accordingly 300 talents for 342/341. Such revenue may seem high but the surviving income and expenditure figures of the Athenian state show that such revenue from the mine leases is quite moderate. In the mid-340s, the income of the state was 400 talents, while a few years later under Lykourgos it had reached 1200 talents. The expenditures were equally high at 180 talents for an expeditionary force, 3,000 *drachmai* state subsidy per trierarch and several hundred talents for jury and assembly pay.[19] Furthermore, one other set of figures needs be mentioned as a comparison. Demosthenes 37 refers to the value of an *ergasterion* and slaves as no less than 20,600 *drachmai*, while the return payment for the loan on the *ergasterion* (washery) is 105 *drachmai* per prytany.[20] If the owner of an *ergasterion*, whose profits depended not on the profits from ore but on the services provided to miners, had an income of more than 105 *drachmai* per prytany, one would expect the lessee of a mine to be able to make payments of 20 *drachmai* per prytany for the proceeds of a mine.[21]

This discussion of the classification and pricing of the mines provides us with a keyhole view into the finances of production in Athens. We get an idea of the sums involved and the detailed framework provided by the state for the exploitation of the primary resource of the Athenians. The involvement of the state was not restrictive to production but fundamental to providing it with a firm and stable basis. The large sums involved as payment to the state and for services testify to the large profits of the industry and consequently to the appeal, volume and value of the trade in silver.

---

[19] Revenues: Demosthenes 10.38 (400T); Plutarch *Lives of the Ten Orators* 842F (1200T); Andreades (1933: 354, 376–381). Expenses: Demosthenes 4.48, 51.11.

[20] Demosthenes 37.31 for the value and 37.5 for the prytany payments. Note that the price of the *ergasterion* is larger than any price for agricultural land or other such endeavour recorded in the evidence: Osborne (1987: 77). For the value of and wealth generated from *ergasteria* (not only *plynteria* but generally) see Stanley (1990). For an account of the lending process on the *ergasterion* of Demosthenes 37, see Harris (2006: 190–197).

[21] Note that the only reference to a supposed profit from a mine is 300 talents over a 3-year period (Hypereides 4.35), which means at least 50 talents per year (if the 300T is a doubled fine) that makes a revenue for the state of 10 talents seem quite reasonable (using the highest amount mentioned in the leases, 6,100 *drachmai*: Agora 19 P26.569; Crosby (1950: 289)).

I have to note here Faraguna's suggestion of a tax on the produce of the Laurion mines based on references in the lexicographers.[22] Faraguna's suggestion has merit and is evidence of greater involvement of the state in the mining industry; however, the use of lexigographical evidence is inadequate to assume such intervention on the part of the state. State resources, according to archaic and classical evidence, were either exploited directly or, more commonly, by lease arrangement without recourse to a known tax regime. Consequently, although a tax on the produce of the mines is a possibility that cannot be discounted, it is necessary to provide evidence of a parallel practice or further, chronologically nearer, evidence before accepting the testimony of the lexicographers.

The leases were not the only source of revenue from the mines, as Xenophon informs us:

> The revenues of the polis will increase not only from the leasing of the slaves, but also from the population increase in the mining district and from the agora there and from the public houses near the mines and from the *kaminoi* and from all other revenues, which will increase.[23]

Apparently, the state had other investments in the mining region, including public accommodation and revenue from the *kaminoi* (smelting installations).[24] These mystery revenues from the *kaminoi* are particularly interesting, since unlike mines and *ergasteria*, *kaminoi* were few.[25]

The obvious solution to revenue from *kaminoi* is that *kaminoi* were state-owned and either state-operated or leased out to private individuals.[26] There are two pieces of evidence against this solution, both seeming to testify to the private ownership of *kaminoi*. Firstly, a Demosthenic speaker seems to refer to a privately owned *kaminos*: κἄπειτα πείσας τοὺς οἰκέτας τοὺς ἐμοὺς καθέζεσθαι εἰς τὸν κεγχρεῶνα ἐπὶ βλάβῃ τῇ

---

[22] Faraguna (2006: 148–152). Harpocration s.v. ἀπονομὴ; Suda s.v. ἀγράφου μετάλλου δίκη.

[23] Xenophon *Ways and Means* 4.49–50: Οὐ τοίνυν μόνον ἡ ἀπὸ τῶν ἀνδραπόδων ἀποφορὰ τὴν διατροφὴν τῇ πόλει αὔξοι ἄν, ἀλλὰ πολυανθρωπίας περὶ τὰ μέταλλα ἁθροιζομένης καὶ ἀπ' ἀγορᾶς τῆς ἐκεῖ καὶ ἀπ' οἰκιῶν περὶ τἀργύρεια δημοσίων καὶ ἀπὸ καμίνων καὶ ἀπὸ τῶν ἄλλων ἁπάντων πρόσοδοι ἂν πολλαὶ γίγνοιντο.

[24] Public houses for rent were a rare phenomenon according to Andreades (1933: 136) but Athens certainly had some not only in the mining region but also in the Piraeus: Xenophon *Ways and Means* 3.12–13.

[25] Kakavoyiannis (2005: 261–262), although further investigations in the region may reveal more. For the location of *kaminoi*, as against mines and *plynteria*, see Konophagos (1980: Carte Topographique Moderne Avec Des Ruines Des Installations Metallurgiques Et Des Puits Antiques, in back cover pocket).

[26] Thiel (1922: 32); Wilsdorf (1952: 157, 161).

ἐμῇ.[27] Usually this sentence is translated as "And then having persuaded my slaves to sit in the foundry to my prejudice".[28] However, the precise meaning of the pivotal word, *kegchreon*, is unknown. It has been proposed that it means either the pit into which the silver was run when melted or the furnace in which it was refined.[29] This is based on the quoted continuation of the complaint by the speaker, which mentions the reducing of the ore.[30] Yet nowhere in either passage is a *kaminos* or smelting mentioned. *Kegchreon* is a variant of *kegchros*, which originally meant 'millet' but came to be used for anything in small grains. In a mining context, small grains do not invoke the image of a furnace but rather the sorting out and grinding process that took place immediately after the digging of the ore and in the washeries. This meaning of the word ties in well with the speech, since the case refers to an *ergasterion*, a washery, and has no mention of a *kaminos* beyond the modern interpretation of *kegchreon*.

Secondly, a *horos* inscription found in Laurion probably refers to the security of a loan on a *kaminos* and the surrounding property.[31] However, it is not certain whether this inscription refers to a silver *kaminos*, since the word is generic and there is no reason to suppose that there were no *kaminoi* for other materials in Attika, especially in the industrial area.[32] Similarly, the *horoi* inscriptions referring to *ergasteria* are not necessarily connected with the silver industry.[33] Thirdly, there are a few mentions in the *poletai* lists of *kaminoi* followed by a name, which is considered to be that of their owner.[34] However, it must be noted that at least in one instance the mine in question is identified by the name of its lessee rather than some other designation: "the mine of Epikrates of Pallene."[35] Additionally, in the *poletai* lists there are several references to a person working a mine (*ergazetai/ergasato*) apparently without being the lessee.[36] Conceivably, accepting our lack of knowledge on the particulars of loan security in Athens, leased public property could become security

[27] Demosthenes 37.26.

[28] Translation: Murray (1939).

[29] Murray (1939: 37.26, note 2).

[30] Demosthenes 37.28.

[31] IG II^2 2750.

[32] For example, IG I^3 435.16–17 on a coal *kaminos*.

[33] IG II^2 2677, 2746–2749, 2752, 2760 are a few examples.

[34] Agora 19 P5.54, P13.81, P38.28.

[35] Hypereides 4.35: τὸ Ἐπικράτους μέταλλον τοῦ Παλληνέως.

[36] Agora 19 P9.41; P10.8, 25; P12.10; P18.8; P20.20, 27, 50, 74; P21.5, 12; P26.265; P27.7, 53; P29.9, 24, 55; P34.6.

for a loan, while in case of default the lender took over the property and its produce for the remaining of the lease period. The only other solution to this problem is that Xenophon refers to a tax rendered on *kaminoi* but such a tax in an industrial setting would be unique in Athens or any polis, since direct taxation was generally avoided.[37] Since both the Demosthenic passage and the loan on the *horos* (boundary stone) cannot be shown to refer to a silver *kaminos* or to prove the exclusive private ownership of *kaminoi*, the public ownership and leasing of *kaminoi* remain the best solution to the revenue mentioned in the *Ways and Means*.

Such intervention in the smelting of silver is the key to the quality control of Athenian coinage silver. One of the few concrete conclusions established by the analysis of the silver of the Athenian owls is that all tetradrachms were made of a specific alloy of a very high level of purity with little copper and gold.[38] The Athenian mint must have had a way to distinguish 'mint' silver from other silver. It follows that the state had imposed specifications of quality on the smelting of Laurion silver. Otherwise, the only possible solution for the constant standard quality of the coinage is to resmelt the silver in the mint. There is no evidence of such a process in the sources, and until the Athenian silver mint is found, there can be no archaeological solution either. Assuming a regulating process for the *kaminoi* provides a better and more functional system of quality control.

The next step in the process of creating coins, the mint, was also controlled by the state as the *demosioi* (public) status of the *argyrokopoi* (slaves in the mint) reveals.[39] A major issue is whether private individuals, particularly the lessees, could use the Athenian mint to create private supplies of coinage and, consequently, the control that the government could exercise over them. On the one hand, the process described in the Coinage Decree for the reminting of allied coinage provides a framework for private individuals to use the Athenian mint.[40] On the other hand, some finds in Laurion may imply that such a process was not available to the lessees. Clay bowls with hemispherical indentations, which resemble coin blanks, have been found in Laurion and in Brauron. These led

---

[37] Rihl (2001: 118).

[38] Kraay & Emeleus (1962: 16).

[39] SEG 26: 72.54–55.

[40] IG I^3 1453B. 16–17, 1453C. 9–10, 1453B/G. 5.1. For the allied coins, resmelting would have been necessary to uphold the quality of Athenian coinage.

Konophagos to suggest that the Athenian silver mint was situated in Laurion not in the *astu* (city).[41] Such a location for the silver mint is problematic, since Laurion lies outside the protective walls of the *astu*, making a mint vulnerable to a sneak naval attack or even bandits.[42] However, the bowls remain a mystery. Kakavoyiannis in a recent study has pointed out that the Brauron bowl seems to have been made totally by litharge not clay and that a similar bowl was found in the Middle Helladic strata of Thorikos.[43] Kakavoyiannis admits that the chronology of the Thorikos strata could have been contaminated by later disturbances.[44] These bowls are not identical, although they all have the telltale indentations. Although I accept Kakavoyiannis' misgivings for the Brauron bowl, since the three rows of mildly interconnected indentations do not seem to have any practical use as such, I am reluctant to accept a similar explanation for the bowl in the Laurion museum. Oikonomakou, who excavated it at Thorikos, is convinced that the bowl is connected with minting and my own impression at the Laurion museum leads me to agree.[45] Only a fragment of the bowl survives but it was obviously flat-bottomed and the indentations are on the flat surface and, although clustered, they are clearly distinguished from each other by raised ridges. The only explanations of the bowl which do not necessitate a mint in Laurion, are either that it was part of a process of private export of silver in blanks, or that blanks were provided to the Athenian mint by the entrepreneurs. In the second case, the problems of such a process particularly in relation to adulteration and weight are insurmountable, which make it very difficult to envision its use for such a well-regulated coinage as that of Athens. Alternatively, although more sinister, the bowls may have been part of a forgery ring, which would easily explain the find without need for elaborate explanations of its relation to official minting. Without further evidence, reconstructing the minting regime of Athens is very difficult, particularly in identifying the role of private individuals. The evidence from

[41] The location of the Athenian silver mint is a matter of debate, since only the bronze mint has been found in the agora: Camp & Kroll (2001). Mint in Laurion: Konophagos (1976: 371), (1980: 369). Note that Konophagos did not follow Svoronos (1915), (1916/1917), who had made a similar assumption, but based himself on other considerations.

[42] The lack of any reference to a mint in the mining region in *Ways and Means* 4.43–48, where Xenophon outlines his solution to the problem of security in the mines, tips the balance against Konophagos' argument.

[43] Kakavoyiannis (2005: 280).

[44] Kakavoyiannis (2005: 280).

[45] Personal correspondence and (forthcoming) *Archaiologikon Deltion* (1998) p. 84.

the leases and the large estimated profits in silver metal of the lessees suggest that they had access to the mint, although it is probable that Athens imposed some limits on the extent of minting of privately owned silver.

The role of the Athenian government in the silver industry, although pervasive, was not particularly pronounced. The state owned the silver mines, administered the leases, legislated on the safety of the works, regulated the quality of silver produced and controlled the minting process. However, it does not appear to have intervened or regulated the internal or exporting trade in silver. As was mentioned earlier, this lack of intervention is surprising. The easiest of explanations is that the nature of our sources, the leases and the speeches, do not concern export and are focused internally on exploitation; thus, it is expected that any governmental intervention in trade remains unknown to us. Since it is impossible to argue that the whole or even the bulk of Athenian legislation has survived, any regulation of the silver trade may have been lost. Nevertheless, such explanations of silence are weak, thus, pending further evidence, it is better to assume that the Athenian government did not intervene officially in silver exports. The reason for this lack of intervention can arguably be found in the role of silver in the Athenian economy.

The revenue from the silver mines certainly played a major role in the finances of the Athenian state. For the majority of states, the influence of their products on their economy, their exportability and the views of contemporaries have been lost. For Athens and silver, however, Xenophon's *Ways and Means* offers glimpses not only of silver's importance in the Athenian economy as an export, but also on the contemporary views of the industry. The *Ways and Means* is a political pamphlet written in the period immediately after the Social War (357–355) and its author is generally accepted to be Xenophon.[46] The purpose of the pamphlet, a type of literary document of which the *Ways and Means* is the only surviving example, was to present a series of proposals for the revival of Athenian state finances. At the time, the Athenian state was under financial strain due to the extreme expenditures of the previous years and the considerable decrease in state revenues during the war.[47] The proposals tackle various sources of revenue, including metics, trade and the silver mines; Xenophon proposes an alternative way to increase revenue from the mines without changing the existing framework of exploitation. The

---

[46] On the authorship and date of the *Ways and Means* see Gauthier (1976: 1–6) and Thiel (1922: viii–xxiii).

[47] State income in 355 had fallen to 130T: Demosthenes 10.37.

specifics of the proposal are outside the scope of this work but several passages testify to the importance of silver as an exportable commodity in the Athenian economy, and thus are of interest. Xenophon extols the commercial advantages of silver, presenting us with a contemporary view of its production and export from the largest producer in the eastern Mediterranean:

> First, it (Athens) has the best and safest harbours, for no matter where they (the ships) anchor they can rest for the winter. And for the *emporoi* in most of the poleis, there is need to take a return cargo, since their coins are not useful outside (their borders). In Athens, on the contrary, there are as many commodities as people want to take as return cargo. And if they do not want to take a return cargo, those who export silver have a good export trade. For wherever they sell it, they receive more than they expended.[48]

This is a view of the silver trade defining the importance of silver as an export product and the advantages it provides to a producer. No other Athenian product is mentioned in such a capacity. Silver is presented as the balancing card of Piraeus, the greatest entrepôt in the Aegean. This lends credibility to the view that silver was the primary exportable product of Athens.

The passage also testifies to the laws of supply and demand in the silver trade and the Greek economy. Xenophon's statement that the price of silver outside Athens is higher than in Athens shows that silver was cheaper for the producer. The situation must have been similar for the other silver producers as well. Silver in this passage is bullion not coins; *nomisma* (coin) is readily contrasted with *argyrion* (silver). Xenophon's statement on the sale price of *argyrion* in Athens and elsewhere ("For wherever they sell it, they receive more than they expended") clearly implies that traders would buy silver bullion in Athens and sell it elsewhere. Coinages, Xenophon states, are of limited commercial value but silver as bullion could be traded anywhere and could fetch a good price. The finds of silver bullion in hoards also suggest that there was a large market for bullion, not only by governments for their coinages but also in

[48] Xenophon *Ways and Means* 3.1–3: πρῶτον μὲν γὰρ δήπου ναυσὶ καλλίστας καὶ ἀσφαλεστάτας ὑποδοχὰς ἔχει, ὅπου γ' ἔστιν εἰσορμισθέντας ἀδεῶς ἕνεκα χειμῶνος ἀναπαύεσθαι. ἀλλὰ μὴν καὶ τοῖς ἐμπόροις ἐν μὲν ταῖς πλείσταις τῶν πόλεων ἀντιφορτίζεσθαί τι ἀνάγκη· νομίσμασι γὰρ οὐ χρησίμοις ἔξω χρῶνται· ἐν δὲ ταῖς Ἀθήναις πλεῖστα μὲν ἔστιν ἀντεξάγειν ὧν ἂν δέωνται ἄνθρωποι, ἣν δὲ μὴ βούλωνται ἀντιφορτίζεσθαι, καὶ [οἱ] ἀργύριον ἐξάγοντες καλὴν ἐμπορίαν ἐξάγουσιν. ὅπου γὰρ ἂν πωλῶσιν αὐτό, πανταχοῦ πλέον τοῦ ἀρχαίου λαμβάνουσιν.

private enterprise for jewellery and plate.[49] Finally, Xenophon here does not argue in order to persuade of the importance of the silver trade, but on the contrary uses the exportability of Athenian silver as an argument on general trade policy. So, the importance of silver as a major export commodity was readily recognised.

Another passage reinforces this presentation of the economics of the silver trade and industry:

> When the coppersmiths become numerous, the value of copperware falls and the coppersmiths go out of business and the same holds true for the ironsmiths. And when there is lots of grain and wine, the value of the crop falls, and the farmers go out of business, so that many abandon working the land and turn to trade and retail and money lending. But the more ore is mined and more silver is produced, the more people go into business in the mining industry. And for furniture, when people have enough to fill the house, they stop buying more; but for silver no-one thinks that he has too much so that he stops getting more, but even if it becomes a lot, the extra they bury thinking that this is as good as using it. And when the poleis do well, the people want silver. The men spend money on fine weapons and beautiful horses and great houses and buildings, while the women turn to luxurious clothes and gold jewellery. And when the poleis are not doing well either because of a dearth of crops or because of war, then since lots of the land remains uncultivated and they need victuals and mercenaries, then again they need money. And if someone says that gold is as useful as silver, I do not gainsay that, but I know that when there is too much gold, then its value falls, and silver becomes more valuable. And I have presented these facts so that we do not cower before bringing more people to the mines, not cower before making more out of them, for the ore will never run out nor will silver ever become valueless.[50]

---

[49] Hoards with metal bars and/or ingots: IGCH 1035, 1182, 1478, 1482, 1636, 1637, 1639, 1640, 1644, 1645, 1647, 1649, 1651, 1874, 2172(AU), 2259, 2313.

[50] Xenophon *Ways and Means* 4.6–12: καὶ γὰρ οὐδ' ὥσπερ ὅταν πολλοὶ χαλκοτύποι γένωνται, ἀξίων γενομένων τῶν χαλκευτικῶν ἔργων, καταλύονται οἱ χαλκοτύποι, καὶ οἱ σιδηρεῖς γε ὡσαύτως· καὶ ὅταν γε πολὺς σῖτος καὶ οἶνος γένηται, ἀξίων ὄντων τῶν καρπῶν, ἀλυσιτελεῖς αἱ γεωργίαι γίγνονται, ὥστε πολλοὶ ἀφέμενοι τοῦ τὴν γῆν ἐργάζεσθαι ἐπ' ἐμπορίας καὶ καπηλείας καὶ τοκισμοὺς τρέπονται· ἀργυρῖτις δὲ ὅσῳ ἂν πλείων φαίνηται καὶ ἀργύριον πλέον γίγνηται, τοσούτῳ πλείονες ἐπὶ τὸ ἔργον τοῦτο ἔρχονται. καὶ γὰρ δὴ ἔπιπλα μέν, ἐπειδὰν ἱκανά τις κτήσηται τῇ οἰκίᾳ, οὐ μάλα ἔτι προσωνοῦνται· ἀργύριον δὲ οὐδείς πω οὕτω πολὺ ἐκτήσατο ὥστε μηκέτι προσδεῖσθαι· ἀλλ' ἤν τισι γένηται παμπληθές, τὸ περιττεῦον κατορύττοντες οὐδὲν ἧττον ἥδονται ἢ χρώμενοι αὐτῷ. καὶ μὴν ὅταν γε εὖ πράττωσιν αἱ πόλεις, ἰσχυρῶς οἱ ἄνθρωποι ἀργυρίου δέονται. οἱ μὲν γὰρ ἄνδρες ἀμφὶ ὅπλα τε καλὰ καὶ ἵππους ἀγαθοὺς [τε] καὶ οἰκίας καὶ κατασκευὰς μεγαλοπρεπεῖς βούλονται δαπανᾶν, αἱ δὲ γυναῖκες εἰς ἐσθῆτα πολυτελῆ καὶ χρυσοῦν κόσμον τρέπονται. ὅταν τε αὖ νοσήσωσιν ⟨αἱ⟩ πόλεις ἢ ἀφορίαις καρπῶν ἢ πολέμῳ, ἔτι καὶ πολὺ μᾶλλον, ἀργοῦ τῆς γῆς γιγνομένης, καὶ εἰς ἐπιτήδεια καὶ εἰς ἐπικούρους νομίσματος δέονται. εἰ δέ τις φήσειε καὶ χρυσίον

This passage touches upon various issues concerning the trade in silver. Firstly, Xenophon attempts a comparison between the various metals in terms of their commercial value. Copper, iron and gold are adversely affected by increased supply because their demand is inelastic. For the base metals, this is expected, since their uses and presumably their rate of wear created a steady but definite demand. In other words, there was only so much armour, weapons and tools needed in a polis; while demand may rise, for example in war or for large building projects, there are definite limits to its increase. The case is similar for gold, because gold was used primarily for jewellery and decoration. For all three metals, Xenophon thinks that demand regulated supply, describing a buyer's market.[51]

Silver, on the other hand, has an infinitely elastic demand. This is explained because of the use of silver for coinage, which is needed equally in times of plenty and hardship. This ever-increasing demand for silver is the direct result of a steadily increasing demand for coinage. The position of silver as a market commodity is seen as completely opposite to that of the other metals, signifying a predominantly seller's market. Secondly, the passage testifies to the main use of silver in the ancient world as perceived by contemporaries. The phrase "they need money", which defines the uses of *argyrion* in the rest of the passage, shows that in Xenophon's thinking, the people desire/need silver as money.

Modern opinions on the value of the *Ways and Means* as evidence for the Athenian economy vary widely, depending mainly on scholarly opinion on the proposals themselves. Boeckh argued that the proposals were impracticable and, thus, the *Ways and Means* has little value, while Cawkwell, Momigliano and others argued the opposite, viewing the *Ways and Means* as the basis of Euboulos' economic reforms.[52] The substantivist scholars of the latter half of the 20th century CE tend to view Xenophon's proposals as correct but impracticable in his period;

μηδὲν ἧττον χρήσιμον εἶναι ἢ ἀργύριον, τούτῳ μὲν οὐκ ἀντιλέγω, ἐκεῖνο μέντοι οἶδα, ὅτι καὶ χρυσίον ὅταν πολὺ παραφανῇ, αὐτὸ μὲν ἀτιμότερον γίγνεται, τὸ δὲ ἀργύριον τιμιώτερον ποιεῖ. ταῦτα μὲν οὖν ἐδήλωσα τούτου ἕνεκα, ὅπως θαρροῦντες μὲν ὅτι πλείστους ἀνθρώπους ἐπὶ τὰ ἀργύρεια ἄγωμεν, θαρροῦντες δὲ κατασκευαζώμεθα ἐν αὐτοῖς, ὡς οὔτε ἐπιλειψούσης ποτὲ ⟨τῆς⟩ ἀργυρίτιδος οὔτε τοῦ ἀργυρίου ἀτίμου ποτὲ ἐσομένου.

[51] Note that I fully agree with Samuel (1983: 24) that what Xenophon does in this passage is economic analysis, if without the common modern nomenclature.

[52] Boeckh (1886: 698–708); Momigliano (1966: 481–487); Cawkwell (1963: 63–64). Also Lewis (1990: 251) for a more moderate view of the influence of Xenophon on Euboulos.

thus Finley argued that Xenophon anticipated later developments, while Polanyi considered that Xenophon's vision, although correct, was never realised in the ancient world.[53] Other scholars view the *Ways and Means* as part of a shift in Greek thinking concerning revenue in general in the period from imperialism to self-containment.[54] Whether the proposals were capable of being implemented in the mid-fourth century is uncertain, although certainly at least one person, with the necessary education, considered them to be so. On the other hand, they certainly were never implemented in their entirety, although some of the proposals relating to trade and metics may have been.[55] The substantivist views of Xenophon as a pioneer in the generation of revenue are dependent on the loss of other proposals and on the interpretation of evidence both from Athens and from other poleis. Lastly, the argument in favour of a shift in Greek thought against imperialism in the mid-fourth century can only be argued for Athens, since the majority of other poleis, except for a brief period in Spartan history, never relied on imperial revenue.

The specific proposals aside, it could be argued that Xenophon's statements do not reflect the reality of the silver industry at Athens, or that since they seek to persuade his audience, they exaggerate the importance of silver in the Athenian economy and its lure to foreign traders. Xenophon indeed seeks to persuade his audience and that creates a certain bias in his arguments. He may have been overly enthusiastic over the effects and prospects of the silver industry, and similarly for the commercial lure of Athens as an entrepôt. However, it is difficult to substantiate that Xenophon lied or grossly changed the facts. His target audience was not modern scholarship or people who had no knowledge of the economic position of Athens and the particulars of the silver industry. On the contrary, the arguments are meant to incite the interest and reaction of those in control, politicians, rhetors and demagogues; those who could implement such changes as Xenophon proposes. Most of them would be members of the upper classes, and possibly would have had some connection to the silver industry, either directly or indirectly through relatives and friends.

The common citizen in Athens had probably never seen a talent of silver but it is impossible to gauge how much he knew about the sil-

[53] Finley (1973: 164), followed by Humphreys (1978: 138); Polanyi (1957: 196), followed by Samuel (1983: 22–23).

[54] Dillery (1993).

[55] Cawkwell (1963: 64).

ver industry. For the upper classes and the mobile segments of society though, Laurion was not an unknown quantity. The fact that Xenophon's suggestion for increasing profits clearly avoids any controversial subjects, such as actually imposing taxes or increasing the rent of the leases, shows that he is mindful of the interests of at least part of his audience, who probably had investments in the industry. Xenophon's picture of Laurion and silver as a commodity may be enthusiastic but not a lie or an exaggeration, since either would not be conducive to his argument. Moreover, although parts of his reasoning are naïve, for example the assertion that the mines would never be exhausted, they are not more naïve than hundreds of decisions and plans by leaders and their advisors over the centuries. Common sense could predict 60 years ago that oil reserves would eventually be exhausted; that did not stop the vast majority of governments worldwide from promoting the use of cars, or the producers of the Middle East from basing their economies on oil exports. From the perspective of two and half millennia of hindsight, of course, Xenophon's suggestions seem naïve and his belief in Athens' advantages wrong, but at the time the situation was very different. When the *Ways and Means* was initially read, or heard, plans to rebuild Athenian finances must have been numerous. Eventually, some of these plans succeeded in bringing an economic revival initially under Euboulos and later, more successfully, under Lykourgos. Xenophon's suggestions on the silver industry were never fully adopted, as far as we know, but someone else's were and by *stele* XVI of the *poletai*, the number of leases per year had tripled. The ideas in the *Ways and Means* may have been too revolutionary for Athens, or simply unworkable, but the facts upon which they were based were common knowledge in Athens, so the possibility that Xenophon is lying or exaggerating is small.[56] The overall picture in the two passages is of silver as a strong commercial commodity. The existence and widespread appeal of trade in silver is presented as an undoubted fact. Additionally, silver has a steady, ever-increasing demand which can withstand any increase of supply, due to its use for coinage.

Although basing his argument on the profitability and exportability of silver, Xenophon at no point mentions intervention by the government in the silver trade, which lends further credence to the impression that governmental intervention was lacking. Of course Xenophon, like the rest of the surviving sources, focuses internally and his references to the

[56] On Xenophon reflecting nature and conditions of trade in the fourth century: Osborne (1991: 138).

silver trade are complementary, not fundamental, to his argument. Nevertheless, Xenophon's picture does not include the government and his plan to increase revenue contains no reference to increases from the silver trade. The explanation of this surprising lack of governmental intervention, however, can be found in Xenophon's picture of the role of silver in the Athenian economy and particularly the public economy. The laws of supply and demand, to whose power Xenophon testifies, made silver the major Athenian commodity. The high demand for silver and the Piraeus' position as one of the great ports in the Mediterranean made governmental intervention largely unnecessary. There was no need for the Athenian government to intervene in order to make silver a more attractive commodity, as silver already had a high demand and no other producer could compete with the commercial position of the Piraeus. The aim of the government is practically confined in creating and assuring an adequate supply of the commodity. Since mining, ancient or modern, is hazardous, the Athenian government, especially without modern technology, could not guarantee a steady supply on the ground. The available options for intervention were limited to encouraging prospecting and creating a safe environment for exploitation. Athens clearly did that by legislating to protect the works and offering short leases for the *ergasima* mines. In addition to this, Athens, through its control of the *kaminoi*, regulated the quality of the product, thus ensuring that Athenian silver had an extra edge in the market. It is impossible to estimate how far these measures were intended to secure a high quality supply for export, since they also secured continued internal revenue and the high quality of Athenian coinage, but these issues are interconnected. Revenue depended upon the continuation of mining concerns and mining depended, on the part of the prospector, upon demand. Thus, ensuring a safe environment for the prospector and assuring the quality of the product benefited the government in terms of revenue, while simultaneously affecting exports.

CHAPTER THREE

THE IMPORTERS OF GOLD AND SILVER

The majority of poleis did not have precious metal resources, yet many managed to acquire metal for coinage. This chapter concentrates on the methods of acquisition of precious metal employed by the poleis. There were four possible methods of acquisition: import of bullion, import of coins, loans from temples and booty from war. Temple loans were employed by poleis in financial straits since any such loans in the sources are usually connected with times of war or famine.[1] War booty, although probably important in particular cases, was not a regular method of supply since it depended on the vagaries of war. Only the first two methods can be considered as regular means of acquisition. The use of coinage as evidence for the study of metal acquisition is not without problems, since for most Greek coinages there can be no certainty as to the number of issues, the interval between them or the number of individual coins within each issue.

For the acquisition of gold two case studies are examined, Asia Minor and Sicily/Magna Graecia, since the numismatic profile of gold/electrum coinages in these areas is starkly different, and thus two very different acquisition profiles can be discussed. Note that although part of the discussion relates to archaic electrum coinages, the debate on the birth of coinage in the Greek World is not touched upon, since the reasons for the invention and adoption of coinage, whether standardization of state payments or gifts and medals, did not change the fact that the state had to procure metal for the coins.[2] In the study of Asia Minor, I have included mints from the Asiatic shore of the Propontis to Kilikia, the islands of the Propontis and the eastern Aegean. The southern shore of the Black Sea and the island of Cyprus are excluded (for a full list of minters, see Table 1 below).

---

[1] For example, the use of the Athenian reserves in the Peloponnesian War: Thucydides 2.13.4–5. Loans from temples for non-emergency reasons, see Aristotle *Oeconomica* 1349a20–23 but this is a case of a tyrant using the reserve.

[2] Note that early coins of possibly private mints are not discussed: Kraay (1976: 23). For the two major explanations of the creation of coinage see Kraay (1976: 320–328), Price (1981). For another explanation (stabilising price of electrum) see Wallace (1987).

Most of the early electrum coins are not securely attributed to a polis, since they do not carry legends and their devices could belong to a variety of cities, whilst the dating of most of the attributed coins is uncertain. Kraay lists seven poleis minting in electrum in the first half of the sixth century, Ephesos, Halikarnassos, Phokaia, Miletos, Samos, Kyzikos and Chios, while another four, Lampsakos, Abydos, Klazomenai and Priene, minted at the time of the Ionian Revolt; Head also attributed some early electrum coins to Erythrai, Smyrna and Teos.[3] Electrum minting was concentrated in Ionia and the islands with only Halikarnassos and Kyzikos in other areas of Asia Minor, at least for early electrum. The means of acquisition of gold employed by these poleis have not survived in the sources, although some could have minted from their own resources, such as Smyrna, Abydos and possibly Lampsakos and Samos.[4] For the other poleis, trade was certainly a viable possibility, as was shown by the Lydian sale to Sparta.[5]

Table 1. Minters in Asia Minor, sixth to fourth centuries (minting in gold or electrum in bold for ease of reference)

ID	Area	Polis	6th EL	6th AR	5th EL	5th AU	5th AR	4th EL	4th AU	4th AR
1	Aiolis	Elaia	No	No	No	No	Yes	No	No	Yes
2	Aiolis	Hekatonnessi Nesos	No	No	No	No	Yes	No	No	Yes
3	Aiolis	Kyme	No	No	No	No	Yes	No	No	Yes
4	Aiolis	Larissa Phrikonis	No	No	No	No	No	No	No	Yes
5	Aiolis	Lesbos	No	Yes	No	No	No	No	No	No
6	Aiolis	Methymna	No	No	No	No	Yes	No	No	Yes
7	Aiolis	Myrina	No	No	No	No	No	No	No	Yes
8	Aiolis	Mytilene	No	No	**Yes**	No	Yes	**Yes**	No	Yes
9	Aiolis	Temnos	No	No	No	No	No	No	No	Yes

[3] Ephesos: Kraay (1976: 25); Halikarnassos: Kraay (1976: 23, nos. 1, 53, 54); Phokaia: Kraay (1976: 26, nos. 13, 70); Miletos: Kraay (1976: no. 55); Samos: Kraay (1976: 26, nos. 66–67); Kyzikos: Kraay (1976: no. 71); Chios: Kraay (1976: no. 72); Lampsakos: Kraay (1976: nos. 73–74); Abydos: Kraay (1976: no. 75); Klazomenai: Kraay (1976: no. 76); Priene: Kraay (1976: no. 77); Erythrai: Head (1911: 578); Smyrna: Head (1911: 591); Teos: Head (1911: 595).

[4] Kraay & Hirmer (1966: 368) and Boardman (1996: 310) both assume mines in the territory of Kyzikos but there is no literary, archaeological or geological evidence to suggest that Kyzikos was a gold producer, except through domination of Abydos, of which I have found no evidence.

[5] See page 45.

ID	Area	Polis	6th EL	6th AR	5th EL	5th AU	5th AR	4th EL	4th AU	4th AR
10	Ionia	Chios	**Yes**	Yes	**Yes**	No	Yes	No	No	Yes
11	Ionia	Ephesos	**Yes**	Yes	No	No	Yes	No	No	Yes
12	Ionia	Erythrai	No	Yes	No	No	Yes	No	No	Yes
13	Ionia	Ikaria (Oinoe)	No	No	No	No	No	No	No	Yes
14	Ionia	Klazomenai	No	Yes	No	No	Yes	No	**Yes**	Yes
15	Ionia	Kolophon	No	No	No	No	Yes	No	No	Yes
16	Ionia	Leukai	No	No	No	No	No	No	No	Yes
17	Ionia	Magnesia	No	No	No	No	Yes	No	No	Yes
18	Ionia	Miletos	**Yes**	Yes	No	No	Yes	No	No	Yes
19	Ionia	Phokaia	**Yes**	Yes	**Yes**	No	No	**Yes**	No	Yes
20	Ionia	Phygela	No	No	No	No	No	No	No	Yes
21	Ionia	Samos	**Yes**	Yes	No	No	Yes	No	No	Yes
22	Ionia	Smyrna	**Yes**	No	No	No	No	No	No	Yes
23	Ionia	Teos	**Yes**	Yes	No	No	Yes	No	No	Yes
24	Karia	Astyra	No	No	No	No	Yes	No	No	No
25	Karia	Euromos	No	No	No	No	Yes	No	No	No
26	Karia	Halikarnassos	**Yes**	No	No	No	Yes	No	No	Yes
27	Karia	Ialysos	No	Yes	No	No	No	No	No	No
28	Karia	Iasos	No	No	No	No	No	No	No	Yes
29	Karia	Idyma	No	No	No	No	Yes	No	No	No
30	Karia	Lindos	No	Yes	No	No	No	No	No	No
31	Karia	Kalymna	No	Yes	No	No	No	No	No	No
32	Karia	Kamiros	No	Yes	No	No	No	No	No	No
33	Karia	Knidos	No	Yes	No	No	Yes	No	No	Yes
34	Karia	Knidian Chersonese	No	Yes	No	No	No	No	No	No
35	Karia	Kos	No	No	No	No	Yes	No	No	Yes
36	Karia	Megiste	No	No	No	No	No	No	No	Yes
37	Karia	Mylasa	No	Yes	No	No	No	No	No	No
38	Karia	Nisyros	No	No	No	No	No	No	No	Yes
39	Karia	Poseidion	No	Yes	No	No	No	No	No	No
40	Karia	Rhodos	No	No	No	No	Yes	No	**Yes**	Yes
41	Karia	Rhodian Peraia	No	No	No	No	Yes	No	No	No
42	Karia	Termera	No	Yes	No	No	No	No	No	No
43	Kilikia	Aphrodisias	No	No	No	No	No	No	No	Yes
44	Kilikia	Holmi	No	No	No	No	No	No	No	Yes
45	Kilikia	Issos	No	No	No	No	No	No	No	Yes
46	Kilikia	Kelenderis	No	No	No	No	Yes	No	No	Yes
47	Kilikia	Mallos	No	No	No	No	Yes	No	No	Yes
48	Kilikia	Nagidos	No	No	No	No	Yes	No	No	Yes
49	Kilikia	Soloi	No	No	No	No	Yes	No	No	Yes
50	Kilikia	Tarsos	No	No	No	No	Yes	No	No	Yes
51	Lykia	Aperlai	No	No	No	No	Yes	No	No	No

ID	Area	Polis	6th EL	6th AR	5th EL	5th AU	5th AR	4th EL	4th AU	4th AR
52	Lykia	Limyra	No	No	No	No	No	No	No	Yes
53	Lykia	Patara	No	No	No	No	No	No	No	Yes
54	Lykia	Phaselis	No	Yes	No	No	Yes	No	No	Yes
55	Lykia	Telmessos	No	No	No	No	Yes	No	No	No
56	Lykia	Tlos	No	No	No	No	No	No	No	Yes
57	Lykia	Xanthos	No	No	No	No	No	No	No	Yes
58	Mysia	Atarneus	No	No	No	No	No	No	No	Yes
59	Mysia	Gambrion	No	No	No	No	No	No	No	Yes
60	Mysia	Kyzikos	**Yes**	Yes	**Yes**	No	Yes	**Yes**	No	Yes
61	Mysia	Lampsakos	No	No	**Yes**	No	Yes	No	**Yes**	Yes
62	Mysia	Parion	No	No	No	No	Yes	No	No	Yes
63	Mysia	Pergamos	No	No	No	No	No	No	**Yes**	Yes
64	Mysia	Pitane	No	No	No	No	Yes	No	No	No
65	Mysia	Prokonnesos	No	No	No	No	No	No	No	Yes
66	Mysia	Teuthrania	No	No	No	No	No	No	No	Yes
67	Pamphylia	Aspendos	No	No	No	No	Yes	No	No	Yes
68	Pamphylia	Side	No	No	No	No	Yes	No	No	Yes
69	Pisidia	Etenna	No	No	No	No	No	No	No	Yes
70	Pisidia	Selge	No	No	No	No	Yes	No	No	Yes
71	Propontis	Astakos	No	No	No	No	Yes	No	No	No
72	Propontis	Byzantion	No	No	No	No	Yes	No	No	Yes
73	Propontis	Chalkedon	No	No	No	No	Yes	No	No	Yes
74	Propontis	Kios	No	No	No	No	No	No	**Yes**	Yes
75	Propontis	Perinthos	No	No	No	No	No	No	No	Yes
76	Propontis	Selymbria	No	No	No	No	Yes	No	No	No
77	Troas	Abydos	No	No	No	**Yes**	Yes	No	**Yes**	Yes
78	Troas	Antandros	No	No	No	No	No	No	No	Yes
79	Troas	Assos	No	No	No	No	Yes	No	No	Yes
80	Troas	Dardanos	No	No	No	No	Yes	No	No	Yes
81	Troas	Gargara	No	No	No	No	No	No	No	Yes
82	Troas	Gergis	No	No	No	No	No	No	No	Yes
83	Troas	Kebren	No	No	No	No	Yes	No	No	Yes
84	Troas	Lamponeia	No	No	No	No	No	No	No	Yes
85	Troas	Neandreia	No	No	No	No	No	No	No	Yes
86	Troas	Ophrynion	No	No	No	No	No	No	No	Yes
87	Troas	Rhoeteion	No	No	No	No	No	No	No	Yes
88	Troas	Sigeion	No	No	No	No	No	No	No	Yes
89	Troas	Skepsis	No	No	No	No	No	No	No	Yes
90	Troas	Tenedos	No	Yes	No	No	Yes	No	No	Yes

Table 2. Hoards with Lydian coins[6]

Number	Findspot	Date	EL	AU	AR
1176	Gordion, Phrygia	c. 610	Y	N	N
1153	Ephesos, Artemision deposit	c. 600–590	Y	N	N
1155	Asia Minor, western?	c. 600–590	Y	N	N
1156	Asia Minor, western?	c. 600–575	Y	N	N
1157	Priene	c. 575–560	Y	N	N
1162	Sardis, Lydia	c. 546	N	Y	N
1879	Persepolis	before 511	N	Y	N
689	Sveti Vlas, Bulgaria	6th	Y	N	N
1632	Egypt	6th	N	Y	N
1637	Hermopolis minor, Egypt	500	N	N	Y
1166	Smyrna	c. 500–490	N	N	Y
1175	Asia Minor, western	c. 480	Y	N	Y
1178	Çal dag, near Sardis, Lydia	c. 470	N	N	Y
1639	Xois, Egypt	Early 5th?	N	N	Y

The supplier of electrum for the early sixth-century coins is generally accepted to be Lydia, based on its proximity to the minters and Herodotos' testimony of its function as a gold market.[7] The concentration of electrum minters in Ionia is considered indicative of the metal's provenance, especially since the Greek poleis of Asia Minor are reported to have had close relations with Lydia. Kroisos discontinued the minting of electrum coinage in Lydia, replacing it with gold and silver and many poleis in Asia Minor followed the Lydian example in the second half of the sixth century.[8] The change in Lydian coinage has been explained as the result either of the exhaustion of the Paktolos deposit or of Kroisos targeting the markets of the Greek mainland, which were unused to electrum.[9] However, there is no evidence to suggest either that the Paktolos deposit was exhausted at the time of Kroisos, especially since Sardis remained a major minting centre after the Persian conquest, or that there was widespread numismatic contact between mainland Greece and Lydia, as the hoards show a definite trend towards Asia Minor and Egypt (for the dispersal of Lydian coins in hoards, see Table 2 above).

6 The hoard numbers in this table are those of IGCH.

7 Herodotos 1.69. Kraay (1976: 28); Boardman (1996: 126); Treister (1996: 172).

8 Kraay (1976: 29).

9 Kraay (1976: 29).

Nevertheless, the influence of Lydian numismatic practice on the minting of the Asia Minor poleis does suggest some relation between the two, which could be the supply of electrum. Equally possible however, is that the poleis followed Lydian numismatic practice because of trade links with it or because of its political dominance over them.

The main objection to the Lydian provenance of the electrum used by all the Asia Minor poleis is that close relations between the Greeks and the Lydians are attested mainly for the reign of Kroisos, while the majority of electrum issues are dated to an earlier period:

> This man Kroisos was the first of the barbarians to come in close contact to us, destroying some of the Greeks to exact tribute, whilst making friends of others.[10]

The Lydian kings before Kroisos, according to the Hellenocentric account of their reigns in Herodotos, were intermittently in conflict with many of the Ionian cities, such as Smyrna, Miletos, Kolophon, Priene and Klazomenai.[11] One supplier need not be assumed for all the different coinages of the period, especially since some of the minters were in contact with other gold producers, and at times their relations with Lydia, if any, were strained. Ephesos could have been supplied by Lydia, since the scanty evidence suggests amiable and possibly close relations before Kroisos; the Lydian kings attacked various poleis but not their nearest neighbour. Beyond pure aggression or empire building as explanations for attacking the Greek poleis, which cannot be discarded out of hand, the Lydians, like many landlocked states, may have been attempting to gain access to the Aegean coast with its maritime wealth and communications. Therefore, not attacking Ephesos could mean that it was the main entrepôt for them in the period. Such close relations, and the wealth they brought, could explain not only the many Lydian coins in the Artemision hoard but also Ephesos' notable absence from the colonisation movement and of the Greek enclave in Naukratis.[12]

Miletos and Phokaia were connected with far-flung colonies which, although not state foundations, had strong connections with the poleis they considered their metropoleis. The Milesian colonies in the Black

[10] Herodotos 1.6.2: Οὗτος ὁ Κροῖσος βαρβάρων πρῶτος τῶν ἡμεῖς ἴδμεν τοὺς μὲν κατεστρέψατο Ἑλλήνων ἐς φόρου ἀπαγωγήν, τοὺς δὲ φίλους προσεποιήσατο.

[11] Herodotos 1.14–22.

[12] Artemision hoard: IGCH 1153. Kraay (1976: 24–25); Robinson (1951: 161, 163); Kagan (1982: 356–359).

Sea and the Propontis, especially Abydos and Trapezous, could have had access to gold/electrum through either their own mines or trade with native tribes respectively.[13] Similarly, Massalia was in position to trade with native tribes not only in Gaul but also in Iberia.[14] The means or articles of exchange in such transactions have not survived, but there is evidence of a brisk trade between the Greeks in Asia Minor and the colonial foundations in both the Black Sea and the west; additionally, depending on the date of formal acknowledgement of the *apoikia-metropolis* (colony-mothercity) relation, gifts could account for part of the supply.[15] Another possible supplier of gold was Egypt, where the Greeks traded from the late seventh century onwards, especially since seven of the twelve traditional founders of the Greek *emporion* in Naukratis were electrum minters (Klazomenai, Chios, Teos, Phokaia, Halikarnassos, Miletos and Samos).[16] The Egyptian exports of the archaic period are debated, since Milne, the pioneer in Greek-Egyptian relations before Alexander, argued against the export of grain, while Boardman proposed that grain was the main export to the Greek world.[17] Although grain could have been imported from Egypt, the quantity could not have been as large as in the classical period; allowing gold as the other major export solves the lack of valuable exports from Egypt and, simultaneously, does not necessitate the assumption of large-scale imports of grain in the early archaic period.

Except for Smyrna, Samos and Abydos, which possibly had resources of their own, the rest of the poleis imported the necessary metal from

---

[13] Strabo 11.2.19, 11.14.9, 11.41.9; Appian *Mithridatic Wars* 103; Pliny 6.14, 6.30, 33.52; Aristotle *On Marvellous Things Heard* 26; Forbes (1964: 166); Healy (1978: 47); Tsetskhladze (1998: 64); Treister (1996: 172).

[14] On the reasons for the Phokaian foundation of Massalia, I think Hodge's (1998: 7–8, 168) argument, that Massalia and Ampurias were stepping-stones on the journey to Iberia, is preferable to that of Shefton (1994: 72) that the Phokaians used a north African route.

[15] Gifts to metropolis: Bury & Meiggs (1994: 71). Trade with Iberia: Shefton (1994: 72). Trade with Gaul: Boardman (1996: 274–275). Tribute could also be a possible means of acquiring gold, but the only case of tribute exacted by a metropolis I have found is the case of the Kotyoran *dasmos* paid to Sinope, which is an exceptional case in that it is a permanent rent for the *chora* and was administered separately by the Sinopeans [Xenophon *Anabasis* 5.5.3, 5.5.10; Hansen & Nielsen (2004: 722)].

[16] Trade before Naukratis: Boardman (1994: 141). Poleis involved in Naukratis' foundation: Herodotos 2.178.2–3; Boardman (1996: 180).

[17] Milne (1939: 177 ff.); followed by Roebuck (1950: 236 f.) and Sutherland (1943: 143). Against see Boardman (1999: 129).

long-distance suppliers. For the majority of poleis, trade was the best acquisition method, since the greatest suppliers, Lydia and Egypt, were not amenable to other forms of acquisition, such as booty or tribute. Following the Spartan-Lydian example, direct state-to-state transactions without private intermediation were the norm for precious metal import in the archaic period.[18] This contrasts readily with the prevailing situation in classical Athens, where the evidence suggests that all trade was conducted through private enterprise.

In the fifth century, more poleis in Asia Minor began to mint, most of them in silver, while the minting of electrum/gold also revived, after its decline in the second half of the sixth century. Following the trend of the Ionian Revolt coinages, the axis of gold/electrum minting moved to the north of region, where Kyzikos, Abydos and Lampsakos minted, with only Phokaia and Chios remaining in Ionia, while gold/electrum minting disappeared entirely in the south of the region. The fifth century witnessed great political and economic upheavals in the eastern Greek world, and especially in Asia Minor and the eastern Aegean, with the aftermath of the Ionian Revolt, the Persian Wars, the rise and demise of the Athenian Empire, as well as numerous expeditions, local wars and revolts. In this century, the economy of the poleis of Asia Minor and their coinages were mainly influenced by Athens, through both the *phoros* (tribute) and other measures, such as the Coinage Decree. The *phoros*, although probably not debilitating, was burdensome and a constant drain in the finances of any polis, since the precious metal left the local economy and a constant supply had to be secured. The Coinage Decree is a controversial and debated document, since, while some of its provisions are clear, its reasoning and practical effects are not.[19] The aim of the Coinage Decree has been variously interpreted as the formalisation of an existing practice, a purely political measure and a sign of commercial imperialism.[20] The main problem with all three interpretations is their adamantly exclusive nature; there is no need to assume that Athens as an imperial power failed totally to examine and evaluate all the possible effects of the decree or that all the allies had the same numismatic practice. As Finley noted, many allies had

[18] See page 45.

[19] On the problems of dating the decree see Mattingly (1961), either date does not affect the discussion.

[20] IG I[3] 1453. Formalisation: Austin & Vidal-Naquet (1977: 57); Political: Finley (1965: 22–24).

either stopped minting locally before the Coinage Decree or did not start minting until after the end of the Peloponnesian War, thus they probably used owls or other large coinages, possibly Aiginetan, for their transactions.[21] For them, the Coinage Decree would signify no more than the formalisation of their existing practices, while such practices could possibly have initially alerted Athens to the possibilities available if the whole of the empire used their coinage.[22] For those allies who had kept their numismatic independence, the political impact of the Coinage Decree would have been great, in that it was an obvious curtailment of their independence, both political and economic. The Coinage Decree would have influenced commerce within the empire considerably, not only for the individual trader, who now had the freedom of trading under one universal currency, but also for the poleis, which were now forced to acquire all silver from Athens for their own transactions.[23] No single motive or consequence should be assigned to a measure as influential and pervasive as the Coinage Decree was designed to be; on the contrary, the various simultaneous and merging causes and objectives provide us with a better understanding of the workings of both the empire and its economy.

Electrum and gold coinages were not affected by the Coinage Decree and some of them flourished in the fifth century, such as the Kyzikene *stater* and the Phokaian/Mytilenian *hektai*. Local gold resources could account for the coinage of Abydos. Phokaia probably utilised her relations with the far west, as in the previous century, and supplied Mytilene under their monetary union. A fragment of the decree of the monetary union has survived concerning alloying; the inscription cannot be securely dated and whether this is the initial decree or a copy is debated:

> ... (and whatever) both cities (by means of a compact add in writing to the stelai or erase), let it be valid. And the official responsible for the alloying of the gold is to be answerable to both cities. For the official who alloys the gold at Mytilene, a majority of the judges is to come from all the magistrates at Mytilene; at Phokaia, also, a majority of the judges is to come from all

[21] Finley (1965: 23).

[22] Athenian coins were the most widely dispersed in the Greek World in the fifth century as shown by the surviving hoards, since Athenian coins are found in 18.8 % of the total (46 of 244 from IGCH).

[23] Finley (1965: 23) rightly noted that such a measure would be beneficial to all traders, Athenian and non-Athenian, although it must be noted that, firstly, the adoption of the Euro has shown how much trade can benefit from a universal currency and, secondly, benefiting non-Athenian traders is not a problem as long as Athenian traders benefit as well.

> the magistrates at Phokaia; and the trial is to occur within six months after the end of the year (in which the official served at Mytilene or Phokaia). If the official on trial is convicted of having wilfully lowered the quality of the alloy, let him suffer the death penalty; but if he is acquitted on the basis of not having wilfully done wrong, let the court determine whether he is to suffer or to be fined. But let the city be considered guiltless and not subject to penalty. The Mytilenians obtained by lot the minting of the coinage for the first time. The prytany after that of Kolonos (in Mytilene) inaugurates this compact, in Phokaia (the prytany) after that of Aristarchos.[24]

Mytilene started minting electrum *hektai* as early as 485, but in the middle of the century a change of type was effected, which made the coinage correspond roughly to the types of Phokaia, although they never became identical. Possibly at that time the monetary union was initially enacted, while the surviving decree dates from the period after the Mytilenian revolt and the alloying regulations correspond to the emergency minting of electrum staters with a large copper content during the revolt itself.[25] The monetary union is undoubtedly a significant development in Greek numismatic practice but can be variably interpreted economically. The simplest explanation is that of a bilateral agreement between the two poleis for reasons of convenience without any further connotations or targets.

However, such a simplistic explanation, although attractive, does not fully conform to the use and spread of Mytilenian/Phokaian *hektai*. The change of type in the Mytilenian *hektai* in the middle of the century marks a development, and the correspondence of the new types with the types of Phokaia suggests that this development was a union agreement. Consequently, for a period of as much as half a century, the two poleis minted separately and for some reason decided to enter into a monetary union. I would suggest that the reasoning behind the union is connected

---

[24] Tod II 112: - - - - - - E[- - - - - - - - - - ὄττι] | [δέ κε αἰ] πόλις [ἀμ]φότ[εραι] | [ ] γράφωισι εἰς τὰ[ν στάλαν ἢ ἐκκ|ολάπ]τωισι, κύ[ρ]ιον ἔστω. [τὸν δὲ κέρναν|τα τὸ] χρύσιον ὐπόδικον ἔ[μμεναι ἀμφο|τέρ]αισι ταῖς πολίεσσι· δι[κάσταις δὲ] | [ἔμ]μεναι τῶι μὲν ἐμ Μυτιλήναι [κέρναν|τι] ταὶς ἄρχαις παίσαις ταὶς ἐμ Μ[υτιλ|ή]ναι πλέας τῶν αἰμίσεων, ἐμ Φώκαι δὲ τ|αὶς ἄρχαις παίσαις ταὶς ἐμ Φώκαι πλ[έ]|ας τῶν αἰμίσεω[ν]· τὰν δὲ δίκαν ἔμμεναι | ἐπεί κε ὠνίαυτος ἐξέλθηι ἐν ἐξ μήννε⟨σ⟩|σι· αἰ δέ κε καταγ[ρέ]θηι τὸ χρύσιον κέρ|ναν ὐδαρέστερον θέλων θανάτωι ζαμι|ώσθω, αἰ δέ κε ἀπυφ[ύ]γηι μ[ὴ] θέλω⟨ν⟩ ἀμβρ[ό]|την, τιμάτω τ[ὸ] δικαστήριον ὄττι χρὴ α|ὖτ⟨ο⟩ν πάθην ἢ κατθέ[μ]εναι, ἀ δὲ πόλις ἀναί|τιος καὶ ἀζάμιος [ἔσ]τω. ἔλαχον Μυτιλή|ναοι πρόσθε κόπτην. ἄρχει πρότανις ὀ | πεδὰ Κόλωνον, ἐ[μ Φ]ώκαι δὲ ὀ πεδὰ Ἀρίσ[τ]|αρχον. On the debate, see Heisserer (1954).

[25] Kraay (1976: 266–267 and no. 982).

to the main use of the *hektai* as unofficial denominations of the daric.[26] The main gold coinage in Asia Minor was the daric which, however, suffered from a lack of fractions. The Phokaian *hektai* in the late archaic-early classical periods probably functioned as unofficial fractions, and at some point in the beginning of the fifth century Mytilene entered the equation by also minting *hektai*. The obvious and immediate consequence of the Mytilenian minting would be the creation of a competitive relation between the two poleis. The effects of such competition cannot be reconstructed, but by its nature competition is detrimental to the supplier. Consequently, the monetary union redressed the balance by merging the two coinages in a joint responsibility of minting, as the decree specifies minting was not simultaneous in the two poleis but alternated at fixed intervals, possibly every year ("The Mytilenians obtained by lot the minting of the coinage for the first time"). The monetary union between Phokaia and Mytilene is best interpreted as an effort to monopolise electrum currency in Asia Minor and provide the much-needed fractions of the daric. To a large extent, if not totally, the union succeeded since no other polis minted *hektai* and the spread of Phokaian/Mytilenian *hektai*, at least in the hoards, dominates Asia Minor. More importantly, the Kyzikene stater did not penetrate efficiently in the region, as shown by the dispersal of electrum hoards (Table 3, below). Geographically, the hoards containing Kyzikene coins are quite widespread, ranging from mainland Greece to inland Asia Minor and from Lebanon to the Ukraine; however, there is a very strong division between silver and electrum coins. Silver coins are found routinely south of Kyzikos itself, mainly in Asia Minor, while electrum coins are mainly found in the Black Sea area, north of Kyzikos. Apparently, Kyzikos had relations with the poleis of Asia Minor and did not concentrate exclusively on the Black Sea, yet only two electrum hoards are found in Asia Minor and one in the Aegean islands. On the one hand, the explanation may be the dominance of the daric in Asia Minor, but since Kyzikos minted in the Phokaian standard, the *hektai* could easily have functioned as its fractions as well, particularly since in practice the Kyzikene stater and the Persian daric, in spite of their difference in value, were considered interchangeable.[27]

---

[26] Kraay (1976: 262): "They appear to have provided a local 'gold' coinage in north-west Asia Minor, and were probably rated as fractions of the Persian gold daric, of which true fractions were hardly ever minted."

[27] Kraay (1976: 262).

Table 3. Hoards containing Kyzikene coins[28]

Number	Place	Date	EL	AR
689	Sveti vlas BUL	6th	Y	N
1638	Delta EGY	500	N	Y
7	Santorini	500–490	N	Y
8	Melos	500–490	N	Y
1168	West Asia Minor	500–490	N	Y
1171	Chios	480	Y	N
1175	West Asia Minor	480	N	Y
1234	Apameia-Myrlea	460	Y	Y
1183	Kolophon	450	N	Y
1188	Troas	450	N	Y
1002	Olbia	450–400	Y	N
1194	Klazomenai	410–400	Y	N
43	Elis	400	Y	N
47	Piraeus	400–380	Y	N
714	Givkovo BUL	400–350	Y	N
1011	Pantikapaion	400–350	Y	N
1201	Abbaitis	390	N	Y
1012	Taman peninsula	M4th	Y	N
1013	Hermonassa	M 4th	Y	N
1212	Abydos	350	N	Y
807	Thracian Cher	350–300	N	Y
726	Orlovka UKR	340–330	Y	N
1239	Pityoussa	335–334	Y	N
1500	Beirut	332	N	Y
734	Ioan corvin ROM	330–320	Y	N
1045	Kobuleti GEO	Bef 325	Y	N
1281	West Asia Minor	320–300	N	Y
1792	Susa	Bef 311	N	Y
1223	West Asia Minor	5th/4th	Y	N
1233	West Asia Minor	4th	N	Y
1248	Kotiaeum	4th	N	Y

Beyond the practical aspects, the theoretical insight provided by the monetary union is particularly important, since it shows not only the understanding by the Phokaians and the Mytilenians of their competition and its effects, but also their willingness to redress the situation using economic rather than political or military measures.

The Kyzikene stater and its fractions was the main trade coinage in Thrace, the Propontis and the Black Sea, as well as an acceptable

[28] The hoard numbers in this table are those of IGCH.

currency in Athens and Asia Minor. The suppliers of gold to Kyzikos are most probably found in the Black Sea, in Pantikapaion, Trapezous and Phasis, since the nearest other suppliers were Macedon and the Strymon region, of which the former had a large gold coinage of its own and the later was under Athenian domination.[29] The electrum issue of Chios has been variously dated by scholars, whilst the latest opinions tend towards associating it with the Coinage Decree and encumbering it with the decree's dating problems.[30] Since stylistically the coin belongs to the mid-fifth century, it can be connected with the Egyptian Expedition and specifically with booty collected there.[31] In general terms, the situation did not change dramatically in the fifth century, with most of the minters relying either on their own resources or on trade for the procurement of precious metal; the lone exception is Chios, which possibly procured metal for its single electrum issue through booty.

The fourth century witnessed an increase in gold/electrum minters and although the majority of minters are found in northern Asia Minor, where Kyzikos, Lampsakos, Pergamos, Kios and Abydos minted, central and south Asia Minor were also represented by Mytilene, Klazomenai, Phokaia and Rhodos. Kyzikos, Mytilene and Phokaia probably utilised the same links to the Black Sea and Iberia respectively as in the previous century. Abydos certainly used its own mines at Astyra, while Klazomenai could have exploited Karşikaya, as the most powerful polis in the Gulf of Smyrna. Rhodos, as the main port of call between Egypt and the Aegean, could have been supplied from there.[32] The suppliers of Kios and Pergamos cannot be identified.

From the beginnings of coinage to the end of the classical period various poleis in Asia Minor minted in gold and electrum, and some of them, namely Kyzikos, Phokaia, Mytilene, Lampsakos and Abydos, exhibit remarkable regularity of minting. Abydos, Smyrna and possibly Klazomenai used local gold resources, while the majority of other minters had to rely on long-distance contacts and trade to acquire the precious metal for their coinages. The only coinage for which an irreg-

[29] Gardner (1920: 166) argued that Kyzikos was supplied by Persia, not an independent source; although the proposal is attractive, there is no evidence supporting it.

[30] Baldwin (1915: 44–45); Gardner (1920: 165); Kraay (1976: 242–243).

[31] On the stylistic grounds, see Baldwin (1915: 44). The Egyptian Expedition lasted six years, and for four and a half of these, the Athenians and their allies were winning (Thucydides 1.104.2). On the allies being in favour of the expedition for financial reasons, see Meiggs (1972: 95).

[32] Demosthenes 56.30.

ular supply can be postulated is the mid-fifth-century electrum coinage of Chios. Electrum and gold minting in Asia Minor depended on trade, and although it is difficult to pinpoint the trading partners, such evidence as the Spartan purchase from Lydia, the monetary union of Phokaia and Mytilene and, more importantly, the regular large-scale minting of poleis with no resources of their own, testify to the importance and volume of trade in gold/electrum between states.

However, Asia Minor represents only one end of the spectrum, where trade was the preferred and only practical means of acquisition; a similar solution cannot be inferred for all minters of gold/electrum in the Greek World. The best example of the other end of the spectrum is minting in Sicily and Magna Graecia. The western colonies rarely minted in gold or electrum, with only seven poleis irregularly minting in gold in the course of three centuries.[33] In the archaic period, there were no gold or electrum coinages in Sicily and Magna Graecia, probably due to the late appearance of coinage in the region and the influence of coinages of mainland Greece rather than Asia Minor or Lydia.

The first gold coinages in Sicily appear in the late fifth century in Syracuse, Akragas, Gela and Kamarina. The coinages of Akragas, Gela and Kamarina have been dated to immediately before the Carthaginian invasion, while that of Syracuse has been connected to both the Athenian and the Carthaginian invasions.[34] The weight standard and denominations of these coinages are the same, all having 2-Litra, 1⅓-Litra and 1-Litra coins that appear to have been designed with a standard relation to silver.[35] Both the similarity of weight standard and denominations, and the time of minting, suggest that these coinages were emergency measures for the procurement of supplies and payment of mercenaries at a time of extreme pressure, similar to the gold coinage of Athens in the 400s.[36] The emergency nature of these coinages suggests an irregular means of acquisition, probably through loans from local temples, confiscations of property or emergency taxation.[37]

---

[33] The situation was probably accentuated by the sparser Greek settlement of Italy and Sicily as against Asia Minor: Snodgrass (1994: 1). Against, see Boardman (1994).

[34] Akragas, Gela, Kamarina: Kraay (1976: 226, 228). Syracuse: Kraay (1976: 228); Jenkins (1972: 175) (1970: 99).

[35] Jenkins (1970: 99).

[36] Kraay (1976: 228); Jenkins (1972: 175); Holloway (1990: 135). Athenian: Thucydides 2.13.4–5 (contingency); Aristophanes *Frogs* 721 f. (gold coinage).

[37] Confiscation of properties in Gela: Diodoros 13.93.2; possible relation with the Sosipolis issue: Jenkins (1970: 15).

In the fourth century, the balance of power had changed in Sicily, with only Syracuse and Messana remaining independent. Dionysios I of Syracuse introduced a bimetallic coinage of gold and silver; the gold coinage consisted of 100- and 200-Litra coins, which have been calculated to be of equal and double value respectively to the silver decadrachm.[38] The value of the gold coins, their ready relation to silver and the wars against Carthage suggest that the gold coinage was used for the procurement of supplies, and more importantly for the payment of mercenaries. Additionally, the secession of minting in the reign of Dionysios II, simultaneous with the secession of hostilities with Carthage, also suggests that the gold coinage of Dionysios I was used for the payment of mercenaries and supplies.[39] The means of acquisition employed by Dionysios I are not certain; however, the considerable amounts of booty gained through the wars with Carthage and numerous raids, as well as the portrayal of Dionysios in Aristotle's *Oeconomica* as constantly devising new methods to acquire precious metal from the upper classes and the temples, tip the scales in favour of irregular means of acquisition.[40] The later gold coinages of Syracuse are connected with Timoleon's campaigns and the reign of Agathokles; Timoleon's campaign was again a time of emergency, while the coinage of Agathokles has more in common with the coinages of the Hellenistic kings than with that of the polis.[41]

The gold coinages of Magna Graecia seem inextricably linked with periods of turmoil, namely the campaigns of Timoleon, Alexander the Molossian and Akrobatos, when Taras and Metapontion asked for help from mainland Greece against the Italiote tribes.[42] The emergency nature of the coinages suggests irregular local means of acquisition, similar to those employed for the late-fifth century coinages in Sicily and Athens.

For the gold coinages of both Sicily and Magna Graecia, irregular means of acquisition have been postulated due to the emergency nature of the coinages themselves. If the gold was acquired through loans from temples and confiscations, then initially the metal would have entered the area either as bullion or as ready ornaments; the nearest gold deposits

[38] Kraay (1976: 224, 231–232); Holloway (1990: 134).

[39] Kraay (1976: 233).

[40] Aristotle *Oeconomica* 1349a14–1950a6. Although the stories are probably exaggerated, there must be a grain of truth in the various stratagems attributed to Dionysios.

[41] The gold coinage of Tauromenion in c. 300 is part of the Agathoklean expansion.

[42] For the dating of these coinages and their relation to campaigns see: Kraay (1976: 191–192) for Timoleon, Kraay (1976: 192, 195) and Jenkins (1972: 197) for Alexander the Molossian and Kraay (1976: 202) for Akrobatos.

Table 4. Hoards with gold and electrum coins in Sicily and Magna Graecia

Number	Findspot	Date	Coins
1932	Taras, Italy	315	Taras, Philip II, Alexander III
1937	Tiriolo, Bruttium, Italy	late 4th	Lokroi
1943	Campiglia Maritima, Etruria, Italy	4th	Etruscan
1944	Rhegion, Bruttium, Italy	*c.* 300	Syracuse (EL)
1945	Pazzano, Bruttium, Italy	*c.* 300	Syracuse (EL), Carthage (EL)
1946	Cariati, Bruttium, Italy	*c.* 300	Syracuse (EL)
1950	Monteparano, Calabria, Italy	*c.* 300	Taras
2093	Catania, Sicily	*c.* 405	Akragas, Kamarina, Gela, Syracuse
2094	Sicily	*c.* 405	Akragas, Gela, Syracuse
2122	Avola, Sicily	*c.* 370	Syracuse, Persia
2124	Avola, Sicily	*c.* 360	Syracuse, Amphipolis, Abydos, Lampsakos, Persia
2142	Selinous, Sicily	*c.* 325	Carthage
2143	Gela, Sicily	*c.* 320	Philip II, Alexander III, Carthage, Flamininus
2153	Palma di Montechiaro, Sicily	*c.* 300	Carthage (EL)
2158	Sicily	*c.* 300	Syracuse (EL)
2159	Buccheri, Sicily	*c.* 300	Philip II
2172	Selinous, Sicily	Late 4th	Carthage (EL)

were in northern Italy and in Iberia and Gaul. However, during the wars with Carthage, imports from Iberia are less likely due to the Phoenician presence there. On the other hand, after the 370s gold in the form of coinage could have been acquired in Sicily, either through customs or, more probably, through confiscations (see Table 4 above). For Italy, such means of acquisition can only be assumed for the later coinage related to the campaign of Akrobatos, since the first gold coinages in hoards are found after the 330s (see Table 4 above).

Turning to silver, a quantitative approach is used to examine the possibility of the import of coins for reminting, and the influence of the geographical distribution of minters on the silver trade. Quantification of ancient data, especially coins, is a method fraught with difficulties, both practical and theoretical. Practically, the lack of total output data means that any results can be considered interim only, pending further evidence. Theoretically, the main problem with any attempt at quantification is the relation of the objects to the economy that produced them. As McClellan pointed out recently, quantification of archaeological remains must be shown to be representative of the real economy and not merely the result of survival. The production of silver coinage, due both to its relation to the state and its overall role in the economy of a polis, is definitely "a representative of real economic activities" and as such can provide key evidence on the economic realities of the trade in silver.[43]

This is an effort to quantify the production of silver coins. The sample collected is from the collection of hoards as found in Thompson, Morkholm & Kraay (1973). Hoards as a statistical sample have their own problems, mainly the hoarding practices of different eras and areas, and the relative volumes of discovery and loss in the modern period. However, hoards account for the vast majority of known and documented ancient coins; thus they are the best available sample source for coinage production, at least until detailed data of die sequences become available. The major theoretical issue concerning the statistical uses of hoard evidence is whether they represent a typical or biased sample and, consequently, whether they retain the representative nature of the real economic activity of coinage production. The typicality of statistical samples is dependent upon their randomness. The randomness of the sample created by the hoards as relating to coinage production is particularly potent since hoarding depends on availability, which in turn depends on volume of production. Consequently, for the purposes of this investigation, until die-sequence evidence becomes available, hoards provide the best available random sample.

The mints selected fall into two categories: firstly, all poleis known to produce silver as well as poleis in silver producing areas where the exact ownership of the mines and the exploitation regime are unknown to us, and, secondly, all poleis that appear in more than five hoards. The count of poleis is based on the general hoard population without a metal bias, thus if a polis is found in five or more hoards irrespective

[43] McClellan (1997: 174).

of the coinage metal, it is included in the count. For example, Olbia is included, since Olbian coins are found in 30 hoards although only one of them is silver. The hoards considered are those from the sixth century to 330 according to the dating in Thompson, Morkholm & Kraay (1973). The lower chronological limit is set in order to avoid contaminating the study with the Alexandrian mints and the wealth procured during the conquest of the Persian Empire. The large variety of denominations and weight standards cannot be directly compared, thus the coins have been translated into units. One unit equals 4grs of silver, so a tetradrachm of 17 grs equals 4.25 units.

Sixty-nine poleis were thus selected and examined (see Table 5 below). Below the poleis are presented according to their geographical position. Group I includes the poleis of mainland Greece, the Peloponnese, the Cyclades, the Ionian Islands, Macedon and Thrace. Group II includes the poleis of Asia Minor, the Aegean islands, the Black Sea, Cyprus and Kyrenaike. Finally, Group III includes the poleis of Italy, Sicily and the Far West.

Of the first ten poleis, only Athens is a silver producer, which is also the only polis to have more than 10,000 units. In the whole sample, only eleven possible silver producers are found, of which the majority are in the bottom half of the list. These data provide us with some important insights in the world of the silver trade, primarily the levels and importance of imports for many of the poleis. The volume of coins produced by the importers is staggering. Some 51,000 units were produced by the importers, or in other words 1½ times the output of Athens. This alone shows the importance of the silver trade, its large volume and value, and lends credence to Xenophon's statement that exporting silver from Athens was always good business. Another indication of the large volume of imports is the large denominations used by the major importers, such as Syracuse, Aigina and Corinth.

Secondly, the issue of the export of silver in the form of coins is at least partly resolved. If the trade in silver was conducted mainly in the form of coins and not bullion then we would expect more of the producers to be prominent in the list. The situation is quite the opposite: the importers are the main coin-producers. If we exclude Athens from the calculations, Syracuse alone (7,327 units) produced more than all the producers together (5,314 units) and Aspendos (5,169 units) about the same total units. The first nine importers on the list produced 33,121 units, or almost the total of Athens and six times the total of all other producers together. The total volume of coinage from the silver producers

Table 5. 69 Silver minters according to total units

Key to Table:

Col. I	ID	Col. VIII	Staters in Hoards
Col. II	Polis	Col. IX	Staters in Hoards (in Units)
Col. III	Geographical Group	Col. X	Drachmai in Hoards
Col. IV	Number of Hoards	Col. XI	Drachmai in Hoards (in Units)
Col. V	Number of Silver (Ag) Hoards	Col. XII	Fractions in Hoards
Col. VI	Total Coins in Hoards	Col. XIII	Fractions in Hoards (in Units)
Col. VII	Standard(s) used in the Polis	Col. XIV	Total Units

All producers in the table are italicized

I	II	III	IV	V	VI	VII	VIII	IX	X	XI	XII	XIII	XIV
1	*Athens*	*I*	*95*	*94*	*8397*	*Tetradrachm -17 grs*	*0*	*0*	*32445*	*34472*	*262*	*32*	*34504*
51	Syracuse	III	76	68	1381	Tetradrachm -17 grs	0	0	6488	7299	160.5	28.5	7327.5
39	Aspendos	II	13	13	1743	Double siglos -11 grs	3407	5169	0	0	0	0	5169
2	Aigina	I	49	49	1660	Stater-12 grs, Drachm-6 grs	1576	4728	89	133	14.5	2	4863
14	Boiotia	I	13	11	1141	Stater-13 grs	1120	3640	2	2	57	7	3649
36	Knidos	II	14	13	2141	Drachm-6 grs	0	0	2120	3180	21	2.5	3182.5
50	Kelenderis	II	8	8	1119	Double siglos-11 grs	2085	3135	0	0	47	9	3144
53	Taras	III	38	38	1965	Stater-9 grs	944	2124	2	2	35	4	2130
8	Mende	I	12	12	465	Tetradrachm-18 grs	0	0	1708	1921	38	5	1926
60	Akragas	III	41	39	724	Tetradrachm-18 grs	0	0	1538	1730	9	1	1731
4	*Thasos*	*I*	*27*	*26*	*979*	*Stater-9/10 grs*	*698*	*1570*	*122*	*122*	*301*	*37*	*1729*
3	Corinth	I	31	30	789	Stater-9 grs	704 (of which 557 Pegasi)	1584	22	16	91	11	1611
57	Gela	III	39	37	625	Tetradrachm-18 grs	0	0	1425	1603	52	6.5	1609.5

I	II	III	IV	V	VI	VII	VIII	IX	X	XI	XII	XIII	XIV
55	Metapontion	III	37	36	1390	Stater-8 grs	667	1334	5	4	720.5	90	1428
58	Kroton	III	38	37	374	Stater-8 grs	655	1310	6.5	6	21	2.5	1318.5
41	*Sinope*	*II*	*9*	*9*	*822*	*Drachm-6 grs*	*6*	*10.5*	*815*	*1222.5*	*1*	*0.1*	*1233.1*
6	*Akanthos*	*I*	*29*	*28*	*367*	*Tetradrachm-17 grs*	*0*	*0*	*944*	*1003*	*89*	*11*	*1114*
52	Messana	III	43	42	233	Tetradrachm-18 grs	1	2	904	1017	5	1	1020
7	Thebes	I	16	15	317	Stater-12 grs, Drachm-6 grs	293	951	1	1.5	69	8	960.5
42	Rhodos	II	8	8	222	Tetradrachm-15 grs	0	0	928.5	870	0	0	870
12	Elis	I	16	16	311	Stater-13 grs	236	767	20	20	103	13	800
5	Sikyon	I	20	20	321	Stater-13 grs, Drachma-6 grs	209	679	11	16.5	289	36	731.5
59	Kaulonia	III	32	32	327	Stater-9 grs	317	713	8	8	1	0.1	721.1
62	Selinous	III	22	22	264	Tetradrachm-18 grs	0	0	618	695	1	0.1	695.1
32	Ephesos	II	17	14	193	Tetradrachm-15 grs	0	0	650.5	610	14	2	612
11	Larissa	I	15	14	364	Stater-7 grs, Drachm-6 grs	3	5	361	541	0	0	546
63	Poseidonia	III	24	24	270	Stater-8 grs	241	482	19	19	13	1.5	502.5
13	Chalcidian League	I	15	13	423	Tetradrachm-15 grs	0	0	428	401	724	90	491
56	Leontinoi	III	34	33	164	Tetradrachm-18 grs	0	0	394	443	65	8	451
64	Himera	III	23	21	139	Tetradrachm-17 grs	0	0	246	369	16	2	371
67	Velia	III	16	15	401	Stater-8 grs	78	156	122	122	400	50	328
30	Chios	II	28	27	253	Didrachm-8 grs	59	118	110	110	500	62	290
9	Leukas	I	17	16	127	Stater-9 grs	127 (of which 122 Pegasi)	285	0	0	0	0	285
16	*Abdera*	*I*	*15*	*14*	*67*	*Drachm-4 grs*	*15*	*30*	*253*	*253*	*5*	*0.5*	*283.5*
38	Kition	II	16	16	413	Double siglos-11 grs	90	234	0	0	337	42	276

I	II	III	IV	V	VI	VII	VIII	IX	X	XI	XII	XIII	XIV
65	Katana	III	23	23	62	Tetradrachm-18 grs	0	0	208.5	234	5	1	235
54	Rhegion	III	31	30	62	Tetradrachm-18 grs	0	0	189.5	213	6	1	214
28	Salamis	II	23	23	230	Stater-7 grs	116 (of which 6 sigloi)	176	4	4	268	33.5	213.5
29	Miletos	II	25	24	233	Stater-12 grs	50	150	33.5	33.5	159	20	203.5
37	Klazomenai	II	10	10	77	Drachm-4 grs	2	6	191	191	15	2	199
34	Kyrene	II	13	13	73	Tetradrachm-14 grs	0	0	220	192.5	8	1	193.5
17	Paros	I	8	8	118	Stater-8 grs, Drachm-6 grs	7	14	111	166	0	0	180
20	*Maroneia*	*I*	*10*	*4*	*51*	*Tetradrachm-15 grs*	*7*	*14*	*176*	*165*	*0*	*0*	*179*
10	*Lete*	*I*	*11*	*11*	*69*	*Stater-10 grs*	*66*	*165*	*6*	*6*	*0*	*0*	*171*
31	Samos	II	21	17	53	Drachm-4 grs	0	0	170.5	170.5	6	0.5	171
33	Kyzikos	II	20	14	371	Tetradrachm-15 grs	6	12	94	88	304	38	138
22	Corcyra	I	9	9	37	Stater-12 grs	37 (of which 2 Pegasi)	111	0	0	0	0	111
15	Ambrakia	I	14	13	42	Stater-9 grs	42 (of which 41 Pegasi)	94.5	0	0	0	0	94.5
49	Byzantion	II	5	4	128	Tetradrachm-15 grs	0	0	68	64	187	23	87
66	Kamarina	III	14	12	19	Tetradrachm-18 grs	0	0	72	81	0	0	81
61	Thurii	III	22	22	315	Stater-8 grs	21	62	7.5	7.5	2	0.25	70
19	Naxos	I	8	8	28	Stater-9 grs	27	60	0	0	1	0.1	60.1
18	*Neapolis*	*I*	*8*	*8*	*83*	*Stater-8 grs*	*8*	*16*	*24*	*24*	*155*	*19*	*59*
48	Phaselis	II	8	8	16	Stater-11 grs	18	54	0	0	0	0	54

I	II	III	IV	V	VI	VII	VIII	IX	X	XI	XII	XIII	XIV
43	Olbia	II	30	1	16	Stater-13 grs	16	48	0	0	0	0	48
24	Anaktorion	I	6	6	19	Stater-9 grs	19 (of which 15 Pegasi)	43	0	0	0	0	43
40	Teos	II	9	9	71	Stater-12 grs	8	24	2	3	63	8	35
69	Herakleia	III	9	9	17	Stater-8 grs	17	34	0	0	0	0	34
35	Kos	II	11	11	13	Tetradrachm-17 grs	4	8	18	19	3	0.3	27.3
27	*Siphnos*	*I*	*2*	*2*	*7*	*Stater-12 grs*	*7*	*21*	*0*	*0*	*0*	*0*	*21*
21	Eretrea	I	9	9	14	Didrachm-8 grs	0	0	18.5	18.5	7	1	19.5
26	*Aineia*	*I*	*5*	*5*	*5*	*Hemidrachm-3 grs*	*0*	*0*	*12*	*18*	*5*	*0.5*	*18.5*
23	Argos	I	7	7	41	Stater-13 grs, Hemidrachm-3 grs	1	3	1	1.5	111	14	18.5
25	*Amphipolis*	*I*	*5*	*5*	*59*	*Tetradrachm-14 grs, Drachm-4 grs*	*1*	*2*	*14*	*14*	*4*	*0.5*	*16.5*
47	Erythrai	II	5	4	6	Drachm-4 grs	0	0	9	9	1	0.1	9.1
46	Lampsakos	II	10	6	42	Drachm-4 grs	0	0	2	2	54	6.75	8.75
45	Magnesia	II	5	5	37	Hemidrachm-2 grs	0	0	3.5	3.5	36	4.5	8
44	Pantikapaion	II	8	5	25	Hemidrachm-3 grs	0	0	1	1.5	25	3.1	4.6
68	Massalia	III	5	3	7		0	0	0	0	7	1	1

can in no way be considered enough to supply the needs of the importers. Kraay's suggestion that the poleis of Magna Graecia and Sicily particularly relied on import of foreign coins for their coinages cannot be substantiated.[44] The relative amounts of coins produced by the importers in general, and the poleis of Italy and Sicily particularly, are too large to be explained by chance acquisition. There are three poleis from Italy/Sicily in the first 10 of the list and 12 in the first 30. The Italian/Sicilian poleis in the first 30 have a cumulative total of more than half that of Athens and 3½ times that of all the other producers together.

Athens is clearly an exceptionally prolific minter, which creates the immediate question of whether Athens did export silver in the form of coins. In addition to the practical problems of such a practice, which are discussed below, such an explanation of Athenian minting volumes disregards the position of Athens in the Mediterranean. Throughout the classical period, when the vast majority of Athenian coins were minted, Athens was one of the most powerful poleis in the Greek world. In addition to its political and military prominence, Athens was also an economic giant and the Piraeus the central node in the Aegean trading lanes and one of the most important in the whole of the Mediterranean. Athens a had vast need for cash to pay for its fleet, its campaigns, its building programs and of course its imports. In addition to such large expenses, during the fifth century the Coinage Decree testifies, as Finley rightly argued, that many of the allies primarily used Athenian coins and stopped minting their own, which was probably a consequence of the need to pay tribute.[45] Athens, although a producer and exporter of silver, has a minting profile akin to that of the great importers such as Aigina, Corinth and Syracuse. Athens' variance with the other exporters brings into sharp relief its other common characteristics with the large importers. These were the great trading powers in the Mediterranean with large fleets and many regional and interregional connections. Seen in this light, the main difference of Athens was its silver resources, which allowed it to mint prolifically without the need to secure imports of silver. The prolific minting of Athens is best explained not in connection with silver exports in the form of coins but rather in relation to its economic, political and military importance in the Greek world.

In addition, the practical problems of reminting foreign coins are particularly acute and have not been addressed in scholarship. The main

---

[44] Kraay & Emeleus (1962: 35); Williams (1997: 27–28).

[45] Finley (1965: 23).

problem is the means a state could acquire quantities of foreign coins. Stocks of foreign coins could be found mainly in banks and certainly not in state coffers. For a state to acquire foreign coins, it must have accepted foreign currency as payment, which contradicts one of the fundamental reasons of minting coins, the surety of recognised legal tender. The evidence suggests that the poleis were very keen to keep their markets free of foreign coinages.[46] Moreover, the evidence suggests that very few coinages had the prospect of an interregional market: the exceptions are the Aiginetan turtles, the Athenian owls, the Corinthian Pegasi and the Kyzikene staters. Other major coinages, such as the Syracusan silver and the Phokaian/Mytilenian *hektai*, never achieved that stage and remained confined to one region. For the poleis to have used foreign coinage as bullion for their own mints implies that the exporters of silver had also an interregional market. The evidence, however, does not support an interregional market for any possible exporter except Athens, which in addition to its place as a silver exporter was also a major commercial hub in the eastern Mediterranean. The only instance of actual reuse of foreign coins is overstriking, which is different from an elaborate process of importing and reminting. Overstriking was not common practice and is best explained as a temporary measure in times of silver shortage.[47] Simultaneously, the various finds of hoarded silver bullion, in the form of ingots and bars, show that bullion was in circulation and could be easily procured not only by states but also by individuals.[48]

The hoard data also provide a valuable insight into the routes of the silver trade. Among the importers in the first thirty poleis, twelve are from the western colonies, seven from Greece and five from Asia Minor. The west was the region with the majority of silver importers on a large scale, which balances to some extent the import-export equation of these poleis, since to this date there has been no explanation of the return cargoes for the export of commodities, primarily grain, to the east. The importers of Group I are numerous but not particularly prominent. This is explained by the relatively smaller size of the poleis and thus lesser demand for coins and smaller financial strength.

---

46 Olbia: IOSPE I(2) Bl Sea Sc Min 24.1; Byzantion: Aristotle's *Oeconomica* 1346b24–27.

47 Kraay (1976: 12).

48 Hoards with metal bars and/or ingots: IGCH 1035, 1182, 1478, 1482, 1636, 1637, 1639, 1640, 1644, 1645, 1647, 1649, 1651, 1874, 2172(AU), 2259, 2313.

Table 6. Silver minters hoard distribution

Minter	Greece	North	Thrace	Asia Minor	Levant	Egypt	East	Italy	Sicily	West	Total
Athens	18	3	1	18	10	15	4	6	18	1	94
Syracuse	0	0	0	2	1	2	1	6	55	1	68
Aigina	26	0	0	4	2	10	5	1	0	1	49
Messana	0	0	0	0	1	1	2	4	33	1	42
Akragas	0	0	0	0	1	0	0	4	32	2	39
Taras	0	0	0	0	0	0	0	37	0	1	38
Kroton	0	0	0	0	0	1	0	36	0	0	37
Gela	0	0	0	0	0	0	0	4	31	2	37
Metapontion	0	0	0	0	0	1	0	33	1	1	36
Corinth	7	0	0	2	1	6	0	5	9	0	30
Akanthos	0	9	0	2	4	6	3	1	3	0	28
Thasos	0	0	13	3	2	6	1	1	0	0	26
Thebes	14	0	0	0	0	0	1	0	0	0	15
Abdera	0	0	5	2	2	4	1	0	0	0	14
Aspendos	0	0	0	11	0	0	2	0	0	0	13
Knidos	0	0	0	9	0	1	3	0	0	0	13
Mende	0	3	0	2	1	5	0	1	0	0	12
Boiotia	10	1	0	0	0	0	0	0	0	0	11
Lete	0	0	1	1	2	5	1	1	0	0	11
Sinope	0	0	0	6	0	2	1	0	0	0	9
Neapolis	0	2	0	1	0	5	0	0	0	0	8
Kelenderis	0	0	0	6	0	0	2	0	0	0	8
Rhodos	0	0	0	8	0	0	0	0	0	0	8
Amphipolis	0	4	0	0	0	0	0	0	1	0	5
Aineia	0	2	0	0	0	3	0	0	0	0	5
Maroneia	0	0	4	0	0	0	0	0	0	0	4
Siphnos	2	0	0	0	0	0	0	0	0	0	2

The major minters in Group I are characterised by a tight dispersal of hoards in the region, as seen in Table 6. Aigina, Boiotia, Thasos and Thebes are characteristic examples, especially in comparison with Corinth or Mende. This tight dispersal exemplifies the potential of interchange of coinages in the region, in other words it shows that foreign coins circulated widely within the region and their use was widespread.

Lastly, the least voluminous production appears to be in Group II. This can be explained by the prevalence of Persian coinage in the area for the larger part of the period, which created an expectedly lesser demand for large-volume local coinages. Moreover, the main large-scale coinages in Asia Minor and the Black Sea area were the Kyzikene stater and the Phokaian *hektai*, both in electrum.

A further problem is the case of non-poleis. It has been argued by scholars that Egypt and other areas of the eastern Mediterranean imported silver in the form of coins from the Greek poleis. This argument was precipitated by the discovery of particularly large hoards in Egypt, many of Athenian coins. Egypt had no silver resources of its own and was prime importer material for the silver-rich Greeks. It is generally thought that the import of silver to Egypt was in the form of coins. However, in spite of the prevalence of Athenian coins in some Egyptian hoards, a study of these hoards reveals that they contain a wide variety of coins, in many cases only a few specimens of each (see Table 7, below). The variable nature of these hoards raises the question of whether this was an intentional public import of foreign coins to use as bullion or an unintentional private import through traders and mercenaries. The dearth of any commodity leads to higher value; in other words, the lack of silver supplies in Egypt made silver more valuable there in contrast to Greece or the Aegean. That would make individual transactions rather more attractive to both parties, since both would be profiting, the Greeks by exchanging their 'low-value' silver with high value commodities and the Egyptians by exchanging their commodities with 'rare' metal. That means that any silver coins, regardless of provenance, would fetch good prices; traders, and mercenaries, would get more for them than if they used or exchanged them in the Greek World. Additionally, there is no reason to suppose that the export of silver to Egypt was in the form of coins since many ingots and bars are found in Egyptian hoards.[49]

[49] IGCH 1636, 1637, 1639, 1640, 1644, 1645, 1649, 1651.

Table 7. Greek coins found in hoards in Egypt

Polis	1633	1634	1635	1636	1637	1638	1639	1640	1641	1642	1643	1644	1645	1646	1647	1648	1649	1650	1651	1652	1653	1656	1659	1660	1661	1662
Abdera	N	N	N	N	Y	N	Y	Y	N	N	N	Y	N	N	N	N	N	N	N	N	N	N	N	N	N	N
Abydos	N	N	N	N	N	N	N	N	N	N	N	Y	N	N	N	N	N	N	N	N	N	N	N	N	N	N
Aigai	N	N	N	N	N	N	N	N	N	N	N	Y	N	N	N	N	N	N	N	N	N	N	N	N	N	N
Aigina	N	N	N	Y	Y	N	Y	Y	N	N	N	Y	Y	Y	Y	N	N	Y	N	Y	N	N	N	N	N	N
Aineia	N	Y	Y	N	N	N	N	N	N	N	N	Y	N	N	N	N	N	N	N	N	N	N	N	N	N	N
Akanthos	N	N	N	N	N	N	Y	Y	N	N	N	Y	Y	Y	N	N	N	N	N	Y	N	N	N	N	N	N
Alexander I (of Macedon)	N	N	N	N	N	N	N	N	N	N	N	Y	N	N	N	N	N	N	N	N	N	N	N	N	N	N
Arados	N	N	N	N	N	N	N	N	N	N	N	N	N	N	N	N	N	Y	N	N	N	N	N	N	N	N
Athens	N	N	N	N	N	Y	Y	Y	N	N	N	Y	Y	Y	Y	Y	Y	N	Y	Y	N	Y	Y	Y	Y	N
Barke	N	N	N	N	Y	N	N	N	N	N	N	Y	N	N	N	N	N	N	N	Y	N	N	N	N	N	N
Bisaltai (tribe)	N	Y	N	N	N	N	N	N	N	N	N	N	N	N	N	N	N	N	N	N	N	N	N	N	N	N
Chalkis	N	N	N	N	N	N	N	Y	N	N	N	Y	N	N	N	N	N	N	N	N	N	N	N	N	N	N
Chios	N	N	N	Y	Y	Y	Y	Y	N	N	N	Y	Y	Y	Y	N	N	N	N	N	N	N	N	N	N	N
Corcyra	N	N	N	N	N	N	N	N	N	N	N	Y	N	N	N	N	N	N	N	N	N	N	N	N	N	N
Corinth	N	N	N	Y	Y	Y	Y	N	N	N	N	Y	Y	N	N	N	N	N	N	N	N	N	N	N	N	N
Cyclades uncertain	N	N	N	N	N	N	Y	N	N	N	N	N	N	N	N	N	N	N	N	N	N	N	N	N	N	N
Cyprus uncertain	N	N	N	Y	Y	N	N	Y	N	N	Y	Y	N	N	N	N	N	N	N	N	N	N	N	N	N	N
Delos	N	N	N	N	Y	N	N	N	N	N	N	N	N	N	N	N	N	N	N	N	N	N	N	N	N	N
Delphi	N	N	N	N	N	N	N	N	N	N	N	Y	Y	N	N	N	N	N	N	N	N	N	N	N	N	N
Derrones	N	N	Y	N	N	N	N	N	N	N	N	Y	Y	N	N	N	N	N	N	N	N	N	N	N	N	N
Dikaia (Macedonia)	N	N	N	N	N	N	N	N	N	N	N	N	Y	N	N	N	N	N	N	N	N	N	N	N	N	N
Dikaia (Thrace)	N	N	N	Y	Y	Y	Y	N	N	N	N	Y	N	N	N	N	N	N	N	N	N	N	N	N	N	N
Elis	N	N	N	N	N	N	N	N	N	N	N	N	N	N	N	N	N	N	N	Y	N	N	N	N	N	N
Eretreia	N	N	N	N	N	N	Y	Y	N	N	N	Y	N	N	N	N	N	N	N	N	N	N	N	N	N	N

Polis	1633	1634	1635	1636	1637	1638	1639	1640	1641	1642	1643	1644	1645	1646	1647	1648	1649	1650	1651	1652	1653	1656	1659	1660	1661	1662
Euesperides	N	N	N	N	N	N	N	N	N	N	N	N	N	N	N	N	N	N	N	Y	N	N	N	N	N	N
Gaza	N	N	N	N	N	N	N	N	N	N	N	N	N	N	N	N	N	N	Y	N	N	N	N	N	N	N
Golgi	N	N	N	N	N	N	N	Y	N	N	N	N	N	N	N	N	N	N	N	N	N	N	N	N	N	N
Himera	N	N	N	N	N	N	N	N	N	N	N	Y	N	N	N	N	N	N	N	N	N	N	N	N	N	N
Ialysos (Rhodos)	N	N	N	N	Y	N	Y	N	N	N	N	Y	N	N	N	N	N	N	N	N	N	N	N	N	N	N
Ichnai	N	N	N	N	N	N	N	N	N	N	N	Y	N	N	N	N	N	N	N	N	N	N	N	N	N	N
Idalion (Cyprus)	N	N	N	N	N	N	N	Y	N	N	N	Y	N	Y	N	N	N	N	N	N	N	N	N	N	N	N
Idyma	N	N	N	N	N	N	Y	N	N	N	N	N	N	N	N	N	N	N	N	N	N	N	N	N	N	N
Imitation Athens	N	N	N	N	N	N	N	N	N	N	N	N	N	N	N	N	Y	N	N	N	N	N	N	N	N	N
Ionia uncertain	N	N	N	N	N	N	Y	N	N	N	N	N	N	N	N	N	N	N	N	N	N	N	N	N	N	N
Kamiros (Rhodes)	N	N	N	N	N	N	Y	N	N	N	N	Y	Y	N	N	N	N	N	N	N	N	N	N	N	N	N
Karia uncertain	N	N	N	Y	Y	N	N	N	N	N	N	Y	N	N	N	N	N	N	N	N	N	N	N	N	N	N
Karpathos	N	N	N	N	N	N	N	N	N	N	N	Y	Y	N	N	N	N	N	N	N	N	N	N	N	N	N
Karystos	N	N	N	N	N	N	N	N	N	N	N	Y	N	N	N	N	N	N	N	N	N	N	N	N	N	N
Kaulonia	N	N	N	N	N	N	N	N	N	N	N	Y	N	N	N	N	N	N	N	N	N	N	N	N	N	N
Klazomenai	N	N	N	N	N	N	Y	N	N	N	N	Y	N	N	N	N	N	N	N	N	N	N	N	N	N	N
Knidos	N	N	N	N	N	N	N	N	N	N	N	Y	N	N	N	N	N	N	N	N	N	N	N	N	N	N
Kolophon	N	N	N	N	N	N	Y	N	N	N	N	N	N	N	N	N	N	N	N	N	N	N	N	N	N	N
Kos	N	N	N	Y	Y	Y	N	N	N	N	N	Y	N	N	N	N	N	N	N	N	N	N	N	N	N	N
Kroton	N	N	N	N	N	N	N	N	N	N	N	Y	N	N	N	N	N	N	N	N	N	N	N	N	N	N
Kyrene	Y	N	N	Y	Y	N	Y	N	Y	Y	N	Y	Y	N	Y	N	N	N	N	Y	N	N	N	N	N	N
Kyzikos	N	N	N	N	N	Y	N	N	N	N	N	N	N	N	N	N	N	N	N	N	N	N	N	N	N	N
Lampsakos	N	N	N	N	N	N	N	N	N	N	N	Y	N	N	N	N	N	N	N	N	N	N	N	N	N	N
Lapethos	N	N	N	N	N	N	N	N	N	N	N	Y	N	N	N	N	N	N	N	N	N	N	N	N	N	N
Leontinoi	N	N	N	N	N	N	N	N	N	N	N	N	N	N	N	N	N	N	N	Y	N	N	N	N	N	N
Lesbos	N	N	N	N	N	N	N	N	N	N	N	Y	N	N	N	N	N	N	N	N	N	N	N	N	N	N
Lete	N	N	N	Y	Y	Y	Y	Y	N	N	N	N	N	N	N	N	N	N	N	N	N	N	N	N	N	N

Polis	1633	1634	1635	1636	1637	1638	1639	1640	1641	1642	1643	1644	1645	1646	1647	1648	1649	1650	1651	1652	1653	1656	1659	1660	1661	1662
Leukas	N	N	N	N	N	N	N	N	N	N	N	Y	N	N	N	N	N	N	N	N	N	N	N	N	N	N
Lindos (Rhodos)	N	N	N	N	N	N	N	N	N	N	N	Y	N	N	N	N	N	N	N	N	N	N	N	N	N	N
Lydia	N	N	N	N	Y	N	Y	N	N	N	N	N	N	N	N	N	N	N	N	N	N	N	N	N	N	N
Lykia uncertain	N	N	N	N	Y	Y	Y	N	N	N	N	N	Y	Y	Y	N	N	N	N	N	N	N	N	N	N	N
Lykian Dynasts	N	N	N	N	N	N	N	N	N	N	N	Y	N	N	N	N	N	N	N	N	N	N	N	N	N	N
Macedonia uncertain	N	N	N	N	N	N	N	N	N	N	N	Y	N	N	N	N	N	N	N	N	N	N	N	N	N	N
Mantineia	N	N	N	N	N	N	N	N	N	N	Y	N	N	N	N	N	N	N	N	N	N	N	N	N	N	N
Melos	N	N	N	N	N	N	N	N	N	N	N	Y	N	N	N	N	N	N	N	N	N	N	N	N	N	N
Mende	N	N	N	N	N	N	N	Y	N	N	N	Y	Y	Y	N	N	N	N	N	N	N	N	N	N	N	N
Messana	N	N	N	N	N	N	N	N	N	N	N	N	N	N	N	N	N	N	N	Y	N	N	N	N	N	N
Metapontion	N	N	N	N	N	N	N	N	N	N	N	Y	N	N	N	N	N	N	N	N	N	N	N	N	N	N
Miletos	N	N	N	N	Y	Y	N	N	N	N	N	Y	N	N	N	N	N	N	N	N	N	N	N	N	N	N
Naxos	N	N	N	Y	Y	N	Y	Y	N	N	N	Y	N	N	N	N	N	N	N	N	N	N	N	N	N	N
Neapolis	N	N	N	N	Y	Y	Y	Y	N	N	N	N	N	Y	N	N	N	N	N	N	N	N	N	N	N	N
Olynthos	N	N	N	N	N	N	N	N	N	N	N	Y	N	N	N	N	N	N	N	N	N	N	N	N	N	N
Orreskioi	N	N	N	N	N	N	N	Y	N	N	N	Y	N	Y	N	N	N	N	N	N	N	N	N	N	N	N
Paphos (Cyprus)	N	N	N	N	N	N	N	N	N	N	Y	Y	N	Y	N	N	N	N	N	N	N	N	N	N	N	N
Parion	N	N	N	N	N	N	N	N	N	N	N	Y	N	N	N	N	N	N	N	N	N	N	N	N	N	N
Paros	N	N	N	Y	Y	N	Y	N	N	N	N	Y	Y	N	N	N	N	N	N	N	N	N	N	N	N	N
Peparethos	N	N	N	N	N	N	N	N	N	N	N	Y	N	N	N	N	N	N	N	N	N	N	N	N	N	N
Persia	N	N	N	N	N	N	N	N	N	N	N	Y	N	N	N	N	N	N	N	N	N	N	N	N	N	N
Phaselis	N	N	N	N	Y	N	N	Y	N	N	N	Y	Y	N	N	N	N	N	N	N	N	N	N	N	N	N
Philisto-Arabian	N	N	N	N	N	N	N	N	N	N	N	N	N	N	N	N	Y	N	N	N	N	N	N	N	N	N
Potidaia	N	N	N	Y	N	N	N	N	N	N	N	Y	Y	N	N	N	N	N	N	N	N	N	N	N	N	N
Rhegion	N	N	N	N	N	N	N	N	N	N	N	Y	N	N	N	N	N	N	N	N	N	N	N	N	N	N
Sabakes	N	N	N	N	N	N	N	N	N	N	N	N	N	N	N	N	N	N	N	N	N	N	N	N	N	Y

Polis	1633	1634	1635	1636	1637	1638	1639	1640	1641	1642	1643	1644	1645	1646	1647	1648	1649	1650	1651	1652	1653	1656	1659	1660	1661	1662
Salamis (Cyprus)	N	N	N	N	Y	Y	N	N	N	N	N	Y	Y	Y	N	N	N	N	N	N	N	N	N	N	N	N
Samos	N	N	N	N	Y	Y	Y	N	N	N	N	Y	Y	N	Y	N	N	N	N	N	N	N	N	N	N	N
Selge	N	N	N	N	Y	N	N	N	N	N	N	N	N	N	N	N	N	N	N	N	N	N	N	N	N	N
Sermyle	N	N	N	N	N	Y	N	N	N	N	N	Y	N	N	N	N	N	N	N	N	N	N	N	N	N	N
Sidon	N	N	N	N	N	N	Y	N	N	N	N	N	N	N	N	N	N	Y	Y	N	Y	N	N	N	N	N
Sinope	N	N	N	N	N	N	N	N	N	N	N	N	Y	N	N	N	N	Y	N	N	N	N	N	N	N	N
Skione	N	N	N	N	Y	N	N	N	N	N	N	Y	N	N	N	N	N	N	N	N	N	N	N	N	N	N
Stageira	N	N	N	N	Y	N	N	N	N	N	N	Y	N	N	N	N	N	N	N	N	N	N	N	N	N	N
Syracuse	N	N	N	N	N	N	N	N	N	N	N	N	N	Y	N	N	N	N	N	Y	N	N	N	N	N	N
Syria uncertain	N	N	N	N	N	N	N	N	N	N	N	N	N	N	N	N	N	Y	N	N	N	N	N	N	N	N
Tanagra	N	N	N	N	N	N	N	N	N	N	N	Y	N	N	N	N	N	N	N	N	N	N	N	N	N	N
Tenos	N	N	N	N	N	N	N	N	N	N	N	Y	N	N	N	N	N	N	N	N	N	N	N	N	N	N
Teos	N	N	N	N	Y	N	N	N	N	N	Y	Y	Y	N	N	N	N	N	N	N	N	N	N	N	N	N
Terone	N	Y	N	N	N	N	N	Y	N	N	N	Y	Y	N	N	N	N	N	N	N	N	N	N	N	N	N
Thasos	N	N	N	N	Y	Y	Y	Y	N	N	N	Y	Y	N	N	N	N	N	N	N	N	N	N	N	N	N
Thracian Chersonese	N	N	N	N	N	N	N	N	N	N	N	Y	N	N	N	N	N	N	N	N	N	N	N	N	N	N
Thraco-Macedonian uncertain	N	Y	N	Y	Y	Y	Y	Y	N	Y	N	N	Y	N	N	N	N	N	N	N	N	N	N	N	N	N
Tyre	N	N	N	N	N	Y	N	N	N	N	N	N	N	N	N	N	Y	N	Y	N	N	N	N	N	N	N
Zankle	N	N	N	N	N	N	N	N	N	N	N	Y	Y	N	N	N	N	N	N	N	N	N	N	N	N	N

GOLD AND SILVER: CONCLUDING REMARKS

The presentation and discussion of the exporters of gold and silver illuminates how the geopolitical distribution of silver and silver resources influenced the development of coinage in the Greek world. Although the original coinage metal was electrum, which is mainly gold, the majority of Greek poleis from the middle of the sixth century onwards minted mainly in silver. The choice of silver, as against gold or electrum, by the majority of the Greek poleis is consistent with the geographical distribution of resources. The major gold resources, mainly those of Tmolos, Gallikos, Egypt and Colchis, were outside the *chora* (countryside) of any individual polis and belonged in their majority either to kingdoms or to tribes. The gold resources belonging to the 'polis' part of the Greek World were less productive and most of them were in regions dominated by silver mines, such as the Pangaion and Siphnos. The unequal geopolitical distribution of resources is the explanation for the evolution of coinage metal use in the Greek World. The prime example is the Macedonian gold coinage of Philip II, which is connected within the tradition with more intensive exploitation of the Pangaion mines, presumably the gold ones.

Gold and silver resources were invariably owned by the state, both in the Greek world and in its periphery, as the evidence for Lydia, Athens, Siphnos and Thasos testifies. The system of exploitation, however, was different between poleis and non-Greek kingdoms. As far as we can infer from the Lydo-Spartan transaction and the large reserves of gold bullion that Kroisos possessed, Lydia employed direct exploitation of its gold resources. The polis on the other hand, as seen in the case of Athens, employed a complex system of indirect exploitation through leasing. Athens, unlike Lydia, did not pursue a monopoly policy and its intervention in production was not pronounced.[1] On the one hand, the differences in policy stem from the differences in the nature of the precious metal reserves themselves, since alluvial gold is easier to exploit and less

[1] Note that throughout I am using monopoly as that of the state against private individuals for foreign trade, rather than the idealised monopoly exhibited by the existence of the *emporion* as argued by Bresson (1993: 168).

risky than vein mining. On the other hand, minimum intervention in exploitation was better financially for the polis, since it required less complex institutions and less bureaucracy. The mining legislation ensured protection of the resources and of the state's investment profits. As was mentioned above, any threat to the safety of miners and mines would adversely affect the revenue of the state. On the other hand, the revenue of the state was guaranteed by the state debtor legislation. There was no need for the state to make special laws in the case of default of payment since far-reaching legislation for state debtors already existed. It is probable that similar legislation was in force for other exporters.

Athens also regulated the quality of the silver surplus, through ownership and leasing of *kaminoi*. Involvement in this instance aimed not merely to increase revenue but more importantly to regulate the quality of silver. For the state, this had a double purpose. Firstly, it meant that Athenian coinage would remain of a high standard of quality without the need for resmelting in the mint; something that I do not doubt was the major consideration of Athens as a major coinage producer in the eastern Mediterranean. Secondly, the involvement of the state in smelting had the further incentive of keeping Athenian silver in general of high quality even if not used for coinage. This may have been an inadvertent consequence of an original decision regarding coinage quality but eventually must have been realised as an important commercial advantage of Athenian silver as an export. Although the involvement of the state is more pronounced in smelting, because it exceeds the traditional directive of ultimate ownership of the resources of the country, the extent of involvement must have been small if effective, which would account for the lack of extensive references. The equilibrium of intervention and involvement in the silver industry in Athens was quite successful, since not only did the state get revenue from the mines and assured the quality of her legal tender but also the investors were not hemmed in by an intrusive governmental policy. The balanced policy of minimal intervention was unsuccessful only in cases where the state stopped being in possession of the mines and could no longer guarantee their safety, as happened in the Dekeleian War.

The disposition of surpluses is difficult to ascertain for any of the exporters, even for Athens. It is certain that the surpluses were disposed widely, for otherwise there would be very few coinages in the Greek World. For Athens, which was an exception in terms of minting, a large part of the silver produced was minted into owls. However, there must have been large amounts of silver in the hands of private individuals, which were offered to the international market as Xenophon testifies in the *Ways and Means*. In the archaic period, part of the surplus revenue acquired by the government was disposed as gifts to the citizens, as seen both in Siphnos and in Athens in 483. The Lydo-Spartan example shows that state-to-state transactions were not unknown in the Greek world and were considered a viable method of disposal. Possibly polis-to-polis transactions also took place but the silence of the sources on the issue leaves this possibility in the balance. In general, non-polis polities had a slight advantage in the disposition of surpluses due to their political profile. A kingdom in the ancient world, since all decisions stemmed from a given individual, was better equipped politically to dispose of its surplus in a more direct manner, as implied by both the Lydian gifts to Delphi and Philip's monetary gifts to supporters abroad. The polis, on the other hand, because of its diffused political power and the public nature of its proceedings, required public deliberation for a similar disposition which, however, did occur, as shown by the Siphnian treasury at Delphi.

The form of precious metal export in the Greek world has been the object of debate among scholars. Current opinion on the issue tends towards export of silver in the form of coins. For gold, the only available evidence, that of Lydia, based on the transaction with Sparta and the gifts to sanctuaries, suggests that bullion was the preferred method of export. For silver, it was shown that the data of coin production in the archaic and classical periods do not support the argument in favour of export in the form of coins. The large amount of silver minted by importing poleis and the corresponding small amount minted by exporters shows that bullion is the better choice. Export in the form of coins and its corresponding import not only invalidates one of the major reasons for minting coins, that is to provide a secure legal tender, but also disregards the issue of reminting expenses.

Turning to the importers, the means of acquisition of precious metal was a major concern for many poleis without native resources. For the majority of gold/electrum coinages of Asia Minor, trade was probably the most practical and favoured means of acquisition, since regularity of issue implies some regularity of supply. The transaction between Lydia and Sparta in the mid-sixth century testifies to state-to-state transactions being conceivable, however it cannot be safely assumed that Lydia was the main supplier of the Asia Minor minters, since relations were strained in the early sixth century. Additionally, the regular minters, namely Kyzikos, Phokaia and later Mytilene, were probably supplied from long-distance trade with the Black Sea and Iberia/Gaul respectively.

On the other side of the Greek world, in Sicily and Magna Graecia, minting in gold and electrum was erratic and connected with periods of emergency. For these minters. supply can only be assumed to have been equally irregular, either through booty, as for Dionysios I of Syracuse, or, more commonly, through temple loans and confiscations. The main differences between minting in Asia Minor and in Sicily and Magna Graecia are the irregularity of issues and the lack of any regular minters, as Kyzikos and Phokaia were in Asia Minor. This difference of practice has a twofold explanation. One the one hand, Sicily and Magna Graecia lacked any gold resources, and had easier contact with silver producers, both east and west. On the other hand, the minting of gold and electrum in Asia Minor was certainly influenced by the numismatic practice of Lydia and later Persia, which had adopted a bimetallic system that made gold and electrum coinages easier to accept and circulate, something readily apparent in the role of Phokaian and Mytilenian *hektai* as unofficial smaller denominations of the daric. Finally, the influence of first contact cannot be ignored, since in Asia Minor the first coinages were electrum under the influence of Lydian practice, while in Sicily and Magna Graecia silver was the initial metal used under the influence of mainland Greek practice.

The variety of acquisition methods employed by different poleis and the differences in basic numismatic practice in different regions are particularly illuminating for our understanding of Greek numismatic practice in general and specifically of the role of the state. Gold coinages afford the opportunity of close study, something impractical for silver coinages due to the large number of mints. There were three main categories of gold/electrum minters: those with local resources, those without and the irregular minters. Those with local resources can be further divided between those with constant access, such as Abydos in Astyra, and those with intermittent access, such as Smyrna and Klazomenai in Karşikaya. The minters without local resources, which had a regular practice, such as the poleis of Ionia in the early sixth century, many of the lesser mints in the fourth and, more importantly, Kyzikos, Mytilene and Phokaia that minted regularly throughout the period, were dependent upon foreign resources and, consequently, on constant close contact with their suppliers. The irregular minters, which outside Asia Minor were the majority, relied upon chance means of acquisition and their use of gold/electrum coinage was limited to emergencies that required larger value coins. Minting in gold/electrum after the middle of the sixth century was a practice against the norm, since silver had become the dominant coinage metal in the Greek World; regular minting was even more of a rarity, since most Greek poleis reserved gold minting for emergencies, probably when all reserves of silver had been exhausted. The different practice of the regular minters in Asia Minor demands explanation. For Abydos, and probably Klazomenai in the fourth century, minting in gold shows elementary economic thinking in preferring to use local resources rather than import silver. However, for the regular minters, particularly Kyzikos, Phokaia and Mytilene, minting in electrum involved complex processes, not least the import of metal. The monetary union between Phokaia and Mytilene reveals a further level of complexity, and implies an understanding of the adverse consequences of competition and the power of monopoly, since the union affected a monopoly of the two poleis in electrum fractions, especially since those fractions had become or were becoming the unofficial smaller denominations of the daric. Kyzikos, on the other hand, succeeded in creating one of the major trade coinages in the Greek World, with particular emphasis on the Black Sea and Propontis areas, whose position in Black Sea trade is best illustrated in the unique attention it receives in the Olbian effort to create a closed monetary system.[2] The behaviour of the regular minters implies a good understanding of the economics of monetization and, more importantly, a rational decision to invest in the creation and maintenance of long-distance contacts in order to fill a niche in the regional market.

For silver, unlike gold, studying specific importers is a mammoth and ultimately pointless task, due to the sheer number of silver minters and the very small number of exporters. Thus, a quantification of coinage production was attempted; admittedly a brief effort at a research area with considerable space for further study. Even so, it becomes obvious that the volume and value of silver trade was considerable, especially in the classical period. The relative volume of coinage produced in Sicily and Magna Graecia was considerably larger than in the rest of the Greek world. Less minting in mainland Greece, the Aegean and Asia Minor is explained by the availability of major coinages in the area, not only the trade coinages, such as the Corinthian *Pegasi* and the Athenian owls, but also the major regional coinages, such as the Boiotian and the Thasian. On the one hand, the volume of coinage production by the importers shows that the exportability of silver was as great as Xenophon claimed in the *Ways and Means*. On the other hand, the importers must

---

[2] IOSPE I(2) Bl Sea Sc Min 24.1.

have expended considerable effort and revenue to import silver. That is especially true not only of the poleis of Sicily/Magna Graecia but also of the great minters such as Aigina and Corinth. In contrast to the modern argument in favour of chance means of acquisition, mainly through foreign coins, the level of coinage production by the importers suggests the employment of regular means. Thus trade, either directly with the exporting state or through private traders, must have been necessary for the import of such quantities of silver. Xenophon's testimony as to the exportability, and consequent importability, of silver, shows that there was a constant incentive for traders to transport silver from the exporters to the importers because of the certain profit created by a limited supply and what seemed like an inexhaustible demand.

PART 2

TIMBER AND GRAIN

INTRODUCTION

In the previous chapters, the role of the government in the trade of precious metals was discussed, specifically the exploitation of mineral deposits and its role in the economy of the polis, and trade as the primary means for the acquisition of precious metals for coinage. Precious metals accounted for a large part of trade in the Greek world in terms of value. However, in terms of volume they accounted for a very small part of the overall traffic in the Mediterranean trading lanes. Other commodities made up the bulk of cargoes in the Greek world, mainly base metals, wood and foodstuffs, and more importantly grain.

This second part of the work discusses such bulk commodities, specifically shipbuilding timber and grain. As mentioned in the introduction, the commodities selected were such that the government would have reason to intervene in their trade. Wood was one of the primary components of Greek material culture, comparable in importance to iron and copper. The discussion concentrates on shipbuilding timber for warships, since they, like coins, were a concern of the government. The importance of naval warfare in the Greek world adds another dimension to the discussion, since the supply of timber and the construction of warships played a pivotal role in the balance of power, particularly in the eastern Mediterranean. Grain, on the other hand, was the main staple food of the Greeks throughout antiquity. For many poleis, it was the major bulk commodity in their ports and markets and its supply a governmental concern, either regularly or under circumstances of crisis. The grain supply, unlike that of other commodities, was in many cases a matter of life or death, and thus governments would, and did, exert considerable force to guarantee it.

The study of both commodities has a defining characteristic, which differentiates them sharply from precious metals. Both timber and grain are perishable materials, which vastly restricts the spectrum of available evidence on their trade. Thus, discussion is limited by the information provided by the surviving literary sources and epigraphical material. Consequently, investigation can be attempted only for those poleis for which information has survived, without the benefit of archaeological evidence, which in both cases means that the discussion centres on Athens. The lack of information on other poleis is lamentable; however, the fact that Athens was probably the greatest importer of both shipbuilding timber and grain makes the loss less debilitating. The types of surviving evidence, literary sources and inscriptions, lead the inquiry towards other aspects of government involvement and intervention.

The main themes explored in the following chapters are intervention through legislation and diplomacy, both peaceful and coercive. Governments could intervene through legislation, such as creating special tax regimes for commodities or restricting the freedom of traders relating to import or export of specific commodities. Intervention through legislation targets members of the community of the polis, both citizens and resident aliens. Governments could also target foreign states or traders through peaceful or coercive diplomacy. Peaceful diplomacy would be expressed mainly through treaties with other states and incentives or honours for foreign states or individuals. Coercive diplomacy implies the use or threat of force, such as the practice of *katagein* and the conquest of areas or resources relevant to the production or trade of one or more commodities.

TIMBER: PROLEGOMENA

In the archaic period, the Greek poleis had not yet developed public fleets but depended upon private captains and ship-owners for naval warfare, since raiding and privateering were culturally accepted.[1] By the end of the sixth century, poleis had, or were beginning to acquire, public fleets due to the development of powerful and centralised governments in conjunction with the invention and spreading use of the trireme. The invention of the trireme was particularly important in this development since its need for larger initial expense and personnel made private ownership more complicated and costly.[2]

In the classical period, on the contrary, fleets were mainly public and, although the maintenance of ships was often partly delegated to private citizens, such as the trierarchs in Athens, their construction was clearly a government responsibility. The following chapters discuss timber as a commodity for both exporters and importers with particular attention paid to the policies of Athens, the greatest naval power in the period. In chapter 4, the exporters of shipbuilding timber are discussed, mainly the Macedonians. The surviving evidence on the exploitation of timber resources and the export of timber and timber products provide a unique opportunity to explore the policies of Greek non-polis polities and particularly the phenomenon of monopoly. In chapter 5, the timber supply and fleet construction of the greatest naval power in the Greek world, Athens, are discussed. The policies of Athens are explored not only on the purely trade-related levels but also on grounds of general policy decisions, particularly during the fifth century. In chapter 6, other major fleet builders in the classical period are discussed, particularly the eastern Greeks and the Peloponnesians; of specific interest are the differences and similarities between these maritime poleis and Athens.

Before continuing, some practical questions of the timber trade and ship construction must be examined. Estimating the exact timber re-

[1] van Wees (2004: 203).

[2] van Wees (2004: 206–207). Some navies did continue to be partly dependant on private initiative in the classical period: van Wees (2004: 208).

quirements for any Greek fleet is beyond our current state of knowledge; however, generic calculations are possible.[3] The basis of the following estimations is the *Olympias*, the modern reconstruction of an Athenian trireme, serving as a model for a generic trireme.[4] The hull of the *Olympias* weighed 25 tonnes.[5] For 25 tonnes of used wood, the original weight in logs would be approximately 50 % higher; for ease of calculation 35 tonnes of wood in logs is assumed throughout.[6] Of the other wooden equipment of the trireme, the most important was the *tarros*, the oar-set, which weighed 1400–2000kgs and needed 2–3 tonnes of wood in logs.[7]

Beyond the initial building of a fleet, further construction annually or at regular intervals was necessary to ensure the maintenance of a fleet, as testified by Themistocles' proposal to build 20 triremes every year to maintain and increase the Athenian fleet.[8] The average life of a trireme was 20 years excluding losses due to weather or warfare. Thus, for the maintenance of a 200-ship fleet at least 10 new ships must have been built every year. For the Athenian fleet of 300 triremes in the Peloponnesian War, regular maintenance necessitated the annual construction of 15 triremes, while for the larger fleet of the second half of the fourth century 18 were needed.[9] Similarly, for a 90-ship fleet, such as that of Chios and Corinth in the Peloponnesian War, five new ships must have been built every year.[10]

It is not asked often enough where and with what resources fleets were built. The building of a trireme could be accomplished either in shipyards near or at the resource areas or in local shipyards at the polis concerned.

---

[3] No remains of a trireme have yet been discovered and it is doubtful that such a discovery is possible, given the trireme's lightness and lack of ballast: Morrison, Coates & Rankov (2000: 127–128).

[4] The Olympias is not an exact replica of an Athenian trireme: Morrison, Coates & Rankov (2000: 267–273).

[5] The basic hull weighed 15 tonnes and the outrigging, seats, decks, stanchions and braces 10 tonnes: Morrison, Coates & Rankov (2000: 210). The Olympias is now considered to be slightly smaller than an Athenian trireme [Morrison, Coates & Rankov (2000: 267–273)].

[6] Personal conversation with Mr. N. Koupetoris (elder), an experienced wooden *kaiki* builder, at Koupetoris shipyard in Salamis, Greece.

[7] Each trireme carried 200 oars, each weighing 7–10kgs: Morrison, Coates & Rankov (2000: 240).

[8] Diodoros 11.43.3.

[9] 300 triremes in Peloponnesian War: Thucydides 2.13. 349 triremes in 353/352: IG II[2] 1613.302, 392 in 330/329: IG II[2] 1627.269 and 360 in 326/325: IG II[2] 1628.489.

[10] Corinth: Thucydides 1.46. Chios: 60 in 412 (Thucydides 8.6) plus 30 lost in the Sicilian Expedition (Thucydides 6.31, 7.20), assuming that half the allied fleet was Chian.

The use of *naupegia* (shipyards) at or near the resource areas implies either domination over these areas or financial transactions between poleis and foreign *naupegia*. Use of local *naupegia* implies long-haul transport of timber from the resource areas to the polis concerned; such transport could be accomplished either by ship or by raft. Specialised timber carriers do not appear in the sources before the second century CE, and thus it must be assumed that they were not used in the classical period.[11] The size of the average merchant ship has been estimated at 120 tonnes, although all the wrecks that have been recovered to date from the classical period are considerably smaller than that.[12] Carrying timber aboard means that the ship must carry more ballast, especially since the long timbers of the trireme could only be carried lashed on deck.[13] The average merchant ships could ideally carry 17 cunits, enough for three triremes, but the need for more ballast and compartmentalization, as well as the lack of long cargo spaces, meant that a merchant ship could not practically carry as much.[14] Freight by raft avoided all problems of cargo space and ballast but was a dangerous enterprise for both ships and cargo. A large raft needed cabled ships both at the front and back to stop it turning sideways, while breaking up was a constant danger in heavy or choppy seas.[15] Both forms of transport entailed considerable costs, a large number of merchant ships and protection from pirates or enemies.

---

[11] Meiggs (1982: 338–339) argued in favour of specialised timber carriers used in the classical period, pointing out that specialised marble carriers are not attested in the sources before Pliny. However, assuming that technology did not progress in the course of antiquity is difficult to believe and specialised carriers cannot be rightfully placed in the classical period without some evidence of their existence.

[12] Casson (1995: 456).

[13] The long timbers of the trireme were about 40 m long, while the average merchant ship was only c. 24 m long (ex. Marseille Bourse wreck): Casson (1995: 458).

[14] For Douglas-fir [the type of timber used in the Olympias: Coates & Morrison (1987)] saw-logs of 10-inch diameter in the Scribner Decimal C Rule Westside scaling method (Long Log Scale), one cunit (100 cubic feet) weighs 7 tons [Log scaling determines the quantity of wood in individual logs. A formula, which closely estimates the Scribner rule, is $Log\,Volume(bd.ft) = (0.79D^2 - 2D - 4) - L/16$, where D is the diameter inside the bark measured in inches at the small end of the log and L is the nominal log length measured in feet. Source: http://www.utextension.utk.edu/publications/pbfiles/Pb1650.pdf. The Westside scaling method is the scaling principle used in pines and firs in the Western Cascades.] A 120-ton ship could carry up to 17 cunits (ideal full capacity, not practical) or 1,700 cubic feet in logs. For the Olympias 2,750 cubits (1,220 m) of plank and 500 cubits (220 m) of thick timbers were needed: McKee (1985: 49). Note that all transport must have been in logs, since construction from ready parts is not considered probable in the period: Steffy (1985: 36).

[15] Theophrastos *Enquiry Into Plants* 5.8.2. For a modern example see Meiggs (1982: 337).

CHAPTER FOUR

THE EXPORTERS OF TIMBER

The producers of shipbuilding timber can be securely identified, since a list has survived in the work of Theophrastos from the late fourth century:

> It is a narrow space, which produces shipbuilding timber. In Europe, it is found in Macedon and in parts of Thrace and Italy, while in Asia, in Kilikia and in Sinope and Amisos. There is also timber in the Mysian Olympos and in Mount Ida, but not a lot. In Syria, there is cedar, and that they use for triremes.[1]

Theophrastos specifically notes that it is a very narrow zone that produces the necessary timber, mainly because triremes were preferably constructed of silver-fir or fir, which can be found in the Mediterranean only above 800 m in altitude:

> In general, silver-fir, fir and cedar are used for shipbuilding. Triremes and long ships are made of silver-fir because it is light, while the round ships are made of fir because it does not decay. Sometimes triremes are also made of fir when they cannot get silver-fir. Those in Syria and Phoenicia made them of cedar because even fir is rare. In Cyprus, they use pine, for the island has a lot and it is considered better than its fir.[2]

Relating to Italy, Theophrastos later specifies that the areas producing shipbuilding timber were south Italy, Latium and Corsica:

---

[1] Theophrastos *Enquiry Into Plants* 4.5.5: Βραχὺς δ' ἐστὶ τόπος ὃς ἔχει καὶ ὅλως τὴν ναυπηγήσιμον ὕλην· τῆς μὲν γὰρ Εὐρώπης δοκεῖ τὰ περὶ τὴν Μακεδονίαν καὶ ὅσα τῆς Θρᾴκης καὶ περὶ Ἰταλίαν· τῆς δὲ Ἀσίας τά τε ἐν Κιλικίᾳ καὶ τὰ ἐν Σινώπῃ καὶ Ἀμίσῳ, ἔτι δὲ ὁ Μύσιος Ὄλυμπος καὶ ἡ Ἴδη πλὴν οὐ πολλήν· ἡ γὰρ Συρία κέδρον ἔχει καὶ ταύτῃ χρῶνται πρὸς τὰς τριήρεις.

[2] Theophrastos *Enquiry Into Plants* 5.7.1–2: Ἐλάτη μὲν οὖν καὶ πεύκη καὶ κέδρος ὡς ἁπλῶς εἰπεῖν ναυπηγήσιμα· τὰς μὲν γὰρ τριήρεις καὶ τὰ μακρὰ πλοῖα ἐλάτινα ποιοῦσι διὰ κουφότητα, τὰ δὲ στρογγύλα πεύκινα διὰ τὸ ἀσαπές· ἔνιοι δὲ καὶ τὰς τριήρεις διὰ τὸ μὴ εὐπορεῖν ἐλάτης. οἱ δὲ κατὰ Συρίαν καὶ Φοινίκην ἐκ κέδρου· σπανίζουσι γὰρ καὶ πεύκης. οἱ δ' ἐν Κύπρῳ πίτυος· ταύτην γὰρ ἡ νῆσος ἔχει καὶ δοκεῖ κρείττων εἶναι τῆς πεύκης. Altitude: Meiggs (1982: 119); note that the quality of the fir is dependent on climate, temperature and soil conditions. Note that Greek botanical nomenclature was as complex as modern; in translations, I use 'silver-fir' for *elate* meaning *abies cephalonica* and *abies pectinata*, 'fir' for *peuke* meaning mainly *pinus laricio* (Corsican pine) and 'pine' for *pitys* meaning *pinus halepensis* (Aleppo pine), following Hort (1968).

> They say the largest and most are in Corsica; those of Latium are of very good quality, both the silver-firs and the firs there are larger and better than the south Italian but even these are nothing compared to those of Corsica.[3]

Relating to Thrace, other sources pinpoint the Strymon area as the primary timber producer.[4] Since Theophrastos was writing late in the classical period, other areas probably produced shipbuilding timber in earlier times but had been overexploited by his time, such as Arkadia.[5] It is safe to assume that most areas with access to forests of sufficient altitude would be able to construct a limited number of triremes; however, large building programmes or continuous supply must have been dependent on the larger producers. The most striking feature of Theophrastos' testimony is the absence of any major navies in the territories he lists as the major producers of shipbuilding timber, at least for the Greek world. The great naval powers of the Greek world are well known, Athens, Corinth, Aigina, Chios, Mytilene, Samos, Syracuse and Rhodes. None of them, with the partial exceptions of Corinth and Mytilene, had native timber resources. Most of these poleis had large navies in the archaic period as well, which probably accounts for the depletion of their native resources. However, the fact that their naval power continued after the depletion of their native resources is the most powerful testimony of the effort they expended to acquire sufficient timber for their navies.

Most of the evidence of timber as an export commodity concerns the Macedonian Kingdom. In Macedon, the king owned the forests and had control over the production and export of timber:

> Then I imported oars to your troops in Samos, when the Four Hundred had already taken over here. For Archelaos was my family's *xenos* and he gave me rights to cut and export as many as I wished. I imported those oars, and at a price of five *drachmai*, because I did not want to sell them at a higher price than they cost me.[6]

---

[3] Theophrastos *Enquiry Into Plants* 5.8.1: μέγιστα δὲ καὶ παρὰ πολὺ τὰ ἐν τῇ Κύρνῳ φασὶν εἶναι· τῶν γὰρ ἐν τῇ Λατίνῃ καλῶν γινομένων ὑπερβολῇ καὶ τῶν ἐλατίνων καὶ τῶν πευκίνων—μείζω γὰρ ταῦτα καὶ καλλίω τῶν Ἰταλικῶν—οὐδὲν εἶναι πρὸς τὰ ἐν τῇ Κύρνῳ.

[4] Herodotos 5.23.2 on Myrkinos and Thucydides 4.108.1 for Amphipolis.

[5] Theophrastos *Enquiry Into Plants* 5.2.1.

[6] Andokides 2.11: ἀλλ' αὐτίκα μὲν τότε εἰσήγαγον εἰς ⟨τὴν⟩ στρατιὰν ὑμῶν οὖσαν ἐν Σάμῳ κωπέας, τῶν τετρακοσίων ἤδη τὰ πράγματα ἐνθάδε κατειληφότων, ὄντος μοι Ἀρχελάου ξένου πατρικοῦ καὶ διδόντος τέμνεσθαί τε καὶ ἐξάγεσθαι ὁπόσους ἐβουλόμην. Τούτους τε εἰσήγαγον τοὺς κωπέας, καὶ παρόν μοι πέντε δραχμῶν τὴν τιμὴν αὐτῶν δέξασθαι οὐκ ἠθέλησα πράξασθαι πλέον ἢ ὅσου ἐμοὶ κατέστησαν.

Andokides boasts that his familial ties of *xenia* (guest-friendship) with the Macedonian royal house were the basis of Archelaos' grant of exploitation and export rights. His comment that the grant had no limitations implies that usually limits were imposed on the exploitation and subsequent export of silver-firs. Andokides' testimony is the only available evidence on the exploitation system employed by the Macedonians. His case may be unique due to his special status as a royal *xenos* but his emphasis is on the unlimited quantity rights he was granted not on the permission itself. This implies that the Macedonians used a controlled leasing system with exploitation and export rights granted to individuals by royal decree. Andokides as a royal *xenos* was probably given in addition to the export rights, which any trader could potentially receive, also exploitation rights, which could have been reserved for Macedonian contractors only. Certainly, the direct giving of concessions as gifts to friendly individuals recalls the oriental practice, especially of the Persian king, to reward loyal subjects, such as happened in the cases of Histiaios and Themistocles.[7] The use of a controlled leasing system directly administered by the king can also be inferred from Alexander's ban on all sales of timber from Mount Dysoron, while presumably allowing for local private uses of the woodland.[8] However, it is possible that some of the exploitation was done directly by the king, in the same manner as the exploitation of the Pangaion mines by Philip.

If his price of five *drachmai* per unshaved oar at cost is truthful, and allowing for an increase in prices during the war, then the trade in oars must have been particularly lucrative, since outfitting a new trireme could cost 1000 *drachmai* or more. Oars were mainly made of silver-fir and their cutting and preparation required considerable skill:

> For this reason those who shave the wood try to take out each layer smooth and by itself because if they take it out like that the oar will be strong, if however they take it out roughly and with more than one layer, then the oar will be weak, the one being a wound, the other an operation.[9]

---

[7] The Achaemenid policy in this matter was similar to that of earlier oriental empires, such as the neo-Assyrians: Falles (1984: 212) for large-scale gifts of land to loyal supporters.

[8] Hammond (1988: 383, lines 25–26).

[9] Theophrastos *Enquiry Into Plants* 5.1.7: δι' ὃ καὶ τὰς κώπας ξύοντες ἀφαιρεῖν πειρῶνται καθ' ἕνα καὶ ὁμαλῶς· ἐὰν γὰρ οὕτως ἀφαιρῶσιν, ἰσχυρὸς ὁ κωπεών, ἐὰν δὲ παραλλάξωσι καὶ μὴ κατασπῶσιν ὁμοίως, ἀσθενής· πληγὴ γὰρ οὕτως, ἐκείνως δ' ἀφαίρεσις.

Theophrastos clearly states that oar-making needed specialist labour, at least in the initial stages after cutting the tree; note particularly the use of a medical parallel in the words 'wound' against 'operation'. That such operations are apparently best done *in situ* in the forest, combined with Andokides' testimony that he was able to transport unshaved oars to Samos, suggests that there was a pool of expert oar-makers in Macedon. Whether these people were in the employ of the king cannot be ascertained; however since the kings imposed limits on exploitation and export, it is a viable possibility that their main means of control were the expert woodcutters and foresters, who were necessary in any attempt at exploitation.

The Macedonian kings gave rights of export not only to individuals but also to poleis, as Perdikkas did with Athens: "And I will not export [oa]rs [to anyone] but an Athe[nian]"[10] The inscription recording the treaty is too fragmentary to be securely dated beyond the long reign of Perdikkas, 440s–413.[11] Notably, the treaty provides exclusive export rights to Athens, although the provision refers only to oars. Perdikkas does not grant rights of exploitation but, under a controlled leasing system, some Athenians probably were granted such rights. Both Andokides' testimony and the treaty with Perdikkas show the importance of the oar trade in the period. In addition to regular wear and tear, which the *Olympias* trials showed resulted in frequent breakages, warfare also accounted for the need for a constant supply of oars.[12] One of the tactics of trireme warfare was disabling the ship by breaking the oars on one side, which necessitated the existence of reserves beyond the *perineos* (reserve oars) at key staging areas and *neoria* (shipyards), and thus, a regular supply.[13] Under these circumstances, it is not surprising that major importers, such as Athens, desired a monopoly of supply, or that the Macedonian kings would consider such as a major concession to an ally.

In the early fourth century, Amyntas provided export rights to the Chalcidian League for all timber and related products:

> Let there be import of pitch and timber, all types of timber for building, and for building ships except for silver-fir, as the *koinon* wants. And for

---

[10] IG I[3] 89.31: καὶ οὐδένα κο]πέας ἐχσάγεν ἐάσο ἐὰμ μὲ Ἀθε[ναίο.

[11] Borza (1987: 44) argued in favour of a date after 424 but any suggestion is as valid as another. See further page 125.

[12] Morrison, Coates & Rankov (2000: 240).

[13] Morrison & Coates (1996: 368–369).

> those let there be export to the *koinon*, having informed Amyntas before the export, paying the taxes that have been agreed. And for the others let there be export and transport, paying the taxes, both for the Chalcidians from Macedonia and for the Macedonians from the Chalcidians.[14]

The treaty was probably concluded in 391, after Amyntas had managed with Thessalian and Chalcidian help to regain his throne from the usurper Argaios, who was supported by the Illyrians.[15] The treaty was possibly the repayment to the Chalcidians for taking care of part of Macedonian territory in the preceding years after Amyntas' request. Of particular interest is the care, even in such hard times, provided by the Macedonian kings for the exploitation of silver-fir and their insistence, even under the terms of an exclusive export treaty, on keeping some control over its export. Of equal interest is that in both treaties only export rights are granted; neither Athens nor the Chalcidians are allowed to directly exploit the Macedonian forests. The policy adopted by the Macedonian kings was not a closed monopoly policy like that pursued for gold.[16] The Macedonians apparently employed a controlled lease exploitation regime which, on the one hand, allowed the king almost total control of both production and export, and, on the other, avoided the need for large numbers of public employees and associated levels of bureaucracy.

The Macedonian insistence on keeping strict control over exploitation rights, even when surrendering the exports, is reflected in the similar policy of the Cypriot kings:

> In Cyprus, the kings did not cut down timber because, on the one hand, they took care and husbanded it, and, on the other, it was difficult to transport.[17]

Cyprus was not one of the major timber producers but had suitable reserves and trade in timber from the island is attested from the early archaic period.[18] The Cypriot kings like the Macedonians had control over both exploitation and export. The Cypriot reserves were of very high

[14] RO 12.9–18: ἐ̣σαγωγὴ {ΕΞΑΓΩΓΗ} δ' ἔστω καὶ πίσσης καὶ ξύλων, | ο̣ἰκοδομιστηρίωμ πάντων, ναυπηγη|σ̣ίμων δὲ πλὴν ἐλατίνων, ὅ τι ἂμ μὴ τὸ | κοινὸν δέηται, τῶι δὲ κοινῶι καὶ τούτων | εἶν ἐξαγωγήν, εἰπόντας Ἀμύνται πρὶν ἐξ|άγειν, τελέοντας τὰ τέλεα τὰ γεγραμμέν[α]. | καὶ τῶν ἄλλων ἐξαγωγὴν δὲ εἶν καὶ δια|{α}γωγήν {[26]διαγωγήν}[26], τελέουσιν τέλεα καὶ Χαλκιδεῦ|σι ἐκγ Μακεδονίης καὶ Μακεδόσιν ἐκ̣ | Χαλκιδέων.

[15] Diodoros 14.92.3–4; Hammond (1979: 174–175).

[16] On this see page 37.

[17] Theophrastos *Enquiry Into Plants* 5.8.1: ἐν Κύπρῳ γοῦν οὐκ ἔτεμνον οἱ βασιλεῖς, ἅμα μὲν τηροῦντες καὶ ταμιευόμενοι, ἅμα δὲ καὶ διὰ τὸ δυσκόμιστον εἶναι.

[18] Raaflaub (2004: 205).

quality mountain pine, which apparently was as good as fir for triremes and was utilised by the Persians during the Persian domination of the island: "In Cyprus, they use pine, for the island has a lot and is considered better than its fir."[19]

The south Italian producers, Sybaris/Thurii, Kroton and Kaulonia, probably also placed restrictions on exploitation, if not export. Very little is known about the exploitation regime and export arrangements of these poleis but the only surviving evidence suggests that foreign states needed permission to exploit the resources and possibly to import as well.[20] The hypothesis of strict control over timber like that of the Macedonians and the Cypriots is not supported by the evidence regarding exploitation and trade policies in polis government. The need for permission, however, suggests that some limitations were imposed upon the timber trade.

Beyond timber and related products, warships were also considered a commodity in the Greek world:

> The Corinthians were at the time close friends with the Athenians and agreed to give them twenty ships, at a price of five *drachmai* each, because by law they could not gift them outright.[21]

In the early fifth century, the Corinthians sold 20 ships to the Athenians. Herodotos clearly narrates this incident as a political gesture not a financial transaction. However, both his lack of comment on the notion of the sale of warships and the Corinthian law testify that such sales were not considered exceptional. Herodotos comments and explains only the nominal price, implying that if the price had been the normal one, then the incident would not be worthy of comment. Similarly, the Corinthian law does not prohibit the sale of warships but only their offer as a gift. The existence of such a law paints an amazing picture of normality with warships being considered items of trade, even as early as the beginning of the fifth century. Further, it provides a rare glimpse of the status of warships as a commercial commodity and the regulation of their disposal by a known ship constructor.

---

[19] Theophrastos *Enquiry Into Plants* 5.7.1: οἱ δ' ἐν Κύπρῳ πίτυος· ταύτην γὰρ ἡ νῆσος ἔχει καὶ δοκεῖ κρείττων εἶναι τῆς πεύκης. Persian ships built in Cyprus: Diodoros 14.39.1.

[20] Diodoros 14.42 on Dionysios of Syracuse needing permission from the south Italian poleis. Note that permission may only be relevant to exploitation, since Dionysios sent his own woodcutters to south Italy. See further page 147.

[21] Herodotos 6.89: Οἱ δὲ Κορίνθιοι, ἦσαν γάρ σφι τοῦτον τὸν χρόνον φίλοι ἐς τὰ μάλιστα Ἀθηναίοισι, διδοῦσι δεομένοισι εἴκοσι νέας, διδοῦσι δὲ πενταδράχμους ἀποδόμενοι· δωτίνην γὰρ ἐν τῷ νόμῳ οὐκ ἐξῆν δοῦναι.

CHAPTER FIVE

TIMBER FOR ATHENS

The greatest naval power in the Greek world in the classical period was Athens. The Athenian fleet was the largest Greek fleet for most of the period, although the allied Peloponnesian fleet in 405 and the Syracusan under Dionysios were close seconds. Athens had no native resources of shipbuilding timber, and thus had to acquire all timber and related products from foreign sources.

The first reference to the Athenian fleet has already been discussed above relating to the buying of 20 Corinthian ships in the early fifth century.[1] The first recorded instance of building is in the late 480s:

> Another proposal of Themistocles before this one managed to be shown best for the polis. When the Athenians had a lot of money in the public treasury, which came from the mines of Laurion, they were going to distribute it among themselves to the amount of ten *drachmai* each. Then Themistocles persuaded the Athenians not to go through with the distribution but instead to use the money to build 200 ships for the war, the one against Aigina. It was that war that then saved Hellas because it made the Athenians go to sea. The ships were not used for the purpose they were built but were there when Hellas needed them.[2]

The exact number of ships built is debated, based on a variant account of 100 ships in the *Constitution of the Athenians*:

> Receiving the money for this purpose, he built 100 triremes, each one of the 100 building one. With these, they fought the naval battle in Salamis against the barbarians.[3]

---

[1] Herodotos 6.89 and page 116.

[2] Herodotos 7.144: Ἑτέρη τε Θεμιστοκλέϊ γνώμη ἔμπροσθε ταύτης ἐς καιρὸν ἠρίστευσε, ὅτε Ἀθηναίοισι γενομένων χρημάτων μεγάλων ἐν τῷ κοινῷ τὰ ἐκ τῶν μετάλλων σφι προσῆλθε τῶν ἀπὸ Λαυρείου, ἔμελλον λάξεσθαι ὀρχηδὸν ἕκαστος δέκα δραχμάς· τότε Θεμιστοκλέης ἀνέγνωσε Ἀθηναίους τῆς διαιρέσιος ταύτης παυσαμένους νέας τούτων τῶν χρημάτων ποιήσασθαι διηκοσίας ἐς τὸν πόλεμον, τὸν πρὸς Αἰγινήτας λέγων. Οὗτος γὰρ ὁ πόλεμος συστὰς ἔσωσε τότε τὴν Ἑλλάδα, ἀναγκάσας θαλασσίους γενέσθαι Ἀθηναίους· αἱ δὲ ἐς τὸ μὲν ἐποιήθησαν οὐκ ἐχρήσθησαν, ἐς δέον δὲ οὕτω τῇ Ἑλλάδι ἐγένοντο.

[3] [Aristotle] *Constitution of the Athenians* 22.7: λαβὼν δ' ἐπὶ τούτοις ἐναυπηγήσατο τριήρεις ἑκατόν, ἑκάστου ναυπηγουμένου τῶν ἑκατὸν μίαν, αἷς ἐναυμάχησαν ἐν Σαλαμῖνι πρὸς τοὺς βαρβάρους.

Unfortunately, neither of the sources mentions the provenance of the timber used for this building program. Until recently, it was generally accepted that the Salamis fleet was built with Macedonian timber, based on Herodotos' praise of Alexander I of Macedon and the *proxenia* he received from Athens.[4]

However, as Meiggs pointed out, the Persians would not allow the export of large quantities of timber from their vassal state to their enemies.[5] Herodotos' praise of Alexander may be a personal opinion of the historian, while the grant of *proxenia* may have been related to other services, possibly the supply of oars, which were an easier cargo to transport clandestinely, or something totally unrelated to timber, such as espionage. However, given Herodotos' favourable stance towards Macedon, which after all medised, it is surprising that he does not mention such a major service to the Athenians as providing the timber for the fleet.

Meiggs argued strongly in favour of south Italy being the main supplier, based, on the one hand, on the implausibility of the suggestion that Persia allowed the export of timber from Macedon, and, on the other, on the evidence that Themistocles had special relations with south Italy.[6] The suggestion that the Persians were deceived by the ostensible purpose of the new fleet as a tool against Aigina presupposes a total lack of foresight on behalf of the Persian Empire.[7] Such lack of foresight is deemed implausible by the Myrkinos affair, where the Persians are shown alert to the potential of the Thracomacedonian timber resources long before Xerxes' expedition.[8] The episode may be an instance of Herodotos' hindsight colouring events, but equally it may be an underhanded apology as to why Macedonian timber was not made available to the Greeks. The presence of a Krotonian ship at the battle of Salamis also indicates a south Italian connection, since Kroton was one of the outlets of the Sila forest via the river Neto.[9]

The discussion raises the question why Herodotos failed to mention the supplier of timber for the fleet he considered "the saviour of Hellas".[10] The solution to the mystery may lie in the later Athenian settlement

[4] Herodotos 8.136.1; Wallace (1970: 199).
[5] Meiggs (1982: 123 f.).
[6] Meiggs (1982: 124–125).
[7] Johnson (1927: 202); Borza (1987: 42).
[8] Herodotos 5.23.2. Borza (1987: 35).
[9] Meiggs (1982: 354).
[10] Herodotos 7.139.

in Thurii, the other outlet of the Sila forest. Herodotos was, according to tradition, one of the settlers there and a possible rivalry between the two cities, Thurii and Kroton, may account for Herodotos' avoidance of the south Italian contribution to the fleet, particularly since Thurii was a supplier of timber for Athens in second half of the fifth century.[11] Equally, however, Herodotos may have neglected to mention the provenance of timber either because there was no single supplier or simply because he thought it an unimportant detail.

The south Italian solution has several practical problems, some of which it shares with other suppliers. As Meiggs noted, the three major problems were lack of time, lack of seasoning and lack of expertise. Meiggs bypassed the problem of inadequate time based on later evidence:

> It is a remarkable fact that in old days in the first Punic War the fleet commanded by Duilius was on the water within 60 days after the timber left the tree, while, according to the account of Lucius Piso, the 220 ships that fought against king Hiero were built in 45 days; also in the Second Punic War Scipio's fleet sailed on the 40th day after the timber had been felled. So effective is prompt action even in the hurry of an emergency.[12]

Pliny represents a Roman tradition which is not encountered in Greek classical history, and there is a distinct possibility of exaggeration. In the classical period, considerable time was allowed for ship construction, thus it is surprising that such a building effort left no trace in Herodotos, when the lesser effort of the Corinthians in 435–433 was mentioned by Thucydides.[13]

Hurried construction is further complicated by the lack of seasoned timber, since for 100 ships 3,500 tonnes of timber would be needed. The problems created by unseasoned timber were known in antiquity but Meiggs suggested that the narrowness of the Salamis strait made any such problems insignificant.[14] Not only is there a tradition of these ships being light and agile, which precludes any possibility of the use of unseasoned timber, but also the battle of Artemision was fought in open waters,

---

[11] IG I[3] 387.101.

[12] Pliny *Natural History* 16.74: mirum apud antiquos primo punico bello classem duilli imperatoris ab arbore lx die navigavisse, contra vero hieronem regem ccxx naves effectas diebus xlv tradit l. piso. secundo quoque punico scipionis classis xl die a securi navigavit. tantum tempestivitas etiam in rapida celeritate pollet. Translation from Rackham (2000). Meiggs (1982: 125).

[13] Thucydides 1.31.1.

[14] Livy 29.1.14; Vegetius 4.36. Meiggs (1982: 126).

where any problems in construction would be immediately apparent: "he launched from Knidos and Triopion 300 triremes, which were specially constructed for speed and lightness by Themistocles."[15] Lastly, expert personnel is needed for trireme construction, which Meiggs supposes that Athens attained through attracting craftsmen from an existing pool of expertise in mainland Greece and the islands, as Dionysios did in Syracuse in the fourth century.[16] Yet, Thucydides' clear statement that the trireme was not the warship of choice before Xerxes' expedition makes the availability of such a pool of expertise doubtful, especially since the majority of fleets at Salamis were of triremes, thus implying a series of building programmes by various poleis at the same time.[17]

The solution to the above problems is that the Athenian triremes were built in the resource areas. Meiggs rightly argues that the solution to the mystery of the Salamis fleet lies in the west, not the Aegean. At the time, the only poleis with large trireme fleets outside the Persian Empire were Corcyra, the Sicilian poleis and presumably Corinth, all in areas with native resources.[18] The Athenians could easily have obtained triremes from more than one area, spreading the need for seasoned timber and expertise over several *naupegia* from Corcyra, or Epidamnos, to Kroton, Kaulonia and the Sicilian cities. The reliance of the Athenians on foreign ship suppliers is testified by the 20 ships they bought from the Corinthians a few years earlier.

The end of the Persian Wars spelled the beginning of a new era for the Greek world as Athens walked the road to empire. The *Pentekontaetia* is one of the most shadowy periods in classical history and yet one of the most important. The Athenians maintained a large fleet throughout the period and probably increased its numbers to reach 300 war-fit triremes in 431.[19] At least one major building program was executed

---

[15] Plutarch *Kimon* 12.2: ὥρμησεν ἄρας ἀπὸ Κνίδου καὶ Τριοπίου τριακοσίαις τριήρεσι, πρὸς μὲν τάχος ἀπ' ἀρχῆς καὶ περιαγωγὴν ὑπὸ Θεμιστοκλέους ἄριστα κατεσκευασμέναις. Meiggs (1972: 76) argued that these triremes were newly built triremes, not those used in Salamis; against see Morrison & Williams (1968: 161–163) and Blamire (1989: 140).

[16] Meiggs (1982: 122) based on Diodoros 14.41.3; however, Dionysios attracted experts from all disciplines of weapon construction.

[17] Thucydides 1.14.2–3; Herodotos 8.45–48.

[18] Thucydides 1.14.2.

[19] Thucydides 2.13.8–9 specifically refers to war-fit triremes (*ploimous*), not the total fleet in the Athenian *neorion*. Judging from the fourth century *epimeletai* accounts, the formal strength of the fleet included non-fit ships as well: Gabrielsen (1994: 127–129).

during the *Pentekontaetia* after the loss of part of the fleet in the Egyptian Expedition.[20] Since Kimon four years later was able to mount another expedition against Cyprus, in the period 454–450 the Athenians must have rebuilt their fleet to a sufficient strength.[21]

Many of the Athenian and allied actions in the period can be connected with resources, and particularly timber. Thucydides' brief account is very selective. According to Hornblower, Thucydides "aims to describe the growth of Athenian power ... we can add that he surely aims to give particular coverage to those events which most alarmed the Spartans."[22] The first act of the Delian League was the capture of Eion on the Strymon, which was still held by the Persians (476).[23] However, the *andrapodismos* of the inhabitants and the resettlement of the site with Athenians testify to its importance. Eion was the gatehouse of the Strymon and its valley with its precious metal deposits and shipbuilding timber reserves, a site comparable in importance to Amphipolis.[24] At the same time, Skyros was captured and resettled, another clearly strategic operation since the island commanded the naval routes to both northern Greece and the Hellespont.[25] The next actions of the Athenians against Karystos and Naxos did not involve resettlement.[26] The major event of the 460s was the revolt of Thasos, motivated solely by economic reasons, specifically its domination of the precious metal deposits and the poleis on the mainland opposite.[27] The Thasian settlements, most importantly Neapolis, later had a reputation as *naupegia* of note, and Athens secured their support throughout the fifth century.[28] Simultaneous with the Thasian revolt, the Athenians tried to settle Ennea Hodoi, the later Amphipolis, but the settlement ended in disaster at the hands of the

[20] According to modern calculations of this hotly debated issue between 100 and 230 Athenian and allied ships were lost in Egypt: Thucydides 1.104, 1.109–110. Meiggs (1972: 107–108); Holladay (1989); Westlake (1969: 66–68); Hornblower (1991: 177).

[21] Thucydides 1.112.

[22] Hornblower (1991: 133).

[23] Thucydides 1.98.1.

[24] Eion as Athenian *emporion*: Thucydides 4.102.3. Control of both Amphipolis and Eion secured domination over the Strymon and the resources of the interior, especially if one took care, as the Athenians did, to build the long walls of Amphipolis: Thucydides 4.102.3.

[25] Thucydides 1.98.2. The Sporades were good pirate bases, for example Halonessos in the fourth century (Demosthenes 7).

[26] Thucydides 1.98.3–4.

[27] Thucydides 1.100.1–2.

[28] *Naupegia*: Strabo 7.F33, 7.F36. Support for Athens: IG I^3 101.

Thracian tribes.[29] The intended size, timing and placement of the settlement testify to the intention of the Athenians in the 460s to acquire full domination of the Strymon valley. The reactions of Thasos and the Thracians show that they exploited the resources of the area and that these played a significant role in their respective economies. The Athenians tried to kill two birds with one stone; on the one hand, remove competition for Laurion and acquire gold resources, and, on the other, dominate both the timber supply and the *naupegia*.

The next event narrated by Thucydides is the Ithome affair, where the settlement of the rebels in Naupaktos is of particular interest.[30] Sometime in the previous years, Athens had taken over Naupaktos, a strategic position without peer, dominating both the Corinthian Gulf and the north-south route of the Ionian Sea, as well as a *naupegion* of note with access to local resources.[31] The Athenians were probably planning a settlement there to control the resources and put pressure on the Peloponnesians, especially the Corinthians. The helots, however, were a better solution since they were certain to oppose any Spartan plan and their alliance with Athens provided a handy base of operations if need arose.[32] In the 450s, the Athenians made two expeditions to Cyprus, the disastrous Egyptian Expedition and fought in the First Peloponnesian War making expeditions to Thessaly and Akarnania.[33] Of particular interest are the expeditions to Cyprus with its large copper resources and timber reserves. In the 440s, the Athenians lost their brief dominion over Boiotia in the battle of Koroneia and had to put down the Euboian revolt.[34] The poleis of Euboia were penalised but not harshly treated, except for Histiaia that suffered *andrapodismos* and resettlement by Athenians. Histiaia commanded the entrance to both the Pagasetic Gulf and the Eurippos strait, and thus gave the Athenians control over the major harbours of the area, Pagasai and Stylis.[35] Athenian interest in Thessaly was seen also

[29] Thucydides 1.100.3. Note that I am retaining the traditional chronology of the beginning of the revolt being earlier than the attempt to colonise Ennea Hodoi, as seen in both Thucydides and Diodoros (11.70), against Rainey (2004: 220).

[30] Thucydides 1.102.1–3.

[31] Ephoros FGrH 70 F121 (Strabo 9.4.7).

[32] Athenian alliance with Naupaktos: Pritchett (1995: 69–72). For the Messenians certain to oppose Sparta at every turn, see the parallel in Diodoros 12.63.5.

[33] Thucydides 1.103–112.

[34] Thucydides 1.113–114.

[35] Stylis is still one of the best moorings in the area and was until the early 1980s a convenient port for loading and repairs by the Greek merchant navy. Volos, ancient Pagasai, remains one of the most used and trusted harbours in Greece.

in the First Peloponnesian War, since Thessaly, in addition to its resources of grain and timber, was the gateway to the north from the Peloponnese, as Brasidas used it in the 420s.[36]

The last events in Thucydides' account are the Thirty Years Peace and the revolts of Samos and Byzantion.[37] A few years later, in 437, the Athenians finally managed to settle Amphipolis on the Strymon. The importance of Amphipolis to Athenian timber supply is illustrated by the reaction to its loss:

> The loss of Amphipolis brought great fear to the Athenians, since the polis was particularly helpful to them for the conveyance of shipbuilding timber and revenue.[38]

The text is often considered evidence of timber import from Amphipolis to Athens based on the interpretation of *pompe* as 'import.'[39] *Pompe* in this case, however, is better interpreted as 'conveyance/escort,' since Amphipolis is not the port from where the 'sending' would take place.[40] Geographically, Amphipolis dominated Lake Prasias and its exit to the Strymon, and thus controlled the flow of timber down the river to the coast; it was ideally suited for *pompe*, conveyance/escort.

The Athenian actions during the *Pentekontaetia*, random as they may seem at first glance, follow a pattern intimately connected with resources and particularly timber. The pattern is best illustrated by the Athenian settlements in Eion, Amphipolis, Skyros, Histiaia and Naupaktos. Four of the five settlements can be connected to timber resources and *naupegia*. Of course, not all expeditions have timber connections, since Athens was an imperial power with political, military and economic concerns and it would be short-sighted to assign one motive to all actions during such a long and volatile period. The settlements are clearly connected with timber and *naupegia* and similar connections are valid for the shattering of Thasian control over Neapolis and the other *emporia* on the

---

[36] Thucydides 4.78. Note also the reasoning for the settlement of Herakleia as guarding the passage northwards and Euboia (Thucydides 3.92.4). Thessalian timber reserves: Meiggs (1982: 128).

[37] Thucydides 1.115–116.

[38] Thucydides 4.108: Ἐχομένης δὲ τῆς Ἀμφιπόλεως οἱ Ἀθηναῖοι ἐς μέγα δέος κατέστησαν, ἄλλως τε καὶ ὅτι ἡ πόλις αὐτοῖς ἦν ὠφέλιμος ξύλων τε ναυπηγησίμων πομπῇ καὶ χρημάτων προσόδῳ.

[39] Smith (1930): "The Athenians were greatly alarmed by the capture of Amphipolis. The chief reason was that the city was useful to them for the importation of timber for shipbuilding and for the revenue it produced."

[40] *Pompe* as conveyance/escort: LSJ s.v. πέμπω III.

Strymon coast. Athens concentrated its efforts on Thrace not Macedon, the greatest timber producer in northern Greece, due to valid strategic reasons. Macedon was a centralised state with a large and experienced army; any expedition was sure to be met with a concerted effort far from the Athenians' favourite battlefield, the sea. In Thrace, on the other hand, Athens could and did dominate the area piecemeal, since the Thasians and the Thracian tribes did not cooperate. Further, as Meiggs rightly pointed out, alliances with the Macedonians were almost impossible to sustain long-term, since foreign policy changed with each holder of the throne, as is best illustrated by the different policies towards Athens of Perdikkas and Archelaos in the Peloponnesian War.[41] Further south, the settlements at Histiaia and Naupaktos were mainly pre-emptive controls on potentially hostile poleis in the Dorian part of the mainland. In addition, Kimon's insistence on the domination of Cyprus is also partly connected to timber.[42]

Another suggestion connecting *naupegia* and timber reserves outside Athens has been made by Unz concerning the tribute imbalance. Unz suggested that part of the tribute was paid not in money but in ships, based on Plutarch's comment on Kimon's behaviour towards the allies that wanted to avoid military service:

> Kimon walked the opposite road in his generalship, committing violence against none of the Greeks and taking money and empty ships from those who did not want to serve.[43]

Blamire argued convincingly that the detail is authentic, in spite of not appearing in Thucydides.[44] It has been suggested that the allies were given the choice of either selling their ships to the Athenians or exchanging them for new ones.[45] However, it is difficult to believe that the Athenians would prefer old ships to money or that they would freely provide the means for the allies to revolt. Further, the Rhodian contribution in the Sicilian Expedition testifies that the tribute-paying allies had warships.[46] Unz's ingenious solution to the tribute imbalance is probably right and

---

[41] Meiggs (1982: 126).

[42] See page 115.

[43] Plutarch *Kimon* 11.2: Κίμων δὲ τὴν ἐναντίαν ὁδὸν ἐν τῇ στρατηγίᾳ πορευόμενος, βίαν μὲν οὐδενὶ τῶν Ἑλλήνων προσῆγε, χρήματα δὲ λαμβάνων παρὰ τῶν οὐ βουλομένων στρατεύεσθαι καὶ ναῦς κενάς. Unz (1985: 36).

[44] Blamire (1989: 137).

[45] Blackman (1969: 189–190); Meritt et al. (1939–1953: 3.246, 250).

[46] Thucydides 6.43.1; note, however, that these were pentekonters, so possibly some of the allies even in the end of the fifth century had still not converted their fleet to triremes.

further connects Athens with allied *naupegia*, since there is no reason to suppose that the 1/60th *aparche* (first fruits) to Athena included payment in services or ships. The contribution of ships, rather than troops and ships, to Athens by the allies is mentioned also in Diodoros again in relation to Kimon's generalship: "... and from the constantly added allies, he received ships, and thus increased the fleet further."[47]

From the Peloponnesian War, treaties and *proxenia* decrees relating to oar supplies and building in foreign *naupegia* survive. During the war, especially after 413, Athens engaged in various large shipbuilding programs. In the Archidamian War, most building was confined to maintenance, while the unexpected windfall of 60 ships at Pylos certainly aided Athenian fleet size.[48] The Sicilian Disaster spelled a large shipbuilding program and the various losses in the Ionian War meant that ships were built throughout the decade until Aigospotamoi.[49]

Most of the evidence concerns the import of oars, starting with the treaty with Perdikkas: "And I will not allow [anyone] but an Athe[nian] to export [oa]rs."[50] As mentioned earlier, the treaty cannot be securely dated beyond the long reign of Perdikkas (440s–413) and although Borza argued in favour of a date in the late 420s, a date in the 430s is equally possible.[51] Borza's suggestion that the treaty also provided for timber supplies, although impossible to disprove due to the fragmentary state of the inscription, cannot be found or plausibly restored in the surviving lines.[52]

The theme of oar supply, again from Macedon, continues with Andokides' testimony.[53] Andokides' position is interesting, since Athens clearly depended upon private traders for its oar supply. Oar supply for the Athenians in Samos in 411 must have been particularly problematic since the regular supply lines stopped in Athens where the oligarchs were in control. The Athenians did not rely only on the goodwill of traders or the odd exile but provided incentives to traders to import oars, as testified by the honours given to Phanosthenes and Antiochides:

[47] Diodoros 11.60.5: παρὰ δὲ τῶν ἀεὶ προστιθεμένων συμμάχων προσλαβόμενος ναῦς ἐπὶ πλέον ηὔξησε τὸν στόλον.

[48] Thucydides 4.16.3, 4.23.1.

[49] In the Sicilian Expedition as many as 170 Athenian ships lost: Thucydides 6.43, 7.16, 7.60. Athenian losses in the period 412–405 reached 305 ships: Thucydides 8.20, 8.34, 8.42, 8.91, 8.102, 8.104; Xenophon *Hellenika* 1.5.14, 1.6.17, 1.6.23, 1.6.34, 2.1.28.

[50] IG I^3 89.31: καὶ οὐδένα κο]πέας ἐχσάγεν ἐάσο ἐὰμ μὲ Ἀθε[ναίο.

[51] Borza (1987: 44).

[52] Borza (1987: 44).

[53] Andokides 2.11.

> ... to [Ant]iochides an[d Phanosthenes] ... to the Athenians ... and the others that ... [the] *demos* of the Athenians ... [alway]s and now he, and [as it appears]. As [the *demos* of Athens], who has the grea[test respect for those importing o]ars [a]nd, thus, desires to return [their] service, [let them have *ateleia* from the *hek*]*atoste* tax [for t]he oars they bring to [the *trie*]*ropoioi* and the *trieropoioi* ... [pu]t in the *na*[*upe*]*gion*. And if they con[sider him the *str*]*ategoi* oug[ht to t]ell the [*boule* and giv]e the appoint[ed] pric[e], and the [*naupegoi* must give the] *trieropoi*[*oi* those ap]pointed ... [Antiochides and] Phanosthenes ... the *hellenotamiai* ... must for ... they broug[ht] ... ho[nour Antiochides and Phanosthenes for tr]ansporti[ng] ... [and] take [it to the *prytaneis*] ... [*ek*]*klesi*[*a*] ... [o]ther ... *3–4vv* ... hon[our them and inscribe them as *proxenoi* a]nd as *euergetai*. [Find what else they w]ant from the Athe[nians. Inscribe ... on the ste]le as *euergetai* of the Ath[enians in the city by the *grammateus* of the] *boule vacat* ... [th]e *boul*[*e*] ... [the *grammateus* of the *bou*]*le* to [inscribe the] de[cree on a ston]e *ste*[*le*] ....[54]

The inscription comprises two decrees, of which the first is too fragmentary for restoration to be attempted and the second is also fragmentary but can be partially restored. The second decree falls in the period 420–405 according to letter forms and if the Phanosthenes honoured is the general of 407/406 then it must surely fall before that year, since Phanosthenes is treated as a non-citizen.[55] The two main issues debated are the circumstances under which the decree was passed, and thus its date, and what was the form of the *hekatoste* (1/100th) tax. The dates proposed

---

[54] IG I^{3} 182.1–31: fr a-b - - - - - - - - - - - - - - - - - | [7 Ἀν]τ̣ιοχίδει κα[ὶ Φανοσθένει 12] | [10]ς Ἀθεναίοις [ ]ι[19] | [10]ορας καὶ τὰ ἄλλα *h*οτ[16] | [9 τὸ]ν δε͂μον τὸν Ἀθεναί[ον 14] | [6 καθάπε]ρ̣ καὶ νῦν αὐτός, καὶ *ḥ*[όπος ἂν φαίνεται] | [Ἀθεναίον ὁ δε͂μο]ς *h*ος περὶ πολλο͂ ποι[όμενος τὸς ἐσάγ] | [οντας κο]πέας [κα]ὶ χάριν ἀποδόσον τὸ λ[οιπόν, ἀτελε͂ς τ] | [όκο ἑκα]τ̣οστο͂ [τὸ]ς κοπέας *h*ὸς ἔγαγον [ἀποδόντον τοῖς] | [τρι]εροποιοῖς, κ[αὶ] *h*οι τριεροποιοὶ #^{7}[12] | [τιθ]έντον ἐς τὸ να[υπέ]γιον, καὶ ἐὰν δέ[ονται αὐτο͂ν *h*οι] | [στ]ρατεγοὶ χρόσθο[ν φρ]άζοντες τε͂ι β[ολε͂ι καὶ ἀποδιδ] | [όν]τες τὲν τεταγμέν̣[εν] τιμέ[ν], καὶ *h*ο[ι ναυπεγοὶ δόντο] | [ν το]ῖς τριεροποιο[ῖς τὰ τε]ταγμέν[α 5 ? Ἀντιοχίδε] | [ς καὶ] Φανοσθένες το[26] | [5]το *h*ο *h*ελλενο[ταμίας 20] | [6]ς χρε͂σθαι ἐς τ[25] | [αὐτ]οῖν ἀγαγόντ[οιν 22] | [7]σ̣οραι, ἐπαιν[έσαι Ἀντιοχίδεν καὶ Φανοσθέν] | [εν ὅτι ἐδια]κονεσάτε[ν 24] | [7 καὶ] προσάγ̣[εν αὐτὸ τὸς πρυτάνες 9] | [8 ἐκ]κλεσί[α 26] | [11 ἄ]λλο - - - - - - - - - - - - - - - - | 3–4 vv. Desunt | fr. c.23 τι· ἐπα[ινέσαι τε αὐτὸς καὶ ἀναγράφσαι προχσένος κα] | ὶ εὐεργέτας. ἒν[αι δὲ αὐτοῖς *h*ευρέσθαι ἄλλο *h*ο͂ν ἂν δέ] | ονται παρὰ Ἀθεν[αίον· ἀναγράφσαι δὲ 8 ἐν στέ] | λει εὐεργέτας Ἀθ[εναίον ἐμ πόλει τὸν γραμματέα τε͂ς] | βολε͂ς ∴ vacat vacat 0.11 fr. d.28 - #^{7}[10] | [- - - - - - - - - - - - - - - - - - - τὲ]ν βολ[ὲν 6] | [- - - - - - - - - - - - - - - - - τό]δ⟨ε⟩ φσέ[φισμα ἀνα] | [γραφσάτο *h*ο γραμματεὺς *h*ο τε͂ς βολ]ε͂ς ἐν στ[έλει λιθί] | [νει - - - - - - - - - - - - - - - - -]ι δὲ τὸς [8].

[55] Walbank (1978: 323–324) on the letterforms and Kirchner (1901–1903: 14083) on Phanosthenes.

are c. 420, 420–415 and after 410; all three based on the need of Athens for oars and the interpretation of the *hekatoste*.[56] The Athenian need for oars has been variously connected to a break in relations with Macedon, the preparations for the Sicilian Expedition and the Ionian War. Athenian relations with Macedon were volatile throughout the period and if the treaty with Perdikkas is not dated to the 420s but earlier, then supply from Macedon cannot be considered a decisive factor for dating the honours to Phanosthenes. Any connection with specific expeditions, either the Sicilian Expedition or the Ionian War, disregards the fact that Athenian need for oars was a constant factor throughout the classical period. Assuming that Athens would have a policy of enticing traders only in times of crisis ignores that oars were as much in constant demand as grain in the fourth century. Times of war heightened the need but such circumstances were more common than peace for the Athenian fleet in the fifth century. The accession of Archelaos in 413 probably made supply easier for Athens, since Archelaos did not share Perdikkas' anti-Athenian prejudices, although Athenian feelings may have taken a while to be soothed after Perdikkas' behaviour. McDonald's argument on the language and spirit of the decree as compared to decrees before the Sicilian Disaster is attempting a comparison between different types of intervention.[57] A comparison between a treaty between states and an incentive to private individuals cannot be successfully argued, since the means of communication and the aims of the respective actions are different. Interstate relations encompass a variety of factors and concerns which cannot be applied to the relations between a government and private individuals or groups.

The other issue of debate, the nature of the *hekatoste*, depends upon the variant interpretations of the *hekatoste* as an import-export tax or a transit/harbour tax and is related to the imposition of the 5 % import-export tax in 414/413 to all harbours in the empire.[58] Firstly, since the 5 % tax was imposed in lieu of tribute, there is no reason to suppose that it included the Piraeus, since Athens did not pay tribute. Secondly, the 5 % tax and the existence of other import-export taxes in the harbours of the empire are not mutually exclusive, since poleis still needed income. Finally, McDonald's note that a tax is not necessarily an import-export

[56] C. 420: Mattingly (1966: 198–201), 420–415: Walbank (1978: 323) and after 410: Meritt (1945: 130–132).

[57] McDonald (1981: 145–146).

[58] Thucydides 7.28.4.

tax is absolutely justified. However, his argument that the *hekatoste* in the Phanosthenes decree is a harbour or transit tax is very difficult to substantiate.[59] On the one hand, an *ateleia* from a transit tax is totally irrelevant to the issues involved in the decree, since the traders are honoured for the import of oars. McDonald implies that the *ateleia* is an empty honour and that "Athens hoped to encourage such import while keeping her financial losses to a minimum."[60] However, if the *hekatoste* is a transit tax, then the grant of *ateleia* would encourage transit not imports, which is patently against Athenian interests in this case. On the other hand, if the *hekatoste* is a harbour tax, then the argument is stronger, although McDonald does not seem to differentiate the two. However, the provisions of lines 8–13 do not support these interpretations, since the officials involved are the *naupegoi*, the *trieropoioi* and the *strategoi*, none of whom are connected to the administration of the harbour or the *emporion*. The initial problem with the interpretation of the decree is that a change of subject is assumed in the middle of a *proxenia* decree, where, presumably, the *boule* encourages the *demos* to confer honours and *ateleia* from the *hekatoste* to those importing oars.[61] However, the references to Antiochides and Phanosthenes in lines 1 and 13–14 respectively, which bracket this perceived hiatus indicate that our perception of the structure of the decree is skewed. Lines 5–7 are instrumental in this case since they have been assumed to advise the *demos*, when they can as easily be interpreted as an explanation of the *demos*' motives in awarding the *ateleia*. Thus, lines 8–13 indicate the procedure through which the *ateleia* can be granted. The end of the decree has been interpreted as a rider including several names of the associates of Antiochides and Phanosthenes, who are granted *euergesia* and are presumably also party to the *ateleia* grant.[62] If the idea of a hiatus is abandoned, then the theme of the decree is clearly discernible. A group of traders, headed by Phanosthenes and Antiochides, are provided with a large financial incentive to continue their services to the Athenian fleet and the decree stipulates the procedure through which the incentive will be granted practically.

---

[59] McDonald (1981: 142–144).

[60] McDonald (1981: 144). For the possible economic importance of *ateleia* to the honorand, see Oliver (2007: 30–37); Oliver is concentrating on the *ateleia* grant to the Spartokids but the argument applies to all recipients.

[61] McDonald (1981: 141): "In the second decree, after a reference to Antiochides and Phanosthenes, the *demos* is instructed to encourage and thank those who import ships' oars by exempting them from the one percent tax."

[62] See Walbank (1978: 313–324) on the various fragments and the rider.

The provisions of the *ateleia* are more in concert with an import-export tax, specifically as in line 12 the issue of price is considered. The level of import-export tax in Athens in the period cannot be securely ascertained, since the first definite mention is dated to 401, when it is a *pentekoste*.[63] Possibly the tax increased after the Peloponnesian War to help state finances. It is equally possible that military supplies were under a different tax provision as a general incentive to traders during the war. If such was the case, then the provisions of the decree are even clearer. The group of traders honoured are provided with an incentive specific to them, which explains why the *ateleia* is so complicated. If this was a general *ateleia* to all importers of oars then it would have been imposed in the *emporion* directly upon import. The decree provides for the special status of this particular group and thus the administering of the *ateleia* falls to the officials accepting the oars and ultimately to the *boule* through the *strategoi*.

The last and most interesting piece of evidence is the infamous Archelaos decree, a horribly fragmentary inscription but with clues tantalisingly tempting to the restorer. This is a very interesting document but extreme caution is necessary, since this is a classic case of history from square brackets. The inscription includes two documents, firstly, a decree detailing emergency finance measures to enable the successful completion of ships built in foreign *naupegia*, and, secondly, a *proxenia* decree relating to services connected to timber and oars. The names of both the archon and the honorary have not survived and most of the provisions of both decrees need heavy restoration. The original restoration by Wilhelm dated the inscription to 411/410 and connected the *proxenia* decree with the Pydna affair.[64]

An alternative restoration by Meritt dated it to 407/406 and this version has been widely accepted by scholars and included in the epigraphic corpora:[65]

---

63 Andokides 1.133.

64 Wilhelm (1922–1924: 122–171).

65 Meritt's original restoration retained the connection with Pydna: Meritt (1932: 110–115). De Sanctis' criticisms relating to the chronology of the Pydna affair and the plausibility of an event four years old being honoured in conjunction to the first decree [de Sanctis (1935: 209)] caused Meritt to eschew the restoration of Pydna in line 28 [Meritt (1936: 246–252)]. Since then, although Meritt's restoration has been widely followed, there have been various versions; Meiggs and Lewis preferred to leave the missing parts of lines 28 and 29 blank [Meiggs & Lewis (1988: 277–280)], while the editors of IG I^3 preferred to return to Meritt's 1932 restoration retaining the connection with Pydna [IG I^3 117].

> [It seemed good to the Boule and th]e demos [what Alkibiades proposed, at the prytany of] Akama[ntis], when [Phe]lleus was [*gr*]*am*[*m*]*a*[*teus*, Antigenes was archon] and [Siby]rtio[s] was [*e*]*pista*[*tes*]. [For the] bui[ld]ing of the shi[ps], [lend to the gen]erals, [fro]m the existing [*apodektai*] of the [money of] Pe[rikles, for the *naupe*]*goi*. What they [lend to be given back to them by the *trieropoioi*. The gener]als to disp[atch] quickly [those sele]cted to sail for t[he completion of the ships.] If not they are to be accu[sed with treason at the c]ourts and the [generals to be accused about n]ot complying. [The *boule* is to ta]ke care [of t]he sending of the shi[ps, those that the *naupegoi*] in Macedonia se[nd], so [that they are sent quick]est to Athens and c[rewed there] for the best dispatch of the g[uarding army to Ion]ia. [If someone does not act] according to these provisions, then he ow[es 10,000 *drachmai*] as sacred money to Ath[ena. Those who co]me first or are first to se[nd a ship are to be given money], as it se[ems best to the *demos*. Archelaos] has been [a good man towards the Athe]nians, [in the p]ast [and in the present]. He too[k care] of the [*naupegoi* who] sai[led out] and sent them [to the *neorion* in ....,] and also [put them up in that] camp an[d gave them timber] and oars and [whatever other] goods [they asked] of him. Pra[ise Archelaos for be]ing a good man [and willing to do wha]tever go[od] he can [and thus he has benefit]ed the polis [and the *demos* of the Atheni]ans. Inscrib[e him and his children on a ston]e [*stele* in the polis as a *proxeno*]*s* and [*euergetes*, and take care of him—].[66]

It is not certain whether the two decrees relate to the same incident. The assumption that they do is implied by the fact that both restorers were inclined to read Pydna as the missing *neorion* in line 28. Even Meritt, after

---

[66] The version used here is Meritt (1936): [ἔδοχσεν τει βολει καὶ το]ι δέμοι· Ἀκα[μα|ν-τὶς ἐπρυτάνευε, Φελ]λεὺς [ἐγρ]αμ[μ]άτ[ευ|ε, Ἀντιγένες ερχε, Σιβ]ύρτιο[ς ἐ]πεστά[τε,| Ἀλκιβιάδες εἶπε· ἐς τ]ὲν πο[ίε]σιν τον [νε|ον δανεῖσαι τὸς στρα]τεγὸς τ[ὸ]ς μετὰ Π[ε|ρικλέος ἀργύριον παρ]ὰ τον {τ̣[ο]ν} ὄντον ἀ|[ποδεκτον τοῖς ναυπεγ]οῖς· hὸ δ' ἂν δανεί|[σοσιν, ἀποδόντον αὐτο]ῖς πάλιν hοι τρι|[εροποιοί· τὸς δὲ τεταγ]μένος πλεν ἐπὶ τ|[ὲν πλέροσιν τον νεον h]ος τάχιστα ἀποσ|[τελάντον hοι στρατεγ]οί· εἰ δὲ μέ, ἐσ-αγό|[σθον προδοσίας ἐς τὸ δ]ικαστέριον· hο[ι| δὲ στρατεγοὶ περὶ το μ]ὲ ἐθέλοντος ἀπι|[έναι ἐσαγόντον· τες δ]ὲ κομιδες τον νε[ο|ν, hὰς ἂν hοι ναυπεγοὶ] ἐγ Μακεδό-νιας στ̣|[έλλοσι, τὲν βολὲν ἐπι]μελεθεναι, hόπος| [ἂν σταλοσιν hος τάχισ]τα Ἀθέναζε καὶ π|[λεροθοσι καὶ ἐπὶ Ἰονί]αν κομίζεται hε| [στρατιὰ φυλάχσοσα φυ]λακὲν τὲν ἀριστ|[εν· ἐὰν δέ τις μὲ ποέσει] κατὰ ταῦτα, ὀφελ|[εν μυρίας δραχμὰς αὐτὸ]ν hιερὰς τει Ἀθ|[εναίαι· τοι δὲ πρότοι ἐλθ]όντι καὶ κομ[ι|σαμένοι ναῦν δοναι δορεὰν κ]αθάπ[ερ ἔδ|οχσεν τοι δέμοι· ἐπειδὲ δὲ Ἀρχέλας καὶ| νῦν καὶ ἐν τοι πρόσθεν χρ]ό̣νοι ἐσ[τὶν ἀν|ὲρ ἀγαθὸς περὶ Ἀθεναί]ος τός τε ἐκπ[λεύ|σαντας ναυπεγὸς ἀνέλ]α̣-βεν καὶ ἐς τὸ [νε|οριον ἐν ....^{9} ......] ἀ̣πέπεμφσεν κα[ὶ| κατέστεσεν ες το hαυτ]ὸ στρατόπεδον κ|[αὶ ἔδοκεν αὐτοῖς χσύλ]α καὶ κοπέας καὶ| [ἄλλα hόσον ἐδέοντο παρ'] αὐτο ἀγαθά, ἐπα|[ινέσαι Ἀρχέλαι hος ὄν]τι ἀνδρὶ ἀγαθοι| [καὶ προθύμοι ποιεν hότ]ι δύναται ἀγαθ|[όν, καὶ ἀνθ' ον εὐεργέτεκ]εν τέν τε πόλιν|[καὶ τὸν δεμον τὸν Ἀθεναί]ον ἀναγράφσα|[ι αὐτὸν καὶ παῖδας προχσένο]ς καὶ ε[ὐερ|γέτας ἐμ πόλει ἐστέ-λεν λιθίνε]ν κ[αὶ ἐπι|μέλεσθαι αὐτον -].

de Sanctis' rightful objection to Pydna, merely left the name unrestored without attempting to include another *neorion* in the equation. Yet the relation of the two decrees is not immediately apparent, since the first decree does not mention where the ships are being built, considering it known or obvious, while the second finds it necessary to name the *neorion* in question. The specific naming of the *neorion* implies that the two events are not directly related, or at least not as closely as commonly assumed. The main reason why Pydna was restored by both Wilhelm and Meritt was that the *stratopedon* in line 29 implies a connection with a military operation. Except the Pydna campaign in 411/410, the only other major operation we know of in northern Greece is the quelling of the oligarchic revolt in Thasos. The main staging area of the Athenians in that incident was Neapolis on the mainland. The assistance of the Neapolitans to Athens in that affair is testified by the Athenian honours to Neapolis in 409–407.[67] Neapolis, in addition to being in a good strategic position to attack Thasos, was also a *naupegion* of note:

> On the coast of the Strymon and the polis of Daton, Neapolis, and Daton itself, there are fertile fields and a lake and rivers and *naupegia* and great gold mines, to the extent that the proverb says 'Rich Daton' as in 'Riches to the rich'.[68]

Epigraphically, the restoration of Neapolis is valid, since the form *Νέαι Πόλει* appears in contemporary inscriptions, and, historically, the use of Neapolis as *naupegion* for the Athenians is not improbable given the Athenian presence in the area since the 460s.[69] The journey of the *naupegoi* would fall either during the suppression of the oligarchic revolution or immediately afterwards. The slight delay of the honours to Archelaos is paralleled by the second decree honouring the Neapolitans and best explained by the unwillingness of the Athenians to extend honours without considerable positive action from the Macedonians. Their experiences of Perdikkas' double-dealings during the last 30 years must have surely taken its toll on relations with the new king. Such positive action would entail Archelaos' active help as presupposed by the first decree,

---

67 IG I^3 101.

68 Strabo 7a.1.36.2–6: παρὰ δὲ τὴν παραλίαν τοῦ Στρυμόνος καὶ Δατηνῶν πόλις Νεάπολις καὶ αὐτὸ τὸ Δάτον, εὔκαρπα πεδία καὶ λίμνην καὶ ποταμοὺς καὶ ναυπήγια καὶ χρυσεῖα λυσιτελῆ ἔχον, ἀφ' οὗ καὶ παροιμιάζονται "Δάτον ἀγαθῶν" ὡς καὶ "ἀγαθῶν ἀγαθῖδας."

69 The dative Νέαι Πόλει as found in IG I^3 101 fits the nine-letter gap in Meritt's restoration. The *iotas* take up one space on the *stoichedon*, as common in the surviving lines.

not merely a small service of conveyance. As was mentioned above, the Archelaos decree is firmly history from square brackets and thus every caution is necessary in dealing with the information it provides.

The decree as restored by Meritt is evidence of the building of ships outside Athens in a *naupegion* in northern Greece. Such building has been considered an extraordinary measure brought about by the inability of Athens to provide secure conveyance of timber from the north to the Piraeus during the Ionian War.[70] However, the problem of secure conveyance was not confined to the Ionian War but persisted throughout the fourth century. Additionally, the decree is dated at a time when Athens enjoyed a temporary supremacy in the Aegean after Kyzikos and before Notion. Thus, the circumstances of the Archelaos decree are more in line with those of the Athenian Empire before the Sicilian Expedition that with later periods when Athenian domination of the Aegean and the north was contested or absent.

Another incident earlier in the Peloponnesian War testifies as to the Athenian policy concerning foreign timber reserves and use of foreign *naupegia*. During the Sicilian Expedition, the Athenians had amassed a quantity of timber in Kaulonia, which was burnt by their enemies: "And chancing upon those ships, they destroyed many and burned the ship-building timber in the territory of Kaulonia, which was ready for the Athenians."[71] Kaulonia was the outlet of the San Bruno fir forest via the Sagra River.[72] Thucydides is vague as to the intentions of the Athenians concerning this timber, particularly as to whether it was seasoned for transport to Athens. The intentions of the Athenians concerning the south Italian and Sicilian timber reserves are revealed earlier in Alkibiades' speech to the Spartans:

> If these matters were successful, either in their entirety or in the most part, we planned to attack the Peloponnese by bringing here the whole force of Greeks who had joined us from there, and to hire many barbarians, both Iberians and others from there who are truly the best in battle of the barbarians of the present day. Further we would build many triremes beyond our own, since Italy has abundant timber.[73]

---

[70] Meiggs (1982: 128).

[71] Thucydides 7.25.2: καὶ τῶν τε πλοίων ἐπιτυχοῦσαι τὰ πολλὰ διέφθειραν καὶ ξύλα ναυπηγήσιμα ἐν τῇ Καυλωνιάτιδι κατέκαυσαν, ἃ τοῖς Ἀθηναίοις ἑτοῖμα ἦν.

[72] Meiggs (1982: 354).

[73] Thucydides 6.90.3: εἰ δὲ προχωρήσειε ταῦτα ἢ πάντα ἢ καὶ τὰ πλείω, ἤδη τῇ Πελοποννήσῳ ἐμέλλομεν ἐπιχειρήσειν, κομίσαντες ξύμπασαν μὲν τὴν ἐκεῖθεν προσγενομένην δύναμιν τῶν Ἑλλήνων, πολλοὺς δὲ βαρβάρους μισθωσάμενοι καὶ Ἴβηρας καὶ

The Athenians never achieved the ambitions set forth by Alkibiades but they apparently considered it a matter of course to build triremes in local *naupegia* in the resource areas after the conquest of a new area. Putting all of Sicily and Magna Graecia under Athenian control can be interpreted as an ambitious plan, and its success would have created a set of extraordinary circumstances comparable to those of the Ionian War when Athenian control of the Aegean was threatened by a Peloponnesian fleet. Simultaneously, however, imperial control over the western Greeks was not truly more extraordinary than control over the Aegean, Asia Minor, northern Greece and the Propontis, which the Athenians had already achieved. A viable interpretation of the relation of Athenian actions during the empire and timber must also include the use of allied *naupegia* for the Athenian fleet.

The Sicilian Disaster also appears to have spurred on a shipbuilding program:

> But as things were, it seemed to them that they must not give in but to prepare a navy, bring in timber from wherever they could, and money, and secure the allies, especially Euboia.[74]

The use of ξυμποϱισαμένους ("bring in") implies construction in Athens itself, which could be considered the model for Athenian fleet construction. However, the situation in Athens at the time was one of intense panic characterised by fear of widespread allied revolt:

> They thought the navy of their enemies in Sicily would immediately sail against the Piraeus, and they must hold, and that their enemies here would double their efforts both by land and by sea, and the allies would go over to them.[75]

If the policy of the Athenians during the empire was to build their fleets in Athens, then it is surprising that they did not have regular supply lines. If however, the opposite was true, that the Athenians relied upon their

---

ἄλλους τῶν ἐκεῖ ὁμολογουμένως νῦν βαϱβάϱων μαχιμωτάτους, τϱιήϱεις τε πϱὸς ταῖς ἡμετέϱαις πολλὰς ναυπηγησάμενοι, ἐχούσης τῆς Ἰταλίας ξύλα ἄφθονα.

[74] Thucydides 8.1.3: ὅμως δὲ ὡς ἐκ τῶν ὑπαϱχόντων ἐδόκει χϱῆναι μὴ ἐνδιδόναι, ἀλλὰ παϱασκευάζεσθαι καὶ ναυτικόν, ὅθεν ἂν δύνωνται ξύλα ξυμποϱισαμένους, καὶ χϱήματα, καὶ τὰ τῶν ξυμμάχων ἐς ἀσφάλειαν ποιεῖσθαι, καὶ μάλιστα τὴν Εὔβοιαν.

[75] Thucydides 8.1.2: τούς τε ἀπὸ τῆς Σικελίας πολεμίους εὐθὺς σφίσιν ἐνόμιζον τῷ ναυτικῷ ἐπὶ τὸν Πειϱαιᾶ πλευσεῖσθαι, ἄλλως τε καὶ τοσοῦτον κϱατήσαντας, καὶ τοὺς αὐτόθεν πολεμίους τότε δὴ καὶ διπλασίως πάντα παϱεσκευασμένους κατὰ κϱάτος ἤδη καὶ ἐκ γῆς καὶ ἐκ θαλάσσης ἐπικείσεσθαι, καὶ τοὺς ξυμμάχους σφῶν μετ' αὐτῶν ἀποστάντας.

dominion of foreign and allied resources and *naupegia* for their fleet, then the implied lack of supplies and the need for fast and imperative action are explained.

The battle of Aigospotamoi deprived the Athenians of both their fleet and their empire. The fourth century was a different era and Athens, whilst remaining one of the major players, never regained the prominence of the fifth century. However, the fleet remained its greatest advantage and, after 378, the largest in the Aegean. In the 370s, Athens got timber from Macedon:

> And consider these points as well, he said, to see whether my thoughts are reasonable. Having Macedon, from where the Athenians get timber, we will certainly be able to build more ships than them.[76]

Here Jason of Pherai contemplates the steps to supremacy and Xenophon of Athens reveals the superstructure of naval dominion. Whether Xenophon represents a specifically Athenian perspective, or a general Greek idea of how to achieve naval power, cannot be ascertained. Either way however, the implication is that dominion over timber resources is a necessary step to achieving naval power. The timing of Jason's comment is particularly significant since at roughly the same time the Athenians had concluded a treaty with Amyntas of Macedon.[77] The provisions of the treaty have not survived but it is valid to assume that some were related to timber or oars. Surely, the renewed opening up of Macedonian timber supplies to the Athenians was a recent event, since a few years earlier the Athenians had a definite anti-Macedonian stance in their support for Olynthos against Amyntas and the Spartans.[78]

The only other literary reference to shipbuilding timber comes from the end of our period after the accession of Alexander:

> When the men who sailed in with the ship, whom you should have immediately destroyed along with their ship, and asked to build small ships in your harbours, was it not obvious that they schemed not to enter the harbour but to be inside it from the start? And if we tolerate small ships, then a bit later we will tolerate triremes, and if in the beginning a few, then later many. And no-one can claim that there is abundant shipbuilding timber in Athens, when we import it with difficulty and from great distance, while

[76] Xenophon *Hellenika* 6.1.11: εἰ δὲ εἰκότα λογίζομαι, σκόπει, ἔφη, καὶ ταῦτα. ἔχοντες μέν γε Μακεδονίαν, ἔνθεν καὶ Ἀθηναῖοι τὰ ξύλα ἄγονται, πολὺ δήπου πλείους ἐκείνων ἱκανοὶ ἐσόμεθα ναῦς ποιήσασθαι.

[77] IG II^2 102.

[78] Xenophon *Hellenika* 5.2.15 and Diodoros 15.19 on the alliance between Sparta and Amyntas; Hornblower (1991b: 206).

> there is none in Macedon, where it is cheap for all who want it. But they planned to build and crew them here, although it is stipulated in the common agreement that such is not allowed, and they assumed that they would be able to do this always and in greater quantity.[79]

Demosthenes 17 is not a genuine Demosthenic work, as recognised since antiquity and supported by stylometric evidence; however, it is a genuine fourth-century creation by a member of the anti-Macedonian party, possibly Hypereides.[80] The speech must have been delivered before the Theban revolt, according to internal references, and is the only evidence of a treaty between Alexander and the Greeks before the destruction of Thebes, possibly during the convention at the Isthmos after Philip's death.[81] The speech provides incontrovertible evidence of the import of timber to Athens for the building of warships. Simultaneously, however, it provides equally incontrovertible evidence that building warships in foreign *naupegia* was such a common occurrence as to guarantee a provision in the treaty between Alexander and the Greek poleis. Possibly, the clause was deliberately inserted against Athenian interests and practice, since Athens was the major naval threat to Macedon.

For the fourth century, our information on the Athenian navy is supplemented by the accounts of the *epimeletai tou neoriou*, a series of inscriptions spanning the period 377–322.[82] Unfortunately, the accounts contain only sparse references to timber, *naupegia* or shipbuilding, since the *epimeletai* were not the officials responsible for building triremes, although the redesigning or repair of ships fell under their jurisdiction.[83] There is only one reference to *naupegia* in the inscriptions: "Another trireme, with the name Boetheia, a work of Archeneides; this one we took

[79] Demosthenes 17.27–28: τῷ γὰρ τὸν τότε ἐπὶ τῆς νεὼς εἰσπλεύσαντα, ὃν ἔδει εὐθὺς μετὰ τῆς τριήρους ὑφ' ὑμῶν ἀπολωλέναι, αἰτεῖσθαι ναυπηγήσασθαι μικρὰ πλοῖα ἐν τοῖς ἡμετέροις λιμέσι πῶς οὐ καταφανὲς ὅτι ἀντὶ τοῦ εἰσπλεῖν τὸ εὐθὺς ἔνδον εἶναι ἐμηχανῶντο; καὶ εἰ λεπτὰ πλοῖα ὑπομενοῦμεν, ὀλίγον ὕστερον καὶ τριήρεις· καὶ εἰ τὸ πρῶτον ὀλίγας, μικρῷ ὕστερον πολλάς. οὐ γὰρ δὴ ἔστι γ' εἰπεῖν ὡς Ἀθήνησι μὲν ἀφθόνων ὄντων τῶν ναυπηγησίμων ξύλων, τῶν μόγις καὶ πόρρωθεν εἰσκομιζομένων, ἐν δὲ τῇ Μακεδονίᾳ ἐπιλελοιπότων, τῇ καὶ τοῖς ἄλλοις τοῖς βουλομένοις εὐτελέστατα καθισταμένῃ, ἀλλ' ᾤονθ' ἅμα τε ναυπηγήσεσθαι ἐνταῦθα καὶ πληρώσεσθαι ἐν τῷ λιμένι [τῷ προειρημένῳ], ἐν ταῖς κοιναῖς ὁμολογίαις διειρημένον μηδὲν τοιοῦτον εἰσδέχεσθαι, καὶ τοῦτ' ἐξέσεσθαι ἐπὶ πλέον ἀεὶ ποιεῖν.

[80] Milne (2000: 205–206).

[81] Vince (1954: 463).

[82] IG II^2 1604–1632.

[83] IG II^2 1612.145–217. There is considerable debate over these *architektones*, since it is apparent in the inscriptions that these people were not the officials mentioned in *Constitution of the Athenians* 46.1, see Jordan (1972: 53–54) and Gabrielsen (1994: 133).

over half-built from the Telegoneia [*naupegi*]*a*, we …"[84] The inscription is dated to 357/356 and the building of the Boetheia to 358/357.[85] The location of the Telegoneia *naupegia* is unknown, although it is a fair inference that they were in Attika. However, Telegonos was not an Attic hero, nor is the name attested among the known Athenian names. Possibly the Telegoneia *naupegia* imply a connection with Torone, which not only had a mythological connection with the hero but also had harbours with maritime opportunities.[86] Torone was conquered by Timotheos in 364 but had probably been lost to Athens by 357.[87] One of the *architektones* who were also *naupegoi* was named Pamphilos and was possibly a Toronean, if we connect him with a gravestone found in Athens, while the other *architekton* who is also a *naupegos* is named Amyntas, a name most common in the peri-Macedonian area.[88] The connections are tentative but it is possible that Torone was used by Athens in the 360s as a *naupegion* and its loss caused the migration of shipbuilders from there to Athens, either voluntarily or not.

The only other relevant reference is to the import of unshaved oars in the early 320s: "15 Oar sets for the *tetrereis*, which Demades bought and where shaved in the archon year of Antikles."[89] Demades was a prominent politician in the 330s and the 320s; it is uncertain whether his purchase of unshaved oars was done in an official capacity or merely the gift of a prominent public figure.[90] The expense was certainly considerable, since fifteen tetreric *tarroi* would cost around 10,000 *drachmai*.[91] Demades was a member of the pro-Macedonian party and had close personal relations with leading figures in Alexander's court and possibly

---

[84] IG II^2 1611.127–133: ἑτέρα τριήρης, ἧι | ὄνομά ἐστιν Βοήθεια, | Ἀρχενηΐδου ἔργον· | ταύτην ἡμίεργον | παραλαβόντες | ἐκ τῶν Τηλεγονείων | [ναυπηγί]ων ἡμεῖς …

[85] Archonship of Kephisodotos (IG II^2 1611.21).

[86] Livy 45.30.4.

[87] Capture: Diodoros 15.81.6; lost by 357: Isokrates 7.9.

[88] Pamphilos: IG II^2 1612.156, 164, 172, 176, 184. Gravestone: IG II^2 10454. Amyntas: IG II^2 1612.202, 207. The name Amyntas is most common in northern Greece and Thrace; there are 42 known in the Aegean area (LGPN Vol. 1), 27 in Attika (Vol. 2), 24 in the Peloponnese and the West (Vol. 3a) 90 in central Greece, mainly in Thessaly (Vol. 3b) and 100 in northern Greece (Vol. 4) [information from statistical service of www.lgpn.ox.ac.uk].

[89] IG II^2 1629.348–351: ταρρούς ἐπὶ τετρήρεις, οὓς | Δημάδης εἰσεπρίατο, | κατειργάσθησαν δὲ ἐπὶ | Ἀντικλέους ἄρχοντος: ΔΠ.

[90] A gap in Demades' official career in 329–326 means he could be one of the *epimeletai*: Develin (1989: 717).

[91] 9,975 *drachmai* to be exact at 665 *drachmai* per *tarros* as in IG II^2 1629.684.

Alexander himself.[92] Possibly these oars are part of a transaction similar to that described by Andokides in 411, where an Athenian uses his personal relations with Macedonians to acquire oar supplies for his city.

The previous two episodes are the only direct evidence relating to shipbuilding and the timber trade in the *epimeletai* accounts; however, two further issues can be indirectly related to the building of the Athenian fleet. Firstly, a captured ship whose name has not survived is mentioned as the work of Eudikos.[93] The assignation of a specific ship, which has been captured from an enemy fleet, to a known shipbuilder, begs the question of how the *epimeletai* knew. The issue is further complicated by the fact that Eudikos can be restored as shipwright of two other Athenian ships.[94] Possibly, the captured *triakontoros* had the name of its shipwright written on the woodwork; that would make it unique among captured ships. Alternatively, since it is difficult to imagine Athenian *naupegia* building ships for Athens' enemies, the *triakontoros* was built in a foreign *naupegion*, which accepted equally Athenian and other orders.

Secondly, none of the makers/builders of triremes is ever graced with a *demotic*. Possibly, the majority of *naupegoi* were metics; that, however, is a surprise since by the middle of the fourth century there should have been a long tradition of shipbuilding in Attica, if we assume that the triremes of the Athenian fleet were being built there since the early fifth century. If we take this one-step further and look into the names of the *naupegoi*, the situation becomes even more interesting. The study of naming patterns and commonality of names in different eras and areas is still an unexplored field, mainly because the major resource on ancient names, the *Lexicon of Greek Personal Names*, is not yet complete. Consequently, any argument utilising name commonality suffers from major methodological problems, mainly relating to the lack of a study of the relation between population densities, survival, excavation and inscriptional patterns and name survival. Acknowledging the above limitations, a study of name commonality of *naupegoi* and *architektones* still affords valuable insights. The only correction to the raw sample in this study is the reduction of the

---

92 Pro-Macedonian like Phokion: Arrian *Anabasis* 1.10.3–5; Plutarch *Demosthenes* 23.2, 28.2, *Phokion* 26.2–3; Diodoros 18.1.1; Demosthenes 18.285. Friendship with Alexander: Plutarch *Demosthenes* 23.6: "as the Athenians were considering and carrying on, Demades, after having accepted a bribe of five talents from the men, agreed to become an ambassador and beg the king on their behalf, either trusting in their friendship or considering that he, like a lion, would be sated of slaughter."

93 IG II^2 1629.145–146.

94 IG II^2 1628.145, 1631.22.

Table 8. Commonality of *naupegoi* names per LGPN volume

LGPN volume	Number of *naupegoi*/ *architektones* names most commonly found in this area
(I) Aegean islands, Cyprus, Kyrenaike	24
(II) Attika	22
(IIIa) Peloponnese, western Greece, Sicily, Magna Graecia	5 or 6*
(IIIb) Central Greece	4
(IV) Macedon, Thrace, northern Black Sea	1 or 2*

*One name is found equally in the two areas.

Athenian sample (Vol. II) by ⅓. The reduction is the smallest possible, as a basic comparison between volumes II (Attika) and IIIa (Peloponnese, western Greece, Sicily, Magna Graecia) of the LGPN suggests.[95]

The sample used is 57 names of *naupegoi* and *architektones* mentioned in the *epimeletai* accounts; Table 8 above demonstrates the commonality of the *naupegoi* and *architektones* names according to LGPN volume.[96]

[95] LGPN figures according to Volume (area):

Volume	Areas	Total people	Men only
I	Aegean islands, Cyprus, Kyrenaike	66489	60249
II	Attika	62361	56618
IIIa	Peloponnese, western Greece, Sicily, Magna Graecia	43261	36848
IIIb	Central Greece	43456	38752
IV	Macedon, Thrace, northern Black Sea	43456	38752

The difference between the figures of volumes II and IIIa is close to ⅓ of the Attic sample. A basic comparison of estimated populations with results biased in favour of Attika, using a mere 10 % of territory under grain cultivation, Columella's lower yields and the highest consumption rates, the estimated population of the Peloponnese and Sicily is 711,000 people, more than twice the projected population of Attika in the fourth century (on this see further page 171). Without considering western Greece and Magna Graecia, volume IIIa should have more than double the individuals in the Attic sample. The correction by ⅓ is most conservative and certainly biases the results towards Attika.

[96] There are 59 names mentioned but two are not used, since the only Lissios in the LGPN database is the one in the accounts and the name Hegesios cannot be entered into the search function.

Attika is well represented in the surviving names but interestingly most of the names are commonly found in Vol. I, the Aegean islands, Cyprus and the Kyrenaike. It is surprising that after a supposed 150 years of ship construction in Attika, still 61 % of *naupegoi* and *architektones* names are more common in other areas. The implication is that a large part of ship construction took place outside Athens, and Athens, in spite of being the greatest naval power in the Aegean, was not the greatest *naupegion* in the Greek world.

The timber policy of Athens in the classical period was quite complex and depended mainly on diplomacy. On the interstate level, Athens employed both peaceful and coercive diplomacy, the latter mainly during its empire. The main aspect of Athenian policy during the fifth century was the domination over resource areas and foreign *naupegia*. In the beginning of the classical period, Athens, not yet a major naval power, did not hesitate to engage in a diplomatic and economic transaction with Corinth for the procurement of ships. Its naval ascendancy during the Persian Wars and its consequent leadership of the Delian League made timber supply and ship construction a major governmental concern. The realisation that Athens did not have the resources to maintain its fleet translated into policy as early as 476, when Eion was captured and resettled. Probably in those early years of the Delian League, the main concern was that the major timber resources in the Aegean area were within the grasp of the Persian Empire in northern Asia Minor, Thrace and Macedon. The lesson of Salamis was not easily forgotten when Athens had to turn to the west, away from its natural allies in the Aegean and Ionia, to build its fleet.

In the *Pentekontaetia*, concern with timber slowly but inexorably turned into an obsession, especially as fear moved from an eastern invasion to one closer to home from the Peloponnese and the allies. Many Athenian actions during the period, particularly the capture and resettlement pattern, show a singular drive to dominate foreign timber resources and *naupegia*, not only for their own use but also to deny them to potential enemies. Although it is not possible to identify securely where Athenian ships were built in the *Pentekontaetia*, Athenian actions and later evidence of building in the resource areas suggest that Athens used allied rather than local *naupegia*.

The Peloponnesian War provides evidence of ship building in foreign *naupegia*, mainly in the Archelaos decree. Interestingly, all evidence of imports concerns oars rather than timber, which is difficult to explain if Athens preferred to construct triremes in Attika. The last three decades of the fifth century provide most evidence of intervention in the timber trade. Athens relied mainly on coercive diplomacy in taking over timber producing areas and *naupegia* but other forms of intervention were also employed. Peaceful diplomacy is testified by the treaty with Perdikkas and the *proxenia* given to Archelaos. Further, Athens legislated to extend honours, privileges and incentives to private traders as shown by the Phanosthenes decree. Probably, Athens also provided general incentives to traders to import oars through a lowering of taxation but the special treatment accorded to Phanosthenes, Antiochides and their associates shows that Athens was willing and able to install complex administrative procedures to secure the oar supply on a personal level.

The fourth century was a different era in fleet-building since imperial access to the resource areas was lost. However, both the Athenian obsession with Amphipolis, which persisted throughout the century, and the treaty with Alexander, suggest that the basis of policy had not truly changed from the previous century, even if its scope had. Athens still tried coercive diplomacy to secure timber and the services of foreign *naupegia*. The treaty with Amyntas of Macedon shows that peaceful measures had not gone out of favour in Athens, although the ascendancy of Macedon and the Athenian defeat in the Social War made Athens operate in a changed environment. Even so, the scant evidence on timber and shipbuilding in the *epimeletai* accounts testifies that Athenian interest in and use of foreign resources and *naupegia* did not dissipate in the fourth century.

CHAPTER SIX

FLEETS OUTSIDE ATHENS

Athens was not the only naval power in the Greek world, yet for very few others has any information on shipbuilding survived. Major naval powers such as Aigina, Chios, Samos and Corcyra have left no record of their timber and shipbuilding arrangements. For other poleis, however, a small amount of information has survived, which exhibits both differences and similarities to Athenian policy.

Corinth was the greatest naval power in the Peloponnese and probably the first place where triremes were built in the Greek world:

> It is said that the Corinthians were the first in arranging ships in the modern way, and it was in Corinth that the first triremes in Greece were built. It also seems that Ameinokles, a Corinthian shipwright, made four ships for the Samians. And there have been more than 300 years to the end of this war that Ameinokles went to the Samians.[1]

The Corinthians had access to timber resources in the mountains of Corinthia and Arkadia and apparently had developed enough expertise in the building of the new type of warships to export shipbuilders.[2] As mentioned earlier, Corinth had legislation pertaining to the sale of warships implying regular construction in the local *naupegia*.[3] Corinth was one of the poleis that contributed to the Greek fleet in the Persian Wars and it continued to support a large fleet during the *Pentekontaetia*. In the battle of Aktion in 435 however, the Corinthians lost a large part of their fleet, which led to a large shipbuilding program in the next two years:

[1] Thucydides 1.13: πρῶτοι δὲ Κορίνθιοι λέγονται ἐγγύτατα τοῦ νῦν τρόπου μεταχειρίσαι τὰ περὶ τὰς ναῦς, καὶ τριήρεις ἐν Κορίνθῳ πρῶτον τῆς Ἑλλάδος ναυπηγηθῆναι. φαίνεται δὲ καὶ Σαμίοις Ἀμεινοκλῆς Κορίνθιος ναυπηγὸς ναῦς ποιήσας τέσσαρας· ἔτη δ' ἐστὶ μάλιστα τριακόσια ἐς τὴν τελευτὴν τοῦδε τοῦ πολέμου ὅτε Ἀμεινοκλῆς Σαμίοις ἦλθεν.

[2] In my reading of the text, Ameinokles built triremes for the Samians, agreeing with Morrison, Coates & Rankov (2000: 38). On the opposite view that Ameinokles built pentekonters see van Wees (2004: 207, n. 21).

[3] Herodotos 6.89 and page 116.

> The year after the battle and the one afterwards, the Corinthians in their anger over the war with the Corcyraeans built and prepared as well as possible a fleet of ships, recruiting rowers from the Peloponnese and the rest of Greece enticing them with high pay.[4]

These ships were probably built in Corinth itself, although some may have been built in Ambrakia, since the Ambrakiotes executed a smaller building program at the same time.[5] The provenance of the timber for the ships built in Corinth is not certain, since the hostility of Corcyra probably stopped any shipments from the Adriatic or northwest Greece. Meiggs argued in favour of local reserves in Arkadia, but it is uncertain whether these had already become overexploited, as they were in the late fourth century.[6]

Legon, in an effort to explain the Megarian decree, argued in favour of imports from Macedon. That argument is based upon the twin assumptions that Corinth had no access to the Aegean and that the Athenians would be covertly hostile.[7] Both assumptions are difficult to substantiate since in the same period Corinth had very close relations with Potidaia and the Athenians sent to help the Corcyraeans in the battle of Sybota were under express orders to avoid aggravating Corinth at all costs.[8] However, the events after Sybota are difficult to explain, not only the Megarian decree but more importantly the combination of the Megarian decree, the Potidaia affair and the break in Athenian relations with Perdikkas, all in the space of one year.[9] Athenian foreign policy was complex, but if it is assumed that the Athenian decision to ally with Corcyra had the aim of using the Corcyraean fleet as a check on Corinthian naval power in the Ionian Sea and the Corinthian Gulf, possibly with the use of Naupaktos as a staging area, then the Corcyraean defeat and the loss of a large part of its fleet at Sybota effectively negated Athenian policy. The

[4] Thucydides 1.31.1: Τὸν δ' ἐνιαυτὸν πάντα τὸν μετὰ τὴν ναυμαχίαν καὶ τὸν ὕστερον οἱ Κορίνθιοι ὀργῇ φέροντες τὸν πρὸς Κερκυραίους πόλεμον ἐναυπηγοῦντο καὶ παρεσκευάζοντο τὰ κράτιστα νεῶν στόλον, ἔκ τε αὐτῆς Πελοποννήσου ἀγείροντες καὶ τῆς ἄλλης Ἑλλάδος ἐρέτας, μισθῷ πείθοντες.

[5] The force contributed by Ambrakia in the battle of Sybota was more than three times the number of ships contributed in the battle of Aktion, which may imply a shipbuilding program: at Aktion 8 ships (Thucydides 1.27.2), in Sybota 27 (Thucydides 1.46.1).

[6] Meiggs (1982: 130). On the problem with the falling quality of Arkadian timber, see: Theophrastos *Enquiry Into Plants* 5.2.1.

[7] Legon (1973) for the argument, Legon (1973: 170) on the inability of the Corinthians to trade in the Aegean.

[8] Thucydides 1.45.3.

[9] Note that I am interpreting the Megarian decree as something recent and current in 432, as seems to be implied by Thucydides 1.67.4, 1.42.2 and Hornblower (1991: 86).

alliance with Corcyra was effected at the same time as the Corinthian shipbuilding program. Possibly the Corinthians had managed, maybe with the help of Megara, to acquire supplies from northern Greece; in that case the most likely candidate would be oars that were easier to transport covertly and were essential in close trireme fighting. The best oars were of silver-fir and apparently were a Macedonian speciality. The nearest harbours were all Athenian allies but Potidaia had strong links with Corinth, possibly strong enough to risk displeasing the Athenians. The scenario is tentative but does explain the swift and mysterious actions of the Athenians. Firstly, they attacked Megarian trading in the Aegean, thus limiting any possibility of last minute supplies entering the Peloponnese for the war that by 432 must surely have been looming at the horizon. Secondly, they neutralised Potidaia, the only polis with strong Peloponnesian ties and an important strategic position in the Chalcidice. Thirdly, they supported a pretender to the Macedonian throne, someone certain to become and stay an ally, since Athens would have been instrumental in his accession. The most risky of the three operations was the one against Perdikkas, since its failure would alienate the Macedonians, which in fact it did.[10] If the treaty with Perdikkas, which provided a monopoly of oars to Athens, was in force at the time, the Athenian reaction becomes more understandable, since Perdikkas had already been shown untrustworthy. All scenarios linking events beyond the information provided by our sources are of course highly speculative, but in this case the scenario, speculative as it is, provides a believable explanation for what otherwise seems like a series of foreign policy blunders that succeeded only in creating enemies and cementing the Peloponnesian alliance, when Athens should have been trying for the opposite.

Mytilene was a major naval power in the eastern Aegean and Asia Minor in the archaic period and one of the ship-contributing allies of the Delian League. Mytilene acquired timber from local resources in its *peraia*:

> Their plan was to free the other poleis, those called Aktaies, which the Athenians had and were formerly dominated by Mytilene, and especially Antandros. And having achieved that (the plan was) to build many ships, since there is timber there and Mount Ida is near, and make other preparations easily; further, from there to attack Lesbos, which is near, and take over the small Aiolian poleis on the mainland.[11]

---

[10] Thucydides 1.57.2–3.

[11] Thucydides 4.52: καὶ ἦν αὐτῶν ἡ διάνοια τάς τε ἄλλας πόλεις τὰς Ἀκταίας

The Mytilenians had dominion over the Aktaies poleis, which were not their colonies as the use of "dominated" (νεμομένων) shows. The Aktaies poleis included Antandros whose dependency Aspaneos was later called the *hulotomion* of Ida and had shipyards.[12] Possibly the Mytilenians sometime in the archaic period had taken over this area, maybe with an eye to its timber resources, which then would have been considerable if by the late fourth century there were still available reserves in spite of regular exploitation. The Athenians, after the Mytilenian revolt, took over these poleis including Adramytion on the other side of the gulf, thus totally cutting off Mytilene from the timber resources of Ida.[13] Taking over these poleis not only ensured that Mytilene would not become a threat again in the future but also provided the Athenians with control over the resources of Ida and the *naupegia* in the gulf of Adramytion.

The Aktaies poleis enjoyed a peculiar status, as attested later in the Peloponnesian War:

> Pharnabazos asked all of the Peloponnesians and their allies not to lose heart over pieces of wood, because there are many in the demesne of the king, as long as they were healthy. And he gave them each a cloak and rations for two months, and gave weapons to the sailors and set them to guard his coast. And he called the *strategoi* of the poleis and the trierarchs and told them to build triremes in Antandros, as many as they had lost, and gave them money and permission to take timber from Ida.[14]

Pharnabazos clearly considers Ida part of the Persian domain. Parallels to this situation can be found in the Myrkinos affair, where the resources of the area were part of the concession of the Persian king to a loyal supporter/governor but were considered to be part of the king's

---

καλουμένας, ἃς πρότερον Μυτιληναίων νεμομένων Ἀθηναῖοι εἶχον, ἐλευθεροῦν, καὶ πάντων μάλιστα τὴν Ἄντανδρον· καὶ κρατυνάμενοι αὐτὴν (ναῦς τε γὰρ εὐπορία ἦν ποιεῖσθαι, αὐτόθεν ξύλων ὑπαρχόντων καὶ τῆς Ἴδης ἐπικειμένης, καὶ τῇ ἄλλῃ σκευῇ) ῥᾳδίως ἀπ' αὐτῆς ὁρμώμενοι τήν τε Λέσβον ἐγγὺς οὖσαν κακώσειν καὶ τὰ ἐν τῇ ἠπείρῳ Αἰολικὰ πολίσματα χειρώσεσθαι.

[12] Strabo 13.1.51; IACP s.v. Antandros.

[13] Thucydides 3.50.3. Athenians taking over Adramytion: Strabo 13.1.51.

[14] Xenophon *Hellenika* 1.1.24–25: Φαρνάβαζος δὲ παντὶ τῷ τῶν Πελοποννησίων στρατεύματι καὶ τοῖς συμμάχοις παρακελευσάμενος μὴ ἀθυμεῖν ἕνεκα ξύλων, ὡς ὄντων πολλῶν ἐν τῇ βασιλέως, ἕως ἂν τὰ σώματα σῶα ᾖ, ἱμάτιόν τ' ἔδωκεν ἑκάστῳ καὶ ἐφόδιον δυοῖν μηνοῖν, καὶ ὁπλίσας τοὺς ναύτας φύλακας κατέστησε τῆς ἑαυτοῦ παραθαλαττίας γῆς. καὶ συγκαλέσας τούς τε ἀπὸ τῶν πόλεων στρατηγοὺς καὶ τριηράρχους ἐκέλευε ναυπηγεῖσθαι τριήρεις ἐν Ἀντάνδρῳ ὅσας ἕκαστοι ἀπώλεσαν, χρήματά τε διδοὺς καὶ ὕλην ἐκ τῆς Ἴδης κομίζεσθαι φράζων.

domain.[15] Neither Thucydides nor Xenophon mentions any significant change in the Persian attitude towards these poleis, although the absence of the Athenian fleet may have altered the balance of power after the Sicilian Expedition. The Aktaies poleis probably secured a concession for the resource from the Great King through the satrapy, and their relationship with Mytilene gave the island access to the resource. The Mytilenian reliance on its *peraia* for timber and *naupegia* serves as a model for the timber supply of the other naval powers of the eastern Aegean, particularly Chios and Samos.

The Peloponnesian League during the Peloponnesian War executed several shipbuilding programmes both in local and foreign territories. The main instance of building from local resources occurs after the Sicilian Expedition:

> The Spartans ordered the poleis to build 100 ships; they and the Boiotians were to build 25 each, the Phokians and the Lokrians 15 and the Corinthians also 15, while the Arkadians, Pelleneans and Sikyonians 10 and the Megarians, Troizenians, Epidaurians and Hermionians also 10. Further, they made all other necessary preparations to continue the war in the spring.[16]

The construction of these 100 ships is indicative of the Peloponnesian League, since every maritime member is appointed a small shipbuilding program. Such diffusion of construction created a diffusion of expenses reflecting the state of the resources of the league. The expectation that local resources would be used is shown by the division and the very small number of ships most of the allies would have to build. Additionally, such diffusion of building provided for the speedy completion of the ships, since most of the poleis would have to build only three or four. The local timber resources and the financial power of the league were not enough for large shipbuilding programs, which accounts for the other building programs of the league, when they got a foothold in the resource areas of northern Greece and Asia Minor.

---

[15] Herodotos 5.23.2. Similar to some extent to the royal monopoly of timber resources documented for the reign of Sargon II of Assyria: Lafranchi & Parpola (1990: xxv, nos. 33–34).

[16] Thucydides 8.3.2: Λακεδαιμόνιοι δὲ τὴν πρόσταξιν ταῖς πόλεσιν ἑκατὸν νεῶν τῆς ναυπηγίας ἐποιοῦντο, καὶ ἑαυτοῖς μὲν καὶ Βοιωτοῖς πέντε καὶ εἴκοσιν ἑκατέροις ἔταξαν, Φωκεῦσι δὲ καὶ Λοκροῖς πέντε καὶ δέκα, καὶ Κορινθίοις πέντε καὶ δέκα, Ἀρκάσι δὲ καὶ Πελληνεῦσι καὶ Σικυωνίοις δέκα, Μεγαρεῦσι δὲ καὶ Τροιζηνίοις καὶ Ἐπιδαυρίοις καὶ Ἑρμιονεῦσι δέκα· τά τε ἄλλα παρεσκευάζοντο ὡς εὐθὺς πρὸς τὸ ἔαρ ἑξόμενοι τοῦ πολέμου.

In 424, after the capture of Amphipolis, Brasidas started to build ships in the Strymon area: "Then he (Brasidas) sent to Sparta asking them to send an army quickly and was himself starting to build ships on the Strymon."[17] These ships were probably never completed but Brasidas' immediate employ of the Strymon resources shows not only the available resources and expertise in the area, which had until then been dominated by Athens, but also the readiness of other powers to utilise conquered timber reserves and *naupegia* immediately upon their acquisition.

The readiness of the Peloponnesians to utilise foreign timber resources and *naupegia* is also evident in the text referring to the rebuilding of the Peloponnesian fleet after the battle of Kyzikos above (page 144). Xenophon names the *naupegion* used: Antandros ("told them to build triremes in Antandros"). The expertise and seasoned timber necessary were readily available in the area, since the Syracusan ships at least were completed within one year.[18]

Peloponnesian shipbuilding during the Ionian War followed the same model, as is testified by the shipbuilding in Ephesos under Lysander in 406:

> When he reached Ephesos and found the city well disposed to him and willing to become a Spartan ally, although at the time it was in a sorry state and was in danger of becoming barbarian and adopting Persian customs because of the intermarriages, since it had become surrounded by Lydia and the King's generals were often camped there. Lysander made camp there, called all the merchant ships to port there and started to build triremes.[19]

Meiggs argued that the timber in this case was imported from other areas of Asia Minor.[20] While that is certainly a possibility, Ephesos had some local resources in the grove of Ortygia and access to the Mesogis Mountains via the river Cayster, since the Peloponnesians were supported by the local satrap, Kyros.[21]

---

[17] Thucydides 4.108.6: ὁ δὲ ἐς τὴν Λακεδαίμονα ἐφιέμενος στρατιάν τε προσαποστέλλειν ἐκέλευε καὶ αὐτὸς ἐν τῷ Στρυμόνι ναυπηγίαν τριήρων παρεσκευάζετο.

[18] Xenophon *Hellenika* 1.2.12. Morrison, Coates & Rankov (2000: 88).

[19] Plutarch *Lysander* 3.2–3: γενόμενος δ' ἐν Ἐφέσῳ, καὶ τὴν πόλιν εὑρὼν εὔνουν μὲν αὑτῷ καὶ λακωνίζουσαν προθυμότατα, πράττουσαν δὲ τότε λυπρῶς καὶ κινδυνεύουσαν ἐκβαρβαρωθῆναι τοῖς Περσικοῖς ἔθεσι διὰ τὰς ἐπιμιξίας, ἅτε δὴ τῆς Λυδίας περικεχυμένης καὶ τῶν βασιλικῶν στρατηγῶν αὐτόθι τὰ πολλὰ διατριβόντων, στρατόπεδον βαλόμενος καὶ τὰ πλοῖα πανταχόθεν ἕλκεσθαι κελεύσας ἐκεῖ τὰ φορτηγά, καὶ ναυπηγίαν τριήρων ἐκεῖ κατασκευασάμενος.

[20] Meiggs (1982: 358).

[21] Strabo 14.1.20.

An episode from the beginning of the Peloponnesian War shows that the Spartans were fully cognizant of the need to utilise foreign resources and *naupegia*:

> The Spartans requested that their allies in Italy and Sicily build ships according to the size of their poleis, to reach a total number of 500, and prepare money contributions, while otherwise that they stay quiet and accept no more than one Athenian ship in their harbours until all preparations were complete.[22]

That is the most ambitious building program of the classical period and, although it was never realised, it shows the capabilities of the resources and *naupegia* of Magna Graecia and Sicily. The Spartans obviously realised that a strong navy was fundamental in order to bring Athens to its knees and possibly tried to emulate Athenian policy regarding building in the resource areas. Of course, the Athenians had already found out that the securest way of accomplishing this was to have direct control over the resource areas, while the league was dependent upon the goodwill of independent allies.

Since all the Peloponnesian examples date to times of war, in times of peace ships may have been built only at local *naupegia*. However, the order to build ships in Sicily and Magna Graecia and the position of the foreign *naupegia* utilised show that employing foreign *naupegia* was a common course of action. Both Amphipolis and Antandros must have been used before, since there was both seasoned timber and expertise available. It would be surprising if both Athens and Mytilene, that dominated these areas before the Peloponnesians, had ignored them. Simultaneously the examples of building in the resource areas, and particularly that of Brasidas in Amphipolis, presuppose control of the area. Thus, it would be surprising if in times of peace control of a resource area did not mean utilizing its resources.

For the western Greeks there is evidence of import of timber to Syracuse and building of ships in the importer:

> He also started to build *tetrereis* and *pentereis*, being the first to invent the building of these ships. Dionysios had heard that the first triremes were built in Corinth, he was eager to build ships of increased size in the city

[22] Thucydides 2.7.2–3: καὶ Λακεδαιμονίοις μὲν πρὸς ταῖς αὐτοῦ ὑπαρχούσαις ἐξ Ἰταλίας καὶ Σικελίας τοῖς τἀκείνων ἑλομένοις ναῦς ἐπετάχθη ποιεῖσθαι κατὰ μέγεθος τῶν πόλεων, ὡς ἐς τὸν πάντα ἀριθμὸν πεντακοσίων νεῶν ἐσομένων, καὶ ἀργύριον ῥητὸν ἑτοιμάζειν, τά τε ἄλλα ἡσυχάζοντας καὶ Ἀθηναίους δεχομένους μιᾷ νηὶ ἕως ἂν ταῦτα παρασκευασθῇ. On the interpretation of the 500 ships, see Hornblower (1991: 244).

> they (i.e. the Corinthians) had founded. Gaining permission from Italy to export timber, he sent half the woodcutters to Mount Aitna, since it had in those times great silver-firs and firs, and the other half to Italy. There he made ready teams to bring the timber to the sea, and sent ships and sailors to escort the rafts as quickly as possible to Syracuse.[23]

Dionysios both imported timber and used local resources in Aitna. The need for permission probably refers to the exploitation of resources, since Dionysios sent his own woodcutters to Italy, rather than import. Further, Diodoros makes clear that the reason for such large-scale import and building in the importer was Dionysios' desire to set Syracuse as equal to Corinth in shipbuilding records.

[23] Diodoros 14.42: ἤρξατο δὲ ναυπηγεῖσθαι τετρήρεις καὶ πεντηρικὰ σκάφη, πρῶτος ταύτην τὴν κατασκευὴν τῶν νεῶν ἐπινοήσας. ἀκούων γὰρ ὁ Διονύσιος ἐν Κορίνθῳ ναυπηγηθῆναι τριήρη πρώτως, ἔσπευδε κατὰ τὴν ἀποικισθεῖσαν ὑπ' ἐκείνων πόλιν αὐξῆσαι τὸ μέγεθος τῆς τῶν νεῶν κατασκευῆς. λαβὼν δ' ἐκ τῆς Ἰταλίας ἐξαγωγὴν ὕλης, τοὺς μὲν ἡμίσεις τῶν ὑλοτόμων εἰς τὸ κατὰ τὴν Αἴτνην ὄρος ἀπέστειλε, γέμον κατ' ἐκείνους τοὺς χρόνους πολυτελοῦς ἐλάτης τε καὶ πεύκης, τοὺς δ' ἡμίσεις εἰς τὴν Ἰταλίαν ἀποστείλας παρεσκευάσατο ζεύγη μὲν τὰ πρὸς τὴν θάλατταν κατακομιοῦντα, πλοῖα δὲ καὶ τοὺς ὑπηρέτας πρὸς τὸ τὰς σχεδίας ἀπάγεσθαι κατὰ τάχος εἰς τὰς Συρακούσας.

TIMBER: CONCLUDING REMARKS

Naval warfare played a major role in the archaic and classical periods. Building and maintaining warships was a state prerogative. Most of the major naval states in the Greek world did not have vast local resources of shipbuilding timber. Thus, a naval state had to acquire the necessary quantities of timber for its fleet on its own account. Shipbuilding timber was not a widely available commodity in the Greek world. As Theophrastos notes, only a few areas were in possession of forested areas with the required timber types. The main producers were Macedon, the Strymon region in Thrace, Mount Ida, the hinterlands of Sinope and Amisos, and Latium, Corsica and Magna Graecia in Italy. Of particular interest is that the great naval powers of the Greek world were situated in other areas, which necessitated their use of the resources of the main producers.

Timber, like metal, was considered a resource of the country, thus, the reserves were owned by the polis or polity in control of them. The exploitation regime employed by the timber producers cannot be fully reconstructed. However, in the best known case, that of Macedon, it appears that all control of the resource rested with the king using a controlled leasing system. In territories under Persian domination however, such as Mount Ida, the ownership and exploitation regime was more layered, as shown by Pharnabazos' assertion that the timber of Ida belonged to the King but apparently was also available to nearby poleis such as Antandros. For reserves under the control of poleis, a leasing system was probably employed but limitations on exploitation were in place, as shown by Dionysios' need for permission in the case of the south Italian poleis.

Export was also regulated by the producing poleis and polities as exemplified in the Macedonian treaties with Athens and the Chalcidian league. The Macedonians provided rights of export to poleis but it was limited, as exploitation was directly controlled by the king. All the evidence concerning timber producers, both poleis and kingdoms, points towards limitations being imposed on exploitation and subsequent export. Timber was a renewable resource, unlike precious metal deposits, and consequently was husbandable. The limitations on exploitation betray a common policy among timber producers, probably aiming at securing future revenues. Such long-term policies, especially for the volatile Macedonian kings, might not seem probable, but the evidence suggests that the producers of timber had the foresight and economic rationality to recognise the need for future revenue and to secure the means. Ships were also items of trade in the Greek world as early as the beginning of the fifth century, as Herodotos and the Corinthian law testify.

Turning to the importers, most of the great naval powers of the classical period, most importantly Athens, had need of foreign timber resources for their fleets. It has generally been assumed that Athens, and other naval powers, imported timber from the resource areas to local *naupegia*. However, there is little evidence supporting such large imports of timber and construction in local *naupegia*. For Athens, the majority of the evidence suggests that the Athenians, particularly during the fifth-century empire, preferred to use diplomacy and acquire control of the resource areas themselves in order to facilitate construction of warships in *naupegia* in the resource areas. Imports during the fifth century appear to have been limited to oars, while for actual ship construction Athens expended much effort in order to dominate the Strymon area. In the fourth century, at least until the advent of Macedon, Athens again tried to control the resource areas and appears to have utilised foreign *naupegia* for ship construction.

The other importers, according to the little surviving evidence, also tried to dominate the resource areas and then utilise the *naupegia* there, as seen in the case of Brasidas in Amphipolis. Additionally they utilised both local *naupegia* according to the resources available and placed orders for ships to be constructed in friendly *naupegia*, such as the Peloponnesian order to the Sicilian cities at the beginning of the Peloponnesian War.

The revealed tendency of both Athens and other poleis to construct ships outside their own *chorai*, albeit usually in a controlled resource area, throws considerable doubt on the extent of the timber trade in the Greek world, at least that relating to warship construction. The difficulties of transporting timber over long distances by ship discussed at the beginning of the chapter help to explain the policy of naval powers. Further, since for poleis with aspirations of naval power or hegemony, timber was a most necessary commodity needing a constant and secure supply, the solution of trying to dominate foreign resource areas on the one hand solved problems of transport, while on the other created a constant threat of losing control of *naupegia* and resources, as Athens feared after the Sicilian disaster. Governmental intervention in the timber trade was quite pronounced in the items, such as oars, which were imported, both through diplomatic ties with exporters and through providing incentives to traders. However, the most important steps taken by naval poleis for securing their timber supply was to eliminate trade as an option as far as they could, since eliminating trade also eliminated most security threats to their timber supply and also provided them with a steady supply of the commodity with very little need to depend on forces beyond their control.

GRAIN: PROLEGOMENA

Grain, mainly wheat and barley, was the main staple in the Greek diet, as well as the main bulk commodity in Greek trade.[1] The trade of grain was a major political concern, at least for those poleis with a permanent, or usual, deficiency of local supply. Thus, grain is the most helpful example for research into the intervention-involvement equilibrium of the government as regulator of trade. Since grain has attracted much attention from scholarship, issues already covered sufficiently will be merely summarised. The availability and variety of evidence available on grain provides us with a unique opportunity to compare the different policies of importers and the responses of the exporters. The following chapters discuss the role of the government in the grain trade, especially as illuminated by legislation. Chapter 7 discusses the exporters of grain, particularly their geographical distribution and their commercial policies. Chapter 8 discusses the most important and well-known importer, Athens, concentrating on its import needs and legislation on the grain trade. Chapter 9 discusses other importers of grain for which information has survived, mainly the quantities of grain imported.

Before continuing, it is necessary to examine briefly the cultivation conditions in the Mediterranean, as they had a direct impact on the production of, and trade in, grain. The climate of the region is diverse but generally characterised by large variability of rainfall, which causes the crop yields to fluctuate widely from year to year, at times up to 50%.[2] The other main climatic feature of the Mediterranean, particularly of its northern coastline, is a systemic diversity of weather patterns on a local scale caused by the mountainous profile of the land, the famous microclimates, which have been recognised as a feature of Mediterranean weather since antiquity.[3] The microclimates are one of the main causes of the regime of estate fragmentation common in the Greek world and the

[1] Foxhall (2003: 76).
[2] Gallant (1989: 395); Osborne (1987: 32–33, 45).
[3] Aristotle *Meteorologica* 2.4.

modern Mediterranean.[4] The mountainous landscape of the region has the added consequence that in most areas only a fraction of the land, between 20 and 30 %, is cultivable and a large part of that needs terracing and irrigation.[5] The agricultural conditions in the Mediterranean result in lower yield ratios than in other parts of Europe or in the Near East. Cereal crops, especially wheat, are particularly vulnerable to rainfall changes and climatic variability, thus creating a never-ending cycle of local shortages, which in turn result in an increased local need for grain imports.

[4] Gallant (1991: 41–45) for a discussion of the surveys of land properties in Greece.
[5] Angel (1972: 88).

CHAPTER SEVEN

THE EXPORTERS OF GRAIN

The main grain-exporting areas in the archaic and classical periods are found in the periphery of the Greek world, in the Black Sea, Egypt and the west. Most of these areas were dominated by Greeks, who had settled there in the archaic period; the phenomenon has become the basis of the debate on the reason and aims of Greek settlement abroad, particularly in the Black Sea. The issue discussed is how far settlement in the Black Sea, and Naukratis in Egypt, was influenced by the needs of poleis in mainland Greece and Asia Minor for imported grain. There is no direct evidence for import of grain in the archaic period; since, however, the Mediterranean climate did not change significantly throughout antiquity, shortages due to weather variability must have been as common in the archaic period as they were in the classical.

The possibility of imports in the archaic period is discussed for each producing area separately in the following sections. However, the main issue of the possibility of trade in grain in the archaic period in general terms must be addressed before continuing with the individual accounts. The paucity of archaic sources makes evidence on specific items of trade very difficult to acquire. Thus, it is particularly fortunate that there is specific evidence on trade in agricultural produce, specifically grain, from the early archaic period.

Hesiod in the *Works and Days* devotes almost 80 lines to advice about sailing and seaborne trade. Garnsey and Morris have argued that Hesiod disapproves of sailing and trade, but the text suggests that trade for profit was common in the period:

> If you desire to turn your silly heart to trading with the thought of escaping debts and sad hunger, then I will guide you to the ways of the roaring sea though I know nothing of sailing or ships.[1]

---

[1] Hesiod *Works and Days* 645–648: Εὖτ' ἂν ἐπ' ἐμπορίην τρέψας ἀεσίφρονα θυμὸν βούληαι [δὲ] χρέα τε προφυγεῖν καὶ λιμὸν ἀτερπέα, δείξω δή τοι μέτρα πολυφλοίσβοιο θαλάσσης, οὔτε τι ναυτιλίης σεσοφισμένος οὔτε τι νηῶν. Garnsey & Morris (1989: 100).

Hesiod was as divorced from the sea, which he freely admits ("though I know nothing of sailing or ships"), as he was from the countryside.[2] The distance of the poet makes his perception of trade particularly valuable, since it is the view of the outsider, and thus better placed to inform us of the common view of trade among contemporaries, than a more expert but engaged opinion, which could easily be accused of bias. Hesiod connects trade with profit and advises in favour of maximising profits at every venture:

> Admire a small ship but put your cargo in a large one, for the greater the cargo the greater will be your profit, if the winds withhold their bad gales.[3]

Even when advising against spring sailing for reasons of safety, Hesiod provides us with the information that it is the prospect of wealth that makes his contemporaries take the increased risks during spring:

> Another season for men to sail is in spring when a man first sees the leaves as large as the footprint of a crow on the top branch of a fig tree, then the seas can be sailed and this is the spring sailing season. Personally, I do not recommend it, for my soul does not like it. Sailing then is hurried and you will not avoid misfortune. But in their ignorance men sail then since the soul of cowardly mortals desires wealth. Yet it is terrible to die in the waves.[4]

Hesiod's views and the space he devotes in the *Works and Days* to advice about trading agricultural produce clearly imply that such trade was a common feature of seventh century society, simultaneous with the great waves of Greek settlement abroad.[5] Consequently, any discussion of the archaic grain trade and its influence on settlement abroad must fall against this background of the commonality of trading in agricultural produce for profit.

Grain was, and still is, one of the principal crops of the Black Sea, since the climate and rainfall, especially in the north and west coasts, are well

---

[2] On Hesiod's view of the countryside, see Osborne (1987: 18).

[3] Hesiod *Works and Days* 643–645: νῆ' ὀλίγην αἰνεῖν, μεγάλῃ δ' ἐνὶ φορτία θέσθαι· μείζων μὲν φόρτος, μεῖζον δ' ἐπὶ κέρδεϊ κέρδος ἔσσεται, εἴ κ' ἄνεμοί γε κακὰς ἀπέχωσιν ἀήτας.

[4] Hesiod *Works and Days* 680–687: ἄλλος δ' εἰαρινὸς πέλεται πλόος ἀνθρώποισιν· ἦμος δὴ τὸ πρῶτον, ὅσον τ' ἐπιβᾶσα κορώνη ἴχνος ἐποίησεν, τόσσον πέταλ' ἀνδρὶ φανήῃ ἐν κράδῃ ἀκροτάτῃ, τότε δ' ἄμβατός ἐστι θάλασσα· εἰαρινὸς δ' οὗτος πέλεται πλόος· οὔ μιν ἔγωγε αἴνημ', οὐ γὰρ ἐμῷ θυμῷ κεχαρισμένος ἐστίν· ἁρπακτός· χαλεπῶς κε φύγοις κακόν· ἀλλά νυ καὶ τὰ ἄνθρωποι ῥέζουσιν ἀιδρείῃσι νόοιο· χρήματα γὰρ ψυχὴ πέλεται δειλοῖσι βροτοῖσιν. δεινὸν δ' ἐστὶ θανεῖν μετὰ κύμασιν.

[5] Wallinga (1993: 4). Against Garnsey & Morris (1989: 100).

suited to cereal cultivation. It must be noted here that the Black Sea, like most regions, at times suffered from grain shortages.[6] However, that does not mean, as Braund infered, that surpluses of grain from the area were irregular.[7]

Most information concerning grain production in the region comes from the Bosporan Kingdom, the modern Crimea, which had two main emporia, Pantikapaion and Theodosia.[8] The other major exporter was probably the west coast, mainly Dacia, which was a large producer in the Roman period; the nearest Greek settlements were Tomis and Kallatis.[9]

Tradition dates the first settlements in the eighth century but the archaeological evidence has suggested later dates for most foundations.[10] The debate on the foundation of these settlements centres on their role as grain producers for poleis in Asia Minor. Roebuck, followed most recently by Boardman, argued in favour of settlement in the region as an effort to alleviate the grain needs of the Ionian cities, particularly Miletos.[11] Noonan soon challenged Roebuck's position, arguing against grain exports from the Black Sea before the late sixth century at the earliest.[12] Recently, Tsetskhladze brought a more political angle into the debate, eliminating grain as a reason for settlement altogether, and identifying instead political pressure from Lydia and Persia on the Asia Minor poleis as the primary motive of the Black Sea settlement.[13]

For a region as large and rich in resources as the Black Sea, such broad categorization of settlement motives greatly restricts the study of settlements, as a recent work has pointed out.[14] Assuming that settlements in the Black Sea were official colonizing ventures, as Roebuck did, disregards the powerful element of individual mobility in the archaic period and tries, not very successfully, to impose later colonization models on

---

[6] Polybios 4.38.

[7] Braund (2007: 41).

[8] On Theodosia as *emporion* in the Bosporan Kingdom, see Demosthenes 20.32. Possibly, Phanagoria was also a Bosporan *emporion*: Bill (1926).

[9] Glodariu (1976); Hind (1998: 140). Coin of Trajan depicting Dacia holding child with ears of grain: BMC. 960v/RIC 621v. Boardman (1999: 247) mentions the wheat-growing region of Dobrudja as a reason for the Greek settlement of the area.

[10] For foundation dates from pottery evidence see Tsetskhladze (1994), although Graham (1997: 250) is right in that Tsetskhladze belittles the literary evidence too much.

[11] Roebuck (1959: 129); Huxley (1966: 68); Solonev (1998: 211); Boardman (1999: 244).

[12] Noonan (1973).

[13] Tsetskhladze (1994: 124).

[14] Vinogradov & Kryzickij (1995: 85–86).

archaic settlement abroad. The later ties of peripheral settlements with poleis in the core of the Greek world are not necessarily evidence of similar ties in the archaic period or indeed of official support for a settlement before its foundation. The debate on the nature of Greek settlement abroad rages amongst modern scholars, with recent studies moving determinedly beyond the traditional explanations of overpopulation, land hunger or hunting for resources, to more composite reasons in tune with an era of high personal mobility, geographic and social, and volatile political and social circumstances.[15]

A closed model cannot encompass all settlements, especially one based on a specific reason or motive for leaving one's polis; flexibility is necessary when studying such a diverse and variable phenomenon as archaic settlement abroad. Tsetskhladze's model of political pressure certainly fits Phokaian actions in the sixth century, but the model implies concentrated political will and organised settlement as early as the seventh century, which is very difficult to substantiate. The prosperity of the Ionian poleis and Herodotos' account of Lydian aggression do not suggest that great political pressure was felt by the Ionians before the Persian onslaught.[16] Roebuck's model of widespread need for imports of grain into Ionia in the middle archaic period, although attractive, presupposes widespread overpopulation and a lack of cultivable land, which is emphatically rejected by the archaeological evidence.[17]

Noonan's argument against trade in grain before the early fifth century, however, is equally difficult to substantiate.[18] The large number of Greek imported wares in the Black Sea settlements, some of them dating before the middle of the sixth century, suggests that trade between the Pontic Greeks and the Aegean or Asia Minor existed from early in the settlements' foundation.[19] The agricultural character of the majority of archaic *chora* settlements in the Olbia/Berezan area combined with the imported wares found there, suggests that agricultural produce was certainly of great importance in the economy of the region.[20] Further, the evidence of trade contacts between Greeks and natives in the

[15] See mainly Osborne (1998), followed most recently by Hall (2007: 93–117, especially 114–117).

[16] See page 72.

[17] Foxhall (2003: 77).

[18] Noonan (1973: 234–235, 238–239, 241) using Herodotos 7.147.2.

[19] Noonan (1973: 237–238, 240); Kryzhytskyy & Krapivina (2003: 515); Vinogradov & Kryzickij (1995: 85–89).

[20] Kryzhytskyy & Krapivina (2003: 513, 528).

Olbia/Berezan area as early as the late seventh century suggest that, since it was one of the main products of the area, grain could have been an item of trade.[21] Tsetskhladze's suggestion that any grain exports from the Black Sea originated in the *chorai* of the poleis certainly has merit, but it is impossible to rule out exports of native grain, since trade with the tribes existed.[22] Grain, along with other commodities, certainly played a role in the economies of archaic settlements in the Black Sea, but it is impossible to argue successfully that the quest for grain, and grain only, was the defining reason for settlement.

Turning to the classical period, exports of grain from the Black Sea are recorded as early as 480: "When Xerxes was in Abydos, he saw ships carrying grain from the Pontus, passing through the Hellespont, headed to Aigina and the Peloponnese."[23] Although the historicity of the passage may be suspect since it assists in Herodotos' characterisation of Xerxes, it is equally possible that Herodotos records a tradition of the area regarding Xerxes' passage.[24] The passage neither implies nor rejects the possibility of regular imports from the Black Sea to Aigina and the Peloponnese before Xerxes' campaign. However, it is in my opinion best to assume that the poleis imported at that time in preparation of potential sieges by the Persian army.[25] Herodotos does not elaborate on the exact provenance of the grain, most of the evidence on export in the classical period relates to the Bosporan Kingdom, so it is a fair inference that grain probably came from the northern Black Sea. The most interesting factor for Bosporan grain exports is the evidence of a specific export policy for grain adopted by the Spartokid dynasty.

A major issue is the ownership of surplus in the Bosporus and the role of the government in production.[26] Since grain was an agricultural product, it is valid to assume that the bulk of surpluses were privately owned. However, some grain was certainly in public hands; the gift of grain provided by Leukon, a member of the Spartokid dynasty, to Athens in a time of crisis shows that the Kingdom had a considerable surplus at its disposal:

---

21 Vinogradov & Kryzickij (1995: 85, 87); Braund (2007: 39).

22 Tsetskhladze (1994: 124).

23 Herodotos 7.147: ἐὼν γὰρ ἐν Ἀβύδῳ ὁ Ξέρξης εἶδε πλοῖα ἐκ τοῦ Πόντου σιταγωγὰ διεκπλέοντα τὸν Ἑλλήσποντον, ἔς τε Αἴγιναν καὶ Πελοπόννησον κομιζόμενα.

24 Doubts on the historicity of the passage: Braund (2007: 44).

25 On this issue, see also Moreno (2007b: 161) with the same conclusion.

26 For an excellent discussion of the Spartokid kingship and system of government, see Moreno (2007b: 144–208).

> In the year before last, when there was famine amongst all peoples, not only did he send you enough grain, but in fact (he sent) so much that Kallisthenes had an extra fifteen talents of silver to dispose of.[27]

Possibly the surplus came from taxes payable in grain, similar to the Athenian *dôdekate* of the islands.[28] Although most taxes in the classical period were paid in coin, the Athenian grain-tax law of 374/373 shows that taxes in kind were known.[29] The influence of the government in the production of grain would have been minimal, since in areas where grain crops flourished, there was no need for the government to impose or encourage its production, as the great demand for grain elsewhere made it a lucrative crop.[30] The main role of the government in production was to protect the land and crops from the ravages of war, as damaging crops was one of the main elements of warfare in our period.[31]

The Spartokids, however, intervened considerably in exports, where the evidence suggests the development of a consistent policy to attract importers. The Spartokids had extended an *ateleia* from export taxes to Athens:

> Not only does that area produce much grain but also Leukon, who controls trade, has decreed that no tax is to be imposed to those transporting to Athens and that those who sail to you shall have priority of lading.[32]

The *ateleia* of the Spartokids was extended to all merchants carrying grain to Athens. Since commercial policies are thought to have been confined to the necessary imports of exceptional poleis, like Athens, the Bosporan *ateleia* has been considered a single exception to the rule of non-intervention.[33]

As long as the evidence was confined to Athens, the Spartokid *ateleia* was justifiably categorised as a unique exception but the discovery of a

---

[27] Demosthenes 20.33: ἀλλὰ πρωπέρυσιν σιτοδείας παρὰ πᾶσιν ἀνθρώποις γενομένης οὐ μόνον ὑμῖν ἱκανὸν σῖτον ἀπέστειλεν, ἀλλὰ τοσοῦτον ὥστε πεντεκαίδεκ' ἀργυρίου τάλαντα, ἃ Καλλισθένης διῴκησε, προσπεριγενέσθαι.

[28] SEG 36.146.6, see further page 188.

[29] Stroud (1998: 27–28).

[30] The production of surplus grain in the Bosporan kingdom may have been further encouraged by the close relationship between the Bosporan aristocrats and Athens as argued by Moreno (2007a).

[31] Destruction of crops: Osborne (1987: 13); Hanson (1998: 49–55). Possibly as a form of economic warfare: van Wees (2004: 122–124).

[32] Demosthenes 20.31: οὐ γὰρ μόνον διὰ τὸ τὸν τόπον τοῦτον σῖτον ἔχειν πλεῖστον τοῦτο γίγνεται, ἀλλὰ διὰ τὸ κύριον ὄντα τὸν Λεύκων' αὐτοῦ τοῖς ἄγουσιν Ἀθήναζε ἀτέλειαν δεδωκέναι, καὶ κηρύττειν πρώτους γεμίζεσθαι τοὺς ὡς ὑμᾶς πλέοντας.

[33] Austin & Vidal-Naquet (1977: 117).

more elaborate parallel at Mytilene throws a different light on the Athenian *ateleia*: "Leukon and [his] sons gave to the [Myt]ilenians a t[ax on wheat] of a simple 1/60th and an *archeion* of [1/90th un]til 10[0,000 — -]"[34] The Mytilenian decree refers to two modes of reduction, a 'simple 1/60th' on wheat and an *archeion* of 1/90th, possibly up to certain amount of *medimnoi*. The reduction to 1/60th effectively halved the export dues for the Mytilenians in the Bosporan Kingdom, since the regular export tax was a *triakoste*. The reduction to 1/90th is more complicated due to the provision of an *archeion*. The usual meaning of *archeion*, administrative building or archive, does not apply here, since its juxtaposition with the *exekoste* clearly implies that the *enenekoste* was a tax.[35] Either *archeion* has a specialised meaning or is the stonecutter's mistake, possibly for *archaion*, capital.[36] Although the *enenekoste* provision is unclear, it is undoubted that Leukon offered an elaborate tax reduction to the Mytilenians.

Reduction of taxes would have been especially welcomed by traders, since the Bosporan Kingdom had the highest rate of taxation known in the period, a *triakoste*.[37] A close reading of Demosthenes' reference to the tax may imply that the *triakoste* applied only to the export of grain and was not levied on other goods: "He imposes on those who export grain from there a tax of one thirtieth (*triakoste*)".[38] In any case, contrary to the common assumption that accepts commercial policies only for the necessary imports of exceptional poleis, the parallel cases of reduction of dues by the Spartokids suggest the existence of a grain export policy in the Bosporus.

Policy implies not only consistency of measures, which is apparent in the case of the Spartokids, but also a reason or rationale leading to its adoption. The reasons for the Spartokid policy are found in the main characteristics of the product itself. Theophrastos notes two main characteristics of the Black Sea; firstly, that it was harvested later than in mainland Greece: "Those of Athens are only about thirty days, or not

[34] IG XII(2)3: Λεύκων καὶ οἱ παῖδες [αὐτοῦ Μυτ]|ιληναίοις ἔδοσαν τελ[εῖν πυρῶ]|ν ἑξηκοστὴν ἁπλῆν καὶ [ἐνενηκο]|[σ]τὴν ἀρχεῖον [μέ]χρι δέ[κα μυριά]|[δων - - -].

[35] LSJ s.v. ἀρχεῖον. I.

[36] LSJ s.v. ἀρχαῖον V.

[37] IG V(1) 1421.1 from Kyparissia in the Peloponnese for a *pentekoste*; Aristophanes *Wasps* 658; [Xenophon] *Constitution of the Athenians* (= Old Oligarch) 1.17 for the *hekatoste*; Andokides 2.11 for the *pentekoste* in Athens.

[38] Demosthenes 20.32.2: ἐκεῖνος πράττεται τοὺς παρ' αὐτοῦ σῖτον ἐξάγοντας τριακοστήν.

much more, earlier than those in the Hellespont."[39] The late harvest in the Black Sea is readily contrasted with the earlier harvest in Egypt, the other great exporter in the Mediterranean:

> As to the development (of the plant) there are also differences from place to place and from climate to climate. Thus, in some soils the crop is quicker, most obviously in Egypt. There barley is reaped in six months and wheat in seven, while in Greece barley is reaped in seven months in some places and in most areas in the eighth month, and wheat takes even longer.[40]

Consequently, by the time Pontic wheat reached the importing markets, demand would not be at its peak, since local, as well as other imported grain would have been on sale already for as long as two months.

The second feature of Black Sea grain noted by Theophrastos is its lightness:

> The lightest (of all wheats) is that of the Pontus, while the heaviest of those imported into Greece is the Sicilian. Yet even heavier is the Boiotian. That is proven because the athletes in Boiotia eat merely one and a half *choinikes*, while when they come to Athens they eat two and a half easily. The Lakonian wheat is also light.[41]

Pontic wheat was not only lighter than the products of other exporters, but also of local producers in Greece, Asia Minor and the Aegean. The lightness of Pontic grain meant that the consumer, given a choice, would prefer other grains, since he would get more calorific intake per measure, one of the drawbacks of measuring by volume not weight.

Reduction of dues provided a powerful incentive to traders, offsetting the natural disadvantages of Bosporan grain and making it competitive in the market. Even in years when Bosporan grain for reasons of price there or elsewhere would have normally been less competitive, the reduction of

---

[39] Theophrastos *Enquiry Into Plants* 8.2.10: προτερεῖ γὰρ ταῖς ὥραις τὰ Ἀθήνῃσι τῶν περὶ Ἑλλήσποντον ἡμέραις τριάκοντα μάλιστα ἢ οὐ πολλῷ πλείοσιν.

[40] Theophrastos *Enquiry Into Plants* 8.2.7: Διαφέρει δὲ καὶ πρὸς τὴν τελείωσιν χώρα τε χώρας καὶ ἀὴρ ἀέρος· ἐν ἐλάττοσι γὰρ ἔνιαι δοκοῦσιν ἐκφέρειν, ὥσπερ ἄλλαι τε καὶ μάλιστα ἐπιδήλως Αἴγυπτος· ἐκεῖ γὰρ κριθαὶ μὲν ἐν ἑξαμήνῳ πυροὶ δὲ ἐν τῷ ἑβδόμῳ θερίζονται· περὶ δὲ τὴν Ἑλλάδα κριθαὶ μὲν ἐν τῷ ἑβδόμῳ παρὰ δὲ τοῖς πλείστοις ὀγδόῳ, πυροὶ δὲ ἔτι προσεπιλαμβάνουσιν. Note that the earliest time, 6 months, refers to the *aparchai* not the bulk of harvest.

[41] Theophrastos *Enquiry Into Plants* 8.4.5: κουφότατος μὲν οὖν ὡς ἁπλῶς εἰπεῖν πυρὸς ὁ Ποντικός· βαρύτερος δὲ τῶν εἰς τὴν Ἑλλάδα παραγινομένων ὁ Σικελός· τούτου δ' ἔτι βαρύτερος ὁ Βοιωτός· σημεῖον δὲ λέγουσιν ὅτι οἱ μὲν ἀθληταὶ ἐν τῇ Βοιωτίᾳ τρί' ἡμιχοίνικα μόλις ἀναλίσκουσιν, Ἀθήναζε δὲ ὅταν ἔλθωσι πένθ' ἡμιχοίνικα ῥαδίως. κοῦφος δὲ καὶ ὁ ἐν τῇ Λακωνικῇ.

dues remained a powerful incentive for traders.[42] The loss of a few talents of dues would be equalised by the increase in total sales, and thus wealth entering the Kingdom, as well as by the increase in traffic resulting in increased dues from imports.[43] The further incentive of priority of lading provided to Athens targets the natural commercial disadvantage of the Black Sea, where early winter and storms threatened to trap ships north of the Dardanelles.[44] The weather was a particularly important factor when competing with Egypt, which had the advantage of continued shipping throughout the year.[45] Priority of lading was a small bonus compared to the *ateleia* but one presupposing a good understanding of traders and their priorities by the Spartokids.

Cyprus was probably an exporter of grain, at least in good years. The only evidence of Cypriot exports is Andokides' reference to grain from the island reaching Athens:

> I ask you to consider this, that the coming grain ships, which are even now entering the Piraeus, are 14, and the remainder will arrive from Cyprus not long afterwards.[46]

Although Cyprus probably served as an entrepôt for Egyptian grain, in the same capacity as Rhodes, Andokides does not provide any such implication. Thus, grain exports from Cyprus probably reached Athens and possibly other areas in the core of the Greek world.

The Phoenician cities were known as producers and exporters of fine flour (*semidalis*).[47] Whether such grain products were exported to the Greek world is a matter of conjecture but the Athenian honours to Strato of Sidon, which guarantee preferential treatment to Sidonian traders, imply a regular trade route between Athens and the Phoenician cities, where grain could have been a commodity.[48]

---

42 For the traders' tendency to roam as price and demand fluctuated, see Braund (2007: 56–57).

43 The dues for 400,000 *medimnoi* (Demosthenes 20.31–33) would be six talents and 3,600 *drachmai* at 3 *drachmai* per *medimnos* (half the subsidized price in Athens, according to IG II[2] 1672.287), while the total sales would reach 200 talents. Of course, the dues for the import of the original cargo would be paid as usual, the Spartokid reduction referring exclusively to the grain export.

44 Demosthenes 35.13.

45 Demosthenes 56.30.

46 Andokides 2.21: τάδε ⟨δὲ⟩ νυνὶ βούλομαι ὑμᾶς εἰδέναι, ὅτι αἱ μέλλουσαι νῆες ἤδη σιταγωγοὶ καταπλεῖν εἰς τὸν Πειραιᾶ εἰσιν ὑμῖν τέτταρες καὶ δέκα, αἱ δὲ λοιπαὶ τῶν ἐκ Κύπρου ἀναχθεισῶν ἥξουσιν ἁθρόαι οὐ πολὺ ὕστερον.

47 Athenaios 1.28a.

48 RO 21.29–36. Note that it is possible that the specific reference to traders in this

The largest exporter of grain in the southern Mediterranean in the classical period was Egypt. For the archaic period, the role of grain in the extensive commercial contacts between Greeks and Egyptians, particularly in the foundation of Naukratis, has been accepted as vital.[49] Naukratis was a unique Greek settlement, not only because it was situated within the sovereign territory of a powerful centralised state but also because its foundation and official status was the product of shared Greek and Egyptian initiative.[50] The extent of the grain trade from Egypt in the archaic period cannot be securely attested, since there is no direct evidence of the need for imports in any archaic polis. It is valid to assume that the grain exports from Egypt were not as large as in the classical period; the Egyptian imports were high-value, mainly silver. Although grain probably made up the bulk of cargoes from Egypt to the Greek world, the remainder probably depended upon luxury items and gold.[51]

The Persian conquest of Egypt in the late sixth century adversely affected the grain trade between Greeks and Egyptians, as is implied by the evidence on grain imports from Egypt, which are confined to the periods of Egyptian revolt from Persia. As Meiggs rightly noted, the allies' willingness to send the expedition to Egypt in the mid-fifth century owed much to the memory of the lucrative trade between the Greeks and an independent Egypt in the archaic period.[52] Psammetichos' gift of grain to Athens in the 440s clearly implies that part of the Athenian motive for the expedition was the prospect of grain imports.[53]

Unfortunately, information on the system of export in Egypt is confined to the beginning of the Hellenistic period, after Egypt had been conquered by Alexander III:

> So that you are not ignorant of the facts, (let me tell you that) these men were operatives and collaborators of Kleomenes, the governor of Egypt. That man, from the moment he became governor, has worked many evils against your city, and many as well to the other Greeks, by buying all the grain and fixing its price, this was done by him and by these men with him. Some of them sent the cargoes from Egypt, others sailed them around the *emporia* and others yet stayed here and distributed the dispatched cargoes.

---

case may be attributed to the existence of traders' guilds in the Phoenician cities, if they continued the same system as that of earlier periods [Kuhrt (1997: 407)].

[49] Austin & Vidal-Naquet (1977: 69).

[50] Herodotos 2.178.

[51] See page 73.

[52] Meiggs (1972: 95).

[53] Plutarch *Pericles* 37.4; Scholia Aristophanes *Wasps* 718.

> Moreover, the ones who stayed here would send letters with the existing prices to those who sailed, so that if grain were dear for you, then they would bring it here, but if its price fell, then they would sail to another *emporion*. This was the main reason, men of the jury, why the price of grain rose, because of such letters and collusions.[54]

The career of Kleomenes, governor of Egypt under Alexander, was rife with economic machinations according to the Aristotelian tradition, rivalling even those of Dionysios of Syracuse.[55] The scheme described in Demosthenes aimed at creating a monopoly of grain in Egypt and manipulating the importing markets. Firstly, Kleomenes bought up the Egyptian surplus and fixed the export price higher than previously. Secondly, he created a network of agents to transport and sell grain in the Greek world. Lastly, further agents were situated at the importing *emporia* from where they communicated to their associates the prevailing grain prices, thus guiding Egyptian grain only to *emporia* with the highest prices.

Kleomenes' grain scheme reveals that the majority of surpluses in Egypt at the time were in private hands, since Kleomenes had to buy them up (παλιγκαπηλεύων). Probably some surpluses were public, since Psammetichos could send grain to Athens in the mid-fifth century. Kleomenes' actions during the 320s famine apparently found no favour with Greek merchants and importing poleis. His scheme, although unique, reveals that the machinery necessary for a full interventionist policy existed, or could be constructed, in the Greek world. The reaction of the Athenians shows that the main obstacle to the widespread use of direct and pervasive intervention was the lack of willingness on the part of governments to take such direct and hostile action. The reason for the unwillingness of governments to adopt policies aiming at monopoly like that of Kleomenes is that they are not sustainable long-term for a commodity with a supply as diffused as that of grain. In other words, a

---

[54] Demosthenes 56.7–9: ἦσαν γάρ, ὦ ἄνδρες δικασταί, ἵνα μηδὲ τοῦτο ἀγνοῆτε, ὑπηρέται καὶ συνεργοὶ πάντες οὗτοι Κλεομένους τοῦ ἐν τῇ Αἰγύπτῳ ἄρξαντος, ὃς ἐξ οὗ τὴν ἀρχὴν παρέλαβεν οὐκ ὀλίγα κακὰ ἠργάσατο τὴν πόλιν τὴν ὑμετέραν, μᾶλλον δὲ καὶ τοὺς ἄλλους Ἕλληνας, παλιγκαπηλεύων καὶ συνιστὰς τὰς τιμὰς τοῦ σίτου καὶ αὐτὸς καὶ οὗτοι μετ' αὐτοῦ. οἱ μὲν γὰρ αὐτῶν ἀπέστελλον ἐκ τῆς Αἰγύπτου τὰ χρήματα, οἱ δ' ἐπέπλεον ταῖς ἐμπορίαις, οἱ δ' ἐνθάδε μένοντες διετίθεντο τὰ ἀποστελλόμενα· εἶτα πρὸς τὰς καθεστηκυίας τιμὰς ἔπεμπον γράμματα οἱ ἐπιδημοῦντες τοῖς ἀποδημοῦσιν, ἵνα ἐὰν μὲν παρ' ὑμῖν τίμιος ᾖ ὁ σῖτος, δεῦρο αὐτὸν κομίσωσιν, ἐὰν δ' εὐωνότερος γένηται, εἰς ἄλλο τι καταπλεύσωσιν ἐμπόριον. ὅθεν περ οὐχ ἥκιστα, ὦ ἄνδρες δικασταί, συνετιμήθη τὰ περὶ τὸν σῖτον ἐκ τῶν τοιούτων ἐπιστολῶν καὶ συνεργιῶν.

[55] Aristotle *Oeconomica* 1352a18–b25.

scheme such as Kleomenes' could work only under famine conditions, since under normal circumstances the importers would be receiving grain from a variety of exporters.

The last grain exporter of note in the southern Mediterranean was the Kyrenaike, which shared with Egypt the remarkable productivity of North Africa.[56] The only evidence of grain exports from Kyrene is the famous gift of grain to the Greek poleis during the 320s famine.[57] The gift, however, presupposes some previous contact between Kyrene and the recipients since, as Leukon's gift to Athens implies, such gifts were usually extended to existing trading partners.[58]

The main grain producers in the western Greek world were Sicily and Magna Graecia, which exported grain to mainland Greece as early as the Peloponnesian War.[59] Possibly Sicilian grain reached mainland Greece earlier, since the Peloponnese had need for imported grain as early as 480, and Sicily had closer relations with the Peloponnesians than those of the Black Sea.[60] In the fourth century, Sicilian grain reached Athens as well; while the grain related themes on the coinage of Sicilian and Italian cities suggest that the western Greeks considered grain one of their most important products.[61] The coast of the Adriatic was another grain exporter but evidence of imports to mainland Greece appears late in the classical period. Probably the pirates infesting the region had an adverse effect on the total volume of Adriatic grain reaching Greece and the Aegean.[62]

In mainland Greece, the only areas mentioned as exporters of grain are Thessaly and Epiros. Both certainly produced and exported grain, at least in the fourth century.[63] However, their inclusion in the Kyrenean

[56] Herodotos 4.158.

[57] RO 96.

[58] Demosthenes 20.31.

[59] Thucydides 3.86.4.

[60] Herodotos 7.147; Foxhall (1998: 302).

[61] Demosthenes 56.9. Coinages: BMC Leontini (all coins), BMC Segesta nos. 36–39, BMC Syracuse nos. 158–161, 208, 224–225, BMC Metapontum (all coins).

[62] RO 100.217–227. Even if the colony is a measure against a specific crisis of excessive piracy in the region [Garnsey (1988: 158)], the Athenian reaction of founding a colony rather than merely increasing the protection of convoys shows that at the time they considered the Adriatic an important supplier. Bresson (1993: 177) is right in that the foundation is part of the general tendency of the Athenians and others to ensure the safety of the main trade routes.

[63] Thessaly: Xenophon *Hellenika* 6.1.11, 5.4.56–57. Epiros: Lykourgos *Leokrates* 26.

gift of the 320s reveals that, unlike other exporters, the Thessalian and Epirote surpluses were very small.[64]

Except for minor exporters, such as Thessaly and Epiros, exporters of grain were situated in the periphery of the Greek world. The position of the majority of exporters as archaic settlements has given rise to a long and fierce debate on the role of grain as a trade commodity in settlement abroad, particularly the Black Sea, western and Egyptian settlements, while the archaic sources certainly suggest that inter-polis and possibly inter-regional trade in grain existed in the archaic period, the role of grain in archaic settlement abroad is impossible to estimate. Settlement abroad had a variety of motives specific to individual cases but in general terms, as long as a surplus of any commodity and the corresponding need for import existed, trade in that commodity is probable even if it were not part of the original decision of settlement.

For the classical period, the picture becomes clearer as the evidence of exports appears in the written and epigraphical sources. Of particular interest are the export policy of the Spartokids and the grain monopoly created by Kleomenes of Egypt in the fourth century. Both cases suggest considerable intervention in the export of grain by governments if under different circumstances and with different ultimate aims. The existence of grain export policies in two exporters raises the question of why the other exporters appear to have had no specific policies. The answer lies in the nature of our sources, as most information on the grain trade is provided by speeches delivered in Athenian courts. In the grain-related speeches, only Kleomenes' scheme survives because it is relevant to the specifics of the speaker's argument. The Bosporan policy is known through an unrelated speech and an inscription, which highlights that the nature of our sources creates a bias towards import policy. Probably other exporters had adopted policies relating to grain but, pending further epigraphic discoveries, these will remain unknown to us.

---

[64] Thessaly: RO 96.8, 25; Epiros: RO 96.10.

CHAPTER EIGHT

GRAIN FOR ATHENS

Athens was the largest polis in the Greek World in the classical period and imported grain from various suppliers, mainly Egypt, the Black Sea and Sicily. More information on the imports of Athens has survived than for all other poleis together. The greater part of the evidence regarding the Athenian grain supply concerns the fourth century, mainly because of the existence of multiple lawcourt speeches relating to the grain trade. The situation before the fourth century is rather obscure. For the archaic period, there is no evidence to suggest that Athens imported grain regularly; however, that does not mean that grain imports were unknown in the period.

In the fifth century, Athens imported a variety of foodstuffs from around the Mediterranean. Most of the surviving evidence refers to luxury products, including grain products, such as *semidalis* from Phoenicia.[1] There is no surviving mention of regular grain imports from abroad, although there is evidence of grain reaching Athens from Egypt and of Athenian interest in the grain production of Sicily in the planning for the Sicilian Expedition.[2] However both the estimated population of Athens in the fifth century (see below page 171) and the reliance of the Periklean strategy on vital imports suggest that Athens imported grain from abroad in significant quantities at least in the second half of the century.

For the fourth century, it is generally agreed that Athens imported grain in large quantities, although the exact volume of the trade is a matter of debate. Demosthenes in his speech *Against Leptines* says that Athens imported 400,000 *medimnoi* per annum from the Bosporus: "Now from there we import 400,000 *medimnoi*."[3] It should be noted at the outset that Demosthenes is arguing in favour of Leukon being a major benefactor, consequently, he would play down or omit anything

[1] Athenaios 1.28a.

[2] Sicily: Thucydides 6.90; Egypt: Plutarch *Perikles* 37.4. For the surviving evidence not providing the necessary basis for identifying any regular contact with a specific producer, particularly the Black Sea, see Braund (2007: 42–51).

[3] Demosthenes 20.32: αἱ τοίνυν παρ' ἐκείνου δεῦρ' ἀφικνούμεναι σίτου μυριάδες περὶ τετταράκοντ' εἰσί.

that detracts from this point.[4] These 400,000 *medimnoi* come, according to Demosthenes, from the Crimean Bosporus only, not from the whole of the Black Sea as some scholars have argued.[5] Athens may well have imported grain from other Black Sea regions as well.[6]

Garnsey has argued that Demosthenes refers to a bad year for local crops, and thus a year of extra imports.[7] However, Demosthenes specifically mentions a bad year later in the passage, and there mentions that Leukon responded to this crisis by sending a large gift of grain to Athens: "But in the year before last, when there was famine amongst all peoples, not only did he send you enough grain, but also ..."[8] Later Kyrene was to do something similar, not just to Athens but to a variety of poleis and kingdoms.[9] The implication is that the import of 400,000 *medimnoi* was common, not a crisis response.[10] Although, as Oliver argued, the exact figure may apply only to the year in question, as per the accounts of the *sitophylakes*, the relative quantity must have been within the usual import quantities from the Bosporus, since an excessive import, probably due to shortage in Athens, would have immediately defeated Demosthenes' argument as the audience would have been aware that the import for that year was exceptionally high.[11]

While it is possible that Demosthenes is lying or trying to mislead his audience, it seems unlikely that the Athenians were so ignorant of their

[4] For Demosthenes' relations with the Black Sea, see Braund (2007: 57–58).

[5] Sallares (1991: 331–332); Whitby (1998: 123); Harris (2003: 3); Braund (2007: 60).

[6] For example from Romania, which is an important producer of wheat in the region, although there is no evidence to my knowledge suggesting grain imports from Tomis or Kallatis. Note that Romania in spite of being almost 3 times smaller than the Ukraine produces on average almost half the wheat that Ukraine produces, according to the data from FAOSTAT (note particularly the relative yields):

Year	Romania production (Mt)	Romania area (Ha)	Romania yield (Hg/Ha)	Ukraine production (Mt)	Ukraine area (Have)	Ukraine yield (Hg/Ha)
2005	7,027,000	2,462,000	28,542	18,700,000	6,570,000	28,463
2004	7,812,428	2,291,650	34,091	17,520,200	5,533,700	31,661

[7] Garnsey (1988: 97).

[8] Demosthenes 20.33: ἀλλὰ πρωπέρυσιν σιτοδείας παρὰ πᾶσιν ἀνθρώποις γενομένης οὐ μόνον ὑμῖν ἱκανὸν σῖτον ἀπέστειλεν, ἀλλὰ ...

[9] RO 96.

[10] Whitby (1998: 124–125) rightly notes that the amount of grain stopped by Philip II of Macedon in the Hellespont supports such large amounts being imported from the Black Sea. See also Moreno (2007a: 69–70).

[11] Oliver (2007: 21).

grain supply that such an exaggeration of figures would pass unnoticed. The grain supply was debated in the *ekklesia* once every prytany, so presumably the majority of the Athenians had at some point participated in these discussions or heard about them.[12] Demosthenes' reference to the accounts of the *sitophylakes* may seem to suggest that the scale of grain imports was not common knowledge but is more likely to have been a rhetorical ploy to bolster his argument by showing that his expertise in the matter went beyond that of the general public.[13] In all probability, Demosthenes accurately reports the amount of grain imported in a normal year, or at least not an extraordinary one.

Demosthenes' claim that the Black Sea provided half of the total grain imports of Athens is a different matter. Gomme thought that Demosthenes was simply lying and that the amount of non-Pontic grain was larger.[14] Since Demosthenes was not debating the import of grain but trying to present Leukon as a major benefactor, it certainly suited his argument to exaggerate the proportion of grain imported from the Bosporus in relation that imported from other areas; note that he appeals only to 'likelihood' (εἰκότως) on this point, not the records of the *sitophylakes*.[15]

In order to arrive at a credible estimate of import volumes, we can try to assess the extent of local production, population size and dietary requirements. Scholars attempting this have reached widely different conclusions, since each variable has a wide range of possible values, which produces exponential differences in the combined result of the calculation. Uncertainty is unavoidable; all that is possible is to caution that any individual estimate may be far off the mark and to estimate both minimum and maximum values.

The size of the Athenian population has been debated amongst scholars for more than 150 years, and no two estimates are the same.[16] Hansen, using as the basis for his estimation political participation requirements, has offered a very convincing argument that puts the number of Athenian

[12] [Aristotle] *Constitution of the Athenians* 43.4.

[13] Demosthenes as a politician was expected to have intimate knowledge of the grain supply, the matter being one of the necessities of political education: Aristotle *Rhetoric* 1360a12; Demosthenes 18.301, Xenophon *Memorabilia* 3.6.13. For the importance of the *sitophylakes* in fourth-century Athens, see Bresson (2000: 133–135); Oliver (2007: 20–21).

[14] Gomme (1933: 32).

[15] For the necessity of considering carefully which statements in the orators are provided with supporting evidence, see Harris (2003: 8).

[16] Beloch (1923); Gomme (1933); Ruschenbusch (1984); Sallares (1991: 79); Hansen (1985).

citizens at more than 30,000 in the fourth century.[17] That would imply a total fourth-century citizen population, including women and children, of 120–150,000. This roughly corresponds to Sallares' top estimate of the maximum number that Attika could feed.[18] Hansen's figures are an estimate but his method is based on well-established figures for political participation and on comprehensive demographic evidence, and as such is more reliable than other estimates based on incomplete figures for military manpower.[19] The number of slaves and metics cannot be securely estimated; Hansen estimates the number of metics as between 33,000 and 46,000 and that of slaves between 66,000 and 93,000.[20]

The variables used are the following:

(a) 150,000: a minimum estimate based on what Attika could feed from its own resources; it is adopted by Osborne as the figure for the total population.[21]
(b) 200,000: Hansen's minimum population of Athens in the fourth century; Garnsey's maximum number of people which Attika could feed from its own resources.[22]
(c) 250,000: this is Hansen's 'probable' estimate for the fourth century.[23]
(d) 300,000: used here as a conservative maximum, Hansen's 'probable' estimate for 431.[24]

---

[17] Hansen (1985: 68). The latest work on Athenian population [Hansen (2006: 19–60)] upholds these figures and presents new arguments in favour of them.

[18] Sallares (1991: 79) at highest yield.

[19] Figures from military manpower are the least helpful since they are by nature incomplete, since they represent only those of hoplite or higher income, thus requiring further guesswork as to the number of non-hoplites. Although Athenian hoplite numbers must have included at least some thetes [van Wees (2001)], the rest of the non-hoplite population cannot be estimated securely, even if we try to combine army and navy figures, since any estimation based on navy numbers is easily doubted because of the use of slaves and hired rowers, as for example in the case of Aigina [Hansen (2006: 12)].

[20] Hansen (1988: 11–12) against Whitehead (1977: 97–98) who estimated 20–25,000 and Osborne (1987: 46), who estimated 20,000 for metics and slaves.

[21] Sallares (1991: 60); Osborne (1987: 99); (1988: 137).

[22] Hansen (1988: 12); Garnsey (1988: 90). Note that Garnsey is leaving a very small margin in his calculations for the type of evidence we have; a mere 50,000 between minimum and maximum.

[23] Hansen (1988: 12).

[24] Hansen (1988: 26). A calculated maximum for the fifth century with 60,000 male citizens and maximum numbers for metics and slaves is 409,000 people. I do not use this figure as a ceiling for the fourth century, although it would be statistically better, in order to keep the figures towards the lower end of the spectrum.

The dietary requirements of this population are another disputed point, with ethnographic studies of various Mediterranean diets being compared with the ancient testimonies. The best treatment of ancient dietary requirements of grain is that of Foxhall and Forbes.[25] Dietary studies in mid-20th century CE Crete found that the projected average cereal requirement of the consumers was 167 kg/year/person or four *medimnoi* of wheat (4.8 of barley[26]); however since that diet included potatoes, in its ancient equivalent grain or pulses would have been more prominent.[27] Foxhall and Forbes, using both the ancient testimonies on grain requirements and modern data, have proposed an average requirement of 212 kg/year/person or 5.3 *medimnoi* of wheat (6.3 of barley).[28] The sources, on the other hand, offer a convenience rule of one *choinix* of wheat per person per day, thus, 7.3 *medimnoi*/year/person (292 kg or 8.7 *medimnoi* of barley, 345 kg).[29] On the extreme end of the spectrum, studies of grain requirements in post-World War II rural Anatolia suggest an average actual consumption of 300 kg/year/person of wheat or 7.5 *medimnoi*.[30] Note that consumption estimates are not helpful in calculating grain imports since, as was shown by ethnographic studies, the amounts stored by the subsistence farmer and bought by the average purchaser are governed by convenience rules not exact calculations of consumption.[31]

The variables used are the following:[32]

(a) 4.8 *medimnoi*: a minimum consumption figure, based on ethnographic studies from modern Greece.[33]
(b) 6.3 *medimnoi*: the figure proposed by Foxhall and Forbes.
(c) 8.7 *medimnoi*: a maximum figure based on 1 *choinix*/ person/day.

Moving from consumption to production, there are two variables to consider: the amount of land cultivated with grain in Attika and the yield of the crop. The amount of cultivable land in Attika has been variously calculated from 17% to 50%, while calculations of land under cereal cultivation have also fluctuated depending on whether biennial fallow

[25] Foxhall & Forbes (1982).
[26] I am using a wheat: barley ratio of 1: 1.2 according to Foxhall & Forbes (1982).
[27] Allbaugh (1953: 106–108).
[28] Foxhall & Forbes (1982: 55, 73).
[29] Foxhall & Forbes (1982: 60).
[30] Hillman (1973: 229).
[31] Allbaugh (1953: 107).
[32] Note that the barley variables are used since the production will also be calculated in barley.
[33] Allbaugh (1953: 98).

is considered normal or extraordinary practice.[34] Jarde calculated the cultivable area as 27 % and the land under cereal cultivation as 10 %, assuming a general practice of biennial fallow.[35] Sallares argued in favour of 30 % cultivable and 15 % under grain cultivation, following Garnsey in his rejection of biennial fallow.[36] Moreno in the most recent discussion of the subject has rejected Garnsey's crop rotation.[37] Moreno makes a good case based on the available evidence but like the other proponents of biennial fallow cannot escape the problem that our sources are from and aimed at an upper class with enough available land to practice biennial fallow. For the average farmer, crop rotation remains the best solution, since even with high probability of crop-failure in more arid areas as Moreno argues, legumes and pulses provide some crop, while fallow provides none.

Osborne and Garnsey have argued in favour of 35–40 % cultivable land with as much as 25 % under grain cultivation.[38] The amount of land cultivated with cereals fluctuated in the ancient world. Pollen counts have shown that in Metapontion multi-crop agriculture was replaced in the mid-fourth century by monoculture of cereals, which could suggest a wide-spread change in patterns of land use in the Greek World.[39]

The variables used for the cultivated area are the following.

(a) 10 % = 240 km^2 = 24,000 ha: a minimum figure for grain cultivation; Jarde's estimation.
(b) 15 % = 360 km^2 = 36,000 ha: Sallares' estimation based on modern data from Attika; Garnsey's minimum estimation.[40]
(c) 20 % = 480 km^2 = 48,000 ha: a maximum figure based on 40 % cultivable land.

Crop yields are the other variable to consider for the total grain production of Attika. The only yields found in the sources are those of Columella, relating to production in Italy, which are 425–530 kg/ha for

[34] I am using Garnsey's 2400 km^2 for the total land of Attika. 17 % in French (1964: 176); 50 % in Osborne (1985: 225). Foxhall (1992: 156) has argued in favour of 50 % of Attika being dedicated to agricultural and pastoral pursuits, which is a considerably better estimate for total land use.

[35] Jarde (1925: 49–52, 142–143).

[36] Sallares (1991: 309–313); Garnsey (1988: 93–94) argued rightly against the wide-spread use of biennial fallow in favour of the modern Greek rotation of suitable crops.

[37] Moreno (2007b: 17–24).

[38] Osborne (1987: 46); Garnsey (1988: 92, 102); Whitby (1998: 104).

[39] Carter (2005: 26).

[40] Sallares (1991: 79); Garnsey (1985: 72).

barley.[41] Estimations of cereal yields in modern scholarship use comparative data from modern Greece, which are considerably higher than those of Columella.[42] The use of modern yields has been rightly suspected since Ruschenbusch noted not only the substantial increase in yields after the introduction of fertilisers in the 1930s but also the evolution of grains over a period of two and a half millennia.[43] Unfortunately, the only figure for ancient Athenian production, the *aparchai* of 329/328, cannot be effectively used as a control, since there is no information on whether 329/328 was a good, average or bad year and since it is debatable whether the *aparchai* represent honest estimates of total production.[44] In addition to the above, an amount of seed stored for next year must be deducted from the figures. I have assumed that the seed kept was 1/8th of total production, halving Columella's figure since light sowing is better in poor soils.[45]

The variables used for the crop yields are the following:

(a) 13.2 *medimnoi*/ha (425 kg/ha): a minimum estimate; Columella's lower barley yield
(b) 16.5 *medimnoi*/ha (530 kg/ha): Columella's higher barley yield
(c) 19.6 *medimnoi*/ha (630 kg/ha): pre-fertiliser average barley yield in 20th century Attika and Boiotia.[46]
(d) 24.7 *medimnoi*/ha (793 kg/ha): maximum barley yield of 20th century Attika.[47]

To arrive to an estimate of possible import quantities the above variables will be combined in Tables 9 and 10.

41 van Wees (2001: 49) on the use of Columella's figures. Note that the recently revealed lightness of north Aegean yields [Stroud (1998: 55)] makes Columella's figures more believable.

42 Gallant (1991: 77).

43 Ruschenbusch (1988: 141–153).

44 Garnsey (1988: 99–100, 1998: 185–187) and Sallares (1991: 394) have argued in favour of 329/328 being a bad year but the issue cannot be resolved without further evidence.

45 On Columella's sowing rate see van Wees (2001: 49). 1/8 is considerably lower than seed ratios in pre-fertiliser modern Greece: Jameson (1978: 129); Sanders (1984: 262). Light sowing being better for poor soils: Theophrastos *Enquiry Into Plants* 8.6.2; Gallant (1991: 46–49).

46 van Wees (2001: 49) based on Ruschenbusch (1988).

47 Gallant (1991: 77).

Table 9. Barley consumption of Attika according to population and diet variables

Medimnoi/people	4.8	6.3	8.7
150000	720000	945000	1305000
200000	960000	1260000	1740000
250000	1200000	1575000	2175000
300000	1440000	1890000	2610000

Table 10. Barley production of Attika according to land cultivation and yield variables, seed subtracted

Medimnoi/hectares	13.2	16.5	19.6	24.7
24000	277200	346500	411600	518700
36000	415800	519750	617400	778050
48000	554400	693000	823200	1037400

Table 11. Combined variables for Attika using minima and maxima of diet and land cultivation estimations

Production/ consumption	277200	346500	411600	518700	554400	693000	823200	1037400
720000	−442800	−373500	−308400	−201300	−165600	−27000	*103200*	*317400*
960000	−682800	−613500	−548400	−441300	−405600	−267000	−136800	*77400*
1200000	−922800	−853500	−788400	−681300	−645600	−507000	−376800	−162600
1305000	−1027800	−958500	−893400	−786300	−750600	−612000	−481800	−267600
1440000	−1162800	−1093500	−1028400	−921300	−885600	−747000	−616800	−402600
1740000	−1462800	−1393500	−1328400	−1221300	−1185600	−1047000	−916800	−702600
2175000	−1897800	−1828500	−1763400	−1656300	−1620600	−1482000	−1351800	−1137600
2610000	−2332800	−2263500	−2198400	−2091300	−2055600	−1917000	−1786800	−1572600

Table 11 is the presentation of the combinations for minima and maxima and presents the range of possible estimations of efficiency/deficiency. The majority of combinations result in negative numbers indicating insufficiency of local production and, consequently, the need for grain imports. The method of variables cannot produce a specific figure beyond an average of projected need. The average import needed would be 936,000 *medimnoi* of barley or, since the imported grain was mainly wheat, 780,000 *medimnoi*. Fluctuations would be normal from year to year and it is possible that in some years the production of Attika would be enough to guarantee minimum imports but the balance of probability implies that in most years Athens would have to import large quantities.

Of interest is the fact that Demosthenes' 400,000 *medimnoi* fits quite well with the average of imports, which may be simply happenstance but even so provides us with a control, since the figures are not widely disparate. An average import of 800,000 *medimnoi* of wheat would mean that between 100,000 and 200,000 people were fed with foreign grain. The combination of variables and the average highlight the probability of regular large-scale grain imports by Athens and a reason for the apparent anxiety of the Athenians concerning their grain supply.

Athens was clearly deficient in local grain and had considerable need for imports, which was expressed in its legislation on the grain trade. There are seven laws relating to the grain trade from Athens. Isager and Hansen have provided the most concise treatment of five of them and the sources in which they appear:

> Finally the grain trade was regulated through legislation. Among the laws on grain the following have been transmitted to us: (1) it is forbidden to export any crop except olives (Plutarch *Solon* 24); (2) it is forbidden to purchase more than 50 *phormoi* of grain at a time (Lysias 22.6); (3) it is a capital offence for persons resident in Athens to ship grain to harbours other than the Piraeus (Demosthenes 34.37, 35.50; Lykourgos 1.27); (4) any grain ship touching in at the harbour of the Piraeus is required to unload at least 2/3 of her cargo and may re-export a maximum of 1/3 (*AthPol* 51 4); (5) it is forbidden for persons resident in Athens to extend a maritime loan unless the ship under contract conveys grain to the Piraeus (Demosthenes 35.51, 56.6, 56.11).[48]

The overwhelming concern of these laws with the import of grain has been the basis of the argument that governmental intervention in trade was exclusively concerned with the import of grain. Combined with the unique position of Athens as the greatest importer of grain in the Greek world, this has given rise to the idea that governmental intervention in trade was limited to the grain imports of extraordinary importers. A close examination of these laws will show that the issue is not as straightforward as it seems at first glance.

The legislation in Athens has been criticized by Moses Finley, as not interventionist enough.[49] As Austin says, the state refrained from creating its own trading mechanisms, preferring instead to manipulate existing ones.[50] This is what Athens can be seen doing in the above laws; using the existing forms of trade and networks and suiting them to her own

---

[48] Isager & Hansen (1975: 28–29).
[49] Finley (1985: 199–200).
[50] Austin (1985: 210).

purposes. In other words, Athens used the networks of trade and the Piraeus' supreme position as an entrepôt to make native and metic merchants bound to transport grain to her.

Law I refers to Solonian legislation and is reported exclusively by Plutarch:

> Of the produce, he allowed only oil to be available to foreigners, while he stopped the export of all others. And he ordered the archon to pronounce curses against those exporting, under pain of paying 100 *drachmai* to the public fund. And this law is found in the first *axon*. Thus, it is not difficult to believe those who claim that in the past even the export of figs was banned, and that the revelation of those who exported them came to be called *sykophantein*.[51]

The authenticity of the law was proved by Michael Gagarin, who based his argument on the mention of the *axon* to which it belonged and on the way it expresses legal procedure.[52] Garnsey believes that this law was:

> ... an ad hoc measure issued in the context of a food crisis and that the shortage had been aggravated by unscrupulous landowners who were sending their grain abroad in search of higher prices.[53]

Garnsey follows the general scholarly idea that this law is grain-related and any explanation, as crisis-measure or just as a general law on exports, seeks to explain it in terms of grain.[54]

However, since the Athenian population in the 590s is impossible to plausibly reconstruct, postulating considerable grain needs can be based only on the later insufficiency of local production in the classical period. It is highly unlikely that Athens in the early sixth century had already exceeded the population of c. 150,000 that could be sustained from local production.[55] Further, if this law targeted grain, then it is surprising that

[51] Plutarch *Solon* 24: Τῶν δὲ γινομένων διάθεσιν πρὸς ξένους ἐλαίου μόνον ἔδωκεν, ἄλλα δ' ἐξάγειν ἐκώλυσε, καὶ κατὰ τῶν ἐξαγόντων ἀρὰς τὸν ἄρχοντα ποιεῖσθαι προσέταξεν, ἢ τίνειν αὐτὸν ἑκατὸν δραχμὰς εἰς τὸ δημόσιον· καὶ πρῶτος ἄξων ἐστὶν ὁ τοῦτον περιέχων τὸν νόμον. οὐκ ἂν οὖν τις ἡγήσαιτο παντελῶς ἀπιθάνους τοὺς λέγοντας, ὅτι καὶ σύκων ἐξαγωγὴ τὸ παλαιὸν ἀπείρητο, καὶ τὸ φαίνειν ἐνδεικνύμενον τοὺς ἐξάγοντας κληθῆναι συκοφαντεῖν. Note that the numbering of the laws in the following discussions is not that of Isager & Hansen (1975).

[52] Gagarin (2006: 267). Stanley (1999: 230) also argued in favour of the authenticity of the law based on the type of penalties imposed. For the general problems with the authenticity of Solonian legislation, see Harris (2006: 290).

[53] Garnsey (1988: 75).

[54] For example see Ehrenberg (1973: 73); Isager & Hansen (1975); Jeffery (1976: 92); Jameson (1983: 11); Austin & Vidal-Naquet (1977: 69). Garnsey (1988: 107) is right in pointing out that the law does not imply an absolute shortage of cereals in Athens.

[55] Garnsey (1988: 109), against Rhodes (1981: 95–96).

grain is not mentioned, as in the export ban of Selymbria.[56] Unless Attika in the 590s is envisioned as deficient not only in grain but also in all other agricultural products, then a general export ban is not only senseless but also inhibitive of growth.

Instead of postulating a cunningly disguised grain law, the Solonian legislation should be considered as it appears, as an oil law. Solon's 'economic' measures, as reported by Plutarch, appear singularly oriented towards manufacture, which can be explained by Solon's perspective on the economy as an occasional trader.[57] Oil in the Greek world was a multifaceted commodity that had a variety of uses, many of them not food related. Good oil could be a major export item as a luxury food product and also as perfume. Of all Athenian agricultural products, oil was the most diverse and the one with the potential to become a major luxury export. The ban on exports of all agricultural products should be seen not as a negative legislation but as an encouragement towards greater production of oil and the creation of an oil-related industry in Athens.[58] As Stanley showed, the adoption of Corinthian pottery types in this period signifies a turn of Athenian industry towards perfume and bathing oils, which can be related to Solonian legislation.[59] Neither can it be considered as an effort by the Athenians to control who consumed the produce of the land, as suggested by Sallares, since in that case a simple general ban would suffice without any mention of oil.[60] Moreover, an export ban on agricultural products was bound to encourage manufacture.

Such a ban with the exceptional push for olive cultivation is extremely interventionist. That such was possible and acceptable in the early sixth century is very interesting since such amounts of intervention would barely seem credible in fourth-century Athens. On the other hand, such extreme intervention is a sign of immaturity.[61] The fact that such an export ban was abandoned (I would assume quickly) is expected, since to concentrate on only one product closes all avenues for growth and evolution. The main reason why Stanley and Garnsey have argued in favour of the law targeting grain is its perceived place in Solon's socio-economic reforms to alleviate the debt and poverty crisis in Athens by

---

[56] Aristotle *Oeconomica* 2.2.17.

[57] Plutarch *Solon* 22.1, 24.2. On Solon's perspective on the economy, see van Raalte (2005: 81–82).

[58] Murray (1980: 46).

[59] Stanley (1999: 249).

[60] Sallares (1991: 304–309); Schaps (2004: 169).

[61] For the opposite view see Descat (1993: 155).

providing cheap grain and other agricultural products to the populace.[62] Possibly the law had this effect to some extent, at least on a short-term basis, but equally its encouragement of oil production and related industries would also have helped the poor escape the vicious circle of land-related debt by opening other avenues of income in trade and manufacture.

Law II fixes the profit margin of retail grain dealers: "they can increase the price only by an obol".[63] The speaker does not specify the measure the law applies to but later in the same speech, he applies it to the *medimnos* ("Yet they increased the price by a drachma several times in one day, as if they had been buying together one *medimnos* at a time"), where the lack of an explanation to the audience suggests that application to the *medimnos* was common.[64] The intervention of the government in this instance is clearly in the interest of the consumer, while at the same time allowing for changes in the market, which would be reflected in the price paid by the *sitopolai* to the *emporoi*.

Law III is mentioned only in Lysias *Against the Graindealers* (22) and its provisions and meaning have long been debated. The speaker quotes the law twice in the speech with a slightly different wording each time, which has created contention on the exact meaning of the words *sumpriasthai/sunoneisthai* and *phormos*:

> Answer me then, do you not confess that you bought together more than 50 *phormoi* of grain, which the law orders you not to do? ... For our part, we bring before you the law, which bans anyone in the city to buy together more than 50 *phormoi* of grain.[65]

Traditionally, the law has been interpreted as forbidding any individual to buy more than 50 *phormoi* of grain at once, thus opening a loophole in Athenian legislation, which would allow bulk-buying cartels.[66] Figueira, however, conclusively showed that the meaning of *sumpriasthai/sunoneisthai* encompasses the creation of a cartel, thus showing that the law forbade any effort to corner the market.[67]

---

[62] Stanley (1999: 232); Garnsey (1988: 75–76).

[63] Lysias 22.8: δεῖν γὰρ αὐτοὺς ὀβολῷ μόνον πωλεῖν τιμιώτερον.

[64] Lysias 22.12: νῦν δ' ἐνίοτε τῆς αὐτῆς ἡμέρας ἐπώλουν δραχμῇ τιμιώτερον, ὥσπερ κατὰ μέδιμνον συνωνούμενοι.

[65] Lysias 22.5–6: Ἀπόκριναι δή μοι, εἰ ὁμολογεῖς πλείω σῖτον συμπρίασθαι πεντήκοντα φορμῶν, ὧν ὁ νόμος ἐξεῖναι κελεύει ... ἡμεῖς γὰρ ὑμῖν παρεσχόμεθα τὸν νόμον, ὃς ἀπαγορεύει μηδένα τῶν ἐν τῇ πόλει πλείω σῖτον πεντήκοντα φορμῶν συνωνεῖσθαι.

[66] McDowell (1978: 157); Seager (1966: 173–176).

[67] Figueira (1986: 153–155).

The *phormos*, whose size is unknown, is presented as a measure familiar to the audience. The *phormos* is often equated in modern scholarship with the *medimnos*, based on a comparison of prices in the Attic *stelai* and Aristophanes' *Assemblywomen*.[68] In the Attic *stelai*, the *phormos* costs six *drachmai* while in the *Assemblywomen* the *medimnos* costs three *drachmai*, which is explained by a drop in prices after the end of the Peloponnesian War.[69] However, the equation is not as simple, since in 414 Athens was still the mistress of the Aegean, while in 392 control of the Hellespont and the Aegean sea lanes had been lost; thus, a drop in prices would be surprising. A second problem with the equation is that the *stelai* record an auction price, which could have been adversely affected by the quality of the wheat and the religious undertones of the Hermokopidai affair, while Aristophanes refers to the contemporary market price. Using these prices, the *phormos* must have been at least twice as large as the *medimnos*. Further arguments against the equation are the clear distinction between the *medimnos* and the *phormos* in the speech and the impossibility of cornering the market successfully with such small quantities, as Figueira showed conclusively.[70] In other texts, *phormos* is usually interpreted as a basket, wickerwork or mat, while in the two texts specifically referring to grain the meaning is not clear.[71] In Hesiod, *phormos* is used as a transport vessel large enough to hold a bad year's crop, while in Aristophanes it is a measure of wheat in an otherwise unintelligible joke that the Scholia fail to explain.[72]

Since the *phormos* and the *medimnos* were not equal, the question of the size of the *phormos* becomes paramount. Although other texts may not be helpful, I believe that Lysias 22 holds the answer to our query. The speaker accuses the *sitopolai* of increasing the price dramatically during a day's trade, referring to Law II above:

---

[68] Pritchett & Pippin (1956: 194–195); Johnston (1997: 81); Figueira (1986: 156); Seager (1966: 175); Whitby (1998: 120).

[69] IG I[3] 421.139; Aristophanes *Assemblywomen* 547–548 (using the price of a *hekteus* to calculate the *medimnos*).

[70] Lysias 22.12: "Yet they increased the price by a drachma several times in one day, as if they had been buying together one *medimnos* at a time"; Figueira (1986: 157–158).

[71] Mat: Aristophanes *Wealth* 542; Clothes: Herodotos 3.98.4, Pausanias 10.29.8; Basket (siege): Aeneias Tacticus 32.2, Herodotos 8.71.2. Unhelpfulness of the other sources: Figueira (1986: 155–159).

[72] Hesiod *Works and Days* 473–482, note that Hesiod knows the *medimnos* as a measure: Hesiod F278 (Strabo 14.1.27). Aristophanes *Women at the Thesmophoria* 811–813, by unintelligible I mean that there is no clear meaning and a variety of jokes can be inferred from it.

> This is the most potent evidence of their lies: if they were doing this for your benefit, then they should be selling at the same price for many days until what they had bought together was sold out. Yet they increased the price by a *drachma* sometimes on the same day, as if they had been buying together one *medimnos* at a time.[73]

Scholars who equate the *phormos* with the *medimnos* have suggested that the *sitopolai* broke the one-obol law as well; however, the speaker never accuses them on that account, nor does his argument run along those lines.[74] The speaker's argument is that since the *sitopolai* bought a large quantity of grain, they should have kept the same price until all the grain had been sold; on the contrary, they acted as if they had not bought a large quantity but very small quantities, thus increasing the price constantly. The emphasis is not on the profit ("they increased the price by a *drachma*") but on the frequency it was exacted ("sometimes on the same day") and, consequently, on the implications on the quantity of grain bought ("as if they had been buying together one *medimnos* at a time"). If the speaker refers to profit per *phormos*, then the only way for the price of the *phormos* to increase by a *drachma*, if one is buying by the *medimnos*, is for the two quantities, the *drachma* and *phormos* as against the obol and the *medimnos*, to be in direct correlation; in other words, for the *phormos* to be six *medimnoi*, as one *drachma* is six obols. If the *phormos* equalled six *medimnoi*, the law limited acquisition to 300 *medimnoi*, or 12 tonnes of wheat; a quantity not large enough to corner the market but enough to keep one *sitopoles* busy for a few days.

Law IV covers specifically the import of grain and restricts the commercial ventures open to Athenian citizens and metics: "And the laws have prescribed the severest penalties, if a man living in Athens transports grain to any other *emporion* than the Athenian."[75] The meaning

[73] Lysias 22.12: ἐρῶ καὶ περιφανέστατον τεκμήριον ὅτι ψεύδονται· ἐχρῆν γὰρ αὐτούς, εἴπερ ὑμῶν ἕνεκα ἔπραττον ταῦτα, φαίνεσθαι τῆς αὐτῆς τιμῆς πολλὰς ἡμέρας πωλοῦντας, ἕως ὁ συνεωνημένος αὐτοὺς ἐπέλιπε· νῦν δ' ἐνίοτε τῆς αὐτῆς ἡμέρας ἐπώλουν δραχμῇ τιμιώτερον, ὥσπερ κατὰ μέδιμνον συνωνούμενοι.

[74] Explanation in Lamb (1943: 498, note *a*).

[75] Demosthenes 34.37: τῶν δὲ νόμων τὰ ἔσχατα ἐπιτίμια προτεθηκότων, εἴ τις οἰκῶν Ἀθήνησιν ἄλλοσέ ποι σιτηγήσειεν ἢ εἰς τὸ Ἀττικὸν ἐμπόριον. Also referred to in Lykourgos *Leokrates* 27: καίτοι ὦ ἄνδρες καὶ περὶ τούτων οἱ ὑμέτεροι νόμοι τὰς ἐσχάτας τιμωρίας ὁρίζουσιν, ἐάν τις Ἀθηναίων ἄλλοσέ ποι σιτηγήσῃ ἢ ὡς ὑμᾶς (And yet, men, on these matters your laws prescribe the greatest penalties, if an Athenian transports grain anywhere but to you). Both passages refer to the same law, note the consistent use of ἄλλοσέ ποι.

and the intent of the law is clear: no Athenian or metic is to transport grain to any other *emporion* but the Athenian; Athens regulated closely the activities of merchants with formal ties to her. Jameson argued that this law is a commercial version of *katagein*, 'bringing grain ships to harbour,' and he is right to highlight the shared element of compulsion in both our law and *katagein*.[76] However, it is compulsion at opposite sides of the spectrum, since one targets exclusively local and the other exclusively foreign *emporoi*. No polis could successfully regulate the activities of foreign *emporoi* for any length of time, thus the occasional need for *katagein*, an extremely hostile form of intervention. Athenian legislation, on the other hand, stayed firmly within the prerogative of the polis in regulating its own citizens and metics.

Law V has been interpreted by Isager and Hansen, followed by Garnsey and others, as regulating the re-export of grain from Athens: "to compel the traders to take two thirds of the grain that reaches the grain *emporion* to the *astu*."[77] An alternative interpretation was proposed by Gauthier, who argued that the remaining one-third was destined for sale in the Piraeus and absolutely refused the possibility of re-export.[78]

The law itself mentions neither particulars on re-export nor obligates unloading of fixed quantities, prescribing merely that of the grain which traders did decide to sell in the *sitikon emporion* in the Piraeus, two-thirds should be transported to be sold in the *astu*, i.e. in the city of Athens as opposed to the port of the Piraeus.[79] The state considered the Piraeus and the *astu* separate domains, as shown by the placement of the dole.[80] This law is, therefore, only a regulation of domestic trade. At the same time, there is nothing to suggest that re-export was illegal or restricted in Athens. Foreign traders, who were not covered by Law IV, could stop at Athens and investigate the market conditions, as is shown by the freedom enjoyed by those stopping at the Thieves' Harbour to visit the *deigma* and decide whether to unload any of their cargo at leisure: "And the ship was anchored there for more than 25 days, and these people wandered around your *deigma*."[81] In addition, there must have

[76] Jameson (1983: 11).

[77] [Aristotle] *Constitution of the Athenians* 51.4. Garnsey (1988: 140); Garland (1987: 89); Oliver (2007: 25–27).

[78] Gauthier (1981), followed by Bresson (2000: 189–190).

[79] Whitby (1998: 121, n. 35).

[80] Demosthenes 34.37.

[81] Demosthenes 35.28: καὶ τὸ μὲν πλοῖον ὥρμει ἐνταῦθα πλείους ἢ πέντε καὶ εἴκοσιν ἡμέρας, οὗτοι δὲ περιεπάτουν ἐν τῷ δείγματι τῷ ἡμετέρῳ.

been official re-export of grain when public surpluses were available, as Whitby argued for the case of Kallisthenes' sale of grain sent by Leukon of the Bosporus.[82]

Law VI is quoted in Demosthenes 35.51 and has attracted two interpretations by modern scholars:

> These, men of the jury, are not the only evils I have suffered from this Lakritos. If he had his way not only would I be robbed of my money but also I would be in the greatest danger, if only the contract I made with these men had not come to my rescue witnessing that I gave the money for a voyage to the Pontos and back to Athens. You know, men of the jury, that the law is harsh, if an Athenian transports grain anywhere but Athens, or if he lends money for another *emporion* than the Athenian and what the penalties for such crimes are and how large and severe they are. Better read aloud the law, so that they know it exactly. *Law.* It is not allowed for any of the Athenians, the metics living in Athens, or their dependants, to lend money on a ship, which will not bring grain to Athens and the other things written about each of these. If someone persists in lending, then let any information and an account of the money be submitted to the *epimeletai*, as with the grain and the ship. And let no trial be admitted about the money, if someone lends money for another trip than to Athens, nor any magistrate to admit such a case.[83]

Isager and Hansen, followed by Jameson, Harris and most recently by Morley, excise the phrase "and the other things written about each of these" (καὶ τἄλλα τὰ γεγραμμένα περὶ ἑκάστου αὐτῶν) considering the law dedicated to grain imports.[84] Garnsey and others include the

---

[82] Demosthenes 20.33; Whitby (1998: 125).

[83] Demosthenes 35.50–51: Οὐ τοίνυν ταῦτα μόνον, ὦ ἄνδρες δικασταί, δεινὰ ἐγὼ πάσχω ὑπὸ Λακρίτου τουτουί, ἀλλὰ καὶ χωρὶς τοῦ ἀποστερεῖσθαι τὰ χρήματα καὶ εἰς τοὺς ἐσχάτους ἂν κινδύνους ἀφικόμην τὸ τούτου μέρος, εἰ μή μοι ἡ συγγραφὴ ἐβοήθει ἡ πρὸς τούτους, καὶ ἐμαρτύρει ὅτι εἰς τὸν Πόντον ἔδωκα τὰ χρήματα καὶ πάλιν Ἀθήναζε. ἴστε γάρ, ὦ ἄνδρες δικασταί, τὸν νόμον ὡς χαλεπός ἐστιν, ἐάν τις Ἀθηναίων ἄλλοσέ ποι σιτηγήσῃ ἢ Ἀθήναζε, ἢ χρήματα δανείσῃ εἰς ἄλλο τι ἐμπόριον ἢ τὸ Ἀθηναίων, οἷαι ζημίαι περὶ τούτων εἰσίν, ὡς μεγάλαι καὶ δειναί. μᾶλλον δὲ αὐτὸν ἀνάγνωθι αὐτοῖς τὸν νόμον, ἵν' ἀκριβέστερον μάθωσιν. {ΝΟΜΟΣ.} Ἀργύριον δὲ μὴ ἐξεῖναι ἐκδοῦναι Ἀθηναίων καὶ τῶν μετοίκων τῶν Ἀθήνησι μετοικούντων μηδενί, μηδὲ ὧν οὗτοι κύριοί εἰσιν, εἰς ναῦν ἥτις ἂν μὴ μέλλῃ ἄξειν σῖτον Ἀθήναζε, ⟨καὶ τἄλλα τὰ γεγραμμένα περὶ ἑκάστου αὐτῶν⟩. ἐὰν δέ τις ἐκδῷ παρὰ ταῦτα, εἶναι τὴν φάσιν καὶ τὴν ἀπογραφὴν τοῦ ἀργυρίου πρὸς τοὺς ἐπιμελητάς, καθάπερ τῆς νεὼς καὶ τοῦ σίτου εἴρηται, κατὰ ταὐτά. καὶ δίκη αὐτῷ μὴ ἔστω περὶ τοῦ ἀργυρίου, ὃ ἂν ἐκδῷ ἄλλοσέ ποι ἢ Ἀθήναζε, μηδὲ ἀρχὴ εἰσαγέτω περὶ τούτου μηδεμία.

[84] Jameson (1983: 11): "Residents of Athens only made maritime loans for voyages bringing grain to Athens"; Harris (2003: 7): "There was a law that made it illegal for any Athenian or metic to engage in transporting grain to any port besides Athens or to make a loan for such a trading voyage"; Morley (2007: 71): "Post Imperial Athens sought to

phrase considering the law dedicated to imports in general, with possibly a special consideration for grain.[85] Both interpretations have problems and an analysis of this law is necessary to arrive at a solution.

The law is quoted not in the text of the speech but in the citation. The vast majority of surviving speeches do not include the citations, while this speech includes all citations, agreements and depositions, which immediately creates the suspicion of a later, possibly Hellenistic, insertion. The reference in the speech itself appears to be to two distinct laws, one relating to the transport of grain and the other to loans. The first law, "if an Athenian transports grain anywhere but Athens", has the same meaning and phrasing as Law IV discussed above. The second law refers specifically to lending with no reference either to grain or to ships, which are mentioned only in the citation. The second is mentioned in another speech, where it is specifically contrasted to Law IV:

> And as soon as we found out what happened, we were surprised and immediately went to this instigator of the whole scheme. And we questioned him angrily as to how, when we had stipulated in the contract that the ship should not sail anywhere but to Athens, and we had lent the money according to that agreement, he dared to leave us open to the suspicions of any willing accusers, that we had been part of the transport of the grain to Rhodos. We complained that he and his partner, in spite of the contract, had not brought the ship to your *emporion*.[86]

Isager and Hansen's interpretation has the further problem of limiting investment to imports of grain only. Such limitation of investment is contradicted in the speech itself in which the defendant, Lakritos, is said to have promised to bring to Athens Koan wine and salted fish,

control the activities of grain traders by restricting their freedom of choice, insisting that anyone who borrowed money in Athens to buy grain had to bring their cargo back to Athens."

[85] Garnsey (1988: 139–140): "Any voyage made by a transport vessel that was financed by a maritime loan negotiated by an Athenian, resident alien or one in his power (typically a slave) had to issue in the import of necessities, particularly grain, to Athens." Austin & Vidal-Naquet (1977: 116) argued that the law applied specifically to ships carrying grain; Bonner (1923: 198); Whitby (1998: 121).

[86] Demosthenes 56.11: καὶ ἡμεῖς ἐπειδὴ τάχιστα ἐπυθόμεθα τὸ γεγονός, ἐκπεπληγμένοι τῷ πράγματι προσῆμεν τούτῳ τῷ ἀρχιτέκτονι τῆς ὅλης ἐπιβουλῆς, ἀγανακτοῦντες, οἷον εἰκός, καὶ ἐγκαλοῦντες ὅτι διαρρήδην ἡμῶν διορισαμένων ἐν ταῖς συνθήκαις ὅπως ἡ ναῦς μηδαμόσε καταπλεύσεται ἀλλ' ἢ εἰς Ἀθήνας, καὶ ἐπὶ ταύταις ταῖς ὁμολογίαις δανεισάντων τὸ ἀργύριον, ἡμᾶς μὲν ἐν ὑποψίᾳ καταλέλοιπεν τοῖς βουλομένοις αἰτιᾶσθαι καὶ λέγειν, ὡς ἄρα καὶ ἡμεῖς κεκοινωνήκαμεν τῆς σιτηγίας τῆς εἰς τὴν Ῥόδον, αὐτοὶ δὲ οὐδὲν μᾶλλον τὴν ναῦν ἥκουσι κατακομίζοντες εἰς τὸ ὑμέτερον ἐμπόριον εἰς ὃ συνεγράψαντο.

which he would not have claimed if it was clearly illegal, or if he had, his accuser would have noted it as illegal. Instead, the accuser argues merely on the implausibility of the claim because Koan wine is not usually imported to Athens via the Pontus. Moreover, a law barring investment in other commodities would clearly disregard the considerable needs of Athens for other imports, most importantly metals, since it would place such imports outside the investment sphere of Athenians and generally impede all imports but those of grain.

The second interpretation avoids both of the above problems since import is not legally confined to grain. However, it creates a law concerned exclusively with imports and criminalising export loans. The exclusive regulation of imports is based partly on the text of the law as cited and partly on the phrase "if he lends money for another *emporion* than the Athenian" (ἢ χρήματα δανείσῃ εἰς ἄλλο τι ἐμπόριον ἢ τὸ Ἀθηναίων). The problem with using the citation has already been mentioned. The phrase "εἰς ἄλλο τι ἐμπόριον" has been interpreted as making a loan for a trading voyage 'to the Athenian *emporion*,' thus exclusively denoting imports; similar to the same construction in Demosthenes 34.37:

> αἱ ταῦτ' ἔπραξεν, ὦ ἄνδρες δικασταί, οἰκῶν μὲν Ἀθήνησιν, οὔσης δ' αὐτῷ γυναικὸς ἐνθάδε καὶ παίδων, τῶν δὲ νόμων τὰ ἔσχατα ἐπιτίμια προτεθηκότων, εἴ τις οἰκῶν Ἀθήνησιν ἄλλοσέ ποι σιτηγήσειεν ἢ εἰς τὸ Ἀττικὸν ἐμπόριον.
>
> And he did these things, men of the jury, while he was resident at Athens, having here a wife and children, although the laws prescribe the severest penalties if someone living in Athens transports grain to any other *emporion* than the Attic.

However, the εἰς construction can also be interpreted as in Demosthenes 34.42:

> ὑπὲρ δὲ τοῦ τὴν δίκην εἰσαγώγιμον εἶναι ὁ νόμος αὐτὸς διαμαρτύρεται, κελεύων τὰς δίκας εἶναι τὰς ἐμπορικὰς τῶν συμβολαίων τῶν Ἀθήνησιν καὶ εἰς τὸ Ἀθηναίων ἐμπόριον, καὶ οὐ μόνον τῶν Ἀθήνησιν, ἀλλὰ καὶ ὅσα ἂν γένηται ἕνεκα τοῦ πλοῦ τοῦ Ἀθήναζε.
>
> The law itself declares which are the admissible cases, specifying that the *emporikai dikai* are to be on the contracts made at Athens and for the Athenian *emporion*, and not only those at Athens but also those made on account of a voyage to Athens.

The meaning of 'εἰς τὸ Ἀθηναίων ἐμπόριον' in this case is clearly 'for the Athenian *emporion*' in the sense of 'concerning the Athenian *emporion*,' since otherwise there would be no need for the further explanation that the law covers voyages to the Athenian *emporion* (ἀλλὰ καὶ ὅσα ἂν γένηται ἕνεκα τοῦ πλοῦ τοῦ Ἀθήναζε).[87] This interpretation of the εἰς construction is preferable since there is clear evidence that one-way loans for outward journeys were made in Athens with no accusation of illegality. There are three instances in the speeches where outward only loans are made, of which one is certainly by an Athenian resident and as such would fall squarely under the provisions of the law.[88] Possibly the law allowed lending on outward voyages only if there was an existing loan for the double voyage. However, such a provision would confuse loans on the ship with loans on the cargo, where it could be stipulated in the agreement that the return voyage was to be conducted on a specific ship but it was not illegal to take another ship back even if otherwise stipulated in the agreement; if it were illegal the speaker in Demosthenes 34.39 would have made the point.

I suggest that the law cited in Demosthenes 35.51 is the creation of a Hellenistic scholar who tried to combine the two laws mentioned in the preceding paragraph into one. The second law is neither a grain nor an import law but a general finance law covering both imports and exports and restricting the activities of Athenian lenders to trading ventures which touch on Athens' *emporion*, as opposed to trading ventures taking place entirely abroad, a wise precaution in a polis where many necessary commodities had to be imported. The general nature of the law connects it more closely with the law governing the admissibility of the *emporikai dikai* than with grain or other commodity-oriented legislation. Like the *emporikai dikai* admissibility clause, the lending law accepts both imports and exports and firmly puts the locus of Athenian trade in the *emporion* itself. This law is direct intervention into the basis of commercial exploits, capital, and provides clear boundaries on commercial investment in Athens. Loans provided a large part of the capital needs of trade in the Greek world and here Athens is seen harnessing the financial power of its populace, citizen and metic, into a tight circle centred on the Piraeus. The inclusion of all types of loans as long as they were connected with the Athenian *emporion* in the legislation shows that the government not only did not hesitate to intervene as pervasively as possible but also had the sophistication to recognise and harness the hidden power of finance. Money, unlike cargoes of grain or landed property, is

[87] This meaning of εἰς is covered in LSJ s.v. εἰς IV.2.

[88] Demosthenes 34.8 (two loans) and 35.22. Lampis is certainly a resident (Demosthenes 34.36) and Antipatros of Kition could also be one if we connect Agora 17.521 (tombstone of an Antipatros of Kition) with our Antipatros.

invisible and unidentifiable wealth, which can generate more invisible wealth, making the investor difficult to identify securely in an era when appearance of wealth was the only sign of it. Investors could remain invisible to the government and the public, yet without them commercial ventures would be less numerous and successful. The Athenian government not only observed and recognised this hidden power of the investor but also harnessed it.

Law VII is a recently discovered law that regulates the collection of two taxes, a *dodekate* and a *pentekoste*, in the Athenian cleruchies in the north Aegean.[89] The law, as Stroud convincingly argued, changes the nature of these taxes from cash to kind.[90] The purpose of the reorganisation is stated clearly in the beginning of the law "in order that there may be grain for the people in the public domain" and like the Eleusinian *aparchai* it aims to make available some surpluses to the public at a price, presumably subsidised, decided by the assembly.[91] The exact nature of both the *dodekate* and the *pentekoste tou sitou* has been debated, since these taxes are otherwise unknown. The *dodekate* has been argued to be either a tax on production or a tax on transit shipping through the islands.[92] Moreno most recently argued in favour of the *dodekate* being a rent-like tax on the *pentakosiomedimnoi* of the islands.[93] Although Moreno's argument is attractive, if nothing else in its Solonic parallel and its implication of a direct tax on income at least for the upper classes, direct taxation levied on citizens is virtually unknown in democratic Athens and one would rightly expect that the *pentakosiomedimnoi* on the islands, like their counterparts in Athens itself would be taxed indirectly through liturgies.

Harris rightly notes that a tax on production is unknown in the Greek world; however, since our knowledge of the tax system in Athens, or any polis, is very limited and the status of the cleruchies was special, the possibility must not be discounted. The text of the law itself suggests strongly that Stroud's interpretation is correct, since the specification

---

[89] SEG 36.146. For the *editio princeps* and detailed discussion of the law and its provisions, see Stroud (1998).

[90] Stroud (1998: 79).

[91] SEG 36.146.56: ὅπως ἄν τῶι δήμωι σῖ[το]ς ἦι ἐν τῶι κοινῶι. Translation from Stroud (1998: 9). IG II^2 1672.287 (Eleusinian *aparchai*): πραθέντων ἓξ δραχμῶν τοῦ μεδίμνου ἑκάστου ὡς ὁ δῆμος ἔταξεν (sold at a price of six *drachmai* per *medimnos* according to the orders of the *demos*).

[92] Production: Stroud (1998: 32). Transit: Harris (1999: 271–272).

[93] Moreno (2007b: 105–107).

of the *meridai* according to the barley and wheat measures suggests known quantities.[94] In other words, transit shipping cannot be securely quantified, since it depends on the number and type of cargoes transiting, thus the law's specification of *meridai* would be impractical. Further, if the tax were a transit tax on grain, then one would expect the law to specify that in the same manner as for the *pentekoste* by adding *sito*; yet the law merely specifies the locale of the *dodekate* without any mention of its type. Additionally, Harris' argument that the Athenians would impose such a transit tax on grain in the islands in order to encourage the import of grain there does not conform with the information provided by IG II^2 1672, where it is clear that the islands had considerable grain production of their own.[95] Concerning the *pentekoste* mentioned in the law, Stroud is certainly justified to suggest that it was an import-export tax, similar to that levied in Athens, and since the islands exported grain, it was in reality a tax on the grain export from the cleruchies, presumably to Athens itself.[96] That the *pentekoste* was levied in the islands is testified by the provision of the law itself, where the transport of the grain to the Piraeus at the tax-farmer's own risk and the subsequent transport to the Aiakeion are specified.[97]

The law proves the existence of taxes in kind and that considerable amounts of grain were exported from the cleruchies, since there is a dedicated *pentekoste* of grain, which was such as to allow for collection in kind. The conversion of both taxes from cash to kind reflects partly the anxiety of the Athenians after the near disaster of 376 and partly their realisation that part of Athenian territory was an exporter of grain and as such could provide public grain surpluses.[98] The *dodekate* both shows

---

[94] SEG 36.146.8–10: "each portion will consist of 500 measures (*medimnoi*), 100 of wheat and 400 of barley" [translation from Stroud (1998: 9)].

[95] Harris (1999: 272): "The difference between the rates charged by the two taxes also makes good sense from an economic point of view: it encouraged merchants to sell their grain in the islands for the local market by charging a lower rate for imports (2 %) and discourages them from re-exporting their cargoes to other ports by charging a higher rate for transhipment (8⅓ %)." Harris' argument would certainly work for the Piraeus, where probably a similar transit tax was levied.

[96] Stroud (1998: 38). One has to note here that Braund's (2007: 41) argument that the lack of mention of Black Sea imports in the law can be used as evidence that the islands were not a vital part of the trade-route between Byzantion and Athens ignores the fact that the law is concerned only with the production and export from the islands themselves, not with transit trade.

[97] SEG 36.146.10–15. For the opposite view, that the *pentekoste* is the import tax in Athens itself, see Harris (1999: 271).

[98] 376: Xenophon *Hellenika* 5.4.60–61; Stroud (1998: 119–120).

that the polis could intervene in the production process through taxation and it also provides a framework for the way the exporters acquired public surpluses from a commodity produced privately. Additionally, the inclusion of a specific clause enabling the assembly to fix the price of grain shows that price fixing was not outside either the prerogative or the willingness of the government.[99] The fixing of price in this case, as Harris rightly notes, was designed to keep prices low in the peak pre-harvest period.[100] Similar price fixing of grain can be observed both in the *aparchai* sale of 329/328 and in the actions of the *sitonai* during crisis.[101] Price fixing was not confined merely to crisis measures or public grain but there was legislation fixing the profit margin of grain in retail trade to one obol profit per *medimnos* (Law II). The one obol law did not establish a permanent price of grain in the Athenian market but it did fix profit margins so that prices would not climb artificially. The intervention of the government in prices was pronounced not only in public surpluses but in ordinary grain on retail.

Athenian intervention was not limited to legislation but covered other areas of the grain trade. The Athenians offered incentives to both private foreign traders to bring grain to Athens and to exporters to prefer exporting to Athens. The honours given to the Spartokids and to their envoys testify to the Athenian incentives to exporters.[102] On the other hand, there are various examples of honours to private traders, mainly from the last quarter of the century.[103] Many of these honours coincide with the crisis of the 320s, which shows that the government was particularly cognizant of the effect a widespread crisis could have on the normal flows of trade.[104] Normally, the size of Athenian grain requirements would be an adequate lure for many traders, but in a widespread crisis less distant ports would offer equally high profits. Thus, Athens provided incentives in those times for traders to import grain. The *dikai emporikai* were also within this sphere of incentives, since, unlike other poleis, Athens offered equality of access and judgement to foreign traders as well as a quick procedure allowing them to be ready to sail with the start of the season.

---

[99] On price-fixing in Athens, see Bresson (2000: 182–206).

[100] Harris (2003: 7).

[101] Demosthenes 20.33; IG II^2 1672.287.

[102] IG II^2 212. On the economic benefits of *ateleia* for the Spartokids, see Oliver (2007: 30–37).

[103] IG II^2 360, 400, 407–409, 416, 479.

[104] Tracy (1995: 30–35).

Athens was the largest polis in the Greek world and the greatest importer of grain. The combination of population, consumption and production variables showed clearly that Athens regularly imported large quantities of grain. The Athenian government intervened considerably in imports mainly through legislation. Several laws regulated the import and dissemination of grain in Athens, targeting mainly Athenian citizens and metics. The intervention of the government was pervasive in most aspects of import, including prices and profit margins. Possibly the most interesting of the laws discussed is Law VI, which was shown to be a general trade/finance law, not one exclusively related to the grain trade. The law targeted not a specific commodity but the backbone of Athenian trade, capital, and restricted lending to trading ventures relating to the Athenian *emporion*. Both the breadth and aim of the law shows the rationality and sophistication of Athenian intervention in trade generally; it was not confined to one specific commodity or dictated by the pressure of necessity.

CHAPTER NINE

GRAIN BEYOND ATHENS

For the other known or inferred importers, information is scarce, particularly when compared to Athens. For the majority, little has survived concerning their grain needs beyond a reference that they imported. All known importers are situated in Greece, the Aegean and Asia Minor, which reveals a definite periphery-core relationship in the grain trade. To the extent of the available evidence, the same model of examination used for Athens is used for the other importers as well.

The Peloponnese grew grain of its own, mainly in Lakonia, Messenia and Elis, and there was probably some production in the Argolis. It also imported grain from the Black Sea, Sicily and Egypt.[1] Exact population figures for any polis or area in the Greek World are beyond our present knowledge but merely the number of poleis in the Peloponnese, higher than in any other area in the Greek World with the possible exception of Boiotia, must mean that population density was relatively high and agricultural land a scarcer resource.[2]

Corinth was probably the greatest importer in the Peloponnese and it is valid to assume that a large part of the imports mentioned as going to the Peloponnese were destined for it.[3] Corinth has not attracted as much scholarly attention as Athens, and thus the available variables of its population and grain production are limited. The most recent calculation of Corinthian population is 70,000 including slaves, based upon its known military strength.[4] The cultivation of cereals is estimated from a 30% of total cultivable land as 10%, 12.5% and 15%, making 9,000, 11,250 and 13,500 hectares respectively. Since it is not known whether the Corinthians cultivated more wheat or barley, the safest option of barley is preferred, using Columella's lower (13.2 *medimnoi*/ha) and upper (16 *medimnoi*/ha) barley yields, as well as the barley yield of modern

---

[1] Herodotos 7.147.2; Thucydides 3.86.4; Diodoros 14.79.

[2] Note that here poleis is used generically not politically; the number is 121 according to Hansen & Nielsen (2004).

[3] Herodotos 7.147.2; Thucydides 3.86.4; Lykourgos *Leokrates* 26.

[4] Salmon (1984: 168).

Table 12. Barley consumption of Corinth according to population and diet variables

Medimnoi/ people	4.6	6.3	8.7
70000	322000	441000	609000

Table 13. Barley production of Corinth according to land cultivation and yield variables, seed subtracted

Medimnoi/ hectares	13.2	16	22.1
9000	103950	126000	174037.5
11250	129937.5	157500	217546.8
13500	155925	189000	261056.2

Table 14. Combined variables for Corinth

Consumption/ production	322000	441000	609000
103950	−218050	−337050	−505050
126000	−196000	−315000	−483000
174037	−147963	−266963	−434963
129937	−192063	−311063	−479063
157500	−164500	−283500	−451500
217546	−104454	−223454	−391454
155925	−166075	−285075	−453075
189000	−133000	−252000	−420000
261056	−60944	−179944	−347944

Corinthia (22.1 *medimnoi*/ha).[5] Of the 27 estimations made using these data (see Tables 12–14), all are negative, showing that Corinth suffered from a regular local insufficiency. The average need for import was 289,005 *medimnoi* of barley or 240,837 of wheat.

Megara is not among the poleis mentioned as importers in the sources but it had a reputation, similar to that of Aigina, as a polis dependent upon trade for its prosperity. The most recent estimation calculated the population of Megara at 40,000 people including slaves, based on its known military strength.[6] The cultivable area of Megara has been

[5] On the modern yield, see Gallant (1991: 77).

[6] Legon (1981: 168–169).

Table 15. Barley consumption of Megara according to population and diet variables

Medimnoi/ people	4.8	6.3	8.7
40000	192000	252000	348000

Table 16. Barley production of Megara according to land cultivation and yield variables, seed subtracted

Medimnoi/ hectares	13.2	16
1000	11550	14000
1250	14437.5	17500
1500	17325	21000

Table 17. Combined variables for Megara

Consumption/ production	192000	252000	348000
11550	−180450	−240450	−336450
14437	−177563	−237563	−333563
17325	−174675	−234675	−330675
14000	−178000	−238000	−334000
17500	−174500	−234500	−330500
21000	−171000	−231000	−327000

estimated as a mere 21 % of the total 470 km^2 due to the raggedness of the terrain and the poverty of the soil; the estimations used are 10 %, 12.5 % and 15 %, making 1000, 1250 and 1500 hectares respectively.[7] As with Corinth, the cereal preference of the Megarians has not survived, thus barley estimations are preferred, while due to the lack of modern yield data from the Megarid, only the barley yields of Columella are used. Of the 18 estimations (see Tables 15–17) made using the above data, all are negative, thus showing that Megara suffered from a regular insufficiency of local production. The average need for import was 248,031 *medimnoi* of barley or 206,642 of wheat.

[7] Legon (1981: 23).

Table 18. Barley consumption of Aigina according to population and diet variables

Medimnoi/ people	4.8	6.3	8.7
13000	62400	81900	113100
20000	96000	126000	174000
35000	168000	220500	304500

Table 19. Barley production of Aigina according to Land cultivation and yield variables, seed subtracted

Medimnoi/ hectares	13.2	16
1288	14876.4	18032
1546	17856.3	21644
1718	19842.9	24052

Table 20. Combined variables for Aigina

Consumption/ production	62400	81900	113100	96000	126000	174000	168000	220500	304500
14876	−47524	−67024	−98224	−81124	−111124	−159124	−153124	−205624	−289624
17856	−44544	−64044	−95244	−78144	−108144	−156144	−150144	−202644	−286644
19842	−42558	−62058	−93258	−76158	−106158	−154158	−148158	−200658	−284658
18032	−44368	−63868	−95068	−77968	−107968	−155968	−149968	−202468	−286468
21644	−40756	−60256	−91456	−74356	−104356	−152356	−146356	−198856	−282856
24052	−38348	−57848	−89048	−71948	−101948	−149948	−143948	−196448	−280448

Aigina was in its own way as exceptional a polis as Athens and one of the earliest known importers.[8] Aigina certainly imported grain in the early classical period, and possibly in the archaic, but after its conquest by Athens its population and importance decreased, thus probably in the fourth century its imports were small, if any. The population of Aigina has been variously estimated by modern scholars, based mainly on its naval strength, ranging from a minimum of 13,000 to a maximum of 45,000 people including slaves. The population estimations used here are 13,000, Kalcyk's estimation, 20,000, which has been recently suggested by Hansen, and 35,000, Figueira's minimum estimation.[9] The cultivation of

[8] Herodotos 7.147.2.

[9] Kalcyk (1996: 320); Hansen (2006: 12); Figueira (1981: 38).

cereals is estimated from Figueira's 40 % total cultivable land and, allowing for intense cultivation due to the small size of the island, the variables are 15 %, 18 % and 20 %, making 1288, 1546 and 1718 hectares respectively.[10] Since the cereal preference of the Aiginetans has not survived, barley estimations are preferred, and due to the lack of modern yield data, the barley yields of Columella are used. Of the 54 estimations (see Tables 18–20) made using the above data, all are negative, thus showing that Aigina suffered from a regular insufficiency of local production. The average need for imports was 130,216 *medimnoi* of barley or 108,513 of wheat.

The Aegean islands were probably the most vulnerable area in the Greek world in terms of grain shortages, owing to the relatively small size of the majority of the islands and the poverty of the soil, especially in the Cyclades. Andros is the second largest island in the Cyclades but its cultivable land, like that of the other islands in the region, is not particularly suited to grain crops. The Andrians probably imported grain regularly in the second half of the fourth century and offered incentives to importing traders.[11] A late fourth-century decree from Arkesine on Amorgos honouring importers of grain suggests that this Cycladic island also imported grain, at least in the second half of the fourth century.[12]

The north Aegean islands were larger and more fertile than the Cyclades but also supported larger populations, as testified by their large navies. Mytilene, and possibly the whole of Lesbos, imported throughout the classical period, as testified by Thucydides during the Peloponnesian War and the Bosporan tax reduction discussed earlier.[13] Probably the Mytilenians imported in excess of 100,000 *medimnoi* annually, if the *archeion* in the Bosporan reduction refers to *medimnoi*.

Samos was also an importer of grain, on the evidence of honours it provided to importing traders.[14] Samian relations with Naukratis in Egypt suggest that the main supplier for the island was in the south Mediterranean, but supplies could easily have come from the Black Sea, as those to neighbouring Mytilene.[15] The population of Samos has been estimated at 50,000 including slaves, based on the island's military strength.[16] The cultivation of cereals is estimated from 30 % cultivable land on the island,

---

[10] Figueira (1981: 23).
[11] IG XII(5).714.
[12] IG XII(7).11.
[13] Thucydides 3.2.2; IG XII(2)3, see page 161.
[14] McCabe *Samos* 36.
[15] Herodotos 2.178.3.
[16] Shipley (1987: 15).

in addition to the whole of the *peraia*, which measured about 50 km^2; the variables used are 10 %, 12.5 % and 15 %, making 9,680, 10,850 and 12,020 hectares respectively.[17] Since the cereal preference of the Samians has not survived, barley estimations are preferred, and due to the lack of modern yield data, the barley yields of Columella are used. Of the 18 estimations (see Tables 21–23) made using the above data, all are negative, thus showing that Samos suffered from a regular insufficiency of local production. The average need for imports was 191,391 *medimnoi* of barley or 159,492 of wheat.

Table 21. Barley consumption of Samos according to population and diet variables

Medimnoi/ people	4.8	6.3	8.7
50000	240000	315000	435000

Table 22. Barley production of Samos according to land cultivation and yield variables, seed subtracted

Medimnoi/ hectares	13.2	16
9680	111804	135520
10850	125317.5	151900
12020	138831	168280

Table 23. Combined variables for Samos

Consumption/ production	240000	315000	435000
111804	−128196	−203196	−323196
125317	−114683	−189683	−309683
138831	−101169	−176169	−296169
135520	−104480	−179480	−299480
151900	−88100	−163100	−283100
168280	−71720	−146720	−266720

Teos was a small polis in Asia Minor but particularly important in this discussion, since its legislation on grain imports has survived. The

[17] For the importance of the *peraia* of Samos in times of shortage and the cultivation regime there in the Hellenistic period see Osborne (1987: 97).

inscription dates the imports to the middle of the fifth century and it is doubtful that a polis that imported in the fifth would not continue importing in the fourth; the regular suppliers are unknown. The Black Sea is the better candidate geographically, but Teos' place as one of the founders of Naukratis in the archaic period makes Egypt the most likely candidate because of past relations.[18]

Teos legislated on its grain supply:

> Whoever in the land of Teos stops grain from being imported by sea or land, by trick or device, or when imported forces the price up, let him perish, him and his family.[19]

The law of Teos is part of the well-known imprecations decree, which has attracted much attention among scholars. The inscription is dated to the first half of the fifth century.[20] The exact content of the inscription is debatable, as is its genre. The obvious religious aspect, or the seemingly religious one depending on viewpoint, has labelled the provisions either as 'curses' or as 'imprecations.' It is certain that the inscription is not a law, or at least it is not an obviously recognisable law as is found in other poleis, most usually Athens.[21] The 'curses' theory has been attacked in recent years in favour of the 'imprecations' one. Either way there seems no reason to suppose that the inscription is a decree or law. However, without an inscription of different format from the same period, we cannot argue that this is not the format that legislation took in Teos at the time. Indeed the only roughly contemporary inscription is again one in the same format, and this seems more of a law or decree of some sort rather than a religious observance. The second inscription refers mainly to political offences, revolution amongst them, but the inclusion of trial procedures in both Teos and Abdera creates more of a legal feel than the first inscription.[22] The last clause of the imprecations inscriptions, relating to defacing of the inscription itself, can find a parallel in other Greek laws where part of the law is that no one should propose a law or decree changing the law as it has been voted.[23]

---

[18] Herodotos 2.178.2.

[19] ML 30.6–12: ὅστις : ἐς γῆν : τὴν Τηΐην : κ|ωλύοι : σῖτον : ἐσάγεσθαι : | ἢ τέχνηι : ἢ μηχανῆι : ἢ κατ|ὰ θάλασσαν : ἢ κατ' ἤπειρο|ν : ἢ ἐσαχθέντα : ἀνωθεοίη, : | ἀπόλλυσθαι : καὶ αὐτ|ὸν : καὶ γένος : τὸ κένο.

[20] Meiggs & Lewis (1988: 66).

[21] Thomas (1996: 28); Jeffery (1976: 226).

[22] Loukopoulou & Parissaki (2004: 307–308).

[23] Athens: Demosthenes 23.62; Halikarnassos: Nomima I.19.32–41; Argos: Nomima I. 110.5–9; Lokris: ML 13; Harris (2006: 313).

Concerning the context, as opposed to format, the inscription contains a variety of clauses, only one of them relating to commerce. The others regard poisons, tyranny and military attack on Tean territory respectively. The first two, the one concerning poisons and the one on grain, seem less serious than the last two, which concern military and political matters. Bravo argued against Meiggs & Lewis that the imprecations are the result of a particular grain crisis and specifically a time when the large landowners in Teos hoarded grain and exported it outside of the city in spite of the crisis at home.[24] Jameson agreed with Bravo, considering a drought at the reign of Artaxerxes as the pivotal event that produced the Tean law.[25] Garnsey & Morris have followed Bravo's suggestion and combined it with Plutarch's Solonian law in Athens mentioned above (page 178), to create the image of a specific crisis being the basis of the imprecation.[26]

The use of Solon's law is a double-edged knife. The employment of curses in sixth-century Athens shows nothing more than that the legal formula is archaic and not unique to Teos. Teos continued to have problems with its grain supply at the end of the fourth century, after its *synoikismos* with Lebedos.[27] In the fourth century, Teos dealt with the problem very differently than the solution suggested by the imprecations. Its *synoikismos* and the changing face of the Greek world gave it the power to make demands of the king and to make specific provisions to its merchants. The parallels between the development in Athens and Teos are obvious. Both poleis had grown in the time between the two legislations and become more powerful, which is reflected in their measures. Instead of a cyclical argument, which bases one explanation on another, an evolutionary process of legislation is better.

There are two problems with these arguments. Firstly, if one accepts that the grain imprecation is the result of a particular incident rather than a general and recurring problem, then the same should be held for the other imprecations as well. Thus, an *aisymnetes* should be assumed who desired to become a tyrant and tried to extend his term of office, and in order to create an artificial crisis for the polis, used poison against the people as a whole and against individuals. In addition, he impeded grain

[24] Bravo (1983: 23) against Meiggs & Lewis (1988: 65).

[25] Jameson (1983: 12) citing Strabo 1.3.4.14. The problem with dating from Strabo is obvious and it would mean dating the inscription slightly later than commonly accepted.

[26] Garnsey & Morris (1989: 103).

[27] McCabe *Teos* 59; note that I am accepting the restoration of grain rather than produce in this inscription, see Bresson (1993).

imports possibly with the help of some device, and eventually betrayed some defensive forts in Tean territory to enemies, either other Greeks or barbarians, not to mention at some point managing to recruit the help of bandits with his plans. This man in the end failed in his machinations, but his attempt convinced the Teans that imprecations against such an incident were necessary and had to be proclaimed at three different festivals.

This may not be impossible, after all the history of humankind has preserved circumstances and actions that verge on the ridiculous. However, given the obvious disparity of the offences it may be more acceptable to move in another direction. Instead of some complicated affair that commended this resolution to the Teans, or even worse a set of different affairs, it is better to suppose a more mundane set of circumstances where a variety of imprecations are written on one stone. The poison clause may seem frivolous but if it is acceptable that the Athenians had some rather complicated laws on homicide, as for example homicide by inanimate object, why should the Teans not ensure the illegality and punishment of a rather easier method of disposing of one's enemies? The last two clauses are defence measures for the constitution and the country itself, both quite mundane.

As to the grain clause, the variety of possibilities covered by it points towards general legislation; "By sea or land, by trick or device," as the inscription says, and while poetic (even in translation), the generality of it shows the range of available possibilities which could threaten the grain supply of the city. Although it is possible that this is a reaction to a specific crisis, the generality of the legislation seems more in tune with a recurring problem than with the unique set of circumstances.[28] In this, I agree with Garnsey's interpretation: "such conduct must have been both common and deleterious and judged deleterious to the community."[29] In the Aristotelian treatise *Oeconomica* II, short-term food-shortages or even famines are dealt with by stratagems and short-term solutions, not general legislation which covers every possible eventuality.

The second problem with Bravo's argument, and also Garnsey's, is that they do not follow the text closely. Both works emphasize the export of existing reserves (procured through hoarding) by some nobles or large landowners. Nevertheless, the text of the imprecation does not suggest

[28] Detailed legislation is considered a necessity of law by Aristotle (*Constitution of the Athenians* 9.2; *Rhetoric* 1354a30ff.).

[29] Garnsey (1988: 76).

this, on the contrary, it refers specifically to import of grain ("grain from being imported"). Much like the Athenian law on the transport of grain, which is general and a reaction not to a specific crisis but rather to an inherent and chronic weakness of the polis, the imprecation covers the same ground, though from a different starting point. The Athenians legislated positively, restricting their traders to a single possible destination, while the Teans legislated negatively, forbidding their citizens from creating any obstacle to the grain supply.

This, if nothing else, highlights the great difference between Athens and any other polis, or at least a polis as small and relatively insignificant as Teos. This has been highlighted by Jameson who is amazed at "the Tean reliance on curses while Athens was establishing her muscular control."[30] Yet Athens had enough Athenian or metic traders to guarantee at least part of its import, if of course they did not place profit above their polis.[31] Gallant proposed that the law reflects the power of wealthy individuals to manipulate food supplies.[32] The purpose of such a manipulation is debatable. On the one hand, it may have a political motive, for example to subvert the constitution, government or existing elite by means of a prolonged engineered food shortage. On the other hand, the purpose of the manipulation may have been simply to make grain prices rise, as is mentioned in the inscription itself ("or when imported forces the price up").[33]

Teos, with its small population, must have depended on foreign traders a lot more than Athens, thus it was forced to depend on people who had no true ties to her, and as such could not be restricted in any way but only encouraged. Thus, it could only legislate negatively towards the people that she could control or influence, her own citizens or metics, with the warning not to impede the communal supply in any way. After all, Teos could do little else, although it would be interesting to know what sort of taxation was imposed on imports and exports. Athens ruled the seas for a large part of the classical period, and except for the early and late fourth century, it had a navy able, through provision of convoys for merchant ships, to pressure merchants in ways that other poleis could not.[34]

---

30 Jameson (1983: 12).
31 Schaps (2004: 122–123).
32 Gallant (1989: 408).
33 Garnsey (1988: 76 n. 17).
34 Garnsey & Whittaker (1983: 4).

Ephesos was one of the most prosperous and important poleis in Ionia, rivalling Miletos. The only evidence of the import of grain comes from the very end of our period (302/301) and unfortunately does not mention the supplier.[35] Ephesos, unlike other Ionian poleis, had no part in the establishment of Naukratis in the archaic period.

Klazomenai is one of the few cities that had a regular and regulated grain supply from abroad. In an inscription, dated to 387/386, regarding the relations between Athens and Klazomenai, the import of grain is mentioned specifically:

> On the polei]s from which the Klazome[nians are brought grain, Phokaia, Chios and S]myrna, it is according to the *spondai* that the[y are to sai]l [into the harbours].[36]

The inscription suggests that the bringing of grain is recurrent and regulated by *spondai* between the poleis in question. Garnsey has proposed an alternative explanation of the provision by connecting it with cases of *sitodeia* (food-crisis).[37] Presumably he is using the mention of *sitodeia* in Klazomenai in the *Oeconomica*:

> The Klazomenians at a time of *sitodeia*, when they had no money, voted that all private individuals who had oil should lend it with interest to the city; being there many olive crops in their land. Thus borrowing, they leased ships and sent them to the *emporia* from where they brought grain providing as collateral the price of the oil.[38]

There is nothing to suggest that the provision in the treaty is connected with the extraordinary episode described by the *Oeconomica*. On the contrary, the *Oeconomica* show that there was a common practice regarding where the Klazomenians got their grain ("sent them to the *emporia* from where they brought grain"). The extraordinariness of the situation in the *Oeconomica* depends on the fact that since this is a *sitodeia*, the government had to take direct measures mortgaging the oil. The mention of Smyrna probably means grain from further east, but both Chios and Phokaia were well-known maritime poleis.

---

[35] IEph 1452.

[36] IG II^2 28.17–20: τῶμ πό]|[λεω]ν ὅθεν σιταγωγῦνται Κλαζομέ[νιοι, Φωκάας καὶ Χί]|[ο καὶ Σ]μύρνης, εἶναι ἔνσπονδον αὐ[τοῖς ἐς τὸς λιμένα]|[ς ἐσπλε͂]ν.

[37] Garnsey & Morris (1989: 103); Garnsey (1988: 72); Garnsey & Whittaker (1983: 4).

[38] Aristotle *Oeconomica* 1348b17–23: Κλαζομένιοι δ' ἐν σιτοδείᾳ ὄντες χρημάτων τε ἀποροῦντες ἐψηφίσαντο παρ' οἷς ἔλαιόν ἐστι τῶν ἰδιωτῶν, δανεῖσαι τῇ πόλει ἐπὶ τόκῳ· γίνεται δὲ πολὺς οὗτος ὁ καρπὸς ἐν τῇ χώρᾳ αὐτῶν. Δανεισάντων δὲ μισθωσάμενοι πλοῖα ἀπέστειλαν εἰς τὰ ἐμπόρια, ὅθεν αὐτοῖς ἧκε σῖτος, ὑποθήκης γενομένης τῆς τοῦ ἐλαίου τιμῆς.

Akanthos is a case in point, not because it imported grain as such, but because of the origin of its grain supply. That Akanthos, as a polis in the Chalcidice (and this holds for all poleis in the region), imported grain is expected, since the region is best suited for other crops, mainly olives and vines, and the poleis there cashed in on these crops.[39] The only reference to the imports of Akanthos refers to Pontic grain.[40] One would consider it more logical to find the supplier for Akanthos, and the Chalcidice, in Macedon or Thrace, both regions well supplied in grain. On the other hand, it is possible that the political situation at the time meant that relations with either region were strained, and thus this created the need for Pontic grain.

Methone was the recipient of a grant by Athens of a regulated import of grain from the Black Sea in the 420s.[41] The Methone decrees are very important for our understanding of the interventionist attitude of imperial Athens in the trade relations of the allies. Bonner has argued that the decree suggests that Methone usually imported its grain from Macedon but due to the troubles between Athens and Macedon at the time (because of the campaigns of Brasidas) an alternative supplier was necessary.[42] However, the decree itself gives no such information or indeed any clue towards that conclusion. On the contrary, the fact that it specifically mentions that the provisions are to hold for Methone, in spite of any other resolution affecting the allies in general, shows that this is supposed to be a permanent solution to the problems of the Methoneans.

The Methone case illuminates the role of the otherwise shadowy 'third player' in the grain trade specifically, and Greek trade in general. Normally any transaction has an origin, the exporter, and a destination, the importer, with a route between them, the traders. Geography and politics often conspire to impose a third pole in these transactions, the polis/kingdom controlling an important part of the transport route. Some geographical areas are particularly suited to play such a role: Gibraltar, Panama, the Rio Grande, Suez and, of course, the Bosporan strait and the Hellespont. Controlling such areas invests a state with inordinate power over any transaction, since it controls the transport lanes.

---

[39] The Chalcidice was famous for its wines, as for example those of Mende and Scione (Demosthenes 35.10).

[40] Demosthenes 34.36.

[41] IG I³ 61.

[42] Bonner (1923: 196).

In the Greek world, such control sites created important poleis, both strategically and economically. In the Methone case, the important 'third player' is Athens, which by that time had dominated the poleis of the Bosporos and the Hellespont and imposed its control over the shipping lanes between the Black Sea and the Aegean. Methone, as an importer, was not only obliged to create whichever necessary links to the exporters, but also to gain the support of Athens, as the controlling power in the Hellespont. Other poleis must also have had the same aim, although evidence concerning them has not survived, not only with Athens but also with whichever other polis controlled the straits. From Athens' point of view, control of the Hellespont not only provided security for her own imports but also was a powerful political weapon, since she could at any time cut off supply to any enemy, rival or revolting ally.

Selymbria is mentioned as affecting a ban on grain exports at a time of shortage.[43] Since the ban continued unabated after the end of the shortage, deficiency in grain must have been a common occurrence. Selymbria and her reactions are those of a small importer that occasionally needed no imports.

The known importers are found in the core of the Greek world, and although the level of surviving evidence is low as compared to Athens, both the number and the size of importing poleis is indicative of the need for grain in Greece, the Aegean and Asia Minor. The importers are not exclusively large poleis with known maritime activity, such as Corinth, Aigina or Samos, but include small and insignificant poleis, such as Teos, Methone and Selymbria. In the majority of cases, only single references to imports have survived but in the cases where the projected consumption/production equilibrium can be estimated, the calculations suggest regular insufficiency of local production, which implies that the rare references in the sources are merely the tip of the iceberg of large scale regular imports. More importantly, in the few cases where more information has survived, mainly through epigraphical sources, small poleis are seen legislating and establishing close relationships with exporters and entrepôts to guarantee their imported supplies. The Tean legislation throws the Athenian legislation into sharp relief, while the evidence from Mytilene, Klazomenai and Methone betray the political intervention that small poleis could exert at intergovernmental level. Although nothing as

[43] Aristotle *Oeconomica* 2.1348b25.

pervasive and encompassing as Law VI of Athens has survived for the other importers, the overall picture relating to grain illuminates a complexity of intervention, legislative and diplomatic, which belies the supposed rarity of governmental intervention in trade.

GRAIN: CONCLUDING REMARKS

Grain was one of the most important commodities in the Greek trading lanes, as it was the main staple food of the majority of the population. Scholarship for almost two centuries has concentrated on the trade in grain, spurred by the numerous references in the sources. Its importance in the Greek diet and the common shortages due to climate made grain one of the commodities in which the state was most likely to play a role.

The exporters of grain were not numerous and the majority of them were situated in the periphery of the Greek World, in the Black Sea, North Africa and Sicily. In the Black Sea, the only known exporter was the Bosporan Kingdom in the Crimea, but other poleis, Tomis and Kallatis being the most probable candidates, are likely to have also exported. In North Africa, grain was exported primarily from Egypt, although Kyrene also had a considerable surplus. In the western Mediterranean, Sicily was the main exporter, although the exact exporting poleis cannot be securely identified. One of the major debates regarding these poleis is the relation between grain and their foundation in the archaic period. Although trade, certainly at inter-polis and possibly at interregional level, was known from at least the seventh century as testified by Hesiod, it is impossible to argue successfully that the poleis of the Black Sea and Naukratis were founded with the express purpose of providing grain for poleis in Greece and Asia Minor. However, that does not mean that trade in grain was absent in the archaic period between peripheral settlements and the core of the Greek world, since evidence from both the Black Sea and Naukratis suggests that the settlements had considerable grain production and surpluses. The form of export was generally bulk grain, although it is possible that it could have been transported in sacks. There is no evidence of export in other forms, for example flour, and the practicalities of sea-transport made other forms unviable.

The majority of grain surpluses were privately owned, although some grain was certainly in public hands. The system of *aparchai*, which was effected even in non-exporters, provided the state with some disposable surplus every year. The gifts provided by exporters to importers in times of crisis, such as those of Psammetichos and Leukon to Athens and that of Kyrene to several poleis, show that exporting states had considerable public surpluses. Possibly some exporters had taxes payable in grain, similar to the Athenian *dodekate* of the islands.

The influence of the state in the production of grain must have been minimal. The weather-induced shortages and the existence of many importers made grain a lucrative crop, which needed no major intervention from the state in production. The main role of the state in influencing production was one of its major aims by default: to protect the land from the ravages of war. The state was involved in disposing of the surplus, as shown by the policy of the Spartokids of making their grain attractive to importers. The Spartokids exhibit a sophisticated understanding of the natural disadvantages of their grain, the lateness of harvest and lightness of product. The specific export policies towards Athens and Mytilene show a consistency of intervention in the marketing of grain, mainly through tax reductions. The differences in the trade policy of the Spartokids towards Athens and Mytilene show an understanding of the different status of importers according to their commercial importance and the amount of grain they needed. Lowering export taxes and providing priority of lading gave Crimean grain the edge it needed against other exporters, mainly Egypt.

At the other end of the Mediterranean, the actions of Kleomenes of Egypt show that the apparatus for maximum intervention in disposing of the marketable surplus existed in the Greek world. However, the reactions of the Athenians towards such intervention and manipulation of the existing trade networks show that such tactics were not welcome, at least amongst the importers. The case of Kleomenes is exceptional, since the polis as an institution would not put forward such measures, due to their long-term unsustainability. The exporting states are observed disposing of surpluses in a variety of ways according to circumstance. In addition to providing incentives to their importers they also, in times of crisis, provided them with grain as gifts.

The importers, on the other hand, were numerous in the core of the Greek world, mainly in Greece, Asia Minor and the Aegean, thus providing a convenient locus for traders. For the majority of these, nothing is known beyond who they were and in some cases from whom they imported. For others, with Athens as the prime example, it is possible to make a rough calculation of their import of grain. I adopted a system of variables rather than a specific estimation because production and consumption can not have been static over a period of two centuries. In fact, neither is static from year to year, especially in the Mediterranean, where the microclimatic environment encourages diversity of production figures. The variable system incorporates different figures for population, cultivated arable land, dietary requirements and yield figures as proposed by modern scholars and mentioned in the sources. Under this system most of the problems of adopting a static calculation, as is usual among modern works, are avoided.

For Athens, which is the greater importer in our period, it was shown conclusively that in most years, in the fourth century at least, it had to import large quantities of grain. Unlike other modern calculations, which have argued either for or against self-sufficiency by adopting specific consumption and production figures, with the use of variables the calculations can be adapted to the specifications of any given year, if such becomes available. For other importers for which consumption and production estimations are possible, such as Corinth, Aigina, Megara and Samos, it was calculated that they regularly suffered from insufficiency of local production, and thus had to import annually.

The legislation on the import of grain shows that the importers were anxious to employ every means at their disposal to ensure their supply. The main example is Athens, where the legislation covered most aspects of the importation of grain. Athenian policy regarding the exporters was to provide them with gifts and honours, such as to the Spartokids and their envoys and possibly Strato of Sidon. Most of the Athenian effort, however, was directed towards private traders, particularly those resident in Attika. The legislation on grain coerced local traders into importing grain and provided safeguards for the dissemination of imported grain, including a flexible fixing of market prices. Of greatest interest, however, is that Athenian legislation also regulated lending capital affecting not only grain but all commodities, both exports and imports, thus exhibiting a high level of intervention in trade.

For Teos, the only other polis known to have grain import legislation, the situation is different. Teos had more detailed legislation than Athens but it had less economic scope. The differences between the measures taken by the two poleis are indicative of their larger differences both politically and economically. Athens was a known and respected political power with a powerful fleet, even when at its weakest, and a commercial hub of the Aegean world with a large resident population of traders, citizen and metic. Thus, Athenian legislation approached traders from a position of strength and reached beyond the Piraeus. Teos, on the contrary, a small and insignificant city in Asia Minor, could only prohibit the inhibition of grain imports by its own citizens, the Tean commercial population being less than necessary to provide sufficient imported grain. The different policies employed by the poleis were not the reflection of a lack of a "coherent institutionalised framework" but depended on the power of the polis.[1] Athens developed what we term an institutionalised framework because it had the power to impose it, not because the idea itself was lacking in other poleis.

[1] Gallant (1989: 406).

CONCLUSION

Researching trade in archaic and classical Greece is a multifaceted endeavour characterised not only by the variability of sources and material but also by a multitude of theoretical and methodological debates. The aim of this work has been to explore and discuss the role of the government in foreign trade. The currently prevailing opinion among modern scholars relegates governmental intervention to exceptional circumstances and the necessary imports of extraordinary poleis like Athens. Through the study of four commodities, gold, silver, shipbuilding timber and grain, in whose trade the government was most likely to play a role, the existence, extent and type of intervention were explored. Gold and silver were the main metals used for precious coinage, which as a state initiative made governments responsible for the procurement of metal. Shipbuilding timber was of particular interest to poleis with naval aspirations, especially in the classical period where navies were built and owned by the state. Lastly, grain was the major staple foodstuff of the Greeks and as the climatic, geographic and demographic conditions in the Mediterranean made grain shortages common, many poleis had a vested interest in the grain trade.

The survival rate of evidence from the ancient world is low, thus it is almost impossible to identify precisely the role of the government in any given commodity or, similarly, the policy of any particular polis or polity as to trade. However, the study of four commodities where the government was most likely to play a role provides a mosaic of information on governmental intervention and involvement in trade, which in turn provides a more complete picture of the government as a regulator of trade. In conclusion, the strands of information from the examination and discussion of the four commodities will be woven together in an effort to explore the role of the government more fully.

Distribution of Resources

To begin, the geographical distribution of the exporters of the four commodities will be discussed. The main exporters of gold in the Greek world are found in the Thracomacedonian region, Lydia, the south-eastern shores of the Black Sea and Egypt. The main exporters of silver are found also in the Thracomacedonian region, the Black Sea and Iberia; the main difference with gold being that one of the major exporters was Athens. Shipbuilding timber was found in quantity only in specific regions around the Mediterranean with the main reserves in the Thracomacedonian region, northern Asia Minor, the southern littoral of the Black Sea and Magna Graecia. Grain was produced throughout the Greek world but large-scale production with an adequate surplus was mainly found in the Black Sea, Egypt and Sicily and Magna Graecia.

With the partial exception of silver, the geographical distribution of the main producers of these important commodities highlights the importance of peripheral areas in the Greek world. The geographical position of the resource areas largely conforms to a core-periphery model, with the core being the Peloponnese, central Greece and Euboia, along with the Aegean islands and south-eastern Greek Asia Minor. The periphery, on the other hand, is divided into two zones with northern Greek Asia Minor, the Hellespont, the Thracomacedonian region, north-western Greece, Sicily and Magna Graecia in the inner zone and north Africa, oriental Asia Minor, the Black Sea and the western Mediterranean in the outer. This geographical distribution of necessary resources established the pattern of trade in the Greek world, since it was impossible for the core to sustain its material culture without the periphery. Thus, exchange of products between the core and the periphery was an unavoidable necessity and, consequently, the core was forced to produce exchange articles for the goods provided by the periphery.

Form of Traded Commodities

There was no uniform standard of export in the Greek World, as commodities were exported in various forms according to necessity and convenience. For gold, there is little evidence on the form of export, which, however, suggests that most transactions included bullion, the form in which Lydia probably exported to Sparta. Further, the emergency nature of many gold coinages in the Greek world, which were minted probably from local reserves mainly of plate and temple dedications, also suggests that most transactions were of bullion. For silver, on the other hand, the form of export is widely debated among scholars and currently the majority opinion tends towards coins being the main form of export. The evidence of minting quantities presented, however, shows that export of silver in the form of coins must have been rare, as a relatively small amount of coins was produced by the exporters, as against the large state production by numerous importers, which suggests that export in bullion was more widespread.

Timber for warships is generally supposed to have been exported as raw timber from the exporters to the importers; however, the majority of the evidence of exports relates to oars, mainly unshaved, as implied by Andokides' transportation of oars from Macedon to the Athenians in Samos and the treaty between the Athenians and Perdikkas. Import of timber for the actual construction of warships, however, is attested in only a very few cases, some of them exceptionally motivated, such as the case of Dionysios of Syracuse, or under very constrained circumstances, such as Athens in the last decades of the fourth century, when Macedon had become particularly prominent in Greek politics. On the other hand, there is considerable evidence for the construction of warships in areas where shipbuilding timber was locally available, which negated all need for the export of raw timber to the naval states, except that needed for repairs. Building in the resource areas was more economical and easier in terms of construction, since the resource areas had not only an abundance of timber but also the necessary expertise. In most cases, such shipbuilding areas were brought under the control of the naval powers through military intervention and conquest. Grain, lastly, was exported mainly in bulk, since the commodity in other forms, such as flour or bread, was particularly vulnerable to mildew and rot during long-distance transport by ship. Transport of grain in containers must have been minimal, since both the extra cost and the need for extra cargo-space would be prohibitive to most traders.

The non-uniformity of standards of export and the variety of different forms in which a commodity could be exported show that trade in the Greek world could support a variability of commodity types and forms. Particularly in the case of timber, where export of raw material was eschewed in favour of conquest and export of finished products, considerations of practicality and the ease of transport played a major role in conditions of trade in the Greek world. Similarly, the case of precious metal export in the form of bullion rather than coins suggests that cost and expense variables played a role in the form of export of commodities.

Ownership of Commodities

A major issue in any economy is the ownership and control of the surplus, since governmental control of surpluses gave the state a more direct role in their disposition and a firmer hand in regulating the trade of a commodity. A range of resources, such as mines and forests, belonged to the state under all circumstances. For gold, the information relates to Lydia, a non-Greek kingdom, where the Spartan transaction with Kroisos and the large amounts of bullion owned by the Lydian kings suggest that the Lydian kings exploited the gold resources directly, in a similar manner to the Persian king, who directly exploited mines and quarries. Further, the sparse information surviving on the Macedonian exploitation of the Pangaion and Lake Prasias mines also implies direct exploitation of the resource. The system employed by Persia was also one of direct exploitation, although the King made concessions to public bodies, such as governors and poleis, as is seen in the cases of Histiaios in Myrkinos, Pythios and the Aktaies poleis.

The situation was different for silver, where the evidence relates to Athens, a polis that apparently had ownership of the underground resources of the country, but control of the surplus was widely diffused by the system of leasing. With leasing, the Athenian state spread the surplus through the population, and the policy of minimum intervention in the production and control of the silver surplus gave an incentive to private trading, although through the profits from the leases, and possibly from the *kaminoi*, the polis had control of a considerable part of surplus. It must be noted here that since Athens was radically democratic; it is possible that oligarchic governments employed less diffused systems of exploitation.

With timber, attention focuses on the other political side of the Greek world, from democratic Athens to autocratic Macedon. The Macedonian kings employed a system of exploitation between the close monopoly of the Lydians and the diffused exploitation of the Athenians, by using a controlled exploitation system, which simultaneously afforded them greater control over the exploitation of their timber resources. The details of the exploitation regime of the Cypriot kingdoms have not survived but it appears that monopolic arrangements were in place there as well. Monopoly arrangements are known for the Greek kingdoms in other commodities as well, such as the silphium monopoly in Kyrene.[1]

Andokides' testimony and the insistence of the Macedonian kings on not granting exploitation rights to foreign states, even when surrendering exclusive export rights, suggest that the kings preferred to keep exploitation under close personal control. It is possible that some part of the timber surplus was directly exploited by the king, on the oriental model, but since Macedon did not have a fleet, the degree of direct exploitation must have been small. The existence of a lease-like procedure shows the middle politico-economic ground held by the autocratic regimes of the Greek World between the polis and the oriental kingships. The leasing procedure employed by the Macedonian kings is different from that employed in Athens, since in Athens leasing was open and conducted under a specific set of rules, while in Macedon leasing depended on the king. It was a concession, which could be withdrawn or extended according to the king's wishes rather a specific set of laws or a public auction like that of Athens. The system was similar, albeit on a smaller scale, to the concessions awarded by the Persian king to poleis and individual governors, as seen in the case of Mount Ida, where Pharnabazos assumed the right to exploit the reserve freely, since it was owned by the King, while simultaneously the Greek poleis also had rights of exploitation. The similarities with the oriental practice did not stop there as Andokides testifies, since providing concessions as gifts to *xenoi* was an oriental custom, which is not found in the polis. Possibly, poleis with timber resources, like those of Magna Graecia, also kept close control over exploitation, even if not as close as that of Macedon, as suggested by Dionysios' request for permission to exploit the south Italian reserves. The difference in attitude between the oriental kingdom and the polis is significant; while Pharnabazos had no qualms about exploiting the resource in the name of the king in spite of any concessions to nearby poleis, it is difficult to imagine the Athenian state sending public slaves to mine some extra silver in a leased mine in a case of emergency.

Turning to grain, the situation is very different from the other commodities, since by nature grain presupposes a more diffused ownership, since its cultivation was largely in the hands of private individuals; something especially true in the polis, where public and temple estates

[1] Aristotle *Fragmenta Varia* 8.44.528; Anaxandridas F4.1.

were leased to private individuals. There were surpluses owned and controlled by the polis through the *aparchai* and, wherever they existed, through taxes payable in grain, but these were small in comparison to the large deposits in private hands. As the policies of Kleomenes of Egypt show, while public surpluses in the exporting countries were considerably larger, an effective control of the surplus of the country meant dealing mainly with privately owned grain.

The uniform practice in the Greek world was for the state to own the resources of the country, in other words the resources that did not depend upon human agency, mainly metals, oxides and forest timber. However, the exploitation of resources and the control of the state over the surplus differed considerably among types of polity. The oriental and Greek kingdoms exploited their resources directly and through direct personal concessions to their subjects, either private individuals or public bodies. The polis, on the other hand, as exemplified in the exploitation of the Athenian silver mines, preferred to diffuse the surplus to the population through leasing. The practice between polis and kingdom, oriental and Greek, appears to diverge sharply in the employment of monopoly by the kingdom, a practice unattested in the world of the polis.

Role of Government in Production of Commodities

The interest of the exporter in a commodity can be expressed through the exertion of influence on its production. Unfortunately, for gold any influence exerted by the exporting states on production cannot be detected, since the majority of information refers to archaic Lydia, which employed a system of direct exploitation, where any measures designed to increase productivity were probably handled within the court, thus leaving no trace for posterity. Philip of Macedon, on the other hand, certainly intervened in the production of the Pangaion gold mines and succeeded in increasing production through investment in installations.

The influence of the government on Athenian silver production was minimal and centred on safety and quality control. On the one hand, the state legislated to protect miners and mining from malicious actions, thus providing a safe environment for the exploitation of the Laurion mines, which was paramount in keeping production stable and increasing. On the other hand, the quality control imposed by the government through its leasing and regulation of *kaminoi* enhanced the marketability of silver both in Athens and outside; guaranteed uniform high quality not only assured the mining prospector the marketability of his silver but also provided more extensive opportunities for him to profit. Profit is one of the greatest incentives for increased production.

The influence of the government on production is also evident in timber exporters. Macedon is the best-known example of a state regulating production; the Macedonian kings kept production of timber in their forests as their personal mandate. Andokides' boast that his royal *xenos* allowed him to cut down as many trees as he wished, implies the normal practice in Macedon was for the king to limit such exploitation; similarly in the surviving treaties with foreign states, while the Macedonian kings gave rights of export, they never relinquished control of exploitation. In principle, the Macedonians employed the same reasoning as the Athenians, although tempered by the differences in their respective exports and political realities. Both regulated production with an eye for the protection of both resource and productivity. The differences in their policies result from the difference, on the one hand, between a democracy and an autocracy and, on the other, on the fundamental differences between timber and silver. Thus, where a democracy legislated, the Macedonian autocracy simply kept production in the hands of the king, and, more importantly, where Athens could only protect productivity as long as silver was available, the Macedonians could protect productivity indefinitely, as timber is a renewable resource as long as exploitation does not exceed re-growth. The modern example of the excessive exploitation of the Amazon reserves, the subsequent deforestation and the internationally enforced sanctions on the marketability of the produce testify to the downward spiral affected by a non-husbanding policy. The Macedonians avoided losing a precious resource through direct control and limited exploitation, similar to that of the Cypriot kings who also limited production. Both Cyprus and Macedon were metallurgical centres, thus protection of valuable timber resources was a major internal concern, since metallurgy has a voracious appetite for fuel, which can easily lead to denudation and over-exploitation.

Grain was a difficult commodity to influence directly, since the majority of arable land and its surplus was in private hands. However, grain was a commodity of universal interest in the Greek world and surpluses were eagerly desired by traders, especially in the known exporters. Thus, the influence of the government in production needed to be minimal and concentrated on protecting production through avoiding war or at least limiting the ravages of attacking armies.

The role of the government in the production of commodities differed according to the type of commodity and type of polity. Commodities whose ownership was private, such as grain, were influenced by the state very little, since the resources, which in the case of grain was arable land, were privately owned. Governments played a larger role in the production of commodities from resources owned by the state. In the case of such commodities, influence on production differed according to type of polity. The extent of intervention and involvement of the government in production, as in exploitation, was heavier in the Greek and oriental kingdoms and considerably lighter in the polis.

Role of Government in Export of Commodities

The disposition of available surpluses was also of interest to poleis and polities; here intervention became more pronounced and various means of disposition were employed, including direct transactions with other states. In an autocratic eastern state like Lydia, the disposition of the surplus was squarely in the hands of the king and his court, meaning that the vast majority of surpluses were state-owned, which influenced greatly their disposition. The transaction with Sparta shows that the Lydian kings traded directly with other states; Herodotos' lack of comment suggests that such transactions were not unique and the earlier examples from Israel and the Near Eastern kingdoms suggest the same. If gold were widely available in free market conditions in Lydia, then one would expect the Spartans to have been in the market, not the palace, negotiating on their sale. Such direct trade with other states creates the right climate for direct trade with foreign traders as well and the actions of Kroisos towards both the Spartan delegation and various Greek temples show that the Lydian kings considered gift-giving a valid method of disposing of their precious metal, a practice with important political connotations, as is testified by the reaction of the Spartans to Kroisos' call for help later. The same appears to be the case also for the Greek kingdoms, as seen in the accusation of the bribery of Greek politicians made against Philip II.

Turning to the poleis and the evidence for silver, the situation is quite different. Athens did not prefer direct exploitation, and the leasing system meant that large parts of the surplus entered and remained in private hands. The large scale of minting in Athens suggests that the state disposed of a great part of its own surplus in coinage, although other uses, including temple dedications, must also have been prevalent. The surpluses in the hands of private citizens found their way into the market, as the *Ways and Means* suggests, where they were available to foreign traders and states, as well as into coinage production through the openness of the minting procedure. It is possible that direct trade between states existed but, unfortunately, there is no evidence of such transactions. Furthermore, it was traditional, at least in the archaic period, for part of the surplus of the state to be distributed to the citizenry, as in Siphnos, where again they reached the open market.

The case of timber again exemplifies the middle status of the Greek autocratic states. In Macedon, the king had absolute control over the disposition of timber surpluses, as Perdikkas' treaty with Athens shows; the king negotiated with other states for exclusive disposition of surpluses. Amyntas' treaty with the Chalcidians is more pervasive, since there not only oars but also all types of timber are included, although the Chalcidians did not attain exclusivity like the Athenians a few decades earlier. In addition, the Macedonian kings also dealt with private traders, granting them limited rights of export, as is shown by Andokides' export of Macedonian oars in the reign of Archelaos. The variety of mechanisms employed by Macedon in the disposition of its timber surplus illuminate the choices available to a government and the limitations on export that could be imposed. The difference in disposition is also evidence of the control of production exercised by the Macedonians, since it shows how both exploitation and disposition were under the direct control of the king. The difference with the Athenian treaty concerning *miltos* with the poleis of Keos is particularly illuminating in this case, since the polis could only control export through shipping, not by direct arrangement like the Macedonians:

> ... it will be exported in a ship which the Athenians will designate and in no other ship, the transport price will be an obol per talent to the *naukleroi* who work; if someone exports in another ship, let him be guilty ... [2]

The variety of options available to the state in disposing of surpluses is more pronounced in the case of grain. Grain exporters, unlike those of shipbuilding timber and precious metals, had more competition for their products, and thus the intervention of the government is more obvious, and shows the care shown by the state for the principal exports of the

[2] IG II[2] 1128.12–14.

land. Unfortunately, the practices of polis governments cannot be fully reconstructed, since the evidence relates mainly to the Greek kingdoms. The Spartokids made arrangements with their importers, offering incentives to make their grain more attractive to traders. The difference in their policy towards Athens and Mytilene shows that they had an acute understanding of the different markets for Bosporan grain and a full realisation of how far incentives, which cut into the revenue of the state from customs, could be taken. Further, the Spartokids did not enter into monopolic arrangements, preferring instead to offer incentives, which, however, were in practice exercised by private traders. On the other hand, the actions of Kleomenes of Egypt show that the necessary mechanisms to impose a monopoly on grain, using it to increase governmental revenues, existed. That such methods were not common among poleis was the result of the networks of trade in the Greek World. Kleomenes could employ such tactics mainly because of the famine besetting the poleis at the time. However, under normal circumstances, the exporting states had to rely on incentives rather than monopoly, since traders would not bear the brunt of excess custom when prices were not extraordinarily high and cheaper grain could have been obtained elsewhere. The difference in policy between the Spartokids and Kleomenes is the difference between the market under normal conditions and in times of widespread shortage. In times of widespread crisis, the exporting states could intervene more forcefully and increase their revenue from exports, while in times of plenty the importers had to be attracted and products made desirable through incentives. The differences in intervention are the exporting equivalent of *katagein*, when the state becomes more forceful in times of crisis with relative impunity.

The evidence on the disposition of surpluses refers mainly to the affairs of the oriental and Greek kingdoms with only limited evidence available on the polis. The evidence from gold, timber and grain suggests that the Greek kingdoms intervened considerably in the export of commodities through direct trade, treaties with other states and incentives to states and their affiliated traders. Some of the arrangements of the kingdoms were monopolistic, as in the case of Macedonian timber and Kleomenes' grain scheme, but the Spartokid policy of providing incentives to important importers shows that the kingdoms could also have sustained non-monopolistic export policies. Simultaneously, the differences in the policies of the Spartokids and Kleomenes show how Greek governments adapted their policies according to the circumstances of the market of specific commodities. Again, as in exploitation, the polis adopted more devolved methods for the disposition of surpluses through the use of private individuals and the release of a large part of the surplus into the market.

Role of Government in the Import of Commodities

Turning to imports, firstly the known states with a regular or permanent shortage in each commodity will be briefly presented. The identification of all poleis and polities with shortages in each commodity is an impossible task, since such information rarely survives in the sources. However, for each commodity it was attempted to identify as many importers as possible within the framework of the available sources and material evidence.

For gold, the states with a regular need and shortage were the majority of poleis minting gold and electrum coinages; the poleis examined in this work were those of Asia Minor and Sicily/Magna Graecia, since in those areas gold and electrum coinages were more common than in mainland Greece and the Aegean. In Asia Minor, the known importers were Chios, Ephesos, Miletos, Phokaia, Samos, Teos, Halikarnassos, Kyzikos, Mytilene, Rhodos, Pergamos and Kios. The majority of these minters needed regular imports to sustain their minting; the exceptions were few, such as Chios in the middle of the fifth century. Moreover, some poleis, such as Kyzikos, Phokaia and Mytilene minted continuously throughout the period in considerable volume. In Sicily and Magna Graecia, the situation was different, with most gold coinages being a reaction in times of crisis, with the only exception being the late fifth- early fourth-century gold coinage of Dionysios of Syracuse. Gold minting in Sicily outside Syracuse was confined to the late fifth century in Akragas, Gela and Kamarina in connection with the Carthaginian invasion, and in Magna Graecia to Taras and Metapontion, chronologically connected to the mainland Greek assistance to the colonies against native revolts.

Silver was the main coinage metal in the Greek world from the late sixth century onwards; the large number of poleis minting in silver makes any attempt to identify the importers superfluous. All poleis minting silver coins, except for the few poleis with silver mines in their territories, were importers. The comparative study of the minters according to coins found in hoards showed conclusively that the poleis without resources were the most prolific minters, except for Athens, which both produced silver and minted it in quantity. The study of 69 poleis appearing in hoards more than five times showed that the poleis of Italy and Sicily minted more than those in mainland Greece, the Aegean and Asia Minor. The reason for such prolific minting in an area with no native resources was that the western Greek world did not use the 'international' coinages, such as the Athenian owls, the Kyzikene staters and the Persian darics, which dominated the markets and provided a surplus of large coins in the eastern part of the Greek world.

Many poleis had permanent shortages in shipbuilding timber, since many poleis had considerable navies and the sources indicate that suitable timber could be found only in limited areas. Unfortunately, the only polis for which precise fleet sizes survive is Athens, and even there only for part of the fourth century. For other importing poleis, the only aids are the infrequent, and possibly suspect, references in the literary sources to fleets used in various naval engagements. The greatest fleet in the Greek World throughout the classical period was the Athenian, which often surpassed 300 ships. The other major fleets were the Chian, the Mytilenian, the Samian, the Rhodian, the Corinthian, the Corcyraean and the Syracusan.

The precise number of states with regular or permanent shortages of grain cannot be identified. For many poleis, shortages can be identified through inscriptional evidence but in very few cases can these shortages be identified as permanent or regular, such as Teos in the fifth century and Mytilene in the fourth. For a number of other poleis regular shortages can be inferred from mentions of imports in the literary sources. In very few cases, where the population of the polis in question has been estimated, a comparison between the estimated needs of the population in grain and the production of the polis shows whether the polis was regularly deficient in grain. The identified poleis that had regular or permanent shortages of grain were Athens, Corinth, Megara, Aigina, Mytilene, Andros, Arkesine in Amorgos, Samos, Teos, Ephesos, Klazomenai, Akanthos in the Chalcidice, Methone and Selymbria.

The importers often intervened in the trade of commodities in order to ensure and safeguard the regularity of their imports. The different means employed to ensure imports contained different degrees of intervention in trade, from forceful coercion of exporters to incentives and honours offered to traders. For some commodities there is sufficient evidence to pinpoint the different means employed by the importing states and the degree of intervention enforced. In other cases, however, we can only infer from probability the means employed and their degree of success.

For gold, the two case studies present two very different pictures of the means of import employed by the poleis. In the sixth century, the Spartan import from Lydia sets the background for any further discussion. The Spartans preferred to import directly in a state-to-state transaction, without intermediaries; this import is extraordinary, since the Spartans had no regular need for gold. That even under extraordinary circumstances, trade was the preferred means of transaction and specifically direct public import is illuminating on the means preferred by the polis. For the majority of Asia Minor minters, in the sixth century and later, which had a permanent shortage of gold for their coinages, the exact means employed to ensure import have not survived. In specific cases, such as that of Chios in the fifth century, chance means of acquisition in the form of booty were probably employed. However, for most of the minters in Asia Minor a more peaceful and less risky solution was preferable, implying trade as the primary means of acquisition. The other side of the coin is amply illustrated in the second case study, that of gold minting in Sicily and Magna Graecia. The gold coinages there, with the possible exception of the coinage of Dionysios I of Syracuse, were crisis measures in times of war, most probably for the payment of mercenaries and for supplies. Under critical circumstances, the Greek poleis tended to requisition material through force, either violent, such as booty, or coercive within the polis, such as extraordinary taxation and loans from temples, as Athens did in the last years of the Peloponnesian War.

For silver, the lack of evidence on the importers is problematical. Scholarly opinion in the last few decades has tended to argue in favour of relatively insecure and chance means of import for the poleis, translated into the theory of acquiring existing coinages for reminting. The large scale minting by poleis with no silver resources of their own combined with the small scale of the coinages of most silver producers points towards a different solution. The various finds of silver ingots and bars in hoards testifies to the existence and viability of trade in bullion. Furthermore, the evidence of entry of foreign coins in any polis contradicts the theory that the state had a ready supply of foreign coinage in its coffers, since money-changing was widespread, and in some cases mandatory, and such functions were the province of private banks not the state. In addition, Xenophon's statement that export of silver was bound to bring profits to traders, since silver had a constant demand and high prices, shows that trade in bullion was not only common but also financially advisable. The specific means by which the states ensured imports are not certain, since very little evidence has survived. Xenophon points towards private traders being part of the transaction but, understandably, he does not provide further specifics, since his theme concerns the production and export of the commodity, not its import.

Shipbuilding timber was a necessary commodity for most naval poleis in the Greek world, especially those with large navies. It has been generally assumed that poleis with navies imported timber from the resource areas to build warships in their own shipyards. However, the only specific evidence for the import of timber for shipbuilding from the resource areas to an importer dates from the end of the classical period, when circumstances had changed dramatically due to the advent of Macedon. On the other hand, there is considerable evidence of shipbuilding in or near the resource areas, mainly from the fifth century. The Lesbian exiles in Antandros, Brasidas in Amphipolis and the Peloponnesians after the battle of Kyzikos used, or planned to use, the *naupegia* in the resource areas to build their fleets. Additionally, the evidence on imports of timber products for shipbuilding refers to oars not timber; such a lack of references, especially in the treaty between Athens and Perdikkas, is odd if timber for shipbuilding was imported in the quantities necessary for building a fleet. The evidence as it stands now points towards shipbuilding occurring in *naupegia* in the resource areas, not towards large-scale import of timber to presumed *naupegia* within the importers. The importance of *naupegia* in the resource areas lent even more consequence to these areas. Athens is the prime example of a naval power trying to secure a regular supply of ships. The Athenian efforts during the *Pentekontaetia* in the Thracomacedonian area are largely the story of Athenian timber and ship supply. There are two parallel matters with which Athens was concerned: the ships themselves and special supplies, such as oars. For the ships, Athens preferred extreme intervention in the form of violent coercion of the exporters through conquest and forced settlement of areas, such as Amphipolis and Eion. In addition to ensuring her own supply, Athens made considerable efforts to limit or cut off the supply of her rivals and revolting allies, as is seen in the conquest and settling of Messenian helots in Naupaktos in order to cut off Corinthian access to the *naupegia* of the area and the outlets of the Aitolian mountains, and in the sundering of Mytilenian domination of the Aktaies poleis after the Mytilenian revolt, cutting off Mytilenian access to the *naupegia* and resources of Mount Ida. On the other hand, Athens also tried to secure the import of special timber supplies, such as oars. The best oars came from Macedon, which Athens could not violently coerce in the same way as the poleis in the Strymon area. The size and population of the Macedonian kingdom made it impossible for a naval polis, even one as big as Athens, to conquer the resource areas or their outlets. Even so, the dominion of imperial Athens on the poleis of the Chalcidice and those of the southern Thermaic Gulf meant that Macedon was at a permanent disadvantage against the mistress of the Aegean. Furthermore, the internal weaknesses of the Macedonian royal house, and of monarchy as a constitution, gave Athens multiple opportunities to oblige the Macedonian kings into providing her with special timber supplies. The treaty with Perdikkas shows how deep Athens could cut into the Macedonian oar trade, since Athens managed to secure a monopoly of import. Athens was not always the all-powerful partner, as is shown by the honours accorded to Archelaos. The ability of the Macedonian king to renege on treaties and deals with little to lose meant that Athens also had to attract the private traders of special timber supplies. Although Andokides may have had no further incentive than his patriotism for providing oars to the Athenian fleet in Samos, the same was certainly not true for other traders, such as Phanosthenes. Specific economic incentives, such as *ateleia* from the *hekatoste*, were powerful reasons for private traders to provide Athens with her necessary supplies.

Athens was not unique in the means employed to ensure her supply of ship and timber products, since other poleis followed similar patterns of intervention. Mytilene, one of the primary naval powers in the Aegean, had under its control the outlets of Ida and the *naupegia* in the Gulf of Adramytion. Thasos, an important naval power in the early fifth century in the Thracian Sea, had under its control the Strymon area and was willing to defend its prerogatives there forcefully, as is testified by the Thasian revolt. Such coercive measures, mainly through colonisation rather than outright conquest, are apparent in the sources for poleis other than Athens. The same is not true of more peaceful solutions and treaties, which can only be identified if the inscription recording them has survived and been excavated. The treaty between Amyntas of Macedon and the Chalcidian confederacy shows that other poleis, or political units, could coerce the exporters into providing extended rights of import without violent conquest. Beyond that, clues in the sources also provide relatively wide niches to assume other roles played by the polis in ensuring its timber imports. For example, that Dionysios of Syracuse needed permission to import south Italian timber shows that in this case direct public import between poleis was available.

The role played by the polis in ensuring its grain imports is subtly different from that for other commodities; the main reason for this difference has already been mentioned above relating to production. Since the bulk of production was in private hands, the importing state was obliged to play a role in relation not only to the exporter but also to the trading networks in the Greek world. Direct public trade occurs in several instances in the sources but it is limited to times of crisis, although not necessarily famines; thus, Psammetichos and Leukon gifted grain to Athens in the 450s and the mid-fourth century respectively and Kyrene provided gifts of grain to a variety of Greek states in the 320s. Similarly, during crises, many poleis with an extraordinary shortage at the time intervened forcefully in the grain trade of their general area, as is testified by the various instances of *katagein*, the forceful detainment of grain ships destined for other poleis. Under normal circumstances, the importers preferred more pervasive but less forceful measures. On the one hand, they offered incentives and honours to the exporters, as is shown by the honours accorded to the Bosporan kings by Athens in the fourth century.

On the other hand, as a direct consequence of the private character of the majority of grain production and trade, the importers took a variety of measures to influence and constrain their own traders. The main means of such intervention was legislation, as seen in Athens and Teos. Both in Athens and Teos, two very different poleis in terms of political and economic power, the state legislated to constrain its traders as to the import of grain. In Athens, citizens and metics were obliged not to import grain to any other port but the Athenian, while in Teos citizens, and presumably metics, were obliged not to divert grain imports from the polis. As was mentioned above, the differences between the measures employed by the two poleis were the result of their different political and economic positions in the Greek World, since Athens was a powerful polis with many citizen and metic traders, while Teos was a small polis without the luck of having a large contingent of local traders. Athens regulated further on its importation of grain by outlawing cartels and the cornering of the market, as well as by regulating the maximum profit on imported grain sales. Both pieces of legislation testify to the existence of the notion of a just price in the ancient world and complement the regulation of retail prices of flour and bread.[3] Finley's suggestion that just price was a medieval concept cannot be proven, since not only does the evidence from Athens suggest that the notion existed in the ancient

[3] [Aristotle] *Constitution of the Athenians* 51.3.

world, but also the condemnations of monopoly further suggest that just price was a mercantile and consumer concern.[4]

Of most interest is the Athenian legislation regulating the finance of foreign trading ventures. Athens in this case is seen intervening forcefully in the hidden backbone of overseas trade, lending capital, by regulating the available ventures in which investors based in Athens could participate. Against the common opinion of scholars on the matter, it was shown that this piece of legislation regulated not merely grain imports, or indeed any imports, but both imports and exports from the Athenian *emporion*. Such intervention on the part of a polis state is particularly illuminating, since it pervades every aspect of Athenian trading, whilst simultaneously being within the peaceful prerogative of the polis. This piece of legislation testifies both to the power that the polis could yield in terms of intervention in foreign trade and to the economic sophistication of the legislators, who recognised and harnessed the invisible power of finance.

Models of Governmental Intervention/Involvement in Trade

Thirty-five years ago, Moses Finley devoted a whole chapter of his *Ancient Economy* to the interaction between state and economy in the ancient world. A very small part of that chapter discussed the role of the state in foreign trade and concluded that ancient states, Greek and Roman, intervened only occasionally and on a limited basis, mainly in connection with crisis.[5] This view has become the orthodoxy on the subject and further investigation into the role of governments has been virtually non-existent. Even in works that touch upon the subject and the evidence relating to governmental intervention, Finley's view of occasional and exceptional intervention has been the guiding principle.[6]

The aim of this work has been to explore the role of the state in foreign trade in the archaic and classical periods. In effect, this can be expressed in one simple question: did Greek governments intervene

[4] Finley (1999: 170). Condemnations of monopoly: Demosthenes 56.7–9; Aristotle *Politics* 1259a5–33 (two cases).

[5] Finley (1985: 155).

[6] Most examples of this practice relate to the trade in grain, given the natural preoccupation of our Athenian sources with the matter. On the Tean law on grain: Bravo (1983: 23); Jameson (1983: 12); Garnsey & Morris (1989: 103). On the Solonian ban of exports: Garnsey (1988: 75); Jameson (1983: 11); Austin & Vidal-Naquet (1977: 69).

in trade, and, if so, how? From the above presentation of the various methods and circumstances of governmental involvement and intervention in the trade of commodities, it is evident that governments in the Greek world both were involved and intervened in trade. More importantly, governments did not confine their involvement and intervention to extreme and exceptional circumstances. On the contrary, governments in the Greek world had both the ability and the will to play a role in the trade of commodities, both in imports and in exports.

Since non-intervention by governments is considered a major sign of the primitive economy, then it follows that intervention and involvement by governments denotes a non-primitive economy.[7] Under these circumstances, the conclusion is forced upon us that the current view of the state as a non-intervening entity in the Greek economy is wrong. Yet, the issue is not closed, since the role played by the government differed according to the type of state, the period and the specific requirements of the commodity in question. A government in the Greek world and its fringes had available a wide spectrum of intervention in the trade of commodities, importing or exporting. Different types of poleis and polities used different parts of the spectrum, although they sometimes overlapped.

The oriental kingdoms, such as Lydia, Persia or Alexandrian Egypt, intervened heavily in the exploitation and trading of their resources. Unfortunately, no evidence on their import policies has survived. The oriental kingdoms not only owned their resources but also exploited them directly, thus gaining control of the vast majority of surpluses. Similar direct intervention is exhibited in the disposition of surpluses by oriental states, since the only attested means of disposition are through direct trade with other states and gifts. However, it is probable that the oriental kingdoms also catered to the needs of private traders for products to reach the open market. The system followed by oriental states was clearly monopolistic and at times even extended to resources not owned by the state, as in the grain scheme of Kleomenes of Egypt.

The autocratic regimes of the orient had their counterparts in the Greek world. These Greek kingdoms also had ownership of their resources but employed a mixed system of exploitation and control. They exercised direct exploitation of the resources, as in the case of gold, but also allowed private exploitation under a closed system of limitations controlled directly by the king rather than legislation, as in timber. The

[7] Finley (1985: 154–155); Austin & Vidal-Naquet (1977: 112).

system of exploitation differed from that of the polis, even though both involved concessions, since the kingdoms retained control of exploitation and the disposition of the product as seen in the treaties between the Macedonian king and Athens and the Chalcidian League. Additionally, both in Macedon and in the Cypriot kingdoms, the safety and quality of resources was considered an important issue and was ensured through the control of the king. The concessions of the Greek kingdoms can be paralleled to the oriental, albeit on a smaller scale; where the oriental kingdoms provided poleis and governors with concessions to resources, the Greek kingdoms provided these to private individuals. In the disposition of surpluses, the Greek kingdoms again exhibited a mixed system. They preferred direct trade but through treaty agreements rather than arbitrarily, and also provided marketable surpluses to private traders. There is a definite tendency towards monopoly arrangements, as is also seen in the monopoly of silphium in Kyrene. In the case of grain, where surpluses were mainly in private hands, the kingdoms, as seen in the case of the Spartokids, did make arrangements on the disposition of surpluses, including direct disposition through gifts. Very little information on the import policies of the Greek kingdoms survives; for their arrangements with poleis, it appears that they utilised the existing trading networks, although with the aid of treaties or arrangements with the exporting governments, as in the case of Amyntas and the Chalcidians and Athens and the Spartokids.

The polis had some few common characteristics with the systems of the above categories, most importantly that of ownership of resources. Beyond that, however, the polis exhibited a strongly devolved system of control and exploitation, mainly through an open leasing system. Leasing in the polis was characterised by the lack of exploitation control beyond basic safety issues, a policy of non-control of the disposition of the private surpluses and the concessions through legislative open procedure. In some cases, the polis imposed limitations on exploitation, as the poleis of south Italy did with timber, but probably this was an issue dictated by the nature of the transaction, since Dionysios was not a private individual but the representative of a foreign government. The polis also ensured the safety and quality of its resources, like Macedon, but through legislation rather than direct control. Disposition of surpluses was also widely diffused. The polis allowed private individuals not only to control but also to dispose of surpluses freely. More importantly, it kept only part of the surplus as its own, so its powers of disposition were smaller. Public surpluses were mainly disposed of within the state, either through direct gifts to the populace or through state finances and projects such as coinage. The polis could dispose of public surpluses as gifts to other states, as Kyrene did, but such actions are observed only under exceptional circumstances. Lastly, the polis as exporter provided incentives to importers and through them to private traders to achieve disposition of surpluses, both private and public.

The polis intervened in imports considerably more pervasively than other states. When necessary the polis did engage in direct imports, mainly when dealing with states that preferred monopoly and direct arrangements. Even then, the polis preferred to operate through treaties, since treaties provided the framework for private traders to access the monopolic markets. The reliance of the polis on trading networks is best exhibited by the incentives provided to foreign traders whenever import was necessary and by the coercive legislation aimed at guiding local traders towards specific imports. In addition, the poleis provided incentives to the exporters, mainly through honours.

The polis, however, was not always peaceful in its dealings. Thus, especially in times of crisis, chance and often violent means of acquisition were used against both the local population and foreign traders or states. Such actions were, on the home front, the imposition of extraordinary taxes and the borrowing from temples and, on the foreign front, the use of *katagein* and the acquisition of booty. The level of intervention that the polis could exercise was to some extent dependent on its political and military power, not on economic factors. Thus, some poleis, when they had the ability, engaged in conquest or violent colonisation of the resource areas, thus acquiring disposable surpluses. Such an outlook is exhibited by Athens throughout the classical period and especially during the fifth-century empire.

The differences in intervention and involvement of the three types of polity prominent in the Greek World have created three interlocking models, since all three types of polity were in constant contact with each other, and the economic realities of the Mediterranean required frequent and extensive exchange between them. A major issue immediately apparent is the applicability of the models to other types of polity and other commodities. The first, and probably the least likely to be answered, is the place of tribal organisations in this interlocking mosaic of intervention. In the borders of the Greek world, tribal organisations were the normal 'polity' with which the Greek poleis and kingdoms had to interact. Many of the resources, especially in the Black Sea, Sicily, Magna Graecia and Illyria, were in the traditional territories controlled by tribes. The similar situation in Thrace provides a model for the interaction between tribes and other polities, mainly the polis. The lack of concerted effort against Athens by the Thracian tribes of the Strymon and Thasos highlights the antagonistic relationship between them. Simultaneously the powerful reaction of the tribes against the Athenian incursion in the 460s shows that at least some tribal organisations were very much aware of the economic and political importance of their resources, something further testified by the extensive tribal coinages. The situation in Thrace, however, may not be directly comparable to other regions, especially the Black Sea, where relations between natives and Greeks seem to have been more integrative as shown by the mergence of Greek trade centres in the native settlements of Colchis.

In the same vein, it would be particularly illuminating to know more about the type of intervention and policy of the polis towards the Phoenician city-kingdoms. The Phoenicians were a major trading power in the Mediterranean in the period and were in constant contact with the Greeks, not only in the western but also in the eastern Mediterranean. The interaction between Greeks, Phoenicians and natives in Iberia was explored in relation to silver and gold but the relations between the polis and the Phoenicians outside the Carthaginian sphere of influence were not necessarily the same. The Athenian honours and privileges granted to Strato of Sidon in the fourth century exhibit aspects of the attitude towards the Greek autocratic regimes, both Macedon and the Spartokids. However, the inclusion of privileges granted to Sidonian traders in the same decree can be explained in two very different fashions. On the one hand, the peculiar polity of the Phoenician city-kingdom was readily recognised by the Greeks, or at least the Athenians, and thus privileges to citizens had to be granted semi-independently of those to the king, maybe as an effort to avoid the implication of a direct clientship relation.

The second issue relating to state intervention is the applicability of the models to commodities that were less universally important. On the one hand, the existing resources of a state are its most important asset, even if they are not precious metals, shipbuilding timber or cereals. As such, we would expect, given the above conclusions on the intervention in exports, that the state—polis, Greek or oriental kingdom—would provide for them in the same or similar fashion to that exhibited for gold, silver, timber and grain. Definitive conclusions on this issue are outside the scope of this work but other cases testify to similar policies and pressures by and on the exporters. For example, Thasos legislated in order to safeguard the quality of its wine by regulating the timing of the acceptable sale of grapes in the pre-harvest season and by outlawing the import of foreign wines in its territory (due to the fear of diluting Thasian wines with inferior vintages and of the sale of foreign wines in Thasian amphoras).[8] In the same vein, the case of Kean *miltos* testifies to considerable intervention by the importers, in this case Athens, to create a monopoly of exchange, similar to that exhibited by both Athens and the Chalcidian League in their agreements with Macedon on timber.[9]

One of the most apparent issues highlighted by this work is that information differs according to geographical area. The surviving evidence of the oriental kingdoms is almost exclusively confined to exports, while the information on the polis mainly relates to imports. The Greek kingdoms provide information both on imports and on exports but that on exports is considerably larger. The situation becomes even more apparent when juxtaposing the importers and exporters of each commodity. As was mentioned above, the exporters are in their majority in the outer layers of the Greek world or its fringes, while the importers are almost invariably in Greece, the Aegean and Asia Minor. Of course, the specific geographical parameters change according to commodity but even so, the pattern remains the same with the partial exception of silver. This geographical distribution can be enlightening in the trade of particular commodities and in a variety of other issues, including settlement abroad. In addition to any such information, the geographical distribution also provides a clue as to the distribution of information on trade that has survived. It is generally accepted that the majority of literary works and artefacts from the archaic and classical periods have not survived. However, the laws of probability dictate that in addition to lucky survivals, the most common elements are more likely to survive than the rarer. In other words, since the majority of importers were in the geographical area of Greece, the Aegean and Asia Minor, import information from the states in these areas is be more likely to have survived. Similarly the further out from this centre, the more information on exports will have survived. Simultaneously, this situation has been further aggravated by the archaeological attention paid to Greece, the Aegean and Asia Minor, which makes the discovery of information in this area more likely.

Lastly, and probably most importantly, the disparity of intervention between polities and particularly the limited intervention exhibited by

[8] IG XII, Suppl. 347.

[9] IG II[2] 1128.

the polis in comparison with the Greek and oriental kingdoms must be explained. Moses Finley rightly noted that Greek states had "infinite room for state intervention."[10] Although it has been shown that the polis intervened and involved itself in trade considerably more than Finley suggested, the extent of such intervention and involvement was less than that of other contemporary polities. Finley, in what has been the standard treatment of the subject for 35 years, suggested that the explanation of the phenomenon lies in the difference between 'economic policy' and 'unintended economic consequences' exhibiting the Greeks' conceptual lack of an 'economy.'[11] Finley's explanation not only does not fit the available evidence as presented in the previous chapters, where the polis is seen involving itself and intervening in trade, but also disregards a major historical concern. The polis did not exist in a vacuum but was one of three main polity types that were in constant contact for centuries. A conceptual lack is not a sustainable argument when it applies only to a specifically delimited part of a civilisation. In other words, if the Greeks lacked economic understanding which led to a lack of rational and specific intervention then not only should the existing cases of polis intervention not exist but also the Greek kingdoms, not to mention the oriental, should not exhibit any greater or lesser intervention than the polis. The explanation of this phenomenon and the differences in intervention between the polis and other polities lies not in Finley's 'conceptual lack' nor, as he rightly noted, in theories of public and private sphere demarcation, but rather in the political and communal nature of the polis itself.[12]

The polis, democratic or oligarchic, was a community of individuals and never lost this defining characteristic throughout the period. Other types of polity, and particularly the Greek and oriental kingdoms, were more like modern states than the Greek polis, since there was a definite division between government, centring on the person of the king, and people. In the polis, the state was the people, even if the people can only be defined as a segment of the population. Thus, there was no clear division between government and people, because the government was the people. Even in oligarchic states, the government included assemblies of the people and the ruling councils were more inclusive of the populace than a king's court or a modern parliament. The only possibility of a

[10] Finley (1999: 155).
[11] Finley (1999: 155, 164).
[12] Finley (1999: 155).

polis resembling the modern state is a polis under tyranny, when the government is divorced from the people because of the domination of a given individual.

Consequently, the polis could not control all exploitation of resources and subsequently the available surplus. More importantly, the polis did not want such control either of the resources or of the surplus, since such control would immediately mean a controller, and thus create the possibility of a tyrant. Even in oligarchic poleis such control could not be achieved, since the different factions ensured that there was enough fear of tyranny to avoid placing such power in the hands of one individual or a small group of them. Legislation, especially early laws, testifies to the anxiety of the Greeks in controlling and limiting the power of individuals and groups, as is seen mainly in the various laws penalising and limiting the power of magistrates.[13] From the available spectrum of intervention possibilities, the polis chose what it could use, as the kingdoms, with their different political and ideological structure, chose theirs.

When the polis played a more forceful role in trade and used heavy intervention, such intervention is invariably linked to crisis, power or both. Thus, even the smallest and weakest polis, when famine threatened, would employ *katagein* to bring in grain. Similarly, when a polis achieved power, military and political, it could forcefully colonise or conquer outright the resource areas of the commodity it needed, such as Athens did with the Strymon region. Often a polis in power was also a polis in crisis or threatened by crisis, such as Athens during the empire when shipbuilding timber was a necessity for keeping its power over the allies.

Under regular circumstances, the polis preferred pervasive intervention in trade without being heavy handed. The main instruments of the polis were legislation and incentives. Incentives were aimed at foreign states and traders in order to attract trading partners. Legislation was aimed internally either as a protection mechanism for the resources, for exports, or as a framework of conduct for traders, for imports. The most interesting feature of the role played by the polis, as against Greek and oriental kingdoms, is the effort of the system to target private traders. The current primitivist orthodoxy, as discussed in the introduction to this work, relegates traders to the fringes of polis society, because of the large number of metics and *xenoi* involved in trade and the condemnatory attitude of the philosophical sources towards manual workers and traders.

[13] Harris (2006).

Although the philosophical sources portray traders and manufacturers as socially inferior, the evidence of state intervention shows that governments were particularly interested in attracting traders to their harbours and does not betray an attitude of perceived social inferiority. Further, the reason why the polis never took the obvious step of more pervasive intervention by creating a merchant navy beholden exclusively to it, is that such a move would place too much power in the hands of a small group of people, and also that even Athens, with its large population, did not have all the traders it needed to trade all its necessary imports and available exports. The social position of traders in the polis is outside the scope of this work and largely irrelevant to the issue at hand. Whether traders were acceptable in the *symposia* of the upper echelons of society is immaterial to their role in the economy of the polis and to the behaviour of the polis as an institution towards them. Traders may have been despised by the Athenian aristocrats and even by ordinary citizens; either due to their occupation or to their status, but their necessity in trade was clearly recognised by the polis. At the very least, it is evident that the polis was interested in traders and recognised their power over its economy.

However, since the polis was a polity based on community rather than government, the importance of traders in its survival, and more importantly the extensive use of incentives to individuals as well as communities of traders, create a definite chasm between practice and ideal. Notably, this chasm is not so much the product of the differences between modern theory and ancient evidence but rather that between the ancient philosophical perspective on trade and traders and the hard evidence of ancient oratory and inscriptions.[14] The chasm has been artificially widened by the insistence of the current primitivist theories on the ancient economy of concentrating upon a limited elite moralising perspective found in some philosophical writings. The easy solution is both obvious and easily called upon, in other words to reject the philosophical evidence as an upper class utopian and moralising perspective. Such blanket solutions, however, are as suspicious as imposing economic models from other eras and areas on the Greek world.

The divergence between reality and philosophy on Greek trade can be as illuminating as it is confusing. Morality, conventional or upper class, and economic reality on the ground can be divergent. The didactic nature

[14] For a similar sentiment, see Samuel (1983: 7).

of Greek philosophy meant that moral criticism of 'unnatural' economic pursuits was as valid as providing practical advice for individuals and poleis to increase their revenue or come out of crisis by equally 'unnatural' means. Expecting the Greeks to be consistent between ideal and practice is idealising a culture and a society as flawed as any other. No one would consider valid the argument that since medieval and Byzantine religious belief in Christianity idealised pious poverty, the papal administration or the societies concerned actually practiced it. In a similar vein, communist beliefs did not stop the existence of a definite upper-lower class practical divide in the countries that practiced communism.

The amount of intervention in the trade of commodities, both exports and imports, and the types of intervention employed show that the Greeks were cognizant of the economic situation of their world and the laws of trade. Providing incentives to ameliorate the weaknesses of a primary export, as the Spartokids did, shows that the Greeks understood the weaknesses and strengths of their economic position in the trading networks of the Mediterranean and that they had the economic basis for bettering their position. Similarly, providing incentives to foreign traders and states in conjunction with delineating the operations of local traders shows that the polis realised fully the power of the trading networks of the Mediterranean and the laws of supply and demand.

The polis never created Adam Smith, nor indeed could it. It was, however, a complex economic unit existing in a volatile geographical area with extensive trading networks. The polis did not invent a science of economics nor did it codify the laws of the economy; that was to be delayed until the modern period. It did however recognise the interlocking nature of the economic networks in the Mediterranean and invented sufficient and rational ways to viably use and interact with them. The polis never played the same role in trade as a modern state does. That however was not the result of a lack of understanding of economic laws or the lack of intervention options but rather the consequence of the political nature of the polis itself. The amount, types and pervasiveness of intervention of the polis in trade is a clear indicator of its interest and understanding of trade as an economic force.

WORKS CITED

3day Meeting for the Research for Primary Gold 30/11–2/12/1988 (1989, Athens).

Agard, J. & Emberger, A. (1989) "Introduction to Southwest Europe" in Dunning, F.W., Garrard, P., Haslam, H.W. & Ixer, R.A., *Mineral Deposits of Europe. Volume 4/5: Southwest and Eastern Europe with Iceland*, London, 1–36.

Allbaugh, L.G. (1953) *Crete: A Case Study of an Underdeveloped Area*, Princeton.

Amit, M. (1965) *Athens and the Sea*, Brussels.

Anderson, R.C. (1962) *Oared Fighting Ships*, London.

Andreades, A. (1933) *A History of Greek Public Finance*, Vol. I, Harvard.

Angel, J.L. (1972) "Ecology and Population in the Eastern Mediterranean" *World Archaeology* 4.1, 88–105.

Aperghis, G.G. (1997/1998) "A Reassessment of the Laurion Mining Lease Records" *Bulletin of the Institute of Classical Studies* 42, 1–20.

Arsenic, Mercury, Antimony and Gold Deposits of Turkey (1970) *Publications of Mineral Research and Exploration Institute of Turkey* 129.

Aubet, M.E. (1993) *The Phoenicians and the West*, Cambridge.

Austin, M.M. & Vidal-Naquet, P. (1972) *Économies et sociétés en Grèce ancienne*, Paris.

Austin, M.M. & Vidal-Naquet, P. (1977) *Economic and Social History of Ancient Greece: An Introduction*, London.

Austin, M.M. (1985) "Review: Trade and Famine in Classical Antiquity; Trade in the Ancient Economy" *Journal of Hellenic Studies* 105, 209–210.

Bache J.J. (1987) *World Gold Deposits: A Geological Classification*, Oxford.

Badian, E. (ed) (1966) *Ancient Society and Institutions: Studies Presented to Victor Ehrenberg for His 75th Birthday*, Oxford.

Baeck, L. (1997) "Greek Economic Thought: Initiators of a Mediterranean Tradition" in Price, B.B. (ed) *Ancient Economic Thought*, Vol. 1, London, 146–171.

Baldwin, A. (1915) "The Electrum and Silver Coins of Chios, Issued during the Sixth, Fifth and Fourth Centuries BC" *American Journal of Numismatics* 48, 1–60.

Barbaressos, A. (1933) "The Gold of Greece" *Τεχνικά Χρονικά* ΔΕΚ, 202–230.

Bekker-Nielsen, T. & Hannestad, L. (2001) (eds) *War as a Cultural and Social Force. Essays on Warfare in Antiquity*, Copenhagen.

Beloch, K.J. (1923) *Griechische Geschichte*, Berlin.

Berent, M. (1996) "Hobbes and the "Greek Tongues"" *History of Political Thought* 17, 36–59.

Bill, C.P. (1926) "Bosporus and Phanagoria" *Classical Philology* 21.3, 254–256.

Bingen, J. (1978) *La papyrus revenue laws: tradition grecque et adaptation hellenistique*, Opladen.

Blackman, D. (1969) "The Athenian Navy and Allied Naval Contributions in the Pentekontaetia" *Greek, Roman and Byzantine Studies* 10, 179–216.

Blamire, A. (1989) *Plutarch: Life of Kimon*, London.
Blok, J.H. & Lardinois, A.P.M.H. (2006) (eds) *Solon of Athens*, Leiden.
Boardman, J. (1980) *The Greeks Overseas*, New York.
Boardman, J. (1994) "Settlement for Trade and Land in North Africa: Problems of Identity" in Tsetskhladze, G.R. & De Angelis, F. (eds) *The Archaeology of Greek Colonisation*, Oxford (Oxford University School of Archaeology Monograph 40), 137–149.
Boardman, J. (1996) *The Greeks Overseas*, Athens (Greek translation).
Boardman, J. (1999, 4th edition) *The Greeks Overseas. Their Early Colonies and Trade*, London.
Boeckh, A. (1886) *Die Staatshaushaltung der Athener*, Berlin.
Bonner, R.J. (1923) "The Commercial Policy of Imperial Athens" *Classical Philology* 18.3, 193–201.
Borza, E.N. (1987) "Timber and Politics in the Ancient World, Macedon and the Greeks" *Proceedings of the American Philosophical Society* 131.1, 32–52.
Borza, E.N. & Thomas, C.G. (1995) *Makedonika: Essays by E.N. Borza*, London.
Bouladon, J. (1989) "France and Luxemburg" in Dunning, F.W., Garrard, P., Haslam, H.W. & Ixer, R.A., *Mineral Deposits of Europe. Volume 4/5: Southwest and Eastern Europe with Iceland*, London, 37 f.
Bradeen, D.W. (1974) *The Athenian Agora: Results of Excavations Conducted by the American School of Classical Studies at Athens. Vol. 17, Inscriptions: The Funerary Monuments*, Princeton.
Braund, D. (2007) "Black Sea Grain for Athens? From Herodotos to Demosthenes" in Gabrielsen, V. and Lund, J. (eds) *The Black Sea in Antiquity. Regional and Interregional Economic Exchanges*, Aarhus, 39–68.
Bravo B. (1983) "Le commerce des céréales chez les Grecs de l'époque archaïque" in Garnsey, P. & Whittaker, C.R. (eds) *Trade and Famine in Classical Antiquity* (Cambridge Philological Society Supplement 8), 17–29.
Bresson, A. (1993) "Les cité Grecques et leurs emporia" in Bresson, A. & Rouillard, P. (eds) *L'Emporion*, Paris, 163–226.
Bresson, A. (2000) *Le cité marchande*, Bordeaux.
Bresson, A. & Rouillard, P. (eds) (1993, Paris) *L'Emporion*.
Briant P. (2002) *From Cyrus to Alexander: A History of the Persian Empire*, London.
Bucher, K. (1893) *Die Entstehung der Volkswirtschaft: Vorträge und Versuche*, Tübingen.
Burkert, W. (1992) *The Orientalizing Revolution: Near Eastern Influence on Greek Culture in the Early Archaic Age*, Cambridge.
Bury, J.B. & Meiggs, R. (1994, 4th edition) *A History of Greece*, Oxford.
Cabrera, P. (1998) "Greek Trade in Iberia: The Extent of Interaction" *Oxford Journal of Archaeology* 17.2, 191–206.
Cameron, G.G. (1948) *Persepolis Treasury Tablets*, Chicago.
Camp, M.J. & Kroll, J.H. (2001) "The Agora Mint and Athenian Bronze Coinage" *Hesperia* 70.2, 127–162.
Carter, J.C. (2005) *Discovering the Greek Countryside at Metaponto*, London.
Cartledge, P.A. & Harvey, F.D. (1985) (eds) *Crux: Essays Presented to G.E.M. de Ste. Croix on His 75th Birthday* (*History of Political Thought* 6.1/2), Exeter.

Cartledge, P.A., Cohen, E. & Foxhall, L. (2002) (eds) *Money, Labour and Land*, London.
Casson, L. (1954) "The Grain Trade of the Hellenistic World" *Transactions of the American Philological Association* 85, 168–187.
Casson, L. (1994) *Ships and Seafaring in Ancient Times*, London.
Casson, L. (1995) *Ships and Seamanship in the Ancient World*, Baltimore.
Cauuet, B. (2002) "Ancient Gold Mines of Dacia" National Research Program (Romania) Alburnus Major Report 2002: http://www.rosiamontana.org/documents/pdf/archrep2002eng.pdf.
Classical Studies Presented to Edward Capps (1936), Princeton.
Cawkwell, G.L. (1963) "Eubulus" *Journal of Hellenic Studies* 83, 47–67.
Coates, J. & McGrail, S. (1985) *The Greek Trireme of the 5th Century BCE*, London.
Coates, J. & Morrison, J. (1987) "Authenticity in the Replica Athenian Trieres" *Antiquity* 61, 87–90.
Cohen, E.E. (1992) *Athenian Economy and Society: A Banking Perspective*, Princeton.
Cole, J.W. (1975) "Peisistratus at the Strymon" *Greece & Rome* 22, 42–44.
Cook, J.M. (1973) *The Troad: An Archaeological and Topographical Study*, Oxford.
Crosby, M. (1950) "Leases of the Laurion Mines" *Hesperia* 19, 189–297.
Cunningham, C.J.K. (1967) "The Silver of Laurion" *Greece & Rome*, 40, 150–162.
Davies, J.K. (2005) "Linear and Nonlinear Flow Models for Ancient Economies" in Manning, J.G. & Morris, I. (eds) *The Ancient Economy: Evidence and Models*, Stanford, 127–156.
Dayton, J. (1978) *Minerals, Metals, Glazing & Man, or Who Was Sesostris I?*, London.
de Blois, L., Bons, J., Kessel, T. & Schenkeveld, D.M. (2005) (eds) *The Statesman in Plutarch's Works, Volume 2: The Statesman in Plutarch's Greek and Roman Lives*, Leiden.
de Sanctis, G. (1935) "Epigraphica XIV Contributi epigrafici alla storia della Guerra deceleica" *Rivista di Filologia* 13, 205–213.
Demou, E. & Arvanitidis, N. (1998) "The Ancient Mines in the Region of Macedonia, Greece, and Their Significance for the Geological and Cultural Heritage" *Geologica Balcanica* 28.3–4, 67–70.
Demou, E. (1989) "Αυτοφυή Μέταλλα σε Στρώματα-Μεταλλοφορίες της Ελλάδας και η Σημασία τους" *Δελτίο της Ελληνικής Γεωλογικής Εταιρείας* 33/2, pp. 207–223.
Descat, R. (1993) "La loi de Solon sur l'interdiction d'exporter les produits Attiques" in Bresson, A. & Rouillard, P. (eds) *L'Emporion*, Paris, 145–161.
Develin, R. (1989) *Athenian Officials, 684–321 BC*, Cambridge.
Deuxieme Conference Internationale d'Histoire Economique (1965), Paris.
Dillery, J. (1993) "Xenophon's Poroi and Athenian Imperialism" *Historia* 42, 1–11.
Dominguez, A. (1999) "Hellenisation in Iberia? The Reception of Greek Prod-

ucts and Influences by the Iberians" in Tsetskhladze, G.R. (ed) *Ancient Greeks West and East*, Leiden (Mnemosyne Supplement 196), 301–330.
Dumitru, F.C. (1993) "A Brief History of Mining on Romania's Territory" *Mineral Wealth* 84, 51–58.
Dunning, F.W., Garrard, P., Haslam, H.W. & Ixer, R.A. (1989) (eds) *Mineral Deposits of Europe. Volume 4/5: Southwest and Eastern Europe with Iceland*, London.
Dunning, F.W., Mykura, W. & Slater, D. (1982) (eds) *Mineral Deposits of Europe. Volume 2: southeast Europe*, London.
Ehrenberg, V. (1973, 2nd edition) *From Solon to Socrates*, London.
Elat, M. (1979) "Trade in Ancient Israel" in Lipinski, E. (ed) *State and Temple Economy in the Ancient Near East*, Vol. II Leuven, 527–546.
Eliopoulos, D.G. & Konstantinides, D.K. (1989) "Μεταλλοφορίες Πρωτογενούς Χρυσού στη Ροδοπική Μάζα, Αξιολόγηση—Δυνατότητες Ανάπτυξης" in *3day Meeting for the Research for Primary Gold 30/11–2/12/1988* Athens, 66–92.
Επεξηγηματικόν Τεύχος του Μεταλλογενετικού Χάρτου της Ελλάδος (1973) Αθήνα.
Falles, F.M. (1984) "The Neo-Assyrian Period" in Archi, A. (ed) *The Circulation of Goods in Non-Palatial Context in the Ancient Near East: Proceedings of the International Conference Organized by the Istituto per gli Studi Micenei ed Egeo-Anatolici*, Rome, 207–220.
Faraguna, M. (2000) "Individuo, stato e comunità. Studi recenti sulla polis" *Dike* 3, 217–229.
Faraguna, M. (2006) "La città di Atene e l'amministrazione dell minere di Laurion," in Rupprecht, H.-A. (ed) *Symposion 2003. Vorträge zur griechischen und hellenistischen Rechtsgeschichte*, Vienna, 141–160.
Figueira, T. (1981) *Aigina: Society and Politics*, New York.
Figueira, T. (1986) "Sitopolai and Sitophylakes in Lysias' 'Against the Graindealers': Governmental Intervention in the Athenian Economy" *Phoenix* 40.2, 149–171.
Finley, M. I (1952) *Studies in Land and Credit in Ancient Athens, 500–200 B.C. The Horos-Inscriptions*, New Brunswick.
Finley, M.I. (1954) *The World of Odysseus*, London.
Finley, M.I. (1965) "Classical Greece" in *Deuxieme Conference Internationale d'Histoire Economique* Paris, 11–35.
Finley, M.I. (1970) "Aristotle and Economic Analysis" *Past and Present* 47, 3–25.
Finley, M.I. (1985, 2nd edition) *The Ancient Economy*, London.
Finley, M.I. (1999, updated edition) *The Ancient Economy*, London.
Fisher, N. & van Wees, H. (1998) (eds) *Archaic Greece: New Approaches and New Evidence*, London.
Forbes, R.J. (1964) *Studies in Ancient Technology*, Vol. 8, Leiden.
Forbes, R.J. (1971, 2nd edition) *Studies in Ancient Technology*, Vol. 8, Leiden.
Foxhall, L. & Forbes, H.A. (1982) "Sitometreia: The Role of Grain as a Staple Food in Classical Antiquity" *Chiron* 12, 41–90.
Foxhall, L. & Lewis, A.P.E. (1996) (eds) *Greek Law in its Political Setting*, Oxford.
Foxhall, L. (1992) "The Control of the Attic Landscape" in Wells, B. (ed) *Agri-*

culture in Ancient Greece: Proceedings of the Seventh International Symposium at the Swedish Institute at Athens (16–17 May 1990), Stockholm, 155–159.
Foxhall, L. (1998) "Cargoes of the Heart's Desire" in Fisher, N. & van Wees, H. (eds) *Archaic Greece: New Approaches and New Evidence*, London, 295–309.
Foxhall, L. (2003) "Cultures, Landscapes, and Identities in the Mediterranean World" *Mediterranean History Review* 18.2, 75–92.
French, A. (1964) *The Growth of the Athenian Economy*, London.
Gabelia, A.N. (2003) "Dioscurias" in Grammenos, D.V. & Petropoulos, E.K. (eds) *Ancient Greek Colonies in the Black Sea* 2 volumes Thessaloniki *Publication of the Archaeological Institute of Northern Greece* no. 4, 1215–1266.
Gabrielsen, V. (1994) *Financing the Athenian Fleet*, Oxford.
Gabrielsen, V. and Lund, J. (2007) (eds) *The Black Sea in Antiquity. Regional and Interregional Economic Exchanges*, Aarhus.
Gagarin, M. (2006) "Legal Procedure in Solon's Laws" in Blok, J.H. & Lardinois, A.P.M.H. (eds) *Solon of Athens*, Leiden, 261–275.
Galanopoulos, V. & Theodoroudis, A. (1994) "Gold, Silver and Base Metals in the Manganese Mineral Assemblages of the NE Chalkidiki Ore Deposits" *Δελτίο της Ελληνικής Γεωλογικής Εταιρείας* 30/1, 507–518.
Gallant, T.W. (1989) "Crisis and Response: Risk-Buffering Behavior in Hellenistic Greek Communities" *Journal of Interdisciplinary History* 19.3, 393–413.
Gallant, T.W. (1991) *Risk and Survival in Ancient Greece: Reconstructing the Rural Domestic Economy*, Cambridge.
Gardikas, S.K. (1939) "Η Ἔρευνα τοῦ Ὀρυκτοῦ Χρυσοῦ ἐν Μακεδονίᾳ: Ὁ Χρυσὸς τῆς Λεκάνης τοῦ Λαγκαδά" *Εργαστήρια Γεωλογίας-Παλαιοντολογίας Καὶ Ὀρυκτολογίας-Πετρολογίας* 16.
Gardner, P. (1920) "The Financial History of Ancient Chios" *Journal of Hellenic Studies* 40, 160–173.
Garland, R. (1987) *The Piraeus from the Fifth to the First Century B.C.*, London.
Garnsey, P. & Morris, I. (1989) "Risk and the Polis: The Evolution of Institutionalised Responses to Food Supply Problems in the Ancient Greek State" in Halstead, P. & O'Shea, J. (eds) *Bad Year Economics: Cultural Responses to Risk and Uncertainty*, Cambridge, 98–105.
Garnsey, P. & Whittaker, C.R. (1983) (eds) *Trade and Famine in Classical Antiquity* (Cambridge Philological Society Supplement 8), Cambridge.
Garnsey, P. (1985) "Grain for Athens" in Cartledge, P.A. & Harvey, F.D. (eds) *Crux: Essays Presented to G.E.M. de Ste. Croix on his 75th Birthday* (*History of Political Thought* 6.1/2), Exeter, 62–75.
Garnsey, P. (1988) *Famine and Food Supply in the Greco-Roman World*, Cambridge.
Garnsey, P. (1998) *Cities, Peasants and Food in Classical Antiquity*, Cambridge.
Garnsey, P., Hopkins, K. & Whittaker, C.R. (1983) (eds) *Trade in the Ancient Economy*, London.
Gauthier, P. (1976) *Un commentaire historique des Poroi de Xénophon*, Geneva.
Gauthier, P. (1981) "De Lysias à Aristote Ath.Pol. 51.4: le commerce du grain à Athènes et les functions des sitophylakes" *Revue historique de droit français et étranger* 59, 1–28.
Georgalas, G.C. (1921) "Ὁ Ὀρυκτὸς Χρυσὸς ἐν Ἑλλάδι καὶ αἱ Χρυσοφόροι

Προσχώσεις Νιγρίτης" *Δημοσιεύματα Του Γεωλογικού Γραφείου* 2.
Glodariu, I. (1976) *Dacian Trade with the Hellenistic and Roman Worlds* (British Archaeological Reports Supplement 8), Oxford.
Goldsmith, R. (1987) *Premodern Financial Systems*, Cambridge.
Gomme, A.W. (1933) *The Population of Athens in the Fifth and Fourth Centuries B.C.*, Oxford.
Goyon, G. (1957) *Nouvelles Inscriptions Rupestres du Wadi Hammamat*, Paris.
Graham, A.J. (1997) "Review Article: The Archaeology of Greek Colonisation" *Journal of Hellenic Studies* 117, 250.
Grammenos, D.V. & Petropoulos, E.K. (eds) (2003) *Ancient Greek Colonies in the Black Sea* 2 volumes *Publications of the Archaeological Institute of Northern Greece* 4, Thessaloniki.
Greek Mining Enterprises Association (1979) *The Greek Mineral Wealth*, Athens.
Hadjistavrinou, Y. & Contantinou, G. (1982) "Cyprus" in Dunning, F.W., Mykura, W. & Slater, D. (eds) *Mineral Deposits of Europe. Volume 2: Southeast Europe*, London, 255–277.
Hall, J.M. (2007) *A History of the Archaic Greek World*, London.
Halstead, P. & O'Shea, J. (1989) (eds) *Bad Year Economics: Cultural Responses to Risk and Uncertainty*, Cambridge.
Hammond, N.G.L. (1979) *A History of Macedonia Vol. II, 550–336 BCE*, Oxford.
Hammond, N.G.L. (1988) "The King and the Land in the Macedonian Kingdom" *Classical Quarterly* 38, 382–391.
Hammond N.G.L. (1989) *The Macedonian State: Origins, Institutions and History*, Oxford.
Hansen, M.H. & Nielsen, T.H. (2004) *An Inventory of Archaic and Classical Poleis*, Oxford.
Hansen, M.H. (1985) *Demography and Democracy*, Copenhagen.
Hansen, M.H. (1988) "Three Studies in Athenian Demography" *Historisk-Filosofiske Meddelelser* 56, 1–28.
Hansen, M.H. (1998) *Polis and City-State: An Ancient Concept and Its Modern Equivalent*, Copenhagen.
Hansen, M.H. (2002) "Was the Polis a State or a Stateless Society?" in Nielsen, T.H. (ed) *Even More Studies in the Ancient Greek Polis: Papers from the Copenhagen Polis Centre*, Stuttgart, 17–47.
Hansen, M.H. (2006) *Studies in the Population of Aigina, Athens and Eretreia*, Copenhagen.
Hanson, V.D. (1998) *Warfare and Agriculture in Classical Greece*, California.
Hanson, W.S. & Haynes, I.P. (2004) (eds) *Roman Dacia. The Making of a Provincial Society* (Journal of Roman Archaeology Supplementary Series 56), Portsmouth.
Harris, E.M. (1999) "Notes on the New Grain-Tax Law" *Zeitschrift fur Papyrologie und Epigraphik* 128, 269–272.
Harris, E.M. (2003) "Law and Economy in Classical Athens: [Demosthenes], "Against Dionysodorus""" in C.W. Blackwell (ed), *Dēmos: Classical Athenian Democracy* (A. Mahoney and R. Scaife (eds), *The Stoa: A Consortium for Electronic Publication in the Humanities* [www.stoa.org]), edition of March 22, 2003, last accessed 28/07/2007.

Harris, E.M. (2006) "Solon and the Spirit of the Laws in Archaic and Classical Greece" in Blok, J.H. & Lardinois, A.P.M.H. (eds) *Solon of Athens*, Leiden, 290–320.

Hasebroek, J. (1928) *Staat und Handel im alten Griechenland*, Tübingen.

Hasebroek, J. (1933) *Trade and Politics in Ancient Greece*, London.

Hatzopoulos, M.B. (1996) *Macedonian Institutions under the Kings*, Athens.

Head, B.V. (1911, 2nd edition) *Historia Numorum: A Manual of Greek Numismatics*, Oxford.

Healy, J. (1978) *Mining and Metallurgy in the Greek and Roman World*, London.

Heisserer, A.J. (1954) "The Monetary Pact between Mytilene and Phokaia" *Zeitschrift für Papyrologie und Epigraphik* 55, 115–132.

Higgins, M.D. & Higgins R. (1996) *A Geological Companion to Greece and the Aegean*, Cambridge.

Hillman, J. (1973) "Agricultural Productivity and Past Population Potential at Asvan" *Anatolian Studies* 23, 225–240.

Hind, J. (1998) "Megarian Colonisation in the Western Half of the Black Sea" in Tsetskhladze, G.R. (ed) *The Greek Colonisation of the Black Sea Area: Historical Interpretation of Archaeology*, Stuttgart (Historia Einzelschriften 121), 131–152.

Hodge, A.T. (1998) *Ancient Greek France*, Philadelphia.

Hodges, H. (1970) *Technology in the Ancient World*, London.

Holladay, A.J. (1989) "The Hellenic Disaster at Egypt" *Journal of Hellenic Studies* 109, 176–182.

Holloway, R.R. (1990) *The Archaeology of Ancient Sicily*, Oxford.

Hopkins, K. (1983) "Introduction" in Garnsey, P., Hopkins, K. & Whittaker, C.R. (eds) *Trade in the Ancient Economy*, London, ix–xxv.

Hopper, R.J. (1953) "The Attic Silver Mines in the 4th Century BC" *Annual of the British School at Athens* 48, 200–254.

Hopper, R.J. (1961) "The Mines and Miners of Ancient Athens" *Greece & Rome* 8.2, 138–151.

Hopper R.J. (1968) "The Laureion Mines. A Reconsideration" *Annual of the British School at Athens* 63, 293–326.

Hopper, R.J. (1979) *Trade and Industry in Classical Greece*, London.

Horden, P. & Purcell, N. (2000) *The Corrupting Sea: A Study of Mediterranean History*, Oxford.

Hornblower, S. (1991a) *A Commentary on Thucydides. Volume 1: Books I–III*, Oxford.

Hornblower, S. (1991b) *The Greek World*, London.

Hort, A. (1968 reprint, 1916 original) *Theophrastus. Inquiry into Plants*, Harvard.

Humphreys, S.C. (1964) "History, Economics and Anthropology; the Work of Karl Polanyi" *History and Theory* 8, 165–212.

Humphreys, S.C. (1978) *Anthropology and the Greeks*, London.

Huxley, G.L. (1966) *The Early Ionians*, London.

Isager, S. & Hansen, M.H. (1975) *Aspects of Athenian Society in the Fourth Century BC*, Odense.

Jameson, M.H. (1978) "Agriculture and Slavery in Classical Athens" *Classical Journal* 73, 122–145.

Jameson, M.H. (1983) "Famine in the Greek World" in Garnsey, P. & Whittaker, C.R. (eds) *Trade and Famine in Classical Antiquity* (Cambridge Philological Society Supplement 8), 6–16.
Jardé, A. (1925) *Les céréales dans l'antiquité grecque*, Paris.
Jeffery, L.H. (1976) *Archaic Greece. The City States: c. 700–500 BC*, London.
Jenkins, G.K. (1970) *The Coinage of Gela*, Berlin.
Jenkins, G.K. (1972) *Ancient Greek Coins*, New York.
Johnson, A.C. (1927) "Ancient Forests and Navies" *Transactions of the American Philological Association* 58, 199–209.
Johnston, A. (1997) "Fifth Century Prices" in *Atti del Convegno Internazionale: I Vasi Attici ed Altre Ceramiche Coeve in Sicilia 1990*, Catania, 81–87.
Jones, J.E. (1982) "The Laurion Silver Mines" *Greece & Rome* 29.2, 170–183.
Jordan, B. (1972) *The Athenian Navy in the Classical Period*, California.
Kagan, D. (1982) "The Dates of the Earliest Coins" *American Journal of Archaeology* 86.3, 343–360.
Kakavoyiannis, E.C. (2005) *Μέταλλα Εϱγάσιμα και Συγκεχωϱημένα: Η Οϱγάνωση της Εκμετάλευσης του Οϱυκτού Πλούτου της Λαυϱεωτικής από την Αθηναϊκή Δημοκϱατια*, Αθήνα.
Kalcyk, H. (1996) "Aigina" in Kancik, H., Schneider, H. & Landfester, M. (eds) *Der Neue Pauly Enzyklopädie der Antike Gesamtwerk*, Stuttgart and Weimar Vol. 1, 320–322.
Kancik, H., Schneider, H. & Landfester, M. (1996) (eds) *Der Neue Pauly Enzyklopädie der Antike Gesamtwerk*, Stuttgart and Weimar.
Kelepertzis, A. (1980) "Η Πρόοδος των Ερευνών Χρυσού στις Περιοχές του Παραρτήματος Θεσσαλονίκης" *Ενημερωτικό Δελτίο Ινστιτούτου Γεωλογικών και Μεταλλευτικών Ερευνών* Ιουλ-Νοε, 12–20.
Kim, H.S. (2002) "Small Change and the Moneyed Economy" in Cartledge, P.A., Cohen, E. & Foxhall, L. (eds) *Money, Labour and Land*, London, 44–51.
Kirchner, J. (1901–1903) *Prosopographia Attika*, Berlin.
Konophagos, K. (1974 [1976]) "The Water Cisterns of Ore Washers in Laurion and Their Special Hydraulic Mortar" *Πρακτικά της Ακαδημίας Αθηνών* 49, 251–261.
Konophagos, K. (1980) *Le Laurium Antique*, Athens.
Koshelenko, G.A. & Kuznetsov, V.D. (1996) "Colchis and Bosporus: Two Models of Colonization" in Tsetskhladze, G.R. (ed) *New Studies on the Black Sea Littoral*, Oxford, 17–30.
Kraay, C.M. (1959) "The Composition of Greek Silver Coins" *Archaeometry* 2.
Kraay, C.M. (1964) "Hoards, Small Change and the Origin of Coinage" *Journal of Hellenic Studies* 84, 76–91.
Kraay, C.M. (1976) *Archaic and Classical Greek Coins*, London.
Kraay, C.M. & Emeleus, V.M. (1962) *The Composition of Greek Silver Coins*, Oxford.
Kraay, C.M. & Hirmer, M. (1966) *Greek Coins*, London.
Kryzhytskyy, S.D. & Krapivina, V.V. (2003) "Olbian Chora" in Grammenos, D.V. & Petropoulos, E.K. (eds) *Ancient Greek Colonies in the Black Sea* 2 volumes Thessaloniki (Publication of the Archaeological Institute of Northern Greece, no. 4), 507–562.

Kryzhytskyy, S.D., Krapivina V.V., Lejpunskaja, N.A. & Nazarov, V.V. (2003) "Olbia-Berezan" in Grammenos, D.V. & Petropoulos, E.K. (eds) *Ancient Greek Colonies in the Black Sea* 2 volumes Thessaloniki (Publication of the Archaeological Institute of Northern Greece, no. 4), 389–506.

Kuhrt, A. (1997) *The Ancient Near East: 3000–323 BC* 2 volumes, London.

Labarbe, J. (1957) *La loi navale de Thémistoclé*, Paris.

Lafranchi, G.B. & Parpola, S. (1990) (eds) *The Correspondence of Sargon II, Part II State Archives of Assyria Vol. V*, Helsinki.

Lamb, W.R.M. (1930) *Lysias*, Loeb Classical Library, Harvard.

Lavelle, B.M. (1992) "The Pisistratids and the Mines of Thrace" *Greek, Roman and Byzantine Studies* 33.1.

Leake, M. (1835) *Travels in Northern Greece*, London.

Legon, R.R. (1973) "The Megarian Decree and the Balance of Greek Naval Power" *Classical Philology* 68.3, 161–171.

Legon, R.R. (1981) *Megara, the Political History of a Greek City-State to 336 B.C.*, Ithaca.

Liatsikas, N. (1939) "Περὶ τοῦ Προσχωματικοῦ Χρυσοῦ τοῦ Γαλλικοῦ Ποταμοῦ" *Πρακτικά της Ακαδημίας Αθηνών* 14, 554–565.

Lloyd, G. (2002) "Preface" in Cartledge, P.A., Cohen, E. & Foxhall, L. (eds) *Money, Labour and Land*, London, xi–xviii.

Lockyear, K. (2004) "The Late Iron Age Background to Roman Dacia" in Hanson, W.S. & Haynes, I.P. (eds) *Roman Dacia: The Making of a Provincial Society* (Journal of Roman Archaeology Supplementary Series 56), 33–74.

Loomis, T. (1998) *Wages, Welfare Costs and Inflation in Classical Athens*, Oxford.

Loukopoulou, L. & Parissaki, M.G. (2004) "Teos and Abdera: The Epigraphic Evidence" in Moustaka, A., Skarlatidou, E., Tzannes, M.C. & Ersoy, Y. (eds) *Klazomenai, Teos and Abdera: Metropoleis and Colony*, Thessaloniki, 305–310.

Lyritzis, G. & Lyritzi, V. (1985) "Χρονολόγηση Σκωρίων με Θερμοφωταύγεια και ο Ρόλος τούς στην Αρχαιολογία" in *Πρακτικά 1ου Σεμιναρίου Αρχαιομετρίας: Σκωρίες της Αρχαίας Ελληνικής Μεταλλουργίας ΙΓΜΕ*, Athens, 69f.

Manning, J.G. & Morris, I. (2005) *The Ancient Economy: Evidence and Models*, Stanford.

Mastoris, K., Tsaila, D., Cheilakos, P., Berroiou, G., Foufres, A. & Koutsinos, S. (1979) "Ο Προσχωματικος Χρυσος της Ελλαδας" in Greek Mining Enterprises Association *The Greek Mineral Wealth*, Athens, 264–322.

Mattingly, H.B. (1961) "The Athenian Coinage Decree" *Historia* 10, 148–188.

Mattingly, H.B. (1966) "Periclean Imperialism" in Badian, E. (ed) *Ancient Society and Institutions: Studies Presented to Victor Ehrenberg for His 75th Birthday*, Oxford, 195–204.

Mayor, A. (1994) "Guardians of the Gold" *Archaeology* 47.6, 53–59.

McClellan, M. (1997) "The Economy of Hellenistic Egypt and Syria" in Price, B.B. (ed) *Ancient Economic Thought*, Vol. 1, London, 172–187.

McDonald, B.R. (1981) "The Phanosthenes Decree: Taxes and Timber in Late Fifth-Century Athens" *Hesperia* 50, 141–146.

McDowell, D.M. (1978) *The Law in Classical Athens*, London.

McKee, E. (1985) "Bulding the Trireme" in Coates, J. & McGrail, S. (eds) *The Greek Trireme of the 5th Century BCE*, London.
Meiggs, R. & Lewis, D. (1988, revised edition) *A Selection of Greek Historical Inscriptions to the End of the Fifth Century BC*, Oxford.
Meiggs, R. (1972) *The Athenian Empire*, Oxford.
Meiggs, R. (1982) *Trees and Timber in the Ancient Mediterranean World*, Oxford.
Meijer, F. (1986) *A History of Seafaring in the Classical World*, London.
Meritt, B.D. (1932) *Athenian Financial Documents of the 5th Century BC*, Ann Arbor.
Meritt, B.D. (1936) "Archelaos and the Decelean War" in *Classical Studies Presented to Edward Capps* Princeton, 246–252.
Meritt, B.D. (1945) "Attic Inscriptions of the Fifth Century" *Hesperia* 14, 61–133.
Meritt, B.D., Wade-Gery, H.T. & McGregor, M.F. (1939–1953) *The Athenian Tribute Lists*, Harvard.
Metcalf, D.M. & Oddy, W.A. (1980) (eds) *Metallurgy in Numismatics*, Volume 1, London.
Meyer, E. (1924, 2nd edition) *Kleine Schriften*, Volume I, Halle.
Michael, K. (1989) "Επιθερμικές Μεταλλοφορίες Au στην Περιοχή Κώνου, Ανατολικής Ροδοπης" in *3day Meeting for the Research for Primary Gold 30/11–2/12/1988* Athens, 93–101.
Millett, P. (1991) *Lending and Borrowing in Ancient Athens*, Cambridge.
Milne, J.G. (1939) "Trade between Greece and Egypt before Alexander the Great" *Journal of Egyptian Archaeology* 25, 177–183.
Milne, R.D. (2000) "The Public Speeches of Demosthenes" in Worthington, I. (ed) *Demosthenes: Statesman and Orator*, London, 205–223.
Moller, A. (2000) *Naukratis: Trade in Archaic Greece*, Oxford.
Momigliano, A. (1966) *Terzo contributo alla storia degli studi classici e del mondo antico*, Rome.
Moreno, A. (2007a) "Athenian Wheat-Tsars: Black Sea Grain and Elite Culture" in Gabrielsen, V. and Lund, J. (eds) *The Black Sea in Antiquity. Regional and Interregional Economic Exchanges*, Aarhus, 69–84.
Moreno, A. (2007b) *Feeding the Democracy. The Athenian Grain Supply in the Fifth and Fourth Centuries BC*, Oxford.
Morgenroth, U. (1999) "Southern Iberia and the Mediterranean Trade-Routes" *Oxford Journal of Archaeology* 18.4, 395–401.
Morley, N. (2007) *Trade in Classical Antiquity*, Cambridge.
Morrison, J.S. & Williams, R.T. (1968) *Greek Oared Ships, 900–322 BC*, Cambridge.
Morrison, J.S. & Coates J.F. (1996) *Greek and Roman Oared Warships*, Oxford.
Morrison, J.S., Coates, J.F. & Rankov, N.B. (2000, 2nd edition) *The Athenian Trireme*, Cambridge.
Morrison, J.S. (1987) "Athenian Sea-Power in 323/2 BC: Dream and Reality" *Journal of Hellenic Studies* 107, 88–97.
Morrison, J.S. (1996) *Greek and Roman Oared Warships*, Oxford.
Moustaka, A., Skarlatidou, E., Tzannes, M.C. & Ersoy, Y. (2004) *Klazomenai, Teos and Abdera: Metropoleis and Colony*, Thessaloniki.
Mpitzios, D.K. (1989a) "Κοιτάσματα Au Επιθερμικού Τύπου σε Ηφαιστεια-

κά Περιβάλλοντα. Ερευνα στον Ελληνικό Χώρο" in *3day Meeting for the Research for Primary Gold 30/11–2/12/1988* Athens, 315–319.

Mpitzios, D.K. (1989b) "Οι Κοιτασματολογικοί Τύποι Πρωτογενούς Χρυσού στον Ελληνικό Χώρο—Μεταλλογενετικά Στοιχεία—Μεταλλογενετικός Χάρτης Au Ελλάδας—Προτεραιότητες Ερευνητικών Στόχων" in *3day Meeting for the Research for Primary Gold 30/11–2/12/1988* Athens, 41–53.

Mposkos, E. (1982/1983) "The Gold, Silver and Tellur Minerals from the Koronouda Ore Mineralisation (Central Macedonia, Greece)" *Δελτίο της Ελληνικής Γεωλογικής Εταιρείας* 16, 97–108.

Murray, A.T. (1939) *Demosthenes with an English Translation*, Harvard (used in Perseus http://www.perseus.tufts.edu/cgi-bin/ptext?lookup=Dem.+37+1).

Murray, O. (1980) *Early Greece*, London.

Nafissi, M. (2005) *Ancient Athens and Modern Ideology: Value, Theory and Evidence in Historical Sciences. Max Weber, Karl Polanyi and Moses Finley*, London.

Nelson, R.B. (1973) *Warfleets of Antiquity*, London.

Nielsen, T.H. (ed) (2002) *Even More Studies in the Ancient Greek Polis: Papers from the Copenhagen Polis Centre*, Stuttgart.

Noonan, T.S. (1973) "The Grain Trade of the Northern Black Sea in Antiquity" *American Journal of Philology* 94.3, 231–242.

Oikonomou-Eliopoulou M., Eliopoulos, D., Zhelyaskova-Panayotoma, M. & Perantonis, G. (2000) "Distribution of Precious Metals in Porphyry Cu±Mo Deposits of Greece and Bulgaria" *Proceedings Mineral Wealth*, 143–151.

Oikonomou-Eliopoulou, M. & Eliopoulos, D.G. (2000) "Palladium, Platinum and Gold Concentration in Porphyry Copper Systems of Greece and Their Genetic Significance" *Ore Geology Reviews* 16, 59–70.

Oliver, G.J. (2007) *War, Food and Politics in Early Hellenistic Athens*, Oxford.

Orfanos, V. (1985) "Ερευνα για Προσχωματικό Χρυσό σε Περιοχές της Θράκης" *Ενημερωτικό Δελτίο Ινστιτούτου Γεωλογικών και Μεταλλευτικών Ερευνών* Ιαν-Ιου, 22.

Osborne, R. (1985) "Law in Action in Classical Athens" *Journal of Hellenic Studies* 105, 40–58.

Osborne, R. (1987) *Classical Landscape with Figures: The Ancient Greek City and Its Countryside*, London.

Osborne, R. (1991) "Pride and Prejudice, Sense and Subsistence: Exchange and Society in the Greek City" in Rich, J. & Wallace-Hadrill, A. (eds) *City and Country in the Ancient World*, London, 119–146.

Osborne, R. (1996a) *Greece in the Making, 1200–479 BCE*, London.

Osborne, R. (1996b) "Pots, Trade and the Archaic Greek Economy" *Antiquity* 70, 31–44.

Osborne, R. (1998) "Early Greek Colonisation?" in Fisher, N. & van Wees, H. (eds) *Archaic Greece: New Approaches and New Evidence*, London, 251–269.

Osborne, R. (1999) "Archaeology and the Athenian Empire" *Transactions of the American Philological Association* 129, 319–332.

Papadopoulos, J.K. (2002) "Minting Identity: Coinage, Ideology and the Economics of Colonization in Akhaian Magna Graecia" *Cambridge Archaeological Journal* 12, 21–55.

Papastamataki, A. (1975) *Ἐκμετάλλευσις τοῦ Ορυκτοῦ Πλούτου τῆς Ἀρχαίας Ἑλλάδος, Ἔρευνα ἐπὶ τῆς Περιεκτικότητας είς Χρυσὸν καὶ Ἄλλα Μέταλλα τῶν Σκωριῶν τῆς Ἀρχαίας Ἑλληνικῆς Μεταλλουργίας*, Athens.

Papastamataki, A. (1979) "Οι Σκωρίες της Αρχαίας Ελληνικής Μεταλλουργίας και η Σημασία τους από Οικονομικής Πλευράς" in Greek Mining Enterprises Association *The Greek Mineral Wealth*, Athens, 850–896.

Papastamataki, A. (1983) "Το Ιστορικό του Ἐργου "Αρχαίες Σκωρίες" στο ΙΓΜΕ και οι Μεταλλουργικές Κάμινοι στο Παγγαίο" *Ενημερωτικό Δελτίο Ινστιτούτου Γεωλογικών και Μεταλλευτικών Ερευνών* 10 Apr-Jun, 27–30.

Papastamataki, A. (1985) "Οι Σκωρίες της Αρχαίας Ελληνικής Μεταλλουργίας" in *Πρακτικά Του 1ου Σεμιναρίου Αρχαιομετρίας: Σκωρίες Της Αρχαίας Ελληνικής Μεταλλουργίας ΙΓΜΕ*, 41–67.

Parkins, H. & Smith, C. (1998) (eds) *Trade, Traders and the Ancient City*, London.

Parpola, S. (1987) (ed) *The Correspondence of Sargon II, Part I State Archives of Assyria Vol. 1*, Helsinki.

Patterson, J. (1998) "Trade and Traders in the Roman World: Scale, Structure and Organisation" in Parkins, H. & Smith, C. (eds) *Trade, Traders and the Ancient City*, London, 149–167.

Penhallurick, R.D. (1986) *Tin in Antiquity*, London.

Polanyi, K. (1957) *The Great Transformation*, Boston.

Posener, G. (1936) "La premiere domination perse en Egypte" *Bibliotheque d'etude* 11.

Price, M.J. (1981) "The Uses of Metal Analysis in the Study of Ancient Greek Coinage" in Metcalf, D.M. & Oddy, W.A. (eds) *Metallurgy in Numismatics*, Volume 1, London, 50–54.

Pritchett, W.K. & Pippin, A. (1956) "The Attic Stelai, Part II" *Hesperia* 25.3, 178–328.

Pritchett, W.K. (1995) *Thucydides' Pentekontaetia and Other Essays*, Amsterdam.

Raaflaub, K. (2004) "Archaic Greek Aristocrats as Carriers of Cultural Interaction" in Rollinger, R. & Ulf, C. (eds) *Commerce and Monetary Systems in the Ancient World: Means of Transmission and Cultural Interaction*, Stuttgart, 198–217.

Rackham, H. (1952, 2nd edition) *The Athenian Constitution. The Eudemian Ethics. On Virtues and Vices*, Harvard.

Rackham, T. (2000, reprint) *Pliny Natural History vol. 4*, Harvard.

Rainey, S. (2004) "Thucydides 1.98–118, Diodoros 11.60–12.28, and Their Common Source" *Athenaeum* 92, 217–236.

Reed, C.M. (2003) *Maritime Traders in the Ancient Greek World*, Cambridge.

Rhodes, P.J. (1981) *A Commentary on the Aristotelian Athenaion Politeia*, Oxford.

Rhodes, P.J. & Osborne, R. (2003) *Greek Historical Inscriptions 404–323 BC*, Oxford.

Rich, J. & Wallace-Hadrill, A. (1991) *City and Country in the Ancient World*, London.

Robinson, D.M. (1937) "A New Fragment of the 5th Century Athenian Naval Catalogues" *American Journal of Archaeology* 41.2, 292–299.

Roebuck, C. (1950) "The Grain Trade between Greece and Egypt" *Classical Philology* 45, 236–247.
Roebuck, C. (1959) *Ionian Trade and Colonization*, London.
Rollinger, R. & Ulf, C. (2004) (eds) *Commerce and Monetary Systems in the Ancient World: Means of Transmission and Cultural Interaction*, Stuttgart.
Rostovtzeff, M. (1941) *Social and Economic History of the Hellenistic World*, Oxford.
Rupprecht, H.-A. (2006) (ed) *Symposion 2003. Vorträge zur griechischen und hellenistischen Rechtsgeschichte*, Vienna.
Ruschenbusch, E. (1984), "Zum letztzen Mal: Die Bürgerzahl Athens im 4 Jh. v. Chr.", *Zeitschrift für Papyrologie und Epigraphik* 54, 253–269.
Sallares, R. (1991) *The Ecology of the Ancient Greek World*, London.
Salmon, J.B. (1984) *Wealthy Corinth*, Oxford.
Samuel, A.E. (1983) *From Athens to Alexandria: Hellenism and Social Economy in Ptolemaic Egypt, Studia Hellenistica* 26, Leuven.
Sancisi-Weerdenburg, H. et al. (1993) (eds) *De Agricultura: In Memoriam Pieter Willem de Neeve (1945–1990)*, Amsterdam.
Schaps, D.M. (2004) *The Invention of Coinage and the Monetization of Ancient Greece*, New York.
Schneider, H.J. (1983) (ed) *Mineral Deposits of the Alps and of the Alpine Epoch in Europe*, London.
Seager, R. (1966) "Lysias against the Corndealers" *Historia* 15, 172–184.
Sear, D.R. (1978) *Greek Coins and Their Values* 2 Volumes, New York.
Shefton, B.B. (1994) "Massalia and Colonization in the North-Western Mediterranean" in Tsetskhladze, G.R. & De Angelis, F. (eds) *The Archaeology of Greek Colonisation*, Oxford (Oxford University School of Archaeology Monograph 40), 61–86.
Shepherd, R. (1993) *Ancient Mining*, London.
Shipley, G. (1987) *A History of Samos*, Oxford.
Shipton, K. (2000) *Leasing and Lending: The Cash Economy in 4th Century* BC *Athens*, London.
Smirnov, V.I. (1989) "European Part of the USSR" in Dunning, F.W., Garrard, P., Haslam, H.W. & Ixer, R.A. *Mineral Deposits of Europe. Volume 4/5: Southwest and Eastern Europe with Iceland*, London, 279–360.
Smith, C.F. (1930) *Thucydides*, Harvard.
Snodgrass, A.M. (1994) "The Nature and Standing of the Early Western Colonies" in Tsetskhladze, G.R. & De Angelis, F. (eds) *The Archaeology of Greek Colonisation*, Oxford (Oxford University School of Archaeology Monograph 40), 1–10.
Solonev, S. (1998) "Archaic Berezan" in Tsetskhladze, G.R. (ed) *The Greek Colonisation of the Black Sea Area: Historical Interpretation of Archaeology*, Stuttgart (Historia Einzelschriften 121), 205–225.
Stanley, P.V. (1999) *The Economic Reforms of Solon. Scripta Mercatura Verlag*, St. Katharinen.
Starr, C.G. (1977) *The Economic and Social Growth of Early Greece, 800–500* BCE, Oxford.
Starr, C.G. (1989) *The Influence of Sea Power on Ancient History*, Oxford.

Steffy, R.J. (1985) "Structural Philosophy and Technology" in Coates, J. & McGrail, S. (eds) *The Greek Trireme of the 5th Century* BCE London, 25–38.
Stroud, R.S. (1974) "An Athenian Law on Silver Coinage" *Hesperia* 43.2, 157–188.
Stroud, R.S. (1998) *The Athenian Grain-Tax Law of 374–3 BCE*. Princeton (Hesperia Supplement 29).
Sutherland, C.H.V. (1943) "Corn and Coin: A Note of Greek Commercial Monopolies" *American Journal of Philology* 64, 129–147.
Svoronos, I. (1915) "Laurion: I. L'Atelier monetaire des atheniens dit du Stephanephoros. II. Monnaies de la revolution les esclaves de mines du Laurion" *Διεθνής Εφημερίς Νομισματικής Αρχαιολογίας* 17, 53f.
Svoronos, I. (1916/1917) "Το Μητρώον Του Ηλισσού Και Η Ζωοφόρος Αυτού" *Διεθνής Εφημερίς Νομισματικής Αρχαιολογίας* 18, 109f.
Tandy, D. (2004) "Trade and Commerce in Archilochos, Sappho and Alkaios" in Rollinger, R. & Ulf, C. (eds) *Commerce and Monetary Systems in the Ancient World: Means of Transmission and Cultural Interaction*, Stuttgart, 183–196.
Theofilopoulos, D. & Vakondios, I. (1982) "Γεωλογικές και Κοιτασματολογικές Έρευνες στην Περιοχή Καλλιανού της Νοτιοανατολικής Εύβοιας" *Mineral Wealth* 19, 27–50.
Thomas, R. (1996) "Written in Stone? Liberty, Equality, Orality and the Codification of Law" in Foxhall, L. & Lewis, A.P.E. (eds) *Greek Law in Its Political Setting*, Oxford, 9–32.
Thompson, M., Morkholm, O. & Kraay, C.M. (1973) *An Inventory of Greek Coin Hoards*, Oxford.
Tod, M.N. (1948) *A Selection of Greek Historical Inscriptions Vol. 2: From 403–322 B.C.*, Oxford.
Tracy, S.V. (1995) *Athenian Democracy in Transition. Attic Letter-Cutters of 340 to 290* BCE, Berkeley.
Treister, M. (1996) *The Role of Metals in Ancient Greek History*, Leiden.
Trikkalinos, I.K. (1961) "῾Ο Χρυσός καὶ αἱ ἐν ῾Ελλάδι Χρυσοφόροι ᾿Εμφανίσεις" *Πρακτικά της Ακαδημίας Αθηνών* 36, 381–396.
Tsetskhladze, G.R. & De Angelis, F. (1994) (eds) *The Archaeology of Greek Colonisation*. Oxford (Oxford University School of Archaeology Monograph 40).
Tsetskhladze, G.R. (1994) "Greek Penetration of the Black Sea" in Tsetskhladze, G.R. & De Angelis, F. (eds) *The Archaeology of Greek Colonisation*, Oxford (Oxford University School of Archaeology Monograph 40), 111–135.
Tsetskhladze, G.R. (1995) "Did the Greeks Go to Colchis for Metals?" *Oxford Journal of Archaeology* 14, 307–331.
Tsetskhladze, G.R. (1998) "Trade at the Black Sea in the Archaic and Classical Periods: Some Observations" in Parkins, H. & Smith, C. (eds) *Trade, Traders and the Ancient City*, London, 52–74.
Tsetskhladze, G.R. (1995) (ed) *New Studies on the Black Sea Littoral*, Oxford.
Tsetskhladze, G.R. (1998) (ed) *The Greek Colonisation of the Black Sea Area: Historical Interpretation of Archaeology*, Stuttgart (Historia Einzelschriften 121).
Tsetskhladze, G.R. (1999) (ed) *Ancient Greeks West and East*, Leiden (Mnemosyne Supplement 196).

Tsetskhladze, G.R. (2002) (ed) *Ancient West & East*, Vol. 1, No. 1, Leiden.

Tsompos, P., Epitropou, N., Zachos, S., & Demades, E. (1989) "Νέα Γεωλογικά και Τεκτονικά Δεδομένα στην Νήσο Θάσο και οι Προοπτικές Εντοπισμού Νέων Pb-Zn-Fe-Mn-Au Μεταλλοφόρων Συγκεντρώσεων" *Δελτίο της Ελληνικής Γεωλογικής Εταιρείας* 23/1, 75–88.

Turner, E.G. (1984, 2nd edition) "Ptolemaic Egypt" in *Cambridge Ancient History*, Vol. VII, Cambridge.

Unz, R.K. (1985) "The Surplus of the Athenian Phoros" *Greek, Roman and Byzantine Studies* 26, 21–42.

Van Effenterre, H. (1994) *Nomima: recueil d'inscriptions politiques et juridiques de l'archaïsme grec. 1*, Rome.

van Raalte, M. (2005) "More Philosophico: Political Virtue and Philosophy in Plutarch's Lives" in de Blois, L., Bons, J., Kessel, T. & Schenkeveld, D.M. (eds) *The Statesman in Plutarch's Works, Volume 2: The Statesman in Plutarch's Greek and Roman Lives* Leiden, 75–112.

van Wees, H. (2001) "The Myth of the Middle-Class Army: Military and Social Status in Ancient Athens" in Bekker-Nielsen, T. & Hannestad, L. (eds) *War as a Cultural and Social Force: Essays on Warfare in Antiquity*, Copenhagen, 45–71.

van Wees, H. (2004) *Greek Warfare: Myths and Realities*, London.

Vavelidis, M. & Amstutz, G.C. (1983) "Investigation on the Gold Occurences in the Kinyra and Thasos (City) Area on Thasos Island" in Schneider, H.J. (ed) *Mineral Deposits of the Alps and of the Alpine Epoch in Europe*, London, 385–391.

Vavelidis, M. (1990) "A New Gold Occurrence in the Askos Area, Thessaloniki District, Northern Greece" (in German) *Chemie der Erde* 50, 173–179.

Vázquez Guzmán, F. (1989) "Spain" in Dunning, F.W., Garrard, P., Haslam, H.W. & Ixer, R.A. *Mineral Deposits of Europe. Volume 4/5: Southwest and Eastern Europe with Iceland*, London, 105–127.

Vince, J.H. (1954, revised edition) *Demosthenes Vol. 1*, Harvard.

Vinogradov, J.G. & Kryzickij, S.D. (1995) *Olbia. Eine altgriechische Stadt im nordwestlichen Schwarzmeerraum*, Leiden.

Wagner, G.A., Pernicka, E., Gialoglou, G. & Vavelidis, M. (1981) "Ancient Gold Mines on Thasos" *Naturwissenschaften* 68, 263–264.

Walbank, M.B. (1978) *Athenian Proxenies*, Toronto.

Walbank, M.B., Lalonde, G.V. & Langdon, M.K. (1991) *The Athenian Agora: Results of Excavations Conducted by the American School of Classical Studies at Athens. Vol. 19, Inscriptions: Horoi, Poletai Records, Leases of Public Lands*, Princeton.

Wallinga, H.T. (1993) "Hesiod's Farmer as a Sailor" in Sancisi-Weerdenburg, H. et al. (eds) *De Agricultura: In Memoriam Pieter Willem de Neeve (1945–1990)*, Amsterdam, 1–12.

Wallace, M.B. (1970) "Early Greek Proxenoi" *Phoenix* 24.3, 189–208.

Wallace, R.W. (1987) "The Origin of Electrum Coinage" *American Journal of Archaeology* 91, 385–397.

Westlake, H.D. (1969) *Essays on the Greek Historians and Greek History*, Manchester.

White, M. (1954) "The Duration of the Samian Tyranny" *Journal of Hellenic Studies* 74, 36–43.
Whitehead, R. (1977) *The Ideology of the Athenian Metic*, Cambridge.
Whittaker, D. (1989) "Amphorae and Trade", in *Amphores romaines et histoire économique: dix ans de recherche actes du colloque de Sienne, 22–24 mai 1986* Rome, 537–539.
Wilhelm, A. (1922–1924) "Funf Beschlusse der Athenes" *Jahreshefte des Österreichischen Archäologischen Instituts* 21–22, 122–171.
Williams, D. & Ogden, J. (1994) *Greek Gold: Jewellery of the Classical World*, London.
Williams, J. (1997) *Money: A History*, London.
Worthington, I. (2000) (ed) *Demosthenes: Statesman and Orator*, London.
Yannopoulos, J.C. (1991) *The Extractive Metallurgy of Gold*, New York.
Zuffardi, P. (1989) "Italy" in Dunning, F.W., Garrard, P., Haslam, H.W. & Ixer, R.A. *Mineral Deposits of Europe. Volume 4/5: Southwest and Eastern Europe with Iceland*, London, 221 f.
Λαυρεωτική. Το Μουσειο του Λαυριου, Guide of the Laurion Museum.
Ο Ελληνικός Ορυκτός Πλούτος (1979) Αθήνα.
T.E.E., E.E. μηχ. μετ. μετ. (2000) *3ᵒ Συνέδριο Ορυκτού Πλούτου* Αθήνα.

INDEX

SUPPLEMENTS TO MNEMOSYNE

EDITED BY G.J. BOTER, A. CHANIOTIS, K.M. COLEMAN, I.J.F. DE JONG AND P. H. SCHRIJVERS

Recent volumes in the series

274. PRAUSCELLO, L. *Singing Alexandria.* Music between Practice and Textual Transmission. 2006. ISBN 90 04 14985 6
275. SLOOTJES, D. *The Governor and his Subjects in the Later Roman Empire.* 2006. ISBN-13: 978-90-04-15070-6, ISBN-10: 90-04-15070-6
276. PASCO-PRANGER, M. *Founding the Year: Ovid's* Fasti *and the Poetics of the Roman Calendar.* 2006. ISBN-13: 978-90-04-15130-7, ISBN-10: 90-04-15130-3
277. PERRY, J.S. *The Roman* Collegia. The Modern Evolution of an Ancient Concept. 2006. ISBN-13: 978-90-04-15080-5, ISBN-10: 90-04-15080-3
278. MORENO SOLDEVILA, R. *Martial, Book IV.* A Commentary. 2006. ISBN-13: 978-90-04-15192-5, ISBN-10: 90-04-15192-3
279. ROSEN, R.M. & I. SLUITER (eds.). *City, Countryside, and the Spatial Organization of Value in Classical Antiquity.* 2006. ISBN-13: 978-90-04-15043-0, ISBN-10: 90-04-15043-9
280. COOPER, C. (ed.). *Politics of Orality.* Orality and Literacy in Ancient Greece, Vol. 6. 2007. ISBN 13: 978-90-04-14540-5, ISBN 10: 90-04-14540-0
281. PETROVIC, I. *Von den Toren des Hades zu den Hallen des Olymp. Artemiskult bei Theokrit und Kallimachos.* 2007. ISBN 13: 978-90-04-15154-3, ISBN 10: 90-04-15154-0
282. PETROVIC, A. *Kommentar zu den simonideischen Versinschriften.* 2007. ISBN 13: 978-90-04-15153-6, ISBN 10: 90-04-15153-2
283. GAERTNER, J.F. (ed.). *Writing Exile: The Discourse of Displacement in Greco-Roman Antiquity and Beyond.* 2007. ISBN 13: 978-90-04-15515-2, ISBN 10: 90-04-15515-5
284. KORTEKAAS, G.A.A. *Commentary on the* Historia Apollonii Regis Tyri. 2007. ISBN 13: 978-90-04-15594-7, ISBN 10: 90-04-15594-5
285. BOEKE, H. *Wisdom in Pindar.* Gnomai, Cosmology and the Role of the Poet. ISBN 978 90 04 15848 1
286. LUSCHNIG, C.A.E. *Granddaughter of the Sun.* A Study of Euripides' Medea. 2007. ISBN 978 90 04 16059 0
287. LAZARIDIS, N. *Wisdom in Loose Form.* The Language of Egyptian and Greek Proverbs in Collections of the Hellenistic and Roman Periods. 2007. ISBN 978 90 04 16058 3
288. JENNINGS, V. & A. KATSAROS (eds.). *The World of Ion of Chios.* 2007. ISBN 978 90 04 16045 3
289. DEN BOEFT, J., J.W. DRIJVERS, D. DEN HENGST & H.C. TEITLER (eds.). *Ammianus after Julian.* The Reign of Valentinian and Valens in Books 26-31 of the *Res Gestae.* 2007. ISBN 978 90 04 16212 9
290. VAN MAL-MAEDER, D. *La fiction des déclamations.* 2007. ISBN 978 90 04 15672 2
291. DE JONG, I.J.F. & R. NÜNLIST (eds.). *Time in Ancient Greek Literature.* Studies in Ancient Greek Narrative, volume 2. 2007. ISBN 978 90 04 16506 9
292. KITZINGER, M.R. *The Choruses of Sophokles'* Antigone *and* Philoktetes. A Dance of Words. 2008. ISBN 978 90 04 16514 4
293. CONWELL, D.H. *Connecting a City to the Sea.* The History of the Athenian Long Walls. 2008. ISBN 978 90 04 16232 7

294. MARKOVIĆ, D. *The Rhetoric of Explanation in Lucretius'* De rerum natura. 2008. ISBN 978 90 04 16796 4
295. GEIGER, J. *The First Hall of Fame.* A Study of the Statues in the *Forum Augustum.* 2008. ISBN 978 90 04 16869 5
296. KIM ON CHONG-GOSSARD, J.H. *Gender and Communication in Euripides' Plays.* Between Song and Silence. 2008. ISBN 978 90 04 16880 0
297. KEULEN, W. *Gellius the Satirist.* Roman Cultural Authority in *Attic Nights.* 2009. ISBN 978 90 04 16986 9
298. MACKAY, E.A. (ed.). *Orality, Literacy, Memory in the Ancient Greek and Roman World.* Orality and Literacy in Ancient Greece, Vol. 7. 2008. ISBN 978 90 04 16991 3
299. HORSFALL, N. *Virgil,* Aeneid *2.* A Commentary. 2008. ISBN 978 90 04 16988 3
300. McKECHNIE, P. & P. GUILLAUME (eds.). *Ptolemy II Philadelphus and his World.* 2008. ISBN 978 90 04 17089 6
301. DE JONGE, C.C. *Between Grammar and Rhetoric.* Dionysius of Halicarnassus on Language, Linguistics and Literature. 2008. ISBN 978 90 04 16677 6
302. SCHMALZ, G.C.R. *Augustan and Julio-Claudian Athens.* A New Epigraphy and Prosopography. 2009. ISBN 978 90 04 17009 4
303. DE LIGT, L. & S.J. NORTHWOOD (eds.). *People, Land, and Politics.* Demographic Developments and the Transformation of Roman Italy, 300 BC-AD 14. 2008. ISBN 978 90 04 17118 3
304. EILERS, C. (ed.). *Diplomats and Diplomacy in the Roman World.* 2009. ISBN 978 90 04 17098 8
305. DEMOEN, K. & D. PRAET (eds.). Theios Sophistès. Essays on Flavius Philostratus' *Vita Apollonii.* 2009. ISBN 978 90 04 17109 1
306. SMOLENAARS, J.J.L., H. VAN DAM & R.R. NAUTA (eds.). *The Poetry of Statius.* 2008. ISBN 978 90 04 17134 3
307. SLUITER, I. & R.M. ROSEN (eds.). *KAKOS, Badness and Anti-Value in Classical Antiquity.* 2009. ISBN 978 90 04 16624 0
308. KOVÁCS, P. *Marcus Aurelius' Rain Miracle and the Marcomannic Wars.* 2009. ISBN 978 90 04 16639 4
309. McGOWAN, M.M. *Ovid in Exile.* Power and Poetic Redress in the *Tristia* and *Epistulae ex Ponto.* 2009. ISBN 978 90 04 17076 6
310. KARLA, G.A. (ed.). *Fiction on the Fringe: Novelistic Writing in the Post-Classical Age.* 2009. ISBN 978 90 04 17547 1
311. MURGATROYD, P. *A Commentary on Book 4 of Valerius Flaccus'* Argonautica. 2009. ISBN 978 90 04 17561 7
312. BISSA, E.M.A. *Governmental Intervention in Foreign Trade in Archaic and Classical Greece.* 2009. ISBN 978 90 04 17504 4
313. REECE, S. *Homer's Winged Words.* The Evolution of Early Greek Epic Diction in the Light of Oral Theory. 2009. ISBN 978 90 04 17441 2
314. COUSLAND, J.R.C. & J.R. HUME (eds.). *The Play of Texts and Fragments.* Essays in Honour of Martin Cropp. 2009. ISBN 978 90 04 17473 3
315. GEBHARDT, U.C.J. *Sermo Iuris: Rechtssprache und Recht in der augusteischen Dichtung.* 2009. ISBN 978 90 04 17647 8

www.ingramcontent.com/pod-product-compliance
Lightning Source LLC
La Vergne TN
LVHW080847300926
849162LV00003B/358

* 9 7 8 9 0 0 4 1 7 5 0 4 4 *